America's Half-Century

The American Moment
Stanley I. Kutler, Series Editor

The Twentieth-Century American City, 2d edition
Jon C. Teaford

American Workers, American Unions, 1920–1985, 2d edition
Robert H. Zieger

A House Divided: Sectionalism and Civil War, 1848–1865
Richard H. Sewell

Liberty under Law: The Supreme Court in American Life
William M. Wiecek

Winning Is the Only Thing: Sports in America since 1945
Randy Roberts and James Olson

America's Half-Century: United States Foreign Policy in the Cold War and After, 2d edition
Thomas J. McCormick

American Anti-Communism: Combating the Enemy Within, 1830–1970
Michael J. Heale

The Culture of the Cold War
Stephen J. Whitfield

America's Welfare State: From Roosevelt to Reagan
Edward D. Berkowitz

The Debate over Vietnam
David W. Levy

And the Crooked Places Made Straight: The Struggle for Social Change in the 1960s
David Chalmers

Medicine in America: A Short History
James H. Cassedy

The Republic of Mass Culture: Journalism, Filmmaking, and Broadcasting in America since 1941
James L. Baughman

Uneasy Partners: Big Business in American Politics, 1945–1990
Kim McQuaid

The Best War Ever: America in World War II
Michael C. C. Adams

America's Right Turn: From Nixon to Bush
William C. Berman

Industrializing America: The Nineteenth Century
Walter Licht

Moralists and Modernizers: America's Pre-Civil War Reformers
Steven Mintz

The Jacksonian Promise: American Society from 1815 to 1840
Daniel Feller

Democracy and Diplomacy: The Impact of Domestic Politics on U.S. Foreign Policy, 1789–1994
Melvin Small

America's Half-Century

UNITED STATES FOREIGN POLICY IN THE COLD WAR AND AFTER

Second Edition

Thomas J. McCormick

The Johns Hopkins University Press

Baltimore and London

The Johns Hopkins University Press
2715 North Charles Street
Baltimore, Maryland 21218–4363
www.press.jhu.edu

ISBN 0-8018-5010-X
ISBN 0-8018-5011-8 (pbk.)

Library of Congress Cataloging-in-Publication Data will be found at the end of this book.
A catalog record for this book is available from the British Library.

FOR JERI

One world is enough for all of us.
—"One World (not Three)", *Bring on the Night* record
album, Sting, 1986

Contents

Foreword

As the twentieth century draws to a close, the international dominance the United States enjoyed for much of the previous five or six decades is no more. The United States is neither an unrivaled "Number 1"—however useful that notion may remain as a domestic political slogan—nor is its position analogous to the last days of the Roman Empire. The United States certainly exercises a powerful role in world affairs, but that influence is more limited and less determinative in the internal affairs of other nations than it had been. The American economic colossus, with its seemingly invulnerable dollar, confronts powerful and prized yen and marks. Trade and money, not tanks and missiles, have become the prevailing measures of power. For the United States, the decades of dominance consumed enormous treasure, and an unbalanced allocation of national energies and resources, which contributed to its relative decline.

Thomas J. McCormick has had a longstanding interest in providing a theoretical understanding of American foreign policy. His perception of America's world role is in the realization that it is an extension and a reflection of domestic forces and considerations. Now, more than five years after the first publication of this volume, that insight is even more true. What the United States does in its economy and how it interacts with the rest of the world certainly has an impact on its international relations and, we might note, on the general well-being and stability of the world. McCormick has complemented that insight with a world-system analysis to explain the competition for international hegemony. American policy-makers, he suggests, attempt to serve two (sometimes divergent) masters: domestic imperatives and systemic needs. His suggestions are particularly appropriate in the post–Cold War world. McCormick's concepts for the period not only offer a rational explanation for the forty years after 1945 but also provide important insights into the interdependent global economy and regional power arrangements that characterize the resulting post–Cold War world-system. The Cold War is over; the world is rearranged. There *is* a "new world order," perhaps not one the United States can dominate, but one it must learn to accommodate and use. The time has come for understanding international affairs as something more than reading the ashes of World War II or perceiving international relations as a simple strategic contest between rival ideologies.

Stanley I. Kutler
THE UNIVERSITY OF WISCONSIN
MADISON, WISCONSIN

Preface

This is a book about the evolution and devolution of American hegemony in world affairs during that era known as the Cold War. The Cold War itself, however, is merely a subplot, part of a larger story that some historians call America's "hegemonic project." An important part of that project was managing the Soviet Union, but it was never the only part and not always the most important. That hegemonic project also sought to manage Germany and Japan, America's wartime adversaries, and Great Britain, a wartime ally, as well as the Third World and the American citizenry itself.

The architects of American global dominance viewed those nations and the American public as obstacles to their envisioned world order of economic internationalism and collective security. Nearly without exception, American leaders regarded nationalism as the bane of the twentieth century—the underlying cause of both world wars, the Great Depression of the 1930s, and the epic revolutions in Russia, China, and Mexico. The efforts of individual states to achieve national prosperity through protectionist, colonial, autarkic, or command economies had produced the opposite—inefficient and redundant national economies prone to overproduction and declining rates of profit. That tendency, in turn, tempted some states to use military force, imperialism, or revolution to redivide the global economic pie. The result was a "zero-sum game" that pitted nation against nation in a Hobbesian war of all against all for finite wealth, power, and resources—the have-nots struggling to be winners; the haves struggling not to become losers.

Such was the consensus view of American policymakers. After a half-century of military conflict and economic insecurity, they saw the only hope for long-term peace and prosperity in the abandonment of economic nationalism and the political and military efforts that had promoted it. Only a single, integrated, free world market, organized around the principles of comparative advantage and economies of scale, could realize capitalism's full capacity for prolonged, sustained growth where there would be only winners and no losers. That free world, however, could be achieved only if political and military power was organized globally in a manner that insured that the rules of the new world order were respected and enforced. Only then could there be a secure and stable global environment that might permit the free flow of capital, goods, currencies, people, values, and ideas necessary to make international capitalism viable. In the aftermath of World War II, the objective reality of America's near-omnipotence and the subjective reality of American egoism led its leaders to define American hegemony as the most efficacious and desirable way of organizing global power.

The historical actors targeted by America's hegemonic project had impeded internationalism in the past and retained the potential for doing so again in the future. Japan's "Greater East Asian Co-Prosperity Sphere," Germany's "New Order" in Europe, Britain's "Ottowa system" of imperial preference, the Soviet Union's "Socialism in One Country," Third World experiments in industrialization for the home market, and American isolationist sentiment for a "Fortress America" in the western hemisphere—all had been prewar attempts to organize economic and security systems into national or regional blocs, and they had made the world less free and less whole.

Over time, it was America's containment policy against potential Soviet expansionism that provided the means to contain and manage other powers as well. Acting in its dual role as the world's banker and global policeman, the United States used the sometimes exaggerated threat of international communism to render Germany and Japan dependent on the United States, not only for economic assistance and secure access to global resources, but also for the military protection afforded by America's nuclear umbrella and its alliance system. Containing the Soviet Union thus became the means to manage Germany and Japan in a fashion that permitted their economic revival as important producers and consumers, while safely integrating them into a free world under American aegis—a Pax Americana.

That same liberal hybrid of internationalism and anticommunism also provided the United States with both the leverage and the rationale to co-opt the British into a "special relationship." Even as Britain declined as a significant world player, the United States provided it with a vicarious sense of power and global mission; a former hegemon and senior partner was transformed into the junior partner of the new hegemon. Likewise, that same mixture of internationalism-cum-anticommunism provided the means and the occasion to discipline those parts of the Third World deemed unreasonable or unruly or unstable into accepting the American rules of the international game. Economic and military assistance in nation building were the rewards offered; covert coups and overt interventions were the penalties. Finally, the amalgam of American egoism and anticommunism powerfully aided the American state in its efforts to abort any postwar revival of American isolationism and to create a consensus in support of an American mandated system of economic internationalism and collective security. Without the evocative power of anticommunism, the implementation of the Truman Doctrine, the Marshall Plan, NATO, and the two wars for integration of the Pacific rim (those in Korea and Vietnam) would not have enjoyed the sustained and broad public support they received.

To a considerable degree, America's hegemonic project was a success. To be sure, other nations often simply took advantage of American hegemony when its goals paralleled their own ("empire by invitation," some called the phenomenon) and, when it did not, sometimes successfully resisted it. On balance, however, American hegemony played a major role in fashioning a world order that enjoyed a quarter-century of peace (at least as measured by the absence of East-West world war) and of prosperity (as witnessed by the unprecedented aggregate growth of global capitalism in the 1950s and 1960s).

On the other hand, as we shall see, hegemony carried within it the seeds of its own destruction. Throughout most of the 1970s and 1980s, overspending on military production and overinvestment abroad adversely affected capital expenditures and research and development in the American civilian goods sector. Indeed, a kind of *disinvestment* occurred in that sector that made the United States over time increasingly less able to hold its home market and to compete in the world market. The economic drag and distortions of playing global banker and policeman over several decades manifested itself in the stagflation of the 1970s, in the mounting budget and trade deficits in the paper prosperity of the 1980s, and in the structural recession of the 1990s. The United States had reached a stage of "imperial over-stretch" where sustaining its policing role could only hasten its economic decline, or where efforts to improve its competitive position for increased world market shares could only be achieved by significant cuts in its political and military obligations. It could no longer have its cake and eat it too.

This relative decline of American hegemony over the past two decades has coincided with the even more precipitous collapse of the Russian empire and with the equally impressive rise of Japan and the German-led European Union. From a long-term perspective, it might be argued that both the American and Russian superpowers lost the Cold War and that Japan and Germany, ironically, may have been its winners. What that portends for the future is a matter to be addressed at this book's end. American hegemony may yet be resuscitated with the collapse of the Soviet Union as a countervailing force, and the Gulf War suggests that the hegemonic project might continue through the vehicle of resource wars rather than cold wars. Perhaps Japan and the United States will drift into a transitional period of co-hegemony, during which division of military and economic labor will permit them jointly to set and enforce the rules of the game. Perhaps the world order will fragment into three, four, or five power blocs, with consequences that could be either benign or malignant. Either the world could devolve into another dangerous, unstable, 1914-style balance of power or the multilateral institutions and rules of the game embodied in the General Agreement on Tariffs and Trade, the International Monetary Fund, the World Bank, and trilateral economic summits might survive "beyond American hegemony" and continue to cement a polycentric world with the glue of economic interdependence.

This book employs a modified world-system analysis. Any theory is an invention (as is the antitheory of empiricism). It imposes articulated order on a seemingly random and unconnected body of disparate facts. Social science theory—invention—cannot, of course, be tested and evaluated in laboratory replication. Its only test is a relative and subjective one. Does it seem to explain more of the data in a more plausible way than do alternative explanations?

World-system theory seemed to me the most plausible invention for understanding the subject of this book. It possesses a combination of virtues that competing explanations do not. Its most general but crucial advantage is its axiomatic insistence on locating any study within the *temporal* context of long-term time and within the *spatial* context of a global unit of analysis. It assumes that all time frames and all units of analysis, whatever their size, are important; but it makes the logical argument that it is always best to begin with the longest and largest and then to devolve, through the intermediate, to the short term and the particular.

To do otherwise runs the risk of reinventing the wheel, of misinterpreting short-term trends as self-contained or unique when they are often merely segments of long-term secular change, up-sides or down-sides of repetitive cycles. Similarly, unless one begins with a global unit of analysis, one runs the proverbial risk of missing the forest for the trees. If one begins at the level of discrete individuals and events, one is likely to become trapped and preoccupied in a maze of particularistic detail and idiosyncratic factors. It is therefore very difficult to work from the specific to the general, to write from the inside out. It is far less problematic, however, to write from the outside in.

To be sure, world-system (or systemic) theory is not the only construct that posits the importance of long-term time and a global context. Both the revisionists' dependency theory and the neorealists' hegemonic theory do so as well, and this study integrates aspects of both into its synthesis. Systemic theory, however, differs from and transcends them in several key respects. Like dependency theory, it stresses the uneven development of global capitalism and argues that underdevelopment of the periphery is a function, not of a late start in modernization, but of the symbiotic and often exploitative relationship that the periphery experiences with developed core countries. It parts company with dependency theory, however, in one key regard. The latter denigrates the possibility of mobility within the system and sees Third World revolutions as the only means of escaping dependency; it cites a parallel need for solidarity between those revolutions based on a common outlook of anticapitalism and anti-imperialism. World-system theory, for its part, expresses a friendly skepticism about such Third Worldism. While it accepts the proposition of Third World agency—the capacity and will to resist and actively make one's own history—it doubts that the autarkic, planned economies of revolutionary regimes can overcome both the hostility of global capitalism and the inefficiency of their own undersized economies. Tacitly denying the possibility of socialism in one country, systemic theory suggests that anticapitalist revolution, were it ever to come, would have to wait until capitalism had reached its spatial limits and the whole world was thoroughly integrated into a single global market. Then, without an ever-expanding economic frontier, capitalism as a system might have to confront its own contradictions. In the meantime, countries working from within the world-system, and playing by its rules of specialized production for a world market, are more likely to experience upward mobility and realize a measure of economic success than radical command economies trying to opt out of the system. The showcase nations of the Pacific rim are an obvious case in point.

Like hegemonic theory, world-system analysis emphasizes the issue of systemic stability. Both focus on the key question of what accounts for the rise and fall of great powers (especially hegemonic powers) and for the fluctuations between unicentric hegemony and polycentric balance of power. The chief difference between the two theoretical approaches resides in their relative treatments of politics and economics. For neorealists, the international system is, at heart, a political system: an interstate system of nation-states, driven by imperatives of maximizing national geopolitical gain. While economics is an important factor, neorealists do not define it as a system—neither as a system of capitalist production nor as one of international commodity exchange. On the other hand, world-system analysts see the international system as essentially an economic system: a world-system of multinational manufacturers, international bankers, long-distance merchants, and international economic institutions like GATT and IMF, engaged in an elaborate global network of commodity production and exchange.

This book's modified version of world-system theory accepts the existence of both an economic world-system as well as an interstate system. Indeed, it is the uneasy tension—the mix of coexistence and competition—between the internationalist imperatives of the economic system and the nationalist predilections of the political system that constitutes a major concern of this book. And it is that tension between economic internationalism and political nationalism that U.S. hegemony sought to resolve in America's half-century since World War II.

Acknowledgments

Research on this volume began at the Woodrow Wilson International Center for Scholars in 1981, aided by a generous grant from the Center and stimulated by the exciting intellectual environment put together by Michael J. Lacey, head of the Center's Program on American Society and Politics.

Stanley I. Kutler, the editor of this series, gave generously of his time, energy, insights, and valued friendship in seeing this project through to completion. I owe him a great debt.

A number of fine historians read an earlier draft of this manuscript: Kathy Brown of the University of Wisconsin at Madison, Walter LaFeber of Cornell University, Melvyn Leffler of the University of Virginia, and Takeshi Matsuda of the Osaka University of Foreign Studies. All transcended the bias of friendship to offer pointed and useful criticism that helped make this a better book. More informally, I benefited from the insights and support of William Borden, John Dower of the University of California at San Diego, Lloyd Gardner of Rutgers University, Nathan Godfried of Hiram College, Pat Hearden of Purdue University, Michael Hogan of Ohio State University, and, as always, of Fred Harvey Harrington of the University of Wisconsin at Madison and William Appleman Williams of Oregon State University.

Chapter 10 of the second edition profited from critical reading by two dear and learned friends, Robin Chapman and Frank Siciliano, both of the University of Wisconsin-Madison. I also had the opportunity to preview versions of it in public lectures in Japan, France, and Germany. For making that possible I wish to thank several historians—Takeshi Matsuda once again; Serge Ricard of the Université de Provence, Aix-Marseille; and Hans-Jürgen Schröder of the Universität Giessen.

Preparation of the manuscript was greatly aided by the constructive criticism of Henry Tom, Executive Editor of the Johns Hopkins University Press; by the impressive skills and wise counsel of Anne Whitmore, my copyeditor at the Press; and by the meticulous labor of my typist, Paula Pfannes.

My wife Jeri, to whom this book is dedicated critiqued my writing style, helped correct proofs, and sustained me with her friendship.

1 | The Analytic Framework: The World-System, Hegemony, and Domestic Power

Each time decentering occurs, a recentering takes place.
—*Fernand Braudel*

From the late stages of World War II until the late stages of the Vietnam War, American hegemony—global supremacy—was the driving force in world affairs. In the post–Vietnam War era, however, the decline of American power, the even greater decline of Russian power, and the emergence of Japan and the European Economic Community as rival power centers have produced a far more polycentric world. No one power is able to set the world's agenda and no contending pair of superpowers is free to use the world as the arena for their rivalry. These centrifugal tendencies raise fundamental questions. Is the Cold War over, or merely in temporary abeyance? Will the United States accept the loss of hegemony, and how will it define its new role in world affairs? Will the multicentered world degenerate into another balance of power struggle, similar to the one that produced World Wars I and II, or will global economic integration and interdependence make it no longer practical for great powers to war on each other? The answers to such questions about the present and future are to be found in the relevant past. Present crises spring out of that epoch called the Cold War, which in turn had sprung from a longer-term crisis of political instability and economic malaise, one that left a pockmarked trail of two world wars, traumatic revolutions in Russia and China, and the greatest depression in capitalism's history. Making the best use of that relevant past, however, requires an understanding of two concepts, the world-system and hegemony.

The Modern World-System

Since modern history began in the late fifteenth century, the earth's inhabitants have lived in three distinct types of environments: the capitalist world-system (or world economy), the external world (empires), or the minisystems of subsistence communities. For the past five hundred years,

1

the dynamic growth and expansion of the world-system has been at the expense of the other two. The Ottoman Empire of the Turks disappeared, the Russian Empire of the Romanovs and the empire of the Manchus in China collapsed in revolutionary disarray, all victims of their archaic political systems and the inability of their quasi-feudal economies to compete with or alternatively to insulate themselves from the more dynamic and efficient economies of the capitalist world-system. Likewise, the minisystems of Eastern Europe, Ireland, the Americas, Africa, and Asia were, over time and despite great resistance, wrenched away from their subsistence, village agriculture and integrated into a cash nexus and the world market. By the late twentieth century, the remnants of the external world of empires, the Soviet Union and the Peoples' Republic of China, had emerged from the containment and self-isolation of the Cold War and begun to experiment with market economies in place of command (planned) economies. Also by that time, the remaining isolated pockets of subsistence systems had virtually disappeared from the face of the earth. The revolutionary expansion of European capitalism and Mediterranean civilization, begun a half-millennium earlier, seemed about to reach its final, all-encompassing frontier. The world-system and the world itself seemed almost one—one world rather than three.

Throughout its five centuries, capitalism has been an inherently expansionistic type of economy. The key to accumulating capital, enlarging market shares, and maximizing profits has historically been long-distance trade, especially by large capitalists with political connections and economic reserves. That was true of Baltic merchant capitalists in the seventeenth century rerouting their grain ships to the Adriatic to take advantage of local famine and exorbitant prices. It was true of nineteenth-century British industrial capitalists using their superior technology and economies of scale to wipe out hand-crafted textiles in Turkey, India, and China and to enlarge the British share of the world market. It is true today of finance capitalists in New York whose overseas bank loans to newly industrializing countries give a high rate of return no longer possible at home. In short, capitalism as an economic system has always functioned most profitably and most efficiently when its universe of options has been sufficiently large and fluid for capital, goods, services, and people to move from one place to another in order to secure greater returns, even if that place be both distant and foreign. Moreover, even when capitalism has not functioned efficiently, its spatial expansion into distant empires and subsistence enclaves has fueled its rejuvenation. Periodically, crises of overproduction have resulted from the contradictory instincts of entrepreneurs to keep production high (to enlarge market shares) and wage bills low (to reduce production costs). Historically, however, global expansion of new markets for goods and capital has helped restore demand to the level of supply, raised the rate of profit, and replaced economic depression with economic boom. The long slumps of 1680–1730, 1870–1900, and 1930–50 were all resolved in part by the creation of new economic frontiers: the mercantile empires of the eighteenth century, the new imperialism of the late nineteenth century, and the economic internationalization promoted by American foreign policy in the mid-twentieth century.

During the last decade, a number of academic observers have concluded that capitalism's tendency toward international fluidity eventually produced a configuration that could properly be described as a system, a combination of parts forming a complex, unitary whole. Fernand Braudel and Immanuel Wallerstein, in their epic studies of early European capitalism, concluded that such a system was in place by 1650. Others feel that it was not until the nineteenth century that an integrated global division of labor allowed capitalism to merit characterization as a system.

Studies advancing a world-system analysis (including this study) argue that there are three constants about that world-system, even though the particular forms it takes are always changing. First, there are always implicit geographical boundaries within that system, and they are essentially defined by the spatial limits of the world market economy at any given time. In our contemporary period, the term *free world* is essentially a synonym for the capitalist world-system. Cold War rhetoric may impart a more ideological twist to the phrase, but Nelson Rockefeller's chief aide got at its root in late 1941 when he declared that America was "committed to the fight for freedom of economic life and for freedom of the seas, in a word, the fight for a free world." Second, there is always a center or pole to the system, a dominant city that acts as the coordinating point and clearing house of international capital. Its location has shifted historically from the Mediterranean to Northern Europe to North America (and perhaps yet to Northeast Asia), but there is always a central metropolis, be it London in 1845 or New York in 1945.

Finally, the system consists of three successive zones, each performing a specialized function in a complex, international division of labor. *Core* countries (the First World) own most of the high-tech, high-profit enterprises. The *periphery* (the Third World) specializes in primary production of agricultural commodities and raw materials—they are the "hewers of wood and carriers of water." Between them, the *semiperiphery* (the Second World) performs intermediate functions of transport, local capital mobilization, and less complex, less profitable forms of manufacturing. Historically, there has been some limited mobility of individual nations between zones, including America's own transformation from a semiperipheral country in 1790 to a core country by 1890. Likewise, changing technology continually redefines what constitutes high-, intermediate-, or low-value enterprises. Textiles, steel, and shipbuilding might have been high-value activities in an earlier era but have become low- or intermediate-value in the contemporary age of electrical equipment. What remains constant are the zones themselves and the specialized (and unequally rewarded) division of labor among them. Hence, in 1988 there is a world-system in which North America, Japan, and Europe constitute the core and specialize in electronics, capital goods, diversified agriculture, and finance; the less developed countries (LDCs) of Africa, Southeast Asia, and the Caribbean basin, as the periphery, specialize in nonpetroleum raw materials and single-crop agriculture; and the newly industrializing countries (NICs), Mexico, Brazil, South Africa, Israel, Iran, India, China, and those of Eastern Europe and the Pacific rim, as the semiperiphery, specialize in shipping, petroleum, credit transactions, and consumer goods manufacturing.

Hegemony

The emergence of a capitalist world economy coincided with the emergence of the modern nation-state as the prevailing political unit of governance, and the nation-state has both fostered and inhibited the capitalist world economy. On one hand, nation-states have often provided crucial stimulation of economic growth and development: their banking, taxation, credit, and internal improvement policies have frequently aided domestic entrepreneurs in accumulating capital and minimizing risks. On the other hand, those same nation-states have often interfered with and impeded the fluidity and mobility of capital, goods, and labor across national boundaries. This nationalist bias is caused in part by nation-states being, by definition, wedded to specific territories and committed to the defense and sustenance of their citizens. In part, too, it reflects the uneven pace of capitalist development among countries, and the unequal division of labor and rewards that results from it. The frequent consequence has been an attempt by "have-not" countries to overtake "have" countries through nationalistic economic measures, often referred to as mercantilistic policies in earlier periods and, in our own time, as import-substitution policies (i.e., substitution of indigenous products for those previously imported). Whatever the cause of this nationalist bias, the resulting farm subsidies, military spending, protective tariffs, navigation laws, capital controls, and restricted currency convertibility have constituted serious obstacles to a free world of economic internationalism and interdependence in which capitalism, as a purely economic system, can realize its maximum efficiency and profitability. So, too, have the policies of territorial expansion that often accompany economic nationalism interfered, by seeking to monopolize whole regions of the earth for the benefit of a single national economy. Examples are the British mercantile empire of the eighteenth century and the Japanese Greater East Asian Co-Prosperity Sphere of the twentieth. In sum, nation-states have tended to pursue policies of economic autarky—capitalism in one country or one self-contained trading bloc—and such approaches limit the options of capital in pursuit of maximum rewards.

Hegemony historically has operated to soften the contradiction between the internationalist imperatives of capitalism and the nationalist biases of political nation-states. In the context of the world-system, hegemony means that one nation possesses such unrivaled supremacy, such predominant influence in economic power, military might, and political-ideological leadership, that no other power, or combination of powers, can prevail against it. Economic supremacy is the indispensable base of hegemony, for all other forms of power are possible with it and no others possible, for very long, without it. Any hegemonic power must, simultaneously, contain the dominant financial center, possess a clear comparative advantage in a wide range of high-tech, high-profit industries, and function commercially as both the world's major exporter and its major importer. Beyond mere economic power, it must possess clear military superiority and ideological hegemony as well. By fear or respect, it must be able to exert its political will over the rest of the system and command deference to its principles and policies.

Hegemony and the balance of power have been on opposing sides of the contradiction between economic internationalism and national autarky or self-sufficiency. The balance of power attempts to use the alignment of forces and, if necessary, war, to prevent any one power from achieving such preponderance that it could impose economic internationalism on autarkic-minded nations. A single hegemonic power, however, has a built-in incentive to force other nations to abandon their national capitalism and economic controls and to accept a world of free trade, free capital flows, and free currency convertibility. As the world's dominant economic power, a hegemonic power has the most to gain from such a free world and the most to lose from nationalistic efforts to limit the free movement of capital, goods, and currencies. So the preponderant world power is unequivocally self-interested in using its economic power, as workshop and banker of the free world, to create institutions and ground rules that foster the internationalization of capital. It finds it inherently advantageous to use its political power as ideologue of the world-system to preach the universal virtues of freedom of the seas, free trade, open door policies, comparative advantage, and a specialized division of labor. It finds it necessary to use its military power as global policeman to protect the international system against external antagonists, internal rebellions, and internecine differences: to be judge, jury, and executioner, insuring that the ground rules of internationalism are not impeded by either friend or foe.

Only twice in the history of the capitalist world economy has hegemony triumphed over balance of power as the prevailing structure of the international system. Great Britain functioned as hegemonic center between roughly 1815 and 1870, and the United States did so between roughly 1945 and 1970. (Others argue that the Dutch republic did so as well, in the late seventeenth century, but the argument seems rather forced.) In each instance, world war was crucial to the formation of hegemony. It radically redistributed power and wealth in ironic fashion, denying hegemony to a European continental power while bestowing postwar supremacy on its balance of power adversary.

In the first instance, France attempted through its Napoleonic Wars (constituting the first truly world war) to impose its dominance on the Eurasian heartland, the very center of European capitalism. Great Britain attempted to thwart that ambition through its traditional balance of power politics, and it ultimately prevailed. But the wars and attendant revolutions were so long, so destructive, so destabilizing that they temporarily obliterated the old balance of power system and left Great Britain the tacit sovereign of the post-Napoleonic world. In the second instance (as we shall see in detail later), Germany, under both the Kaiser and Hitler, attempted to impose its dominance on the same Eurasian heartland, while Anglo-American balance of power diplomacy sought to prevent it. But the ironic consequence of World Wars I and II was, by denying hegemony to the Germans, to make it possible for the Americans to become the acknowledged leaders of the free world. In each case, hegemony made it nearly impossible for other core powers to use war as an instrument of diplomacy against each other—a Pax Britannica for the mid-nineteenth century and a Pax Americana for the mid-twentieth. In each case, hegemony blunted the forces of economic nationalism and facilitated greater global interdependence, enabling a freer and easier *exchange* of goods in the nineteenth century and the multinational *production* of goods in the twentieth.

Hegemony is always impermanent, as Great Britain discovered and the United States is discovering. Indeed, hegemony undermines the very economic supremacy upon which it necessarily must rest. Two related tendencies lead the preponderant power to neglect investment in its civilian research and production and to transform itself into a *rentier* nation and *warfare* state. There is a tendency to overinvest and lend overseas and to live off dividends and interests (renting out one's money, hence *rentier*). It happens because it is easy to do, since the hegemonic power is in a position to secure favorable treatment for its capital throughout the free world. It happens also because it is necessary, since higher wage bills make it more profitable to invest overseas than at home. The higher wage bills themselves are part of the burden of power: the necessity to demonstrate to managers and workers that there are ample economic rewards for supporting an internationalist foreign policy with their votes, tax dollars, and conscription.

The tendency to overinvest abroad is compounded by the tendency to overinvest in military production. Essential to the hegemonic power's capacity to act as global policeman, military research and production receive favored treatment from the government in the form of state-subsidized high profits. The government becomes a more predictable and more profitable customer than private individuals and corporate consumers. The end result is to divert capital from civilian to military production, to the neglect of modernization needs of the domestic industrial plant. This disinvestment, as some term it, erodes over time the economic underpinnings of hegemony and makes it more difficult to compete with other core powers who have avoided the pitfalls of similar disinvestment. Moreover, like a snowball rolling downhill, the problems compound as the hegemon grows aware of its decline. Confronted with declining profitability in the civilian sector, it is likely to stress military spending even more as the easiest way to assure its capitalists of adequate returns—often spending far in excess of any plausible military purposes. Relatedly, it is likely to exploit its continuing function as world policeman to extort special privileges from its competitors: favored treatment for its currency, its trade, and its investments in exchange for continued police protection. In short, it is likely to become even more of a rentier or warfare economy and speed up the very decline it is trying to retard.

The Domestic Context of Hegemony

Hegemony does not simply happen, individuals and groups of people make it happen. A sufficient base of power is the prerequisite for global supremacy, but it is insufficient unless the will to use that power is present in those determining public policy for the potential superpower. In the case of the United States since 1945, it is no easy matter to identify who determines policy. The difficulty reflects the existence of two antithetical tendencies, a dominant one toward greater elitism in making foreign policy and a secondary but still powerful one toward residual pluralism. The result, too, has been antithetical: a prevailing consensus that nonetheless contains elements of conflict.

The tendency toward elitism has included centralizing policymaking in the executive branch of the government and limiting the number and intensity of potentially inhibiting influences. One obvious manifestation of this trend has been the gradual conversion of Congress into nearly a rubber stamp, merely approving or acquiescing in actions taken by the executive branch. Executive agreements like those at Yalta and Potsdam, undeclared wars like Korea and Vietnam, nearly carte blanche military spending bills, and sweeping presidential fiats like the Truman, Eisenhower, and Carter doctrines all bore the stamp of what came to be called the imperial presidency. There has also been a marginalization of public opinion and popular voting as shapers of policy. Since World War II, the number of Americans having nil or minimal interest in foreign affairs has significantly increased ("the inattentive public," as political scientists term them), while the extent of voter turnout and intensity of party loyalty have measurably declined.

Another indication of foreign policy elitism has been the privileged influence enjoyed by the "aristocracy" of business and labor—multinational banks and corporations and, to a lesser and less permanent degree, the American Federation of Labor and the Congress of Industrial Organizations (now the unified AFL-CIO). Such broad-based interest groups have replaced political parties as the government's major conduit for mobilizing junior executives, rank-and-file workers, and other interested Americans ("the attentive public") to support the government's foreign policy. Such groups, in turn, have received the lion's share of economic rewards from American internationalism and even, at times, have shared responsibility for implementing policy (as they did, for example, in the Marshall Plan and the Alliance for Progress). A final manifestation of the elitist tendency has been the effort to further centralize policymaking in the National Security Council (NSC) to counteract diffusionist tendencies by new and enlarged bureaucracies concerned with foreign policy. In the immediate postwar period, the proliferation of area and topical desks within the State Department—each with its own perspective and short-term agenda— necessitated the creation of the Policy Planning Staff (PPS), to insure a more global, coordinated approach. By the end of the 1940s, the appearance of bureaucratic players outside the State Department—the Central Intelligence Agency (CIA), the Department of Defense (DOD), the Economic Cooperation Administration (ECA)—had made interdepartmental coordination crucial if American policy was not to become simply the sum of so many bureaucratic territorial battles. For good and sometimes ill, the NSC was created to attempt that coordinating role.

The image this suggests, of an oligarchic foreign policy omnipotent in the face of an enfeebled Congress and an irrelevant public, is partially true, yet partially misleading. Image approximated reality most nearly in the decade between the Korean War and escalation of the Vietnam War. Peace, unparalleled prosperity, and the heady, psychic reward of being leader of the free world ("the arrogance of power," as Senator J. William Fulbright called it) created little receptivity to democratic dissent from mainstream internationalism. Such was not the case, however, in the immediate post–World War II period, when critics on both the right and the left questioned the logic of internationalism and the necessity of American hegemony. Nor has it been the case in the last two decades, when the trauma of the Vietnam War and increasing awareness of American economic decline have begun to raise questions about the morality, profitability, and feasibility of American globalism.

Even when least assertive, Congress and the public have had some influence on foreign policy. Although they did not make policy nor even deter it from its undeviating internationalism, they did sometimes force it to take forms not preferred by the policymakers. Congress did so through two key functions—the power to appropriate monies and the power to investigate. Some of its powerful committees—Finance, Ways and Means, Armed Services, and Military Affairs—had significant say as to how much the United States spent as global policeman (often less than the executive branch desired prior to the 1960s, often more than it wanted thereafter), where that money was spent (predictably and disproportionately in the states and districts of congressmen with the greatest committee seniority), and what rationale justified its spending (usually anticommunism and national security rather than economic internationalism and the needs of free world allies).

Similarly, Congress's committees on un-American activities and internal security, and other ad hoc investigatory bodies, continually confronted the executive branch with charges that its internationalism subverted the national interest: it sold out Eastern Europe to the Russians, lost China to communism, let the secret of the atomic bomb escape, failed to push the Korean War (and later the Vietnam War) to victorious conclusion, and betrayed American allies like Batista, Somoza, and the Shah of Iran while abetting American enemies like Castro, the Sandinistas, and Khomeini. While congressional investigative forays were patently partisan and truly powerful only in the McCarthyite era of the early 1950s, their ever-present possibility clearly reinforced the White House's need to avoid at all costs the appearance of appeasement. This pressure may have meant that some tactical roads were not taken or, if taken, were traveled in secrecy (e.g., the Iran-*contra* affair).

The opinion of the voting public was also of material concern to policymakers. While voter turnout and party loyalty did decrease, those trends actually enhanced the importance of those who continued to vote but whose party loyalty could no longer be taken for granted. To be sure, that voting public was rarely influenced in its electoral choices by foreign policy issues, even during the Vietnam-era antiwar movement. Domestic issues, class mobility, and ethnic identity were far more influential. Indirectly, however, voters did make a connection between domestic concerns and international affairs. Proponents and beneficiaries of the Great Society reform programs of the mid-1960s worried that militarization and the Vietnam War were draining away money, energy, and moral concern from those social endeavors. Victims of inflation and declining real wages in the mid-1970s wondered if that same costly war and the OPEC (Organization of Petroleum Exporting Countries) oil shocks did not demonstrate that American preoccupation with and dependence on the outside world had resulted more in economic sacrifices than in economic rewards.

In addition, specific ethnic blocs of voters developed a direct interest in foreign policy issues relevant to their group. Voters of Eastern European descent were often intensely concerned about the fate of their fatherlands under Russian control. Especially was this true of those with ties to Poland, Hungary, and the Baltic states—nations whose modern existence did not begin until 1919, was snuffed out in 1939, and faced a problematic future. Similarly, Jewish voters generated an even more intense commitment to the establishment and preservation of an independent Israeli state. Long a Zionist dream, the desire for a Jewish homeland took on added urgency with the need to resettle the surviving victims of Hitler's "final solution" Holocaust. Such ethnic groups voted in disproportionately high numbers and clustered in key urban areas in pivotal industrial states with large electoral votes. Jewish voters in particular were the political balance wheel in New York and, to a lesser extent, in Illinois and California. As a consequence, the formulation of American policy in Eastern Europe and in the Middle East had to take into account the political clout of such ethnic groups.

This domestic mix of elitism and pluralism meant that policymakers had to be perpetually aware of the potential for conflict posed by congressional and public opinion. Tactics, rationales, and rhetoric had to be carefully chosen to minimize any such conflict and maximize the extent of domestic support. American globalism required money, personnel, and the mantle of legitimacy, and none of those essentials was possible without legislative and popular consent, sustained at a high level over a long period of time. American leaders were startlingly successful in securing that kind of long-term consensus in support of American internationalism. Politics may not have "stopped at the water's edge" nor pure bipartisan unanimity ever been realized, but American society—from top to bottom—did accept, for more than four decades, both the fact and the desirability of American hegemony. It did so largely because hegemony paid. Its capacity to deliver great and growing material and psychic benefits stood in attractive contrast to the despair and depression of the 1930s. But Americans accepted their global function also because successive administrations were so successful in manufacturing consent. Sensitive to the processes of American politics, they carefully mobilized and rewarded their likeliest supporters in business, labor, and the universities, nullified their potential adversaries through co-optation of the right and suppression of the left, and carefully packaged and boosted their programs in terms that would have the widest public appeal. Not until the Vietnam War and the post-Vietnam economic decline would the legitimacy of hegemony come to be questioned and the political process of generating consensus prove more complex and difficult.

Even single-interest ethnic groups failed to create any major detours in the road traveled by American foreign policy. Where ethnic and national interests coincided, the government gave Eastern European ethnic groups rhetorical flourishes that were satisfying to them and useful to the Cold War policy of containment. Presidents made periodic declarations of support for the liberation of Eastern Europe, secretaries of state preached the virtues of rolling back the Russian empire rather than merely containing it, and the Voice of America encouraged anti-Soviet opinion and behavior behind the Iron Curtain. When ethnic and national interests diverged, however, the ethnic groups came up empty-handed. Central to their concern but marginal to the government's, Eastern Europe was never deemed worth serious risk-taking on the part of American policy. The passive American responses to the crises in Hungary (1956), Czechoslovakia (1968), and Poland (1981) all accentuate this point. Moreover, when détente with Russia seemed desirable in the early 1970s, the American government proved quite vigorous in urging Eastern European ethnics in the United States to embrace that reversal of containment on the grounds that it would facilitate emigration, travel, family contacts, and cultural exchange with their old homelands.

America's Middle Eastern policy offered a similar though more complex pattern. Certainly the potential for conflict between ethnic and national interests always existed. The United States was the first country to recognize the independence of Israel in 1948, and it eventually developed an intimate, special relationship with that new nation. Such developments were consonant with the interests of most American Jews, but there was always concern that they threatened to turn the majority Arab world, with its anti-Israeli hostility, against the United States. Given the importance of Persian Gulf oil and the Suez Canal to America's associates in Europe and Japan, it seemed a hostility that could ill be afforded. For several reasons, however, the complications have thus far proved to be more potential than real.

First, American recognition of Israel carried no Cold War risk of throwing angry Arabs into the Soviet orbit, since Russia was almost as quick as the United States in extending its recognition. Moreover, prevailing wisdom, even in the relatively pro-Arab State Department, viewed the Arab nations as so weak, divided, and generally ineffectual in the late 1940s that they presented no immediate threat to American and Western interests in the area. Second, it must be remembered that the special relationship between the United States and Israel was not a sudden, dramatic development that would have triggered an explosion of Arab anger, but a slow, incremental process nearly two decades in the making. As late as the Suez crisis of 1956, the two countries found themselves in a sharply adversarial position, and the 1958 Lebanon crisis saw the United States use its own troops rather than Israeli surrogates to carry out the so-called Eisenhower Doctrine. In essence, the special relationship did not come to pass until the American preoccupation with Southeast Asia forced the United States to consider the use of regional deputy policemen, and the stunning Israeli success in the 1967 Six Day War demonstrated how well it could play that role.

Finally, when the United States–Israel entente did flower, it served American purposes without endangering the oil resources. Israel's major policing function, in American eyes, was to keep radical, nationalist regimes in Egypt and Syria from stepping out of line and upsetting the regional balance in Russia's favor. Both were non-oil-producing states. The major oil-producing nations, chiefly Saudi Arabia and Iran, were firmly in the American orbit, dominated by conservative regimes and less active in their anti-Israeli diplomacy than other nations in the region. In sum, ethnic and national interests in America's Middle Eastern policy, while always potentially in conflict, have thus far not diverged so sharply that American support for Israel has carried a very high price tag.

Ins-and-Outers

This continuity and consensus, stretched over forty-three years and eight presidents (four from each party) and challenged on the contested terrain of domestic politics, did not happen "in a fit of absence of mind," as the Victorians said of the British Empire. "Nothing much is apt to come into being in that way," noted British historian, A. L. Rowse. Such ideological hegemony at home, matching that abroad, "was the result rather of a conscious, deliberate and tenacious campaign . . . on the part of the elect spirits of the nation." Notwithstanding the tension between concentration and pluralism, there has indeed been an evolution of a loosely integrated foreign policy elite—America's "elect spirits"—who, above all others, have been responsible for the continuity and consensus that spanned decades and administrations.

This foreign policy elite has been concentrated in the upper strata of a hierarchical bureaucracy: the secretaries, under secretaries, and assistant secretaries of state, defense, and the treasury and the administrative officers of the CIA, NSC, ECA, the Agency for International Development (AID), and the President's national security adviser. Since World War II, the elite has been drawn from two quite different sources. About one-third have been career civil service officers who have spent their adult lives climbing the bureaucratic ladder. Moving beyond the middle echelon, where their function was not to make policy but to gather data and implement policy, the more accomplished reached policy-planning levels in the more rarefied upper echelon. These upwardly mobile bureaucrats have been especially evident in the Department of State and have come disproportionately from among the area specialists on the Western European and Russian desks, reflecting the importance attached to those core regions. Classic examples from the early Cold War were George F. Kennan and Charles E. Bohlen, the leading Russian area experts, who came to play key roles in the long-range, globally oriented Policy Planning Staff. They helped conceive the Marshall Plan for Europe and the industrial recovery plan for Japan and lobbied for them with congressional committees. More recent examples have been Alexander M. Haig, Robert C. McFarlane, and John M. Poindexter, who moved up quite a different bureaucratic ladder, through the military services to positions as secretary of state or national security adviser.

The other two-thirds of that foreign policy elite were ins-and-outers. Such individuals move back and forth between the public and private sectors, as though on a perpetual shuttle. Unlike their careerist colleagues, who tend to remain inside only one departmental bureaucracy, ins-and-outers often move from one department to another on their return trips to governmental service. For example, Secretary of State George P. Shultz had earlier stints as secretary of labor, director of the Office of Management and Budget, and secretary of the treasury. The recent director of the Central Intelligence Agency, William J. Casey, served earlier as Arms Control and Disarmament Agency adviser, chairman of the Securities and Exchange Commission, under secretary of state for economic affairs, and president of the Export-Import Bank. Holding these varied roles has tended to make such people less attached to any single perspective, to broaden and integrate their world views by giving them experience in both domestic and international affairs, and to expand their universe of useful political contacts, since they have dealt with a greater variety of congressional committees and private interest groups.

These ins-and-outers have originated in three parts of the private sector, although directly or indirectly almost all have been products of the business world. About 40 percent of ins-and-outers have come directly from corporate management backgrounds. This has been especially true of secretaries of defense: Charles E. Wilson (1953–57), former president of General Motors, Neil H. McElroy (1957–59), former president of Proctor & Gamble, Thomas S. Gates (1959–60), former chairman of the board of Morgan Guaranty Trust, Robert S. McNamara (1961–87), former president of Ford Motor Company, and Caspar W. Weinberger (1981–87), former vice-president of Bechtel Corporation. Another 40 percent of ins-and-outers have come from the nation's most prestigious law firms, invariably ones doing a major amount of business in international corporate law. This has been particularly true of secretaries of state: Dean Acheson (1949–53) had been a senior partner in Covington & Burling, John Foster Dulles (1953–59), a senior partner in Sullivan & Cromwell, William P. Rogers (1969–73), senior partner in Rogers & Wells (where future CIA Director William Casey was also a partner), and Cyrus Vance (1977–80), senior partner in Simpson, Thatcher & Bartlett. Of the remaining 20 percent, more than half have come from academic posts in major universities, usually from political science departments ("defense intellectuals," as they are sometimes called). This background is most often found among national security advisers: McGeorge Bundy (1961–66) had been dean of arts and sciences at Harvard, Walt W. Rostow (1966–69), professor of economic history at MIT, Henry A. Kissinger (1969–75), professor of government at Harvard, Zbigniew Brzezinski (1977–81), professor of government at Columbia, and Richard Allen (1981), a staff member of the Georgetown University Center for Strategic and International Studies. All had close ties to business and business-run foundations. Bundy would head the Ford Foundation after leaving his NSA post, Rostow was America's most famous proponent of procapitalist modernization theory, Kissinger and Brzezinski were both protégés of David Rockefeller, the business patriarch of that famous family, and Allen's private consulting activities in international business were to produce his resignation for alleged conflict of interests.

Of the two subgroups of the elite, careerists and ins-and-outers, the latter has clearly been the dominant group. Achieving prominence and permanence as so-called dollar-a-year men in World War II (Bruce Catton dubbed them "the War Lords of Washington"), these cosmopolitan leaders always carried the day when their views diverged from the expert advice of career bureaucrats. Internal debates over early policy toward communist China, over the 1950 blueprint for militarizing American policy, and over neutralization schemes for Germany, all would amply demonstrate this result. Their repeated triumphs indicated two things. First, their multiple roles, both in the private sector and in varied governmental positions, had given them a broader and stronger base of power than careerists, with their more singular base of power in a particular department. Second, they were always able to fall back on an argument that has proven to be decisive, even in the face of the superior expertise held by the careerists: namely, that their varied portfolios made it easier for them to see the big picture while more narrow experts could not see the forest for the trees. Dean Acheson might agree with Russian experts (like Kennan and Bohlen) that the National Security Council exaggerated the Russian communist menace but argue successfully that the global crisis of the free world in 1950 necessitated mass military spending anyway. Dean Rusk might agree with Asian experts that Ho Chi Minh was more of an Asian Tito than a Russian lackey but argue successfully that Asian neutralism was as dangerous as Asian communism to the essential task of reintegrating the Pacific rim into the world-system. Henry Kissinger might agree with African specialists that America could do business with the Marxist regime in Angola but argue successfully that to do so would set a bad precedent worldwide. ("You may be right in African terms, but I'm thinking globally," he said.)

Such schisms have been the exception rather than the rule. Until the post-Vietnam era, when serious and sustained differences divided even ins-and-outers, there was great homogeneity of opinion within the foreign policy elite. Moreover, this was matched by longevity in power, as its members measured their public service not in terms of one or two presidential administrations but in terms of decades. Paul H. Nitze, for example, chaired the Policy Planning Staff during the second Truman administration, and, still active three and a half decades later, headed the Reagan administration's arms control negotiations with the Russians. That commonality and prolonged tenure helped make the foreign policy elite the very heart of the imperial presidency. Its members became companions and tutors to the presidents, socializing with them and instructing them on their proper world view and on America's place in it. That was true even of chief executives like Dwight Eisenhower, Richard Nixon, and Lyndon Johnson, who brought international experience and a reasonably coherent global vision to the job. It was truer still of presidents like Harry Truman and John Kennedy, whose experience and perspective were more limited; and most true of those like Gerald Ford, Jimmy Carter, and Ronald Reagan, who were virtual neophytes in international affairs. All were intelligent and learned quickly, and even the most ill-prepared left his personal stamp upon American foreign policy. Still, over the course of forty-three years, none of these presidents ever strayed outside the fairly narrow range that constituted mainstream American foreign policy. Each accepted the reality and propriety of American hegemony. Each came to understand, master, and accept the complex but coherent vision of internationalism toward which that hegemonic power was pushing and pulling the world-system. Republicans and Democrats, pragmatists and ideologues, wielders of power and yielders of power—for all, continuity rather than discontinuity marked the presidential changings of the guard. And, more than any other variable, it was the presence and power of that foreign policy elite—those upper-level careerists and those ins-and-outers—that accounted for that striking stability.

What set the foreign policy elite apart from all other groups was its coherent and cosmopolitan world view, a systematic and systemic analysis of foreign policy. The ins-and-outers especially, because of the multiple functions they performed and the double-tracked perspectives they gained from public and private spheres, were stimulated to see the world as a system, a world-system: a kind of ecological whole of moving, dynamic, interconnected parts, in which every part affects every other part, and, in turn, the whole. And, because ecological systems often change slowly over time, they were inclined to project American foreign policy needs over decades-long periods, even, in Henry Luce's famous phrase, an "American Century." It was this *long-term globalism* that set them apart from Congress, the middle bureaucracy, and much of the business community, each of which has a more acute concern for special interests, organizational imperatives, or short-term profits. It is perhaps appropriate, then, that this study employ a world-system analysis, for that was the very analysis used by the group with the most autonomous power to shape and make American foreign policy.

2 | Seeking Supremacy: The Historical Origins of American Hegemony, 1895–1945

> We have a moral obligation to stay out of war if possible. But we also have a moral obligation to keep open the course of our commerce and of our finance.
> —*Woodrow Wilson, 1916*

> If we see that Germany is winning we should help Russia and if Russia is winning we ought to help Germany and that way let them kill as many as possible, although I don't want to see Hitler victorious under any circumstances.
> —*Senator Harry S. Truman, 1941*

In 1895, Brooks Adams published his controversial book, *The Law of Civilization and Decay*, and in 1900, he followed it with a more optimistic message in his *American Economic Supremacy*. Great grandson of John Adams and grandson of John Quincy Adams, the brilliant and eccentric Brooks was, in his own right, confidante and adviser to Theodore Roosevelt—soon to be America's first modern imperial president—and to John Hay, secretary of state *extraordinaire*. The two main theses articulated in Adams' books were to echo resonantly and repeatedly in the thoughts, writings, and uttered words of the subsequent twentieth-century Americans with the most power to shape American foreign policy. In essence, Brooks Adams argued that the international system was in the process of disintegration and that only the United States, with its economic supremacy, could offer the global leadership necessary to stabilize the world order. After a half-century of seeking, America finally would manage to fulfill Adams' prescriptive prophecy with its triumph in World War II.

America as a Regional Power, 1895–1915

Written during the terrible 1890s depression, Adams' first book witnessed his awareness of three interrelated crises. First, all the industrialized core countries were trapped in the last quarter of the nineteenth century in the

"Long Depression." Overinvestment in production systems too small-scale to be efficient and selling in protected, national markets too limited to be sufficient resulted in a steadily declining rate of profit. Worse yet, traditional efforts to raise profits by cutting labor costs produced a bitter working-class backlash whose episodic violence and growing cohesiveness made class conflict a reality and revolution a constant specter. Second, the decline of British hegemony after 1870 meant that no restraining mechanism existed in the world-system to prevent individual nations from using mercantilism and imperialism to revive the rate of profit and pacify working-class discontent. Challenged by the power of newly unified Germany, weakened by a half-century of playing the world's policeman, and debilitated by lowered productivity and declining commercial competitiveness, Britain no longer had either the will or the power to force others to play by its traditional rules of free trade and economic internationalism. Indeed, it haltingly joined other great powers in nationalistic measures to protect their home markets and enlarge their imperial markets in Asia, Africa, the Near East, and Latin America.

Finally, Adams' first book reflected his gloomy conviction that America had not escaped Europe's malaise. Despite its far larger common market, integrated by the recently completed railroad revolution, it too had fallen victim to the Long Depression of declining profits and escalating class conflict—the "year of violence" in 1877, the "great upheaval" of 1886, and the "terrible year" of 1894. Like their European counterparts, American capitalists and conservative politicos embraced the overproduction theory and the belief that a permanent industrial surplus, well in excess of effective domestic purchasing power, required them to monopolize the home market through protective tariffs and to expand the foreign market through participation in the so-called new imperialism. Seeming validation of Adams' analysis was soon to come in the Spanish-American War of 1898 and American colonial dominion over the Philippines, Puerto Rico, Hawaii, Wake Island, and Guam, and its quasi-colonial control of Cuba.

Adams' second book, published in 1900, was far more upbeat. In his first, *The Law of Civilization and Decay*, he had posited that international society, as well as individual nations, moved in "oscillations between barbarism and civilization, or, what amounts to the same thing, . . . from a condition of physical dispersion to one of concentration." British hegemony had provided the concentration—the center—that made civilization (progress and prosperity) possible, but now centrifugal dispersion would reduce the international system to a war of all against all.

In *America's Economic Supremacy*, Adams revealed a way to defy his law of inevitable oscillation. Because of three developments, he was now persuaded that a rapid and peaceful transition from British hegemony to American preponderance could yet turn the world back toward concentration and civilization. Adams' book title identified the most important factor. Economic supremacy, he believed, was the basis of all other forms of power. By 1900, the United States had surpassed Great Britain as the world production leader in iron and steel, coal, and textiles. Moreover, the great merger movement of 1897 onward had made American industry the most large-scale in the world. That emergence of big business made it possible for U.S. Steel, Standard Oil Trust, International Harvester, American Sugar Refining, Northern Securities Company, and many others to generate such cost-saving large production runs that American goods could undersell European ones of comparable quality throughout the world economy.

Coupled with American economic supremacy was a change in its dominant ideology. By 1900, American leaders were moving away from the nationalistic ideology of tariff protectionism and overseas imperialism. The ruling Republican Party moved to embrace a different ideology of tariff reciprocity and the Open Door policy. In the Dingley tariff of 1897 and the Open Door notes of 1899–1900, Adams saw the glimmer of a transformation from defensive nationalism to expansive internationalism, to the ebullient notion that American economic supremacy was best served by an unlimited global market rather than a restricted national and colonial market. The tariff law sought to make it easier for foreigners to sell into the American market so that they could earn some of the dollars necessary to buy America's expanded exports. The Open Door policy in China attempted, in part, to persuade other core powers that imperial competition for exclusive territory was not only confrontational and dangerous but economically inefficient as well. In the first place, formal colonialism was cost-ineffective because it stimulated anticolonial resistance and rebellion that was expensive to control or repress. While perhaps less true in small, isolated islands, important mainly as coaling depots, cable relay stations, and naval bases, it was especially true of heavily populated, established societies, like China, valuable for their potential markets and raw materials. In addition, closed colonial monopolies offered no incentive to core capitalists to become more efficient, while the free market competition of an Open Door context ("a fair field and no favor," as Secretary of State Hay put it) would discipline them to make all their operations, foreign and domestic alike, more efficient and profitable.

Finally, *America's Economic Supremacy* envisioned a third development that could complete America's substitution for Great Britain as the center of the world-system. Persuaded that economic power and ideological persuasion alone would not produce hegemony, Adams argued that the United States must take an increasingly large role in policing the world order. Economic and moral power had to be translated into military power if America was to have, as Franklin Roosevelt later put it, its "rendezvous with destiny." The successful war against Spain in 1898 demonstrated a greater American willingness to use force in the Caribbean and the Pacific, but Adams was less optimistic that the American public would embrace the role of global policeman. Military power potentially demanded great sacrifices, not only by risking human lives, but by endangering America's traditional opposition to standing military forces in times of peace. Consequently, Adams came to believe that only a strong imperial president could carry the day. Only a charismatic leader in the White House, willing to extol masculine, military values and able to make his personal will tantamount to the will of the people, could persuade America to make that choice. Not surprisingly, Adams saw his friend Theodore Roosevelt as the kind of modern president America would require if its citizens were to be persuaded that global policing was a moral responsibility, bearing an economic gain sufficient to offset any necessary sacrifices of life and principle.

Judged against the reality of the period between 1895 and 1915, Adams' prescriptive vision was premature at best. To speak of American economic supremacy was misleading. Still a net debtor itself, the United States lacked the commercial and financial tools to translate its industrial superiority into commensurate export gains. Deficient in marketing networks overseas and wholly lacking foreign branch banks, American capitalists found it difficult to develop markets and to finance sales. Likewise, America's ideological transformation remained incomplete. Protectionism would not fade away, as the Payne-Aldrich tariff of 1907 demonstrated, and open door rhetoric was belied by closed door, imperialistic practices, especially in the Caribbean and Pacific basins.

Finally, even presidential charisma could not generate sufficient domestic support for an American role in global pacification. The attentive public might endorse "big stick" gunboat diplomacy in Cuba and Nicaragua, the Philippines and northern China (the Boxer Rebellion), but Europe was a different matter. The public might applaud Theodore Roosevelt's blustery brag that he took the Canal Zone and let Congress debate, "and while the debate goes on the Canal does also"; and it might approve his mediation of the Russo-Japanese War over dominance in Northeast Asia. But efforts to interject American influence into European and Mediterranean affairs (for example, the Algeciras conference over a Moroccan crisis) ignited no such approbation. Notwithstanding the hegemonic visions of Adams, Roosevelt, and a host of other budding internationalists, American expansionism prior to 1915 remained firmly regional in nature, confined to its traditional nineteenth century spheres of ambition in Latin America and the Pacific basin. Europe beckoned hardly at all. Traditional isolationism warned against European entanglements, while European mercantilism seemed likely to shut American capitalists out of European markets. So, American economic expansion largely restricted its profit-making activities to the developing semiperiphery: to China, where the American Open Door policy followed Marco Polo's dream of Cathay's fabled markets; to Brazil, where Americans encouraged that would-be colossus of the South to break its economic dependence on Great Britain; to Canada, where American goods and capital sought a back door into an increasingly protected British empire; and to Mexico, where $1 billion in American investment—more than Mexico's own investment, more than all other foreign investment combined—made that country an economic client-state by 1910. In sum, the two main pillars of American policy, the Monroe Doctrine and the Open Door policy, retained a firmly regional orientation. Not until Wilson's Fourteen Points would the latter policy be applied more internationally; not until the Truman Doctrine would the Monroe Doctrine be translated into a policy global in scope.

World War I and American Globalism

World War I was a watershed for the world-system and for the American position in it. Climax to a half-century of increasing competitiveness and fragmentation of the world order, World War I began with Germany's first attempt to dominate Europe's industrial heartland (the Stuttgart-Antwerp-Paris "iron triangle") and its Balkan and Near Eastern periphery. This coincided with Japan's first attempt to dominate China and Northeast Asia through its 21 Demands (a virtual ultimatum for a Japanese protectorate in China) and its takeover of the German sphere of influence in northern China. It ended with the Bolshevik Revolution in Russia and eventually, by both choice and coercion, with the partial withdrawal of that nation from the world-system. In short, the interdependent world economy of the mid-nineteenth century, presided over by the British navy, British bankers, and British free trade ideology, seemed to be dissolving into a series of rigid regional economies.

In contrary fashion, however, World War I also marked the emergence of the United States as a truly global power and the attendant possibility that it might replace or join with Great Britain in restoring cohesiveness to the political order and the world economy. American economic supremacy was becoming a reality rather than a precocious notion. Owners of American factories, fields, and mines discovered that the developed European core was a far superior consumer of their products than the more problematic semiperipheral Asia and Latin America. American bankers discovered the enormous profitability inherent in financing such sales, and their war loans and postwar loans to Europe offered leverage that might keep Europe open to American goods in the future. And the American government facilitated these developments by permitting large corporations to ignore the antitrust laws if their overseas operations might thereby be made more efficient and competitive. The government also amended the Federal Reserve banking laws to legalize and encourage establishment of American branch banks overseas. Already the dominant workshop economy, America's mass production technology (Fordism) and scientific management (Taylorism) were the envy of Europe and Japan, and the United States also seemed ready to join Great Britain as the banking and credit center of the world-system.

Equally important were the ideological and military alterations in the American position. Led by a brilliant and strong-willed president, Woodrow Wilson, the United States seemed poised to take the baton of internationalism from the British. Wilson's classic Fourteen Points statement of early 1918 was perhaps the quintessential expression of the newly dominant American world view. Renouncing balance of power politics, that handmaiden of autarkic nationalism, Wilson called for freedom of the seas, free trade ("the removal, so far as possible, of all economic barriers"), a global open door ("an equality of trade conditions among all the nations"), arms reductions, political self-determination, and a gradual end to colonialism. Moreover, Wilson crowned his commitment to an internationalist ideology with a call for American participation in a "general association of nations" and thus a role in "affording mutual guarantees of political independence and territorial integrity to great and small states alike." In effect, the Fourteen Points address called for the very thing that Brooks Adams had deemed crucial to the exercise of American hegemony—an American role in global pacification. A year later, Wilson made clear that he envisioned a joint Anglo-American naval police force to protect and guarantee the new international order. "We should between us," he told one prominent British leader, "do the whole of the marine policing of the world. . . . Together, we should have vastly preponderating navies over any forces that could be possibly brought against us."

These changes in the American economic, ideological, and military positions were necessary preconditions for American hegemony. As postwar events demonstrated, however, they were not yet sufficient. American power in 1919 was still not so preponderant that other nations had to bow to it nor American leaders so experienced that they made the best use of the considerable power they did possess. Erstwhile European allies, principally France, had forced Wilson to accept a peace that compromised many of his internationalist principles. In particular, the Versailles peace treaty assessed Germany $33 billion in reparations to expiate its "war guilt," divided up its empire as spoils of war, reduced its territorial access to raw materials, and denied it membership in the League of Nations and adequate means of national defense. Frustrated in his failure to integrate Germany into the unitary, interdependent world order, Wilson failed as well in his effort to deflect Japan from its continuing strategy of unilateral,

Pan-Asian imperialism. Unwilling to renounce the 21 Demands in China, Japan resisted American efforts to coax or coerce it back into a more collective framework.

The failure to include Germany and Japan made a shambles of Wilson's vision of a unitary world order. He hoped, however, to use American postwar leadership to rectify the inadequacies and then to preside over the final triumph of global integrationism. As he told a group of journalists, America had fought the world war "to do away with an old order and to establish a new one," and "it was my paramount duty . . . to lend such counsel and aid as I could to this great, may I not say, final enterprise of humanity." America's new leverage as world creditor would be one means to that goal. So, too, would American participation in global peace keeping. Especially important would be American membership in the League of Nations and its moral commitment, as a "Great Power" representative on the League's Security Council, to guarantee and protect the integrity of all League member nations throughout the globe. Of additional relevance would be American willingness to ratify a Franco-American alliance guaranteeing the security of western Europe against future German resurgence.

Wilson's hopes were dashed by the refusal of the U.S. Senate to ratify the Versailles Treaty and membership in the League of Nations. (Later, by inaction, it failed to ratify the Franco-American alliance.) The rejection symbolized the lack of an effective domestic consensus in behalf of American internationalism. Indeed, it highlighted the contrary reality, that much of the American public still had not accepted the legitimacy and propriety of American hegemony.

Many political groups did accept the desirability of a global police role for the United States but did not agree with the terms dictated by the Versailles Treaty. Centrist internationalists, like Elihu Root, saw the Versailles system as punitively anti-German and feared that the League's role in enforcing it would trap the United States into supporting a policy of repressing an inevitable German revival rather than encouraging its integration into the collective framework. Right-wing internationalists, like Henry Cabot Lodge, thought the peace treaty protected the status quo of European empires, and they feared that American membership in the League would deny the United States the freedom to encourage the break-up of those colonial systems and their integration into an American imperium or sphere of influence. Left-wing internationalists, like William Borah, saw the Versailles Treaty as an imperialist, antirevolutionary, anti–Third World instrument, whose hypocritical mandate system and rejection of racial equality vitiated Wilson's commitment to self-determination and decolonization. All understood the central reality, that the League of Nations, whose covenant was Article I of the Versailles Treaty, was only as good or as bad as the status quo the treaty was supposed to enforce. All, for different reasons, found it an unacceptable status quo. Had it been more to their liking, all would have been willing to countenance an American role in global pacification.

Another group offered more fundamental opposition to Wilsonian internationalism, some rejecting it altogether and some opposing its prospective requirement that the United States make repressive force a feature of its foreign policy. This loose cluster of so-called isolationists represented a broad spectrum of American society. Manufacturers in industries not competitive in world markets were more concerned with home markets than foreign ones. This was especially true of labor-intensive industries like textiles. In the decade after 1900, Chinese, Indian, and Japanese competition increasingly priced that portion of American industry out of the world market. Pacifist organizations, like the Women's International League for Peace and Freedom, recovered from the repressive wartime atmosphere and parlayed postwar disillusionment with the "killing fields" of Europe into significant support for disarmament and opposition to American military interventionism.

Ethnic groups, unhappy with the postwar prospects for their homelands, voiced concern over policies that would commit the United States to maintain the postwar status quo. Some German-Americans, recovering some measure of respectability, offered misgivings about the anti-German nature of the Versailles Treaty. Many Irish-Americans, their Anglophobia further fueled by repressive British action in Ireland, warned that joining the League could only make the United States an accessory to sustaining a brutal British empire. Russian-American radicals, influential in the American Socialist Party, braved wartime antiradicalism and the postwar Red Scare hysteria to express concern that the peace treaty and the League were instruments of counterrevolution and anti-Russian interventionism. Relatedly, many labor leaders, even in the conservative American Federation of Labor, took exception to the Wilsonian internationalism espoused by Samuel Gompers and the dominant faction on the AF of L executive committee. Motivated by a mix of ethnic and radical perspectives, they articulated an anti-imperialist, anti-interventionist policy abroad and a strategy of income redistribution and nationalization of mines and railways at home.

The 1920s and Semi-internationalism

During the 1920s, Republican presidents Harding, Coolidge, and Hoover labored in the same vineyards as their Democratic predecessor. Centrist internationalists themselves, they fundamentally shared Wilson's vision of a unitary, integrated world, governed by internationalist principles of freer trade, open doors, decolonization, arms controls, self-determination, and a specialized division of labor. On the other hand, they also operated within the same limitations Wilson faced in 1919–20: the lack of clearly preponderant power abroad and of political consensus at home. The consequence was a kind of semi-internationalism; a half-way house between isolationism ("the retreat to normalcy") and full-blown, consistent internationalism.

The overarching goal of American foreign policy was, in the words of Secretary of State Charles E. Hughes, a "Pax Americana," a new world order under American leadership. However, in deference to the domestic reluctance toward a peace-keeping role for the United States, that Pax Americana was not to be maintained by arms but by moral suasion and economic leverage. Moreover, it was to function outside the framework of the League of the Nations and the League's moral commitment to use force in defense of its members. Within those significant limitations, American leaders in the 1920s pursued the primary Wilsonian goal of integrating the diverse parts of the world-system into a single, interdependent whole. Intervening in the pivotal European issue of German reparations, the United States sought to foster German integration through provisional settlement in the Dawes Plan of 1924 and a final arrangement in the Young Plan. The two plans, named after their American financier authors, attempted to alleviate the burden of German economic recovery by scaling down installment payments between 1924 and 1929 and then reducing the remaining demands from $33 to $9 billion thereafter.

American dollar diplomacy resulted in French-Belgian evacuation of the German industrial Ruhr Valley in 1924, occupied the previous year because Germany defaulted on reparations payments. In turn, it promoted an atmosphere of détente between Germany and its wartime opponents that helped produce the Locarno Pact of 1925 guaranteeing the security of the western borders between Germany and France and Belgium. That "Spirit of Locarno" led to German admission to the League of Nations in 1926. Germany was now officially characterized as a "peace-loving" nation and accorded the same commercial terms as other core capitalist powers. The end result, hoped American leaders, would be a Germany prosperous enough to resist the blandishments of bolshevism and to play a key role, as Europe's most efficient economy, in the postwar recovery of that continent. It would also mean, they hoped, a Germany secure enough to turn away from the temptations of right-wing revengefulness and to seek its security within a collective framework.

American foreign policy played an even more direct and important role in the parallel effort to reintegrate Japan into the international order in Asia. Prompted by economic need, concern for national security, and a sense of cultural mission, Japan had sought since the Sino-Japanese War in the 1890s to become the dominant power in Asia. It remained torn, however, between alternative strategies. It could align itself with the dominant capitalist world power and secure its sponsorship or strike out on its own, through either force or diplomacy, to obtain a Pan-Asian system under its own aegis ("our Monroe Doctrine," as some Japanese asserted). From 1902 to 1915, Japan largely followed the first strategy, through alliance with Great Britain. Beginning with the 21 Demands of 1915, however, Japan changed tacks to take advantage of the Western preoccupation with the great war in Europe. One consequence was a rising conflict between Japan and an America that, acting out its own economic and cultural needs, harbored a grand design that saw the whole Pacific rim integrated into an open world market, insuring for the United States equal access to Asia's future economic development. That conflict manifested itself most dangerously in a spiraling naval arms race initiated by the American Naval Bill of 1916.

In the 1920s, the United States took the lead in deterring Japan from unilateral expansionism and promoted anew the alternative of alignment with the dominant Western power. This time, however, the United States, rather than Great Britain, would assume the paramount role. At the Washington Conference in late 1921–early 1922, the United States secured Japanese acceptance of three treaties that together constituted the so-called Washington System. The Four-Power Pacific Treaty abrogated the Anglo-Japanese Alliance and replaced it with a consultative arrangement involving the United States, Japan, Great Britain, and France. The Nine-Power Treaty guaranteed Chinese independence, endorsed the Open Door policy in trade and finance, and renounced new political ventures that might fragment or colonize China. Finally, the Naval Armaments Treaty established a ten-year naval holiday in new capital shipbuilding and established a 5-5-3 size ratio for the American, British, and Japanese navies—large enough for Japan to defend its existing territory but not so large that it could expand unilaterally. The cost to the United States for Japanese acceptance of this system included willingness to give Japan "an extraordinary share" of profit-making opportunities in Manchuria and a commitment that the Second China Consortium, acting as investment clearinghouse for China proper, would accord Japan an equitable share there as well. This was a small price if, as American leaders hoped, the treaties deterred Japanese unilateralism, kept Asia open to general capitalist penetration, and used Japan as role model of procapitalist modernization for the rest of the Pacific rim.

Despite these integrationist ventures in both Europe and Asia, American policy fell well short of achieving a Pax Americana. American economic policy remained strongly influenced by nationalism and parochialism. Tariff protectionism remained the norm, as did American insistence that Europe repay its war debts to the United States. Both inhibited the capacity of major trading partners to earn or retain the dollars necessary to being effective consumers of American exports. Similarly, American governmental pressure on private investors to make only nonmilitary, nonspeculative, "productive" loans met with mixed success. Consequently, from equal parts of greed, inexperience, and inadequate public accountability, private lending by American capitalists put a great deal of money into the world economy, but not always where it did the most good.

The inadequacy of American economic power to promote global integration was matched by America's unwillingness to concern itself with European security matters and by a lack of interest in military spending. For example, its fostering of German integration through Dawes-Young economic diplomacy was not accompanied by any political or military diplomacy. By and large, the United States deferred to Great Britain, the declining hegemon, on issues involving European security. It might approve of British participation in the Locarno arrangements, but it would not play more than an indirect role in boosting the "Spirit of Locarno." Similarly, in Asia the United States declined to build up its navy to even the minimum standards incorporated into the Washington Conference naval disarmament pact, even though Great Britain and Japan engaged in a de facto arms race in smaller, noncapital ships not covered by the treaty. The consequence of American underspending and Anglo-Japanese overspending was the very strategic imbalance the Washington Conference had sought to avoid, lest it undermine the Open Door policy. Given American public opinion, U.S. leaders could address that imbalance only by efforts to persuade the British and the Japanese to enlarge the Washington naval agreement to cover light cruisers, destroyers, and submarines. Their initial efforts at the Geneva disarmament conference in 1927 were a total failure; their subsequent attempt at the London Naval Conference in 1930 met with only limited success.

The gap between the grandiose pretensions of Pax Americana and the more limited reality of American economic amd political actions also manifested itself in core-periphery relations. American policymakers in the 1920s remained committed to earlier Wilsonian policies of informal empire (the substitution of informal financial controls for formal political control), and a collaborative open door policy of equal access to markets and raw materials, seeing these as the most efficient way for the core countries to exploit those of the periphery. Moreover, they met with partial success in breaching European efforts to monopolize Third World resources. For example, American governmental pressure helped American oil companies gain positions as minority stockholders in existing European companies in the Middle East, while it also helped to break down British efforts to create a rubber cartel to manipulate prices to their advantage.

Despite those achievements, most of the periphery remained organized on closed door rather than open door principles. For example, Europe's petroleum deficiency made it unwilling to permit wholly independent American operations in the Middle East, which could have disrupted European control of production, pricing, and marketing strategies. In other instances, private American corporations found it more profitable to collaborate with European resource monopolies than to support their own government's efforts to break them. Just such a business-government schism both delayed and limited the success of the Commerce Department in undermining the British-dominated rubber cartel. In addition, American military interventionism and the financial protectorates in the Antilles and Central America belied the principle of an anti-imperialist, antimilitarist open door. That evident double standard strengthened European and Japanese resistance to the open door, since it produced a pervasive suspicion that the real meaning of that policy was "what's yours is mine, and what's mine remains mine." Finally, the periphery itself refused to play passive performer on America's open door stage. In China, for example, many leading intellectuals came to see the open door as a more insidious form of imperialism (neocolonialism, to use a later term), to be resisted like any other form. Chinese nationalism, generated in part by such views, helped make China so volatile in the 1920s that the Second China Consortium—the financial vehicle for open door collaboration—failed to secure or float any developmental loans there. That failure, contrasted with the profitability of Japanese colonization schemes in Korea and southern Manchuria, suggested to Japan that unilateral force and closed spheres might be more rewarding than open door internationalism.

The 1930s: From Drift to Mastery

The Great Depression began in the United States in the aftermath of the 1929 Wall Street crash and spread to Europe and Japan in 1931–32. International bank lending dried up as central banks attempted to rescue their own prime domestic customers then, after the bank system collapsed in 1932, tried to save themselves. The crumbling of the international gold standard destroyed stability and predictability in currency convertibility and initiated round after round of competitive monetary devaluations. Trade among core powers plummeted sharply, a trend exacerbated by a wave of high protective tariffs led by the American Smoot-Hawley law in 1931. The bottom dropped out of prices for raw materials produced by the periphery. Late in the 1920s, President Calvin Coolidge had concluded that "our investments and trade relations are such that it is almost impossible to conceive of any conflict anywhere on earth which would not affect us injuriously." Now, in the early 1930s, the conflict was not simply "anywhere" but everywhere, and while largely economic in nature for the moment, it would soon become political and military as well.

Domestic opinion differed sharply over the causes of the Great Depression and America's proper response to it. Economic nationalists argued that American manufacturers, bankers, and farmers had become extraordinarily and dangerously dependent on foreign markets, investments, and raw materials during the spectacular global expansion of the American economy between 1915 and 1929. Seeing the origin of the depression as external rather than internal, they concluded that America's vulnerable dependence on the global economy had backfired when international disintegration had dragged the American economy down with it. Those holding such opinions generally opted for a program of capitalism in one country—or at most, one hemisphere. Concretely, that meant prohibitively high protective tariffs on foreign goods to give American businessmen a de facto monopoly of America's continent-spanning common market. It also meant economic planning of the domestic economy so that production would not outrun effective consumer demand—planning carried out on a voluntary basis by businessmen themselves rather than by government agencies.

Economic internationalists had a quite different view, and their views would ultimately prevail during the administrations of Franklin D. Roosevelt. In their opinion, the American economy in the 1920s had been insufficiently internationalized. Its residual economic nationalism, manifested in its policies on tariffs, war debts, and lending, had prevented the United States from playing a consistent leadership role in behalf of an integrated, unitary world economy. Without that leadership, other core nations had been freer to follow autarkic strategies in their domestic economies and their overseas empires. The result had been the partial fragmentation of the world-system into a series of overduplicative, undersized, nonspecialized economies selling to national and imperial markets too limited and small to be sufficiently profitable. Over time, argued these internationalists, such collective inefficiency had depressed profits, discouraged capital spending, and led to stock market speculation, nonproductive corporate takeovers, and unsafe lending as the only means of profit taking. Those holding such opinions favored a vigorous assertion of American leadership in pushing and pulling the world away from fragmentation toward the Wilsonian goal of an interdependent world order with low tariffs, free convertibility, nil capital controls, and open doors. In the meantime, they concluded, the American domestic economy would have to be put back on the track before it could act as the locomotive to pull the rest of the world economic train once more down the internationalist right-of-way. There developed a tacit, temporary agreement between economic nationalists and internationalists that short-term domestic recovery temporarily took priority over efforts to rebuild the shattered world-system.

The Great Depression unleashed centrifugal forces in the world-system, as each core nation sought to save itself through autarkic measures of planned production at home and managed trade abroad. True of the United States, it was even more true of core nations that did not possess the great American advantages of a continental free market and self-sufficiency in food and raw materials. These ventures in managed economies—from more statist versions like Hitler's New Plan to the looser business-government collaboration of Roosevelt's New Deal—floundered on one elemental fact. All tended to further contract the volume of world trade and, in turn, forced individual states to make frightful choices about how to divide the shrunken economic pie. While economic international-ism postulated a rising growth tide that would lift all who rode it, domestic economic planning was essentially a process of deciding who would be the winners and who the losers. Supply-side planning, putting money in the hands of capitalist investors at the expense of workers' wages and welfare, risked the wrath of social rebellion. Demand-side planning, putting money in the hands of working consumers at the expense of capitalists' profits, risked the flight of capital elsewhere in search of better returns.

Eventually, each state would resolve that class contradiction in the only way that capitalism had ever resolved it, by an external expansion that would revive the rate of profit sufficiently to reward both capital and la-bor. In the case of Germany and Japan, the expansion came through mil-itary intimidation and war as a means of redistributing wealth and power in their favor. That choice of militaristic, territorial expansion flowed partly from their status as "have-not" nations, desperately deficient in food and raw materials, dependent on industrial sales abroad to finance pri-mary commodity imports, and thus in a position to either "export or die." It resulted partly from a revengeful revival of earlier attempts to institute a German-dominated continental system in Europe and a Japanese-domi-nated Pan-Asianism from the North China Sea to the Indian Ocean. Finally, it sprang from the nature of their political regimes and the evident predi-lection for the use of force by the brutal Nazi regime in Germany and the ascendant military professionals in Japan. The consequent chronicle is a sad and familiar one: In Germany's case there was its remilitarization of the Rhineland in 1936; its de facto intervention in the Spanish civil war in 1937; absorption of Austria in early 1938; its takeover of the Czechoslova-kian Sudetenland in the Munich agreement of late 1938 and conquest of the rest of Czechoslovakia in early 1939; the invasion of Poland in Sep-tember 1939; the Blitzkrieg onslaught of France, the Low Countries, and Norway in early 1940; the Battle for Britain in late 1940; and the invasion of Russia in June 1941. Similarly, there was Japan's conquest of Manchuria in

1931–32, abrogation of the Washington naval pact in 1934 and full-scale war on China in 1937, its articulation of the Greater East Asian Co-Prosperity sphere goal in 1938, its de facto absorption of French Indochina in 1940, and its general assault on the American, British, and Dutch empires in the western Pacific in late 1941. Together, in late 1940, Germany, Japan, and Italy signed the Tripartite Pact, making common cause against possible American intervention and articulating a vision of Germany's Eurasian common market and Japan's Asian crescent to meet and link in the Persian Gulf. *"Lebensraum,"* as Hiter put it: living space!

Living space for Germany and Japan, however, was dying space for American private enterprise and for capitalism as an integrated world-system. If the two Axis powers succeeded, the world would devolve into four classic empires organized around industrial cores: Western Europe, North America, Russia, and Japan—each empire rationalizing and protecting its own space and resources and pushing and probing that of its rivals. The whole arrangement would obstruct the inherent inclination of capital toward a maximum of profit making options. It would increase exploitation of the periphery by the core and thus heighten the likelihood of social insurgency. It would necessitate garrisoning measures and a sustained, intensive level of military spending that would distort and weaken industrial economies. Called by some Americans "the quarter-sphere" policy and by others a "fortress America," it was rejected by elite leaders on two grounds. First, it could work only with extensive government planning (state capitalism), which might destroy the prerogatives of private enterprise, reduce the rate of profit, and socialize institutions that in turn might later be usurped by leftist governments and used against the interests of capital. Second, it abandoned three-quarters of the world-system at the very moment when all conditions were favorable for American hegemony, when the real possibility existed that America could be master of all it surveyed and not merely be satisfied with its own backyard.

Yet these same hankerers-after-hegemony did not indulge in that role until 1940. Limiting themselves to economic appeasement, they tried to persuade Germany and Japan that open doors, world markets, and disarmament could give rewards as great as closed doors, regional markets, and militarism—and without the unacceptable risks of Armageddon. This American preference for the carrot rather than the stick reflected several factors. First, the United States lacked the credibility to play a more coercive role. It was militarily underprepared and was saddled with an unimpressive record of noninvolvement in European security matters and ineffectual involvement in Asian ones like the 1931 Manchurian crisis. Second, American policymakers feared that coercion would only lead Germans and Japanese to rally around their regimes rather than lead to their unseating. Appeasement, on the other hand, while it might not deter these regimes (perhaps nothing would), might buy time that could be put to good use. Finally, and most importantly, appeasement seemed the only compromise between coercion and doing nothing that could provide some common ground between the contending forces of internationalism and its opponents in American society.

The same tensions that had divided Americans over the Versailles treaty in 1919, and that had produced mixed results in the 1920s, continued to divide America in the 1930s. Indeed, the dichotomy was more sharp and intense now because both groups were stronger than ever before. Stimulated by the depression to look inward, Americans were more attracted to the antiwar, anti-intervention movement. Powerfully represented in Congress, these so-called isolationists shaped the neutrality laws of the mid-1930s, designed to avoid American involvement in future European wars. At the same time, however, internationalists put aside their party differences and their past disagreements over the proper purposes of American police power and expressed their willingness to support a more risk-taking policy by the Roosevelt administration.

Nineteen forty changed all. Western Europe fell before the German onslaught, Indochina slid into the Japanese orbit, and the Axis powers signed the Tripartite pact. "The nightmare of a closed world," as one historian characterized it, had transcended bad dream and become reality. As the prestigious *Fortune Round Table* put it a year and a half before Pearl Harbor, "What interests us primarily is the longer-range question of whether the American capitalist system could continue to function if most of Europe and Asia should abolish free enterprise." With near unanimity, the American foreign policy establishment would answer that very question in the negative. Arguing that "tariff walls—Chinese walls of isolation—would be futile" in a fragmented world, President Roosevelt himself posited the essential internationalist principle: "Freedom to trade is essential to our economic life. We do not eat all the food we produce; we do not burn all the oil we can pump; we do not use all the goods we can manufacture. It would not be an American wall to keep Nazi goods out; it would be a Nazi wall to keep us in."

Nineteen forty did not change things entirely for the worse, however. Britain held up in the face of a concerted German air war, and in holding up left open the option for the United States to enter the war. Not only did Britain provide the United States with a formidable ally, but it offered an island staging ground that would be essential if Germany were to be dislodged from its continental dominance. The nightmare could yet be transformed to dreams of a free world and open doors, the historical conjuncture and opportunity for hegemony not lost. And American leaders seized it with a vengeance and with a vigor that belied all past reservations. America would go to war. Germany would be crushed, and Japan too, if it proved necessary. Peace would be made on American terms. And if antiwar, anti-internationalist sentiment still influenced public opinion, then that opinion would have to be brought around by political socialization where possible or circumvented by deceit where not.

World War II, then, would be the means by which the United States asserted and assumed hegemony in the world-system; it would become global workshop and banker, umpire and policeman, preacher and teacher. The potential for such arrogation of power had existed since 1919, but now war provided the last ingredients: the will to power by elite leaders and the popular acceptance of the legitimacy and propriety of that will. In the fall of 1940, amidst fading fears and rising expectations, two powerful and articulate careerists in the State Department capsulized the revitalized internationalist perspective. "I have been saying to myself and other people," wrote Adolph Berle in his diary, "that the only possible effect of this war would be that the United States would emerge with an imperial power greater than the world had ever seen." Agreeing with Berle that it was now America's historical turn to succeed Britain as hegemonic power, Norman Davis concluded that "we shall in effect be the heirs of Empire, and it is up to us to preserve its vital parts."

World War as Diplomacy

World War II was, for American leaders, a case of "diplomacy by other means." They fought the war not simply to vanquish their enemies, but to create the geopolitical basis for a postwar world order that they would both build and lead. Assuming their victory to be inevitable, they not only planned for peace even as they waged war but also tailored their military strategies to facilitate implementation of those postwar plans. Concretely, American policymakers sought two major goals. They aimed to insure that the periphery in the Pacific rim, the Mediterranean basin, and Latin America would be integrated, under American aegis, into a global market economy, its resources equally open to all core powers. Specifically, that entailed rolling back Japanese expansion in Asia, blunting Germany's military-economic penetration of Latin America, and even preparing the way for the United States to replace its British ally in the Middle East and the Mediterranean. More importantly, they sought to insure that no one core power would dominate the Eurasian heartland, especially its industrial center in the German Rhine-Ruhr region, northeastern France, and Belgium. That required that Nazi Germany be crushed and that no other nation, like Russia, be allowed to fill the void left by Germany's disempowerment.

These were hegemonic goals, awesomely global and omnipresent in nature. American ambitions then knew few bounds; American power would, however, confront very real limits. It was limited externally by the simple fact that no nation, however paramount, has ever had sufficient power to impose its will unilaterally on the entire rest of the world-system. Dislodging Germany, the world's strongest military power and second strongest industrial power, from its entrenched control of Europe was a task difficult enough to tax any power. Doing so while simultaneously fighting a two-ocean war against Japan was an even more staggering assignment. In addition, American power was limited internally by a semi-isolationist public that had never wholly accepted the logic of internationalism or thought it sufficiently rewarding to merit participation in a world war. The Roosevelt administration feared that, even in the unifying aftermath of Japan's attack on Pearl Harbor, the public's essential support for the war would erode if it were required to endure long casualty lists or make significant economic sacrifices in behalf of American globalism.

This conundrum—how to use limited means to meet unlimited ends— was not a new one. Great Britain, on the eve of its global ascendancy, had confronted a similar puzzle in its world war against Napoleonic France. It had evolved a strategy of minimizing its weaknesses and maximizing its strengths to realize its ambitious aims. Now, a century and a half later, the United States adopted a similar strategy to meet similar circumstances to fulfill similar goals. It was chiefly pragmatism that shaped the strategy, but to a modest degree so did American awareness of British precedents.

The British strategy had been a three-tiered one, and the American strategy neatly mirrored it. First, the British had used their financial and industrial supremacy to arm and subsidize their continental allies (ultimately, Austria, Prussia, and Russia) and then let them do the bulk of the fighting and dying against Napoleon's international army. In like vein, the United States used its awesome economy, not only to build a military machine for itself, but to subsidize its allies through the lend-lease program ($31 billion to Britain, $11 billion to Russia) and then let those allies, especially the Soviet Union, bear the major brunt of fighting the *Wehrmacht*.

Second, the British used their seapower to keep open the Mediterranean and the Caribbean, while limiting British army action largely to the periphery of the Iberian peninsula, the Ottoman Empire, and North America. Similarly, the United States used its seapower to keep open the North Atlantic and to reopen the North Pacific, employed its airpower to punish Germany and Japan industrially and psychologically, and limited its land actions to the periphery of the world-system: North Africa in 1942, Sicily and Italy in 1943, and island-hopping in the Pacific after the 1942 naval victory at Midway.

Finally, Britain entered the main European theater only when the war had reached its final and decisive stage. Its direct military presence acted to inhibit any other continental power from attempting to take France's place in the continental power structure and reinforced the legitimacy of Britain's claim to a dominant say in peace negotiations. In parallel fashion, the United States entered the European theater only in the last and determinant phase of World War II. Operation Overlord, its invasion of France in June 1944, and its push eastward into Germany similarly restrained potential Russian ambitions in the west and assured America's seat at the head of the peace table. It had the added advantage of putting the Rhine-Ruhr area—the primary geoeconomic objective of the war—into Anglo-American hands.

Crucial to the American strategy, and central to early Soviet-American conflict, was the issue of the "second front." From early 1942 onward, the Russians urged the United States and Great Britain to open a second front to relieve them of the awful burden of fighting alone against more than two hundred divisions of the German *Wehrmacht.* The Anglo-American response was long on promise but short on delivery. In May 1942, President Roosevelt informed Josef Stalin that he "expected the formation of a second front this year"; and in August, Prime Minister Winston Churchill assured Stalin that the assault on Europe would begin no later than spring of 1943. Instead, the Americans and the British postponed any direct cross-Channel invasion of Western Europe and focused their military action on the Mediterranean periphery: North Africa in late 1942, and Sicily and Italy in the summer of 1943.

This "periphery" strategy, as military historians call it, has been characterized as a British invention, designed to maintain Britain's traditional sphere of influence in the Mediterranean and to keep open the imperial lifelines to India, East Africa, and the Persian Gulf. It was criticized by American military leaders, such as General Dwight Eisenhower, because it delayed a cross-Channel attack into France and the Low Countries. But it was a strategy happily embraced by American political leaders, including President Roosevelt. It dovetailed with their postwar ambitions to join, if not replace, Great Britain as the dominant power in an area rich in oil and situated at the crossroads of world trade. So the military campaigns of 1942–43 were the opening salvo in the historic transformation of the Mediterranean into an American lake. The strategy would mollify the Russians, they hoped, by keeping the letter, though hardly the spirit, of the second front pledge. In so doing, it maintained the status quo whereby the only armies fighting and dying in the European heartland were Russian and German. If the American war aim was the prevention of single-power, regional hegemony in Europe, what better way to achieve it than by letting the two major contenders for the position exhaust themselves in stalemated struggle?

The strategy also maintained popular support for the war at home. It supplied Americans with a sense of action and some progress toward victory after a year of reverses, yet it did not ask for sacrifices that might erode the war's popularity. The pivotal fact is that the United States could truly have fulfilled its second front pledge only by fighting a very different kind of war than the limited one it chose. It would have had to wage an all-out mobilization struggle, which might have radically sacrificed civilian production and civilian standards of living, and an all-out, early attack that might have produced far higher casualties and higher risks of temporary setbacks. That was a choice internationalist leaders would not make. Any strategy that did not keep casualties minimal, produce an unbroken string of victories, and maintain prosperity at home was one, they feared, that would tempt Americans to turn their backs on *The Good War* (as Studs Turkel called it) and resume their traditional affair with isolationism.

This American strategy nearly backfired. Not only did the Mediterranean campaign come upon hard times in the prolonged, indecisive battle for Italy, but it coincided with a definite shift in the Russian war that saw the Red Army obtain clear ascendancy over the *Wehrmacht.* Indeed, even as American troops landed on North African soil in November 1942, a battle had begun that would prove as decisive for World War II as Gettysburg had for the American Civil War—the siege of Stalingrad. When it ended in debacle for the Germans in February 1943, it was clear that the stalemate stage of the Russo-German war was over. No more warm-weather German offensives followed by cold-weather Russian counteroffensives, with death and destruction on astounding scales—and all on Russian soil (to the uncountable sum of at least twenty million Russian lives by war's end). From now on, it was clear that the battle line would move in only one direction—westward. The only questions were how fast the Russians could go and how far they would choose to go. All this at a time when the Mediterranean commitment of forces made it impossible to get an Anglo-American army into Western Europe itself before the spring of 1944.

The shift in the balance of power occasioned by the Stalingrad battle produced a critical reassessment of American strategy. Analysts for the Joint Chiefs of Staff (JCS) projected mounting successes for the Red Army in 1943 and 1944. Not until early 1945, when it had conquered eastern Prussia and reached the Vistula defense line in Poland, would its fighting forces outdistance their logistical support and be required to halt. At that point, one of two things could happen. The Red Army, after regrouping and reorganizing its supply lines, could successfully carry the battle into Germany, and perhaps beyond to the English Channel; or it could force Germany (and through it, the rest of occupied Europe) to make peace on Russian terms. In either case, the result would be tantamount to Russian hegemony in most or all of Europe. In that case, the JCS report declared, "we would have to conclude that we had lost the war." Hitler might be dead, Nazism smashed, and Germany humbled, but America would have lost the war. For, again, as the JCS acknowledged, it was never the destruction of Nazi Germany *per se* that was the American war aim; it was the prevention of any one power from dominating Europe and limiting American access to it.

Faced with this post-Stalingrad situation, American leaders were forced to reconsider their options. Essentially there were three: play the German card, play the Russian card immediately, or play the Russian card later. The first option was to assassinate Hitler and cut a separate deal with the German generals (hence its name, the "Junker option," referring to a type of German officer). Presumably this plan would entail a separate peace similar to that made with Italian Fascists in 1943. Germany would evacuate Western Europe and either continue the eastern front war or work out separate terms with the Soviet Union. Debatable in its political feasibility, the stratagem suffered from the more fundamental flaw that it would merely return Europe to the 1939 antebellum status quo. Germany would still not be integrated into an internationalist structure, and its generals—hardly more trustworthy than Hitler—would be free to replay the same scenes all over again.

The second alternative was to make a territorial and political settlement with Russia in 1943 in advance of any second front invasion. The obvious advantage was that it would guarantee Britain and America a half-loaf share of Europe regardless of the outcome of the cross-Channel attack. More compellingly obvious was the disadvantage. It would require negotiating a territorial settlement of Europe from a position of Anglo-American weakness. Two hundred eighty Russian divisions, counterpoised against an allied army still situated in Britain, was the sort of power imbalance that would put the Soviets in the political driver's seat. What this plan actually offered was a half loaf that would not include the vital Rhine-Ruhr area. Even if Russia consented to Western occupation of that industrial core, it would surely demand guarantees that it be the major beneficiary of that industry through massive reparations, either through dismantling industrial machinery and shipping it to Russia or through appropriating the lion's share of the industrial goods produced in the region. The end result would be the strengthening of the Russian industrial economy and loss of the German productivity that was crucial to the general recovery of capitalism in Western Europe.

The third option was the one finally chosen. The United States would play the Russian card later. In the meantime, it would do two things: (1) postpone all territorial and political settlements until the Allies' power was such that they could cut a better deal with the USSR; (2) launch a maximum-effort, second-front invasion of France with the German industrial heartland as its ultimate objective. An all-out invasion in 1944 that reached the German frontiers by year's end (at the same time the Russians reached the Vistula) would enable the Americans to deal with the Russians from a position of countervailing power. Rather than settle for the half loaf of a 1943 advance deal, the Allies could play the Russian card in early 1945 with some assurance of getting two-thirds of a loaf. Indeed, a better as well as greater portion: industrial Western Europe to the Western Allies; less-developed, primary-commodity Eastern Europe to the Soviet Union. More-over, this option insured that when peace came, the Anglo-Americans would have a respectable military presence on the European continent— perhaps crucial to negating any postwar Russian intimidation of Western Europe that might destabilize the area and undercut American plans for its economic reconstruction.

The Allied invasion of France began on D Day, June 6, 1944. The British and American armies, occupying France and having survived the Battle of the Bulge in December 1944, were ready by January 1945 for the Battle of Germany. So too were the Russians on the eastern front, as the Red Army stood at the gates of Warsaw and entry to the north German plains. In their last significant military move prior to playing the Russian card, the Ameri-cans rejected British plans for a bold, sabrelike move across those same German plains, a move calculated to beat the Russians to Berlin. The rejec-tion was perfectly in keeping with American war aims. Berlin, as the Ger-man capital, was symbolically important, but of little strategic or economic importance. Certainly its capture was not important enough to warrant incurring heavy casualties (it would later cost the Russians one hundred thousand fatalities), especially when the Yalta agreement was to give the Allies half the city without costing the United States a single life. What was important, strategically and economically, was the Ruhr-Rhine industrial core, the Germany that stretched from Stuttgart to Cologne. And that Germany could best be secured by a broad-front advance along the whole German frontier. It was a safe strategy and a sound one, but it could have been jeopardized had the proposed British thrust across the northern plains been outflanked and smashed.

The Yalta System

In early February 1945, just three months before Germany's capitulation, the moment finally came to play the Russian card. At a week-long confer-ence in Yalta, on the Crimean peninsula, the United States, the USSR, and Great Britain constructed what came to be known as the Yalta system. The component parts of that system constituted a series of trade-offs over the future of Poland, Germany, Northeast Asia, and the United Nations Organi-zation (UNO). Poland was the touchiest issue. Poland was vitally important to Russian security, being historically the natural invasion route from the west. For Britain and the United States, Poland was a litmus test of whether

Russia would organize its territorial gains into an autarkic bloc or enter into America's internationalist system. So there was strong Anglo-American displeasure at Russian efforts to install a procommunist government in Poland and to move its boundaries westward, at Germany's expense and to Russia's gain. The compromise settlement constructed at Yalta recognized Russia's de facto capacity to establish a pro-Soviet government in Poland. The agreement counterbalanced that recognition by adding token non-communists to the Polish government and offering vague promises of free elections and self-determination for all of liberated Europe.

The German issue was curiously less divisive at Yalta. Germany was vital to both the United States and the USSR, and within a year of war's end it would become the chief cause of the Cold War. In early 1945, however, internal divisions within each government over German policy inclined each to keep future options open. The dominant opinion in the Soviet government, a subordinate one in the American, favored a hard policy of limiting German economic rehabilitation to light industry that had no war-making potential. The majority view in the American government, a minority one in the Russian, favored a soft policy toward German reindustrialization. Even the soft-liners, however, split sharply along national lines. The American advocates sought to use German industrial production to promote the general recovery of Western European capitalism while the Russian proponents aimed to siphon much of that production eastward as reparations to aid Russian postwar reconstruction. Because of such internal and external divisions, the Yalta accord on Germany was both general and flexible. It agreed to the temporary dismemberment of Germany into four zones of occupation but kept open the possibility of eventual reunification when permanent peace was made. It acceded to Russian demands for reparations but declined to set precise figures or to specify the form the reparations would take until Germany's capacity to pay had been determined.

Northeast Asia would be a crucial element in both the war-at-hand and the postwar political battle to come. The United States wanted two things. First, it wanted the USSR to enter the war against Japan once the Battle of Germany was over. The Red Army could immeasurably facilitate Japan's defeat by tying down the two million Japanese soldiers in Northeast Asia and preventing their use in defense of the Japanese home islands. Second, the United States wanted to make sure that Russian entry into the Pacific war would not bias the outcome of the on-going Chinese civil war by aiding the Chinese communists to undermine the so-called Chinese nationalists. The Soviets, for their part, were willing to meet American objectives, provided the price was right: realization of traditional Russian territorial goals in Northeast Asia and participation in the occupation government of Japan after the war. The resulting trade-off was quite straightforward. The USSR agreed to enter the war in the Pacific within three months of the end of war in Europe and to sign a treaty of alliance and friendship with the noncommunist Chinese nationalist regime. In return, Russia received territorial and economic prizes in Manchuria, Sakhalin, and the Kurile Islands. Significantly, this protocol skirted the issue of Russia's role in postwar Japan.

Finally, the Yalta conference had to make some reply to the American call for a United Nations Organization. American leaders wanted a new league largely for symbolic purposes—to redeem Wilson's unkept pledge of 1919 and to dramatize America's postwar commitment to embrace internationalism and to eschew isolationism. Russia, for its part, was largely indifferent to the proposed UNO, save a desire that it not become an instrument of Western interference in the Soviet sphere in Eastern Europe. The Yalta agreement served both interests. While it approved the creation of a new international organization of nations, it invested real power in its Security Council, to be dominated by the five Great Power permanent members. Moreover, each Council member possessed veto power. Russia's security needs could be protected, and the American public could be reassured that their government had not signed a blank check to join in every future foreign war.

Harry Hopkins, Roosevelt's confidante, hailed the Yalta system as "the dawn of a new day" and "the first great victory of the war." Subsequent critics lambasted it as a sell-out of Poland and Eastern Europe. The leading scholarly authority sees it as neither, but as closer to victory than sell-out: a system marked by significant consensus between the United States and Soviet Union. That consensus, however, was reached at the expense of clarity. Deliberate ambiguity was required to mask existing differences over Poland and likely differences over Germany. Nonetheless, some American leaders, out of either genuine conviction or simply a desire for expediency, hoped the end of war would see that ambiguity resolved in America's favor. They hoped that Russia could be persuaded to tolerate a certain amount of political pluralism and market economy in Eastern Europe, so long as no regime's foreign and military policies were anti-Soviet. (Finland would later be the model of such hopes turned real—a process described as "Finlandization.") American leaders also hoped that Russia could be persuaded to moderate its tough demands on Germany and permit the higher levels of industrial production necessary for the restoration of Germany itself and Europe generally. In short, they hoped to persuade Russia to reenter the world-system on American terms. (If not, they would isolate it outside the world-system; they would "contain" it.)

The major means for realizing these hopes was to be economic diplomacy, linking American aid for Russian reconstruction to modifications in Soviet policy toward Poland and Germany. That took two forms. First, the

United States modified its position on reparations at the Potsdam conference in July 1945, catering to the soft-German policy advocates in the Soviet government. The Americans agreed to let Russia take what it wanted
out of its occupation zone and to take limited industrial reparations out of
the western zones, half of which would be paid for by agricultural exports
from the Russian zone. The trade-off aided both parties by allowing Russia
to obtain some reparations from the western zones while helping the West
solve its food shortage problems in those zones. More importantly, it attempted to give Russia a stake in allowing higher levels of German industrial productivity. Production quotas that exceeded German subsistence
needs would mean a greater industrial surplus available for Russian reparations. The second implement of American economic diplomacy was a
proposed $6 billion reconstruction loan to Russia. Stalin broached the idea
at the Yalta conference, and the Truman administration left the notion to
twist slowly in the wind, saying neither yea nor nay, in an obvious ploy to
exact conditions from the Soviets.

In the six months following Yalta American hopes were not realized nor
was the ambiguity of the Yalta system resolved. Poland continued to be a
non-negotiable issue for the Soviets, who remained impervious to periodic
Anglo-American calls for free Polish elections. On the German issue America drifted toward a soft policy of reindustrialization and Russia slid toward a hard policy of curtailing industrial productivity. In addition, a disturbing tone of acrimony crept into Soviet-American dialogue, sparked in
particular by the "get tough" posturing of Roosevelt's successor, Harry
Truman. Yet considerable give-and-take continued. The Americans did
recognize the pro-Soviet Polish government. The Russians did accept the
limited arrangement for German reparations and did agree to treat all four
occupation zones as a single economic unit. And the acrimony did not end
Russian-American dialogue or prevent the establishment of the Council of
Foreign Ministers as the permanent vehicle for continued talks. In other
words, the Yalta system remained in place even as the Pacific war moved
toward its climactic end. Indeed, the USA-USSR-UK meeting at Potsdam
(outside Berlin) in July 1945 essentially built upon the Yalta accords and
even extended them. Although more cold and formal in tone and less substantial in content, principles of the meeting at Potsdam remained within
the Yalta framework.

The short and sometimes happy life of the Yalta system was due largely
to one factor: it was a reasonably accurate mirror of the balance of power
and forces that existed in Europe in the spring and summer of 1945. The
considerable consensus of the Yalta agreements reflected the parity of
power, while the considerable ambiguity reflected the inability of any
party to alter that balance in its favor. Then, in the immortal words of

Joseph Heller's novel, "something happened!" That something altered the military equation upon which diplomacy rested. It energized America's quest for hegemony, heightened Russian insecurity, and set the stage for the origins of the Cold War. That something happened August 6, 1945, in the skies over Hiroshima, Japan.

3 | Cold War on Many Fronts, 1945–1946

In many ways the whole postwar history has been a process of American movement to take over positions of security which Britain, France, the Netherlands and Belgium had previously held.
—*Eugene V. Rostow*

Should American policy succeed in breaking down the system of imperial preferences and the sterling bloc, and, consequently severing the special economic ties binding the Dominions to Great Britain, the latter will be reduced to a second-rate power with a population of 48,000,000. The United States will then remain the only capitalist Great Power.
—*Eugene Varga, Soviet economist*

In July 1945, at the Potsdam (Berlin) conference with Britain and Russia, President Harry S. Truman received official word that the first testing of an atomic bomb had been "successful beyond the most optimistic expectations of anyone." The military administrator of the atomic bomb project, Major General Leslie R. Groves, estimated "the energy generated to be in excess of the equivalent of 15,000 to 20,000 tons of TNT; and this is a conservative estimate." Science director of the project, J. Robert Oppenheimer, later recalled the impact of the test on those observing it at Alamogordo, New Mexico.

> We knew the world would not be the same. A few people laughed, a few people cried. Most people were silent. I remembered the line from the Hindu scripture, the *Bhagavad-Gita*: Vishnu is trying to persuade the Prince that he should do his duty and to impress him he takes on his multi-armed form and says: "Now I am become Death, the destroyer of worlds."

For President Truman, however, the atomic bomb meant not merely death but life. It meant not only the military capacity to be "destroyer of worlds," but the political capacity to help create a new world, unitary and open, under America's protective aegis. Thus, with an excessive casualness that

43

badly concealed his cockiness, Truman informed Stalin of the American achievement. Atomic diplomacy had begun. The Cold War would not lag far behind.

Atomic Diplomacy

For nine gestating months, President Roosevelt and his successor had anticipated the news Truman received at Potsdam. As early as September 30, 1944, Secretary of War Stimson had told Roosevelt, "There is every reason to believe that before August 1, 1945, atomic bombs will have been demonstrated and . . . that one B-29 bomber [will be able to] accomplish with such a bomb the same damage against weak industrial and civilian targets as 100 to 1,000 B-29 bombers." Indeed, he knew (as would Truman after April 1945) that both the director of the Office of Scientific Research and Development, Vannevar Bush, and the chairman of the National Defense Research Committee, Charles Conant, president of Harvard, believed that the first generation fission bomb would be superseded by a hydrogen "super-super bomb" in which the energy released would be increased by "a factor of a thousand or more . . . equivalent in blast damage to 1,000 raids of 1,000 B-29 Fortresses, delivering their load of explosive on one target." They even alerted the President to the possibility of delivering atomic or hydrogen bombs "on an enemy target by means of a robot plane or guided missile."

Five days after the end of the Potsdam conference, the United States dropped the first atomic bomb on Hiroshima. It was August 6, 1945. Russia entered the Far Eastern war on August 8, the Americans dropped the second atomic bomb, on Nagasaki, on August 9, and Japan sued for peace on August 10. President Truman called those war-ending atomic raids "the greatest thing in history." In two blinding glares—a horrible end to a war waged horribly by all parties—the United States finally found the combination that would unlock the door to American hegemony.

With the atomic bomb, the Truman administration, like Oppenheimer's multiarmed Vishnu, could accomplish several goals simultaneously. Struck by fanatical Japanese resistance at Iwo Jima and Okinawa and unpersuaded by navy and air force arguments that Japan could be bombed and blockaded into submission, Truman unquestionably believed that the atomic raids saved many American lives, by eliminating the need for a land invasion of Japan. Important for obvious reasons of sentiment and humanitarianism, that conviction also had great domestic political significance. The American government had consistently waged World War II in a manner that minimized, as much as feasible, the human and economic sacrifices asked of the American people. To have done otherwise might have jeopardized public support for the war's internationalist objectives and risked revival of prewar isolationism; and to have ended the war with a quantum jump in American casualties, especially after spending two billion tax dollars on a weapon that made such a battlefield price unnecessary, was no way to sustain popular support for American policy. Conversely, a graphic demonstration of the bomb's military power was a means of suggesting to Americans that the role of postwar policeman could be played on the cheap ("More bang for the buck," as a later secretary of defense would say) and at little cost in American lives. Power with perquisites but few prices.

Another goal of the atomic raids was to shock the world, for two diametrically different purposes. The more benign was to give the world "adequate warning as to what was to be expected if war should break out again," as Arthur Compton, one of the bomb project's top researchers, told Secretary of War Stimson. The bomb "must be used" so that it would never be used again. But the shock also was to make clear to the world that the United States was ruthless enough to drop the bomb on live targets. A prearranged demonstration of the atomic bomb on a noninhabited target, as some scientists had recommended, would not do. That could demonstrate the power of the bomb, but it could not demonstrate the American will to use the awful power. One reason, therefore, for American unwillingness to pursue Japanese peace feelers in mid-summer 1945 was that the United States did not want the war to end before it had had a chance to use the atomic bomb.

This less benign purpose sought principally to shock the Soviet Union and Western Europe. From the beginning of the Manhattan Project, which built the bomb, Russia had been excluded from participating in it or sharing the fruits of it, even though Britain and Canada had played significant collaborative roles. The elaborate security programs connected with the project were aimed less at German spies than Soviet sympathizers. It was hoped that the Americans' atomic monopoly (and demonstrated willingness to use it) would make the Russians, as Secretary of State James F. Byrnes phrased it, "more manageable in Europe." Either in tandem with or in place of economic diplomacy, atomic diplomacy might inhibit potential Soviet expansionism and even intimidate Soviet leaders into softening their policies on Eastern Europe and Germany. Put another way, atomic diplomacy might resolve the ambiguity of the Yalta accords in America's favor. It might sufficiently shift the balance of forces that the United States could up the ante in the power game that inevitably occurred in the rearrangement of a shattered world. Such hopes were to be disappointed. If anything, atomic diplomacy reinforced Russia's security fears, strengthened its disposition to control its Eastern European buffer zone more tightly, undermined soft-liners on German policy, and led Soviet leaders to create a crash atomic bomb project of their own.

Western Europe, even more than Russia, was the target of the atomic shock treatments. Persuading Europe to discard its own nationalism and accept American internationalist hegemony was expected to be no easy matter. It would likely prove even more difficult when, as anticipated, American public opinion required the postwar demobilization of the American army and its partial withdrawal from Europe. With the Red Army still mobilized east of the Elbe River, Western Europe might be intimidated into making separate political and economic arrangements with the Soviet Union. The atomic bomb, however, gave the United States a diplomatic tool more powerful than the Red Army presence. If Europe cooperated with the United States, that tool could provide Europe with a nuclear umbrella that would shield it from Red Army diplomacy and provide a psychologically secure environment so that America could get on with the primary task of rebuilding European industry, a vital component of a revivified world-system. In that purpose, atomic diplomacy was no small success. It might not have made Russia more manageable, but it did make Europe more malleable.

Finally, the atomic bomb as diplomatic weapon enabled the United States to exclude Russia from the development of postwar policy toward Japan and to monopolize that sphere itself. While the United States did not want the war to end too quickly, before the bomb could be used, it also did not want it to go on too long. If war in the Far East lasted well beyond Russian entry on August 8, it would not only facilitate Russian military expansion in Northeast Asia but would permit the Soviet Union to stake a substantial claim to sharing in the postwar occupation and governance of Japan. At that early juncture the United States was still unsure what role Japan would be allowed or asked to play in postwar Asia. Few Americans, however, doubted that Japan, with its vast industrial resources at Osaka, Nagoya, and Tokyo, would play an important role. Whatever the role, however, the United States wanted a monopoly on its determination. Viewed in this context, the timing of the atomic raids becomes more explicable. Not only does it help explain the Hiroshima raid on August 6 (two days before the Russian entry), but it suggests an even more pervasive reason for the unseemly haste with which the bomb was dropped on Nagasaki—on August 9, before Japanese authorities had time to make sense of the first raid. Quite simply, the United States wanted the war ended within days (not weeks or months) in order to limit the size and scope of Soviet involvement.

American Power and the American Dream

In his historical novel *Washington, D.C.*, Gore Vidal described the last days of a fictionalized Franklin Roosevelt and the first days of his successor.

The ravaged old President, even as he was dying, continued to pursue the high business of reassembling the fragments of broken empires into a new pattern with himself at center, proud creator of the new imperium. Now, though he was gone, the work remained. The United States was master of the earth. No England, no France, no Germany, no Japan left to dispute the Republic's will. Only the mysterious Soviet would survive to act as other balance in the scale of power.

Vidal's fiction mirrored reality. There was indeed a giddiness among postwar American internationalists that came from possessing vast, preponderant power while the rest of the world possessed so little.

Economic might was the more obvious component of that power. After a decade of depression and underutilized capacity, American industry was running full-bore, while wartime demand and government aid had stimulated extensive capital spending on additional productive capacity. Spurred on by having an integrated, continental market in its forty-eight states, America's industry was the most rationalized in the world. It most approached optimal size and the economies of scale, so it enjoyed advantages over all its global competitors in all of the high-value product lines: steel, farm machinery, machine tools, electrical equipment, construction machinery, and automobiles and trucks. Only in the less profitable lines of nondurable consumer goods, such as textiles, was it unable consistently to out-produce and out-sell its commercial rivals. Compounding U.S. economic supremacy, the American farm belt, in the face of the war's devastation of European agriculture, enhanced its historic position as the world-system's major breadbasket. Likewise, American bankers transcended their previous parity with British counterparts as New York clearly surpassed London as the dominant financial center of the world-system. Thus, unscathed by the ravages of war and only mildly distorted by its limited mobilization for war, the American economy by 1946 was the workshop, the bakery, and the banker of the postwar world. In contrast, Great Britain, the Soviet Union, Germany, and Japan had all been devastated by war and their economies grotesquely distorted by the awful strains of more extensive mobilization.

Military might was the other element of the power that was breeding arrogance among American leaders. Despite the rapid demobilization of the wartime army in 1945–1946, the United States remained the most powerful military force in the world-system. The monopoly of the atomic bomb was central to that superiority—the Aladdin's lamp tucked away in the folds of the American cape, ready to be withdrawn and rubbed if circumstances demanded. Also important were American naval supremacy and continued leadership in strategic air power, providing the greatest mobility and firepower. In contrast, the German and Japanese military machines were defeated and dismantled. The British war engine was significantly reduced and sorely strained in the attempt to protect British interests in the Indian Ocean and the Mediterranean Sea. Even the mighty Red Army, conqueror of the *Wehrmacht* and occupier of Eastern Europe, was partially demobilized in 1946 as the Soviet Union threw itself into the task of postwar economic reconstruction at home. Possessing no atomic bomb, no modern navy, and no strategic air command; decimated by terrible losses of life and equipment in the war with Germany; and handicapped by a poor transport system and technological backwardness (the horse was still on a par with the internal combustion engine as the army's source of power and movement), the Soviet Union was in no position to challenge the United States if the latter chose to play the role of world policeman. Even assuming the worst of Soviet intentions, American military intelligence had already concluded by November 1945 (before partial Soviet demobilization) that the USSR would not have the military power to risk a major war before 1960.

If there was a certain arrogance discernible in American leaders, it was an arrogance of righteousness as well as of power. In the last analysis, American leaders assumed that American power was constructive simply because they believed American intentions self-evidently just and generous. Looking back over the sweep of a half-century, they thought they understood why the world-system had hovered on the brink of self-immolation through two world wars, the great depression, and epic social revolutions. Moreover, they had a vision of how to reorder and manage the world-system in ways they thought would negate its self-destructive tendencies and usher in a golden age of economic profitability, political stability, and social tranquility. While they acknowledged the self-interest that would be served by their new order, they were firm in their proud conviction that other core powers would participate in the benefits of that order, and that even the periphery ultimately stood to gain from "trickle down" effect. In a cost-benefit analysis, the rest of the world would win more than it would lose by acquiescing in American hegemony: greater security and material rewards in exchange for diminished autonomy. The great trade-off!

The postwar American vision was not a new intellectual construct but one largely borrowed from British thought. The old hegemonic power tutored the new. It was Britain past, not Britain present, that did the teaching—not the declining Britain of the twentieth century, of John Maynard Keynes, but the ascending Britain of the eighteenth and nineteenth centuries, the Britain of Adam Smith. The envisioned goals were material rewards and physical security for both the United States and the world as a whole. America had to make a plausible case that its hegemony served systemic interests as well as self-interests if others were to defer to it voluntarily.

The general physical security was contingent in part on nations enjoying adequate material rewards. If the rewards were reasonably satisfactory, then there was less likelihood of nations or peoples using war or revolution to effect some economic redistribution. But security was also contingent on having an umpire or policeman for the system as a whole. American leaders, of course, were determined that the United States should play the role, but changing circumstances would dictate how and to what degree it shared the role with other powers. It might be shared with other Great Powers through the UN Security Council, as the Yalta-Potsdam plan originally envisioned. It might be shared with the UN General Assembly, as it would be during the Korean War. It might be shared through regional alliances such as NATO (the North Atlantic Treaty Organization), SEATO (Southeast Asia Treaty Organization), ANZUS (a mutual defense pact among Australia, New Zealand, and the United States), and the OAS (Organization of American States). But however it was shared, America would be the nexus.

Material rewards, in turn, depended on a certain amount of physical security. Trade and capital would not flow into areas made inhospitable by anticapitalist regimes or made dangerous by war or revolution. As John C. Calhoun noted a century earlier, speaking of slavery's future in America's western territories, "property is inherently timid."—It would go only where the political climate was stable and receptive. The same was true of other forms of property, of goods and gold, in the mid-twentieth century. Capital would not venture into parts of the world-system that were not physically safe and politically stable. The earlier case China in the 1920s was an instructive example. All the Western powers and Japan had accepted the open door principle of free market competition in China. All recognized the independence of China and agreed to forego further efforts at partitioning or colonizing it. And all looked forward to the profitable exploitation of China and to its transformation from Marco Polo's dream to the reality of Asian riches. Yet foreign capital would not enter that free market because the Chinese revolution, with its disunity, xenophobia, economic nationalism, and violence, made China wholly uninviting. American diplomacy and the Washington treaty system had opened the door to China, but none would pass through the portals unless a "fair field and no favor" could be made a safe field as well. From such examples American postwar leaders concluded that global prosperity depended in part on a hegemonic America maintaining global law and order.

Security per se, however, did not guarantee prosperity. To an equal degree, American internationalists believed, the global economy had to be organized on the basis of classic liberal principles of free trade, comparative advantage, and economies of scale. Only a free market economy on a worldwide level, they argued, could maximize profits for the whole system as well as for its specific parts. At the heart of these principles was the concept of "productionism." In essence it was an internationalized version of Say's Law. A nineteenth-century French economist, J. B. Say, had posited that "in an economy characterized by specialization, each producer makes goods, not for his own consumption, but in the expectation of exchanging them for other goods. . . . It follows that the aggregate supply of goods produced is the same thing as the aggregate demand. *Total demand and total supply are identical.* That is Say's Law."

That classic economic theorem had repeatedly broken down in the twentieth century, especially in the depression of the 1930s. National economies were not "characterized by specialization," but by self-sufficiency. They attempted to produce everything needed by their populaces, even those products for which they possessed no natural advantage and which could have been imported more cheaply, and even those goods whose production runs were too small to realize the savings that came with economies of scale. The result was uneconomical production runs of overpriced goods for undersized markets. A further consequence was the very thing Say's Law deemed impossible—supply in excess of available demand that resulted in overproduction crises and industrial depressions of increasing severity and length.

The American dream of a unitary free world reinvoked Say's Law at the global level after it failed at the national. If nations gave up efforts at self-sufficiency (autarky) and specialized in those products they could make as well as and sell for less than anybody else (comparative advantage), and if they produced those items in large volume (economies of scale) for a global market rather than a national market, the end result would be a world economy in which everything that was produced would be consumed. Crises of overproduction would become a thing of the past; production would create its own demand. Maximizing global production would maximize global consumption and per capita standards of living. That was the essence of productionism: producing the largest volume of specialized goods for sale in the widest possible world market.

This international growth strategy employed two favorite metaphors: the world economy as a pie and a rising tide lifting all ships. Scarcity (nongrowth) economics had regarded the economic pie as fixed in size (zerosum) and had espoused national economic planning as a way to slice the pie in favor of this class as opposed to that class, or for this nation as opposed to some other—for winners and losers. The result was class conflict at home in the first case or confrontation abroad in the second. As Cordell Hull, secretary of state from 1933 to 1944, put it, "When nations cannot get what they need by the normal processes of trade, they will continue to resort to the use of force." Making the pie bigger (productionism), however, offered a way out. Even if a given class or nation retained the same percentage of the pie, the pie's absolute increase meant that each slice's size would grow as well. Even if unequal, the material rewards would be sufficiently large to assure that social and international peace would be the natural companions of prosperity.

On the rising economic tide, some ships, to be sure, were bigger than others, and the American ship was the biggest of all. Specialized production for a free worldwide market clearly favored the American economy, since it possessed the natural advantage of being able to outcompete the rest of the world in a wide range of the most profitable products. As a consequence, other core nations suspected American economic policy of being a self-serving device to steal away their old empires and intrude into their home markets. Likewise, peripheral nations feared it as a self-serving means to perpetuate the gap between "rich lands and poor," as Nobel economist Gunnar Myrdal termed them, and to keep the raw material economies of the Third World dependent on the industrial economies of the First.

Given their perception of American intentions, core capitalist nations in postwar Europe were inclined to regulate and limit their trade with dominant America and to plan their domestic economies so that supply and demand were balanced. Given the powerful influence of the working-class in most European governments, that planning generally involved elaborate welfare programs and the nationalization of decaying industries like coal and steel. Similarly, peripheral nations were inclined to regulate and limit their trade with all core countries and to launch planned industrialization programs of their own that substituted indigenous production of goods previously imported (import-substitution policies).

While acknowledging the self-serving character of productionism, American leaders argued that a global growth strategy would not only lift all ships in absolute terms but in relative terms as well. It would do what welfare capitalism or import-substitution could not do. It could enable other core countries to close the gap between the American standard of living and their own, and it would facilitate the transformation of the periphery from raw material production to industrialism. Welfare capitalism that redistributed wealth from capital to labor would, they claimed, prompt domestic capitalists to leave and foreign capitalists not to enter. Capital underinvestment, coupled with higher wage costs, would price such a core nation's goods out of the world market, result in heavy trade deficits, and ultimately depress the economy and the per capita income. Similarly, import-substitution and state-planned industry in the periphery would discourage the import of capital and technology, prompt domestic capitalists to flee in search of higher profits, and rely upon national markets that were too small or poor to generate adequate local demand.

Alternatively, productionism would argue that the way for European working classes to gain was to sacrifice, and the way for the periphery to industrialize was to specialize even further in nonfinished raw materials. If labor in the core made short-term sacrifices (austerity, balanced budgets, diminished welfare programs), the savings would ultimately make it possible for their nations to compete with the United States for a larger share of the world market. Profit rates would be maintained, domestic capital would stay at home, foreign capital would be attracted, and labor's fixed share of an expanding economy would be more remunerative than a larger share of a stagnant one.

Similarly, if the periphery gave up its short-term, uneconomical efforts at forced industrialization, it could make its specialized agricultural and raw materials production more large-scale, more mechanized, and ultimately more profitable. Anticipating the modernization theory of the 1960s, American economists and public figures argued that such primary commodity specialization would attract foreign capital to the road, rail, and harbor improvements that would later have industrial uses. They also pointed out that the profits from raw materials and agricultural sales in an expanding world market could be used to capitalize the next stage of development in light industry and semifinished manufacturing. Specialized production for the world market rather than self-sufficient production for the national market was the better road to modernity. Writing for the powerful, elitist Council on Foreign Relations, famed Harvard economist Alvin Hansen acknowledged that the "legitimate goals" of the periphery included the right to industrialization. That right, however, was limited to "a moderate degree of industrialization consistent with their resources, especially the manufacture of light consumer goods." His view echoed the consensus articulated as early as 1944 by the interdepartmental Executive Committee on Economic Foreign Policy, which praised the virtues of "balanced development" that realized "productivity and . . . income by making economic use of those resources in which a country has a comparative advantage."

Future Secretary of State Dean Acheson summarized America's free market vision of productionism in 1943 when he told a congressional committee that what would be required after the war was "an arrangement which has the effect of increasing production in the world, of consumption and employment, and reducing the barriers of trade and doing away with discrimination." A year later, at the Bretton Woods conference, the United States created the institutional infrastructure essential to the arrangement Acheson envisioned. The International Bank for Reconstruction and Development (the World Bank) was to provide long-term funding for the reconstruction of postwar Europe and, later, for Third World development. Dominated by the United States (which subscribed to one-third of its $9.1 billion capital and held one-third of its directorships), its lending policies were expected to favor those nations that played by the American rules of internationalism and to penalize those that leaned toward economic nationalism and managed trade.

Institutional twin to the World Bank was the International Monetary Fund (IMF). Operating with a $7.1 billion budget, it was designed to induce deficit trading nations to avoid currency devaluation as a means to correct their imbalance and to opt instead for deflationary spending cuts that would make their exports more price competitive. Also dominated by the United States, the IMF aimed at a world of free convertibility. Essential to the maximization of world trade, foreign exchange earned by sales to one trading partner had to be freely convertible to gold or any other foreign currency if it was to be used to buy from yet another trading partner. Aiming also at stable and predictable exchange rates, the IMF sanctified the U.S. dollar as the benchmark against which all other currencies would be valued. No one in 1944 anticipated the events of three decades later when the Bretton Woods system would collapse and the American dollar and American trade would begin their long decline. For the moment, the more pressing issue was how to transform the World Bank and the IMF from paper institutions into functioning ones, how to change the American dream of free trade and free convertibility to the reality of a free world.

Selling the American Dream to Western Europe

Selling the American vision to other members of the world-system was no mean chore. The European core and much of the periphery, especially Asia, had compelling reasons to resist American plans. Similarly, the Soviet Union, with its ambivalent relationship to the world-system, eventually chose not to play by American rules, especially when American policy hardened and made the rules more stringent than those established earlier by the Yalta system. The Soviets ultimately proved the greatest obstacle to American hegemony and its blueprint for a new world order, hence the Cold War. One can make the case, however, that Western Europe was of even greater concern to American policymakers in 1945 and 1946.

Some European leaders endorsed economic internationalism and invited America's hegemonic efforts to impose it on Europe; "empire by invitation," it has been called. Robert Schuman, Georges Bidault, Jean Monnet, and others saw transnational economic institutions and eventual European economic unification as the wave of the future. International control of the Ruhr, the European Coal and Steel Authority, and the European common market sprang, in part, from the minds of such leaders. They reflected three motivations. They sought to stifle the dangerous tendencies of German nationalism by integrating the German economy into a larger European context. They sought to induce Britain to eschew its special relationship to the old British empire and to use its still considerable financial power to stimulate European productivity. Finally, they sought to become competitive with the United States in world markets. These unificationists saw their own historic nationalism as their worst economic enemy. The quest for national self-sufficiency had spawned and artificially protected inefficient and unprofitable industries that sold into limited national markets too small to permit large-scale production and at prices too high to be competitive in a free market. Imperialism had attempted to overcome the handicap by enlarging the market, which made larger production runs possible, and by providing cheap raw materials from within one's own trading bloc. But imperialism's monopolistic character also shut European producers out of global competition, at home and in their empires, that might have forced them to be more efficient. European economic integration, therefore, could become the postwar means to overcome the nationalistic obstacles preventing Europe from wresting its share of world markets from the dominant American economy.

Despite such advocacy of European internationalism, most European governments reembraced their prewar doctrines of economic nationalism and resisted American efforts to change their minds. Such preference grew from pressures at home and from their assessment of their situation abroad. As the American concept of productionism anticipated, much of the internal pressure on these countries came from the European working classes. Empowered by their key role in the war effort and embittered by fifteen years of economic deprivation, they were determined to use their political clout to get government commitment to full employment and social safety net programs. As a consequence, European governments were under great pressure to regulate the economy in ways that insured a larger share of national income for labor. On the other hand, those governments doubted they could generate labor's share through free competition in the world market, at least not in the short run. Free market competition served the United States well, for it possessed comparative advantages in a whole range of high-profit enterprises; but the free market severely penalized those less blessed with such advantages. Forced to compete with the United States in an open, free market world, Europe feared being stripped of its overseas colonies and economic spheres of influence and being threatened even in its own home markets.

Responding to labor pressure from within and fearful of American competition from without, Europe began in 1946 to experiment with nationalistic policies that smacked more of the prewar order than the postwar one desired by the United States. At home, European governments moved toward greater regulation (sometimes even management) of the economy, attempting to raise labor's share of income while restraining the flight of capital. Included in that economic regulation were brief flings with higher tariffs and currency controls to protect the home market for domestic producers, minimize the trade deficit with the United States, and ward off external pressure for deflation and spending cuts. At the same time, they tried to insure themselves of a share of the periphery by exempting their formal administrative colonies from the American open door. Even when they moved toward acceptance of political independence for the colonies (for example, the British in India in 1947), they attempted to retain some arrangement that favored their own trade and capital and discriminated against others, like the Americans. In short, the Europe of 1946 seemed to be moving toward a semiautarkic system somewhere between the German bilateralism of the 1930s and the American multilateralism of the 1940s, but probably closer to the former. European leaders envisioned not a unitary free world but a system divided into compartments and spheres (the Americas, the Russian empire, and Europe and its overseas dependents in Asia and Africa). And while trade among those regional blocs would remain important, individual states would regulate and limit trade in ways that would maintain a trade balance and protect the integrity of their domestic programs.

If all that were so, why then did Europe eventually accept American hegemony and the multilateral vision that went with it? The diplomacy of the British loan in 1946 suggests an answer. Great Britain had an enormous need for American dollars in 1946. Although desperate to import American machinery, electrical equipment, and raw materials for its own industrial revitalization, it lacked sufficient dollars to pay for them and had no immediately prospective means to earn such dollars. The United States, for its part, regarded the British sterling bloc, the Commonwealth, as the chief bottleneck to world trade. The collective sense among American leaders was that eliminating British restrictions on converting Commonwealth pounds to dollars would, in one giant step, unplug the stoppage that kept postwar trade at depression levels.

The British loan of 1946 was the trade-off that gave dollars to the British and greater access to the sterling bloc to the Americans. To describe the loan's essentials, the United States gave Great Britain a long-term, low-interest loan of $3.8 billion. The British paid for that loan with a promise that pounds sterling would be made freely convertible to dollars within a year. That seemingly innocuous concession literally implied the demise of British economic management at home and economic control of its dominions. Up to this juncture, the British had used convertibility controls as the chief means of minimizing their trade deficit with the United States while protecting their labor programs against deflationary tendencies.

Having been faced with the options of cutting back on domestic spending or cutting back on American imports, Britain had chosen the latter. It had rationed the pounds that could be converted to dollars in order to limit how much British consumers could spend on lower-priced American goods. Free convertibility now ruled out that option and left the Labor Party government with no alternative save the ironic and deflationary one of cutting government spending and prolabor programs. In effect, American internationalism required that, when the dictates of the world market and the policies of individual states came into conflict, the former had to prevail.

Free convertibility also threatened British control of its overseas client-states. World War II ended with Great Britain owing significant amounts of money to India, Egypt, Australia, and other overseas dependencies for goods and services provided during the war. Britain had paid for them with a series of paper transactions that deposited funds in what were known as blocked currency accounts. In effect, this practice created a special form of sterling similar to the German aski mark of the 1930s, one that could not be converted to dollars and could be spent only on purchases from Great Britain. It was one way for the British to continue economic dominion even as they lost political dominion over colonies, like India, and protectorates, like Egypt. With the end of convertibility controls, the British faced the certain prospect that India, Egypt, Australia, and others would convert the newly unblocked sterling to dollars in order to buy comparable goods and services from the United States at prices cheaper than Great Britain could offer. Along with this might come a drift of British dependencies out of the sterling trade bloc into a multilateral system dominated by the United States. If that occurred, then the Soviet prediction might well come to pass: that Great Britain would "be reduced to a second-rate power" and the "United States . . . then remain the only capitalist Great Power."

Despite the implications of free convertibility, the British accepted it as a necessary price. Unwilling to adopt a painful, Soviet-style forced reindustrialization, Britain found the transfer of American technology, goods, and raw materials essential to British reconstruction. And borrowing the dollars seemed the only way to pay for them. As it turned out, the British did not have to pay the full freight for the 1946 loan. Free convertibility created such a mass run on the pound sterling by its domestic and foreign holders that it brought the British economy to the brink of financial ruin. So, in order to save its major trading partner, the United States had to let the British revert to controlled semiconvertibility. Indeed, more than a decade passed before, in 1958, the British pound and other European currencies became freely convertible to dollars. So the 1946 loan revealed something of the prematurity of the American effort to convert Europe to its vision of internationalism. Yet it showed some of the potency of American dollar diplomacy in winning over reluctant European critics, and it revealed much about which way the wind was blowing.

Confronting the Periphery: The China Tangle

Converting the periphery to the American way of viewing and doing things presented problems of a different nature. In the immediate postwar period, the issue was less the periphery's dissatisfaction with its specialized role as primary commodity producer (though that would soon become apparent) than the political instability that prevented much of the periphery from playing any economic role at all. This was especially true in Asia where anticolonial uprisings and political independence movements destabilized French Indochina, the Dutch East Indies, and British Malaya and stymied the resumption of traditional core-periphery trade. Most especially was this true of China, where the long-running civil war that began in the 1920s accelerated, nullifying American hopes for the role China might play in the political, military, and economic life of postwar Asia.

Asia presented a dilemma for the United States that it did not face in Europe. In confronting it in 1946, America was forced to make some serious revisions to its postwar dream of an ideal world. The problem with Asia was that it possessed only one industrial nation, namely Japan. That meant that any postwar reindustrialization of Japan presented potential dangers not apparent in German reindustrialization. A reconstructed Germany might be counterbalanced by a reconstructed Britain, France, Belgium, and Netherlands. It could be subsumed within the framework of a larger European industrial core. A reconstructed Japan, however, would have no natural counterweights in Asia. Possessing singular power in the region, it would tend to regain great freedom of action as it regained industrial strength. Past Japanese behavior in the 1910s and 1930s made American leaders fearful that a revivified Japan would be tempted to try unilateral expansion in Asia whenever world circumstances permitted it.

Economic logic had to give way to strategic considerations. Japan seemingly could not be reindustrialized without its becoming an Asian policeman that could not be trusted or easily controlled. So, in 1945–46, America leaned toward a strategy that would contradict Japan's comparative advantage. Japanese industry would be decentralized and scaled down through the break-up of the prewar monopolies and the forfeit of industrial reparations to its wartime Asian victims. Some American policymakers favored the creation of alternative industrial centers in China and perhaps Indonesia, the Philippines, or Korea, partly financed by Japanese reparations. In this Asia of multiple, semideveloped industrial centers, economic power would be somewhat equalized; so political-military power would depend more on population, size, and geography. China, not

Japan, would be the logical Asian peacekeeper, performing the role first envisioned for it in Roosevelt's concept of the Four Policemen.

The Chinese civil war wrecked all. Waged between the Kuomintang (KMT—the Chinese nationalists) and the Chinese Communist Party (CCP), this decades-long struggle renewed itself in scale and ferocity after Japan's defeat in 1945. In this internecine encounter, the KMT enjoyed the moral approval of the United States and a billion dollars of war and postwar aid. It even benefited from the 1945 Treaty of Friendship and Alliance with the USSR and Stalin's efforts to discourage the CCP from a revolutionary attempt to seize power. Nonetheless, the KMT fared poorly, partly because of the burdens of uncontrollable inflation and its own corruption, and partly because of the mass peasant support and superior tactics of the CCP.

By early 1946, American hopes of an outright nationalist victory were dead, and the only hope for China lay in a negotiated stabilization agreement. Consequently, President Truman sent General of the Army, General George C. Marshall on his famous mission to China, to arrange formation of a coalition government dominated by the KMT but with communist participation. The proposed union disintegrated before the incompatible parties even got to the altar. A February cease-fire broke down by midspring, and by the fall the KMT and CCP were waging wholesale war in Manchuria with the latter seeming to have the upper hand. By the end of 1946, it was clear that the nationalists could not win the civil war, and the best the United States could hope for was a long, stalemated struggle that at least avoided a communist triumph. The USSR concurred in that hope, but out of fear that a unified China, even a communist one, might be more of a danger than an aid to Russian interests in Asia. In any case, it was clear that no acceptable Chinese regime would play the role desired for it by American leaders. Spurred on by that realization, in 1947 those policymakers reassessed their Japanese policy and eventually followed the reverse course, reindustrializing Japan after all. Even that flip-flop, however, did not mean that the United States had given up on China. As John Foster Dulles, future secretary of state, put it: "[The United States] must get away from the idea that this . . . is the last word as to what is going to happen in China. There has never been those final last words as regards China in the past, and I do not think it is so now."

Russia and Its Options

The effort to integrate Russia into the world-system on American terms has properly received great scholarly attention, for the failure of that effort produced the Cold War—a prolonged state of belligerency without actual fighting. By the end of 1946, the Yalta system had collapsed and the Cold War had begun. The ambiguity over Germany and Eastern Europe did not

produce a softer Russian policy on Germany nor its acceptance of democratic capitalist regimes in Eastern Europe. Ambiguity instead devolved
into a more hardened bipolarization between Russia and America over the
future organization of Europe and of its Middle Eastern periphery. Neither
economic diplomacy nor atomic diplomacy by the United States persuaded the Soviet Union to make its accommodation with American
preeminence and American prescriptions. Indeed, both strategies might
have been counterproductive. By reviving the specter of "capitalist encirclement," they may have strengthened the political power of those Soviet
authorities who wished to tighten Russian control over its new postwar
spheres, build atomic weapons, modernize the military, and encourage dis-
turbances in the world-system that would preoccupy the United States
and make it less threatening to Soviet security.

The USSR per se was not then very important to the United States. Its
importance derived from the fact that its very existence complicated the
overarching American task of reconstructing Western Europe and integrating it into a global free market. Russia did, after all, control Eastern
Europe, an historic source of food, raw materials, and markets for Western
Europe, and thus important to the latter's recovery. It did possess political
and ideological ties with some political parties and trade unions in Western
Europe and it did possess substantial military power, making it automatically of concern to Europeans. In addition, Russia's example of five year
economic plans and forced industrialization offered Europe an alternative
model of state capitalism and economic autarky to the American model of
economic internationalism. To a Europe, leaning to the left and nationalist
options, these factors constituted an inducement to work out barter arrangements and closer political relationships with the Soviet Union. They
tempted Europe to play the Russian card in ways that might further circumscribe American access to the Eurasian land mass.

In that context, the issue in 1945 and 1946 was whether or not Russian
international goals and policies could be reconciled with the American
goal of rebuilding and reintegrating capitalist Europe. On what terms, if
any, should Russia be readmitted to a world-system that had expelled it
after the Bolshevik Revolution of 1917? To properly understand the issue
one must realize that it was not a new issue but a recurring one. Russia,
both czarist and communist, had always possessed an ambivalent relationship to the world-system. Historically, Russia had evolved as an empire,
fueled by migration and colonization both eastward and westward. Although imposing in size and numbers, Russia was economically backward,
and imperial czars had often tried to nullify the consequences of that
backwardness by attempting to insulate Russia from more modern Europe. As a result, in modern history the Russian empire often functioned as
an area outside the world-system. At other times, Russian leaders self-

consciously opted for closer ties to the West, either out of military necessity (the Napoleonic Wars, for example) or out of nascent modernization
impulses, borrowing from the West (capital and technology) in order to
catch up with the West. In effect, prerevolutionary Russia vacillated between contrary impulses to isolate itself from or integrate itself into the
world-system. And the system itself reacted with equal ambivalence. Mod-
ernizing Russia as part of the system looked to be a profitable undertaking,
but Russian size and military power made it a risky one.

Central Europe's failure to follow Russia's revolutionary example led
the USSR to partially withdraw from the world-system and attempt to
create a socialist enclave—an external world. But foreign intervention and
capitalist encirclement, the decimation of the working class by civil war,
and the opposition of the peasantry all exacerbated an existing distortion
in the Russian economy dubbed *war communism*: inordinate amounts of
scarce resources went into a modern military industry while all too little
went into agriculture and civilian industry. This created a society at once
modern and fearsome yet backward and ineffectual.

Under Stalin, this war communism devolved into another variant of
state capitalism. The state simply replaced private corporations in accumulating capital, disciplining workers, appropriating surplus, and making
investments. This state capitalism, in turn, coexisted in shifting tension and
tolerance with "black capitalism" in consumer goods and services (a black
market version of free enterprise). In effect, Russia was experimenting
with its own varieties of economic nationalism as a strategy to catch up
with and overtake Western capitalism. Save for a radical ideology, which it
used to legitimize its actions, the Russian state under commissars was not
unlike the Russian state under czars. Stalin had more in common with
Peter the Great than with Karl Marx.

Next to the emergence of American hegemony, the reemergence of
Russia as an actor in world affairs was the most significant consequence of
World War II. Its reentry into the world-system left Stalinist Russia with
two options. It could remain inside that system and attempt to realize Russian ambitions through peaceful coexistence with internationalist America, or it could insulate itself from that world-system, integrate its wartime
gains into an enlarged Russian empire, and pursue its goals through an
adversarial relationship with the capitalist world. A number of factors,
both foreign and domestic, pulled the Soviet Union and Stalin in both directions in 1945 and 1946.

Staying inside the world-system offered greater rewards for the USSR
in the first twelve months after the final end of World War II. The greatest
reward was the possibility of influencing public policy and future choices
for the western, industrialized two-thirds of defeated Germany. So long as
coexistence remained the norm, Russia had a chance of benefiting from

German industry, by receiving either dismantled equipment or a significant share of industrial production. Once the Iron Curtain descended, however, the West would be the sole beneficiary of German productivity. It would also be in a position, if it so chose, to rearm the Germans and integrate them politically and militarily, as well as economically, into a transnational framework. Western Europe would be safe from German revanchism, but would Russia be?

In addition, staying inside the system offered the Soviet Union a better chance for realizing the traditional Russian geopolitical desire for warmwater access to the oceanic highways of the world. Russia had historically sought access to the Persian Gulf and the Mediterranean Sea only to be blocked by Britain's containment policy in Afghanistan, Iran, and Turkey. In 1944, Stalin had agreed to respect the British sphere of influence in Greece (a commitment he largely honored), but he had made no such commitments on points east of Greece. Given Russian anticipation of Britain's decline as a world power, the chance to expand Russia's presence in Iran and Turkey was more propitious than it was likely to be in the foreseeable future. But the prospects might improve if Russia maintained a peaceful relationship with the United States. Given American hostility to Britain's closed door policies, the United States might even welcome an Anglo-Russian competition that might reduce British influence in the Near East while keeping Russia's expanded presence within reasonable bounds. On the other hand, a clearly confrontational relationship between Russia and the West would assuredly lead Britain and the United States to bury the hatchet and make common cause against any Russian encroachment. In the end, the USSR would face an American opponent in the Persian Gulf and the Mediterranean far more powerful than prewar Britain had been.

Extending wartime cooperation was also a way for the Soviets to strengthen communist parties in Western Europe. The political left had enjoyed an enormous postwar resurgence, especially in France and Italy. With its stature enhanced by its wartime role in anti-Nazi resistance movements, and that of many conservatives tarnished by pro-Nazi collaboration, the European left was in a position to challenge centrist reformers for the opportunity to lead the reconstruction of the war-torn continent. Often winning 20 to 30 percent of the popular vote, European communists were powerful enough to demand and often get cabinet positions in coalition governments, like de Gaulle's in France. This postwar renewal of popular front governments was likely to enhance the power of the left and put it in a position to influence public policy on reconstruction. Given the traditionally close ties between western European communist parties and Moscow, this was tantamount to saying that Russia could have some say in European policy choices.

All this was partly contingent on Russia's remaining inside the world-system and enjoying a certain legitimacy that then could rub off on its European comrades. If, however, Russia retreated into Stalin's earlier "socialism in one [bloc]," the European left and Soviet influence would face likely demise. First, western European communist parties would become open to charges of disloyalty, of collaborating with an external, alien world whose existence was threatening to European security. Second, it was eminently predictable that any Russian self-isolation would be followed by instructions to western European communist parties to abandon popular front coalition politics and reembrace the revolutionary militancy of the early 1930s (the so-called Third Period of the Communist International). If this happened, the tactic of working outside the system would only isolate European communists on the radical fringe of European politics and further open them to charges of marching to Moscow's orders rather than meeting the needs of their own working classes.

A final reason for Russia to stay on good terms with the West was that sustaining the spirit of Yalta and allied unity would offer more means for promoting Russian growth and modernization. Self-isolation and a hostile relationship with the West would necessitate continued, massive military spending that would further distort the misshapened Russian economy and delay the material rewards ("bread and butter socialism," as Khrushchev later called it) long promised to the Russian people. Peaceful coexistence, however, might not only redirect capital from the military to the civilian economic sector but maintain access to Western economies whose technology transfers were essential if Russian modernization was not to lag hopelessly behind core capitalist countries. Crucial here was atomic technology. Setting aside the issue of military usage, many Russians viewed nuclear power at the cutting edge in the future of industrial energy and propulsion. An adversarial relationship with the West would perpetuate not only an American atomic bomb monopoly but a significant Western technological lead in the refining of fissionable materials and the development of peaceful industrial uses of atomic energy. Coexistence, however, might mean a Russian share in that technology.

While all these factors produced cooperationist tendencies in Russian policy during 1945 and 1946, other elements pushed Stalin in the other direction—toward withdrawal from the world-system—primarily the desire to protect Russian control in Eastern Europe. The problem with coexistence was its two-way character. While cooperation facilitated Soviet input into the German issue and European reconstruction, it also made it possible for the West to insist on some say in Eastern Europe. Anglo-American demands for free elections or for economic open doors kept alive the option of democratic capitalism in Eastern Europe. And that option was anathema to many Soviet leaders who feared that historic hostilities and pro-Western economic ties would ultimately produce governments in Eastern Europe that were not only anticommunist but anti-Russian. The former might be tolerable, but the latter was not. The region was simply too vital as a defensive buffer to be spared, a fact attested to in 1939 when Russia had conquered and absorbed the Baltic republics and the eastern third of Poland. From this viewpoint, withdrawing from the world-system into self-containment offered a seemingly sure means of imposing "Red Army socialism" in Eastern Europe and creating a series of satellite protectorates that would act as a Great Wall between the capitalist world and the Russian empire.

A second factor that favored Russian isolationism was Stalin's enduring need to maintain social control in Russia itself. He had sought to do so through coercion in the purges of the late 1930s, but the exigencies of waging war later forced him to stress consensus-building instead. The basis of that consensus was Russian parochialism—defense of the holy homeland against alien invaders. It was in the name of Russian nationalism rather than international communism that Stalin led his warring country. That sufficed nicely so long as the war was one of self-defense fought on Russian territory, but the transition to an offensive war and the movement of millions of Russian soldiers and their intellectual cadres into Eastern and Central Europe altered circumstances dramatically. Its revolutionary ideology dulled by four years of neglect, Russian national parochialism had no ally in confronting the cosmopolitan forces it encountered in its victorious march. New cultures, new ideologies, new ways of viewing and doing things were strewn in the path of the Russian army, until it met the ultimate "other" when American and Russian soldiers embraced on the banks of the Elbe River. These encounters reinforced parochial suspiciousness, but they also provoked curiosity, and curiosity can kill consensus. The longer the Russian army maintained routine contact with Westerners, friends and foes alike, the more susceptible it would be to variegated, pluralist influences. In that context, dropping an Iron Curtain between Russia and the West and imposing more conformist regimes in the East seemed a way of keeping the other world fearsome rather than fascinating, and a way of buttressing the Stalinist regime inside Russia.

Finally, Russian tendencies to withdraw from the world-system were reinforced by the doomsday thinking prevalent in some Russian intellectual circles at the end of World War II. It held that postwar capitalism would cause the world to drift back into another 1930s-style great depression and that the consequent autarkic tendencies and nationalistic rivalries would produce another global crisis, perhaps yet another global war. If that happened, then Russia would face anew, as it had from 1939 to 1941, the possibility of internecine conflict in the West being redirected against the Soviet Union. To prevent that eventuality, proponents of such theories advised Stalin to consolidate Russia's wartime gains, integrate its new territories into the Russian empire, step up its military spending—to make the Soviet world so impregnable that capitalists would fight only amongst themselves and leave Russia in a position to affect the future direction of a world destroyed by capitalism's third and finally successful try of the century at suicide.

The Beginnings of the Cold War

Such end-of-capitalism millenialism had little impact on Stalin in late 1945 and early 1946. Inherently cautious, the Soviet leader believed "the bourgeoisie is very strong" (as he told Tito) and that capitalism had great resilience as a world economy. Indeed, Western Europe, aided by the lower fuel costs of a mild winter, showed signs of surprising economic recovery rather than of imminent collapse. Moreover, as late as May 1946, Russia still retained some hope that it would influence and benefit from Western policy in Germany and that it might yet share in nuclear technology. The ratio of rewards to liabilities seemed better for coexistence than for confrontation.

Nowhere was this more apparent than in the Russian strategic sphere in Eastern Europe. American demands for political pluralism and market economies proved less substantive than rhetorical and tactical. American leaders invoked them to satisfy domestic voters or as a stalling device to deflect Russian pressure on other issues. For example, the London Foreign Ministers Conference in September 1945 saw the United States bring the meeting to a stalemate partly over the lack of free elections in Bulgaria. Its real purpose, however, was to prevent Russia from adding Japan to the agenda in an effort to secure Russian participation in its occupation. Secretary of State James F. Byrnes privately admitted that the United States was "going off in the same unilateral way [in Japan] as the Russians were going off in the Balkans." Two months later at the Moscow Foreign Ministers Conference, after the Japanese issue was safely resolved in American favor, the United States recognized the Bulgarian government without a murmur of disapproval about the means of its election.

The superficial nature of America's Eastern European policies made them more a nuisance than a threat to Soviet regional interests. That permitted Russia the luxury of approaching Eastern Europe in a more pragmatic way, rather than having to make an all-or-nothing choice between open doors or a closed curtain. As a consequence, Soviet policy differed from country to country. In Poland, Romania, and Bulgaria, the Iron Curtain (Winston Churchill gave it the name) descended harshly and rapidly in 1945–46. Geography and history determined their fate. Poland's northern plains were the natural avenue of invasion into Russia and the one used by the bulk of the *Wehrmacht* in 1941. Romania's and Bulgaria's seacoasts faced Russia across the Black Sea. Both had allied themselves with Nazi Germany, and Romania's Danube River delta had been a jumping-off point into southwestern Russia. Elsewhere in Eastern Europe the Russians operated in more cautious ways. In Finland they tolerated (as they still do) a noncommunist regime that maintained economic ties with the West while it remained firmly committed to a foreign policy friendly toward the USSR. In Hungary they accepted a conservative rout of the communist party at the polls and peaceful relations with a noncommunist government until the spring of 1947, after the Cold War had begun. In Czechoslovakia they lived with a coalition government dominated by independent, democratic socialists until 1948 when a domestic crisis, partly generated by America's Marshall Plan, led to a communist takeover. In Yugoslavia Stalin advised his fellow communist, Josip Tito, to forego a communist revolution and share power with noncommunists—an unwanted piece of advice that helped provoke Yugoslavia's break with Russia in 1948. In its occupied third of Austria, the Russians rang down the Iron Curtain in 1947 only to ring it up again in 1955 by, surprisingly, signing a peace treaty with that country. In many ways, Russian policy in Eastern Europe reminded one of traditional American policy in the Caribbean, where the United States used formal control in some countries and informal control in others, depending on geographic circumstances and local conditions—foreign policy that was more utilitarian than doctrinaire.

This cautious Russian commitment to coexistence eroded throughout much of 1946, chiefly because American policy hardened in ways that implicitly upped the ante for Russia's admission to the world-system. President Truman declared that Yalta was simply a wartime "interim agreement," subject to reassessment in light of the realities of postwar power redistribution. Moreover, he made clear that in any necessary new arrangements he would follow a tough negotiating line. "I am tired of babying the Soviets," said Truman in January 1946. The attitude carried over into American policy on the Middle East, atomic energy, and Germany.

In the Near East, Russian probes into the old British sphere quickly corrected the USSR's mistaken assumption about American policy. While the United States might not have minded some loosening of British control in the area, it had no intention of letting any other nation fill the vacuum. Instead, it wished to supplant the British and to continue their policy of keeping Russia bottled up in the Black Sea and the Caspian Sea. In Iran, Russia used political pressure and military threats to coerce from that country a share of oil concessions comparable to that given the English and Americans. However, American invocation of the UN Security Council and a stern demand that Russia fulfill its wartime pledge to leave northern Iran were sufficient to effect Russian withdrawal—without an Iranian oil concession. In Turkey, Russian pressure to get a share of strategic control over the Dardanelles (an historic Russian objective) produced another American warning and the first postwar dispatch of a carrier task force to the region. The result once more was a Russian tactical retreat. And in Greece, Russia lent only moral support to the civil war waged by Greek communists and other antimonarchists, though it feared that communist Yugoslavia's material aid to that revolution might signal a Pan-Balkan movement independent of Stalin's control. Even Stalin's nominal and indirect involvement, as we shall see, would be sufficient to justify the stern Truman Doctrine response in early 1947.

Nineteen forty-six witnessed a toughening of America's atomic diplomacy as well, after three months of vacillation in late 1945. Most American leaders continued to see America's atomic bomb monopoly as something to hoard and exploit in postwar power brokering with the Soviets. A few, however, shared Secretary of War Stimson's belief that "if we fail to approach [the Russians] now and merely continue to negotiate with them, having this weapon rather ostentatiously on our hip, their suspicions and their distrust of our purposes and motives will increase."

The embodiment of this vacillation was Truman's new secretary of state, James F. Byrnes. At the London Foreign Ministers Conference, Byrnes had warned his Russian counterpart, V. M. Molotov, in humor too black to be funny, that if he did not "cut out all this stalling and let us get down to work, I am going to pull an atomic bomb out of my pocket and let you have it." Sobered by the failure of that conference and the apparent ineffectualness of atomic diplomacy, Byrnes went to the Moscow conference at the end of 1945 in a very different frame of mind. Voicing his opposition to "using the bomb for political purposes," he called for the international control of atomic energy. Promising that the American bomb monopoly would "not be unnecessarily prolonged," he affirmed the ultimate objective of "unlimited exchange of scientific and industrial information."

Byrnes' deviant venture in depoliticizing the atomic bomb brought the whole weight of the American foreign policy establishment down upon him. The bipartisan powers on the Senate Foreign Relations Committee, Arthur S. Vandenberg, Republican from Michigan, and Tom Connally, Democrat from Texas; the State Department professionals, like Roosevelt's former under secretary, Sumner Welles, and Russian expert George F. Kennan; military spokesmen, like Secretary of the Navy James Forrestal and Admiral William Leahy; and a host of leaders from elite organizations like the Council on Foreign Relations, all agreed that the atomic bomb monopoly was crucial to Europe's sense of security and therefore to the success of American reconstruction policies. The monopoly, therefore, was to be sustained until the task was completed.

Providing the rationale for that unyielding approach was George F.

Kennan's "long telegram" from Moscow in February 1946 (later the basis for his famous "Mr. X" article in 1947). Kennan characterized the USSR as an insatiably expansionistic society driven by its revolutionary Marxist-Leninist ideology, its paranoid sense of national insecurity, and its Stalinist totalitarianism. Western reasonableness, he argued, would only whet the Russian appetite in much the fashion that appeasement had done with Hitler in the 1930s. Only Western strength and resolve, applying a counter-force at every weak point between the Russian empire and the free world, could "contain" the Soviet Union. Its expansionism thus frustrated, the communist regime would eventually collapse, be overthrown, or mellow into a form more like those in the West.

That containment policy consensus resulted in Byrnes' fall from favor with President Truman and ended any Soviet hopes that coexistence could lead to a share in atomic technology. The Acheson-Lillienthal plan, put forward in the spring of 1946, still retained some of Byrnes' flexibility, but it sharply upped the price that Russia would have to pay: international control of Russia's essential uranium supplies, international determination of the number and location of nuclear power plants in the USSR, international on-site inspection, and, finally, suspension of the Russian atomic bomb project. In the meantime, the American atomic bomb monopoly would continue, and not until all other stages had been achieved would the United States destroy its nuclear weapons. In turn, the Acheson-Lillienthal proposal was altered and subsumed by the far more rigid Baruch plan. It insisted that Russia give up its UN veto power where atomic energy issues were concerned, and it refused to establish any timetable for the accomplishment of the stages. Bernard Baruch, the plan's author, neither expected Russia to accept the plan nor regretted that it would not. Predictably, Russia said no, and it stepped up the pace of its own atomic bomb project.

Neither the unhappy denouement of this attempt to address the atomic energy issue nor the Middle Eastern competition, in and of themselves, was sufficient to cause the Cold War. The former was as much consequence as cause, and the latter was a predictable part of the power probes and territorial readjustments that take place after any major war that produces a rapid and dramatic shift in the balance of power. But there were other fundamental causes for Cold War, and by 1946 one had emerged from the ashes of World War II that was so crucial as to be irreconcilable. The issue was Germany's future. No one issue would so polarize East and West, in 1946 and on through the Berlin blockade of 1948, the Berlin crisis of 1961, and the missile deployment controversy of the 1980s. Indeed, one can argue without much exaggeration that, before 1950, Germany was considered the *causa belli* of the Cold War, and it has never since been far removed from center stage.

For both the USSR and the United States, Germany was central to their concepts of national security. Two world wars had amply demonstrated to the Soviets the grave dangers and possible consequences of allowing Germany to reindustrialize and rearm, while it perhaps still harbored notions of realizing the German ambitions of 1914 and 1939. Even the unlikely prospect of a German revolution, so dear to Russian hopes in 1919, no longer struck a responsive chord. Given a quarter century to ossify, the communist revolution had become a Russian empire. Communist internationalism had been nationalized into Stalin's "socialism in one country," and new centers of world radicalism were not welcome unless they were clearly subordinate to the Soviet Union. That was true of Mao's China, Tito's Yugoslavia, and of communist guerrillas in the Greek civil war. It would be even more true of a core colossus like Germany.

For the United States, the logic of economic internationalism quickly carried it away from the Treasury Department's hard policy. Germany pastoralized would be a Germany of radically reduced living standards and per capita income, perhaps ripe for a move to the left and rapprochement with Russia. Germany reindustrialized would be Europe's most cost-competitive producer and its most effective consumer. Without full German participation in the European economy there could be no European recovery; without that, there could be no revitalization of the world-system; without that, there could be no American prosperity or any permanency to American free enterprise. Not unmindful of the German role in past intracapitalist wars and aware that France especially shared Russia's fears of German revanchism, the United States thought that reindustrialization (and even remilitarization) could safely be accomplished if Germany were integrated into a collective Atlantic community via a common market or a multinational armed force.

Those contradictory perspectives on Germany clashed frontally in 1946. The key issues were reparations to the USSR and the level of German industrial productivity. Russia actually decreased productivity in its occupation zone and pressured the West to keep its productivity levels as low as possible. At the same time, Russia stripped the meager industrial capability from its eastern zone while prodding the West to deliver to the Soviets plant and equipment from its more industrialized areas of control, all for shipment back to the Soviet Union. In May, any semblance of compatibility vanished when the United States stopped all shipments of industrial reparations from the western zones to Russia and adopted the so-called First Charge Principle: namely, that German productivity and its capacity to pay for Western imports took precedence over Russian reparation demands. By late summer, Secretary of State Byrnes made his famous Stuttgart speech (in the heart of the German industrial region) and publicly affirmed a new priority. It boosted the Germans' right to control their own destiny, withheld approval of Poland's absorption of East Prussia, and promised that American troops would remain in Germany. Finally, in December, the Americans and the British integrated their occupation zones, creating Bizonia and laying the foundation for what would soon be the Federal Republic of Germany. Faced with this fait accompli, Russia stopped its removal of German industry to the east and began producing German goods on German soil. Clearly, the Russians were there to stay as well. By the end of the year, the outlines of two Germanys were visible to one and all. The Russian-American Cold War had begun.

The Cold War at Home

If Russia was now the external devil, there was also an "enemy within" that threatened America's hegemonic internationalism in 1946. It had appeared in 1945 when popular pressure had forced the American government to commence a rapid demobilization of the American armed services. But it became more dramatically apparent in 1946 with the emergence of heterogeneous political groups that did not buy the logic or accept the imperatives of American hegemony, either for their constituents or for the nation as a whole. Representing both the political left and the political right, they seemed, to the centrist liberals who dominated the Democratic party of Harry Truman, to be frightening precursors of a new isolationism.

On the left were labor leaders from the more radical industrial unions, who pushed for Keynesian programs of deficit spending and full employment at home and limited, regulated trade aboard; also New Deal mavericks, like Henry Morgenthau and Harold Ickes, who entertained similar views and who assigned higher priority to German and Japanese deindustrialization than to the restoration of postwar trade; and finally internationalists, like Secretary of Commerce Henry Wallace, who did assign great value to world trade but who feared that the emerging containment policy toward Russia might needlessly sacrifice potential markets in so-called socialist countries. These groups clashed repeatedly with the administration in 1946 over its response to the wave of postwar labor strikes, its equivocation over the full employment act, its failure to prevent the hostile Taft-Hartley labor relations act, and its dismissal of Wallace from the cabinet for his public espousal of renewing Soviet-American cooperation. The clash climaxed in September 1946 when representatives of these groups formed the Progressive Citizens of America (PCA) and collectively criticized the government for retreating from New Deal domestic reform and opting for overseas adventurism instead. The organization was the nucleus of the left-wing Democrats who would bolt the party two years later and run Henry Wallace as the Progressive party candidate against President Truman.

Far more imposing were groups on the right, whose power was evident

in the congressional elections of 1946, which returned control of the legislature to the Republican party for the first time in nearly two decades. Tied
closely to local chambers of commerce and to businessmen selling largely
in the home market, they stressed the need for protective tariffs to safeguard that home market. Distrustful of Europeans and doubtful of America's power to restrain their autarkic tendencies, they saw more danger
than promise in an American globalism and made their wariness clear by
speaking against foreign aid, tariff liberalization, and participation in international banking and monetary agencies. The most principled and elo-
quent of these conservative critics was Senator Robert A. Taft of Ohio
("Mr. Republican"). "Our fingers will be in every pie," said he in his condemnation of American internationalism. "Our military forces will work
with our commercial forces to obtain as much of world trade as we can lay
our hands on. We will occupy all the strong strategic-points in the world
and try to maintain a force so preponderant that none shall dare attack
us. . . . Potential power over other nations, however benevolent its purposes, leads inevitably to imperialism."

Most conservatives did not share Taft's concern for potential American
imperialism. Moreover, they did believe that the American free enterprise
economy needed foreign outlets for its goods and capital if it was to survive. However, they saw that need best served not through a unitary world-
system but through creation of an American-monopolized sphere of
strategic-economic influence in one part of the planet. For them, the Monroe Doctrine was a more appropriate guide for American policy than the
Open Door policy. Most, however, no longer limited their vision of an
American-dominated New World simply to the Western Hemisphere (the
old Fortress America policy of the 1930s). They added another arena to
that of North and South America, enlarging the American sphere to include the so-called Pacific rim, meaning all those economies located on the
rim of the Pacific Ocean—North America on the east and Southeast Asia,
China, Korea, and Japan on the west. Spearheading this enlargement was a
group called the China lobby, a loose coalition of missionary-reform
groups, with sentimental attachments to China, and of West Coast businessmen (like freshman senator William Knowland), whose commercial
horizons followed the course of the setting sun. Already critical of the administration's policy of trying to force the Chinese nationalists into coalition government with the communists, they would later attempt to embar-
rass the executive branch for its alleged loss of China.

These threats from the left and right badly frightened centrist liberals
and threatened their control of mainstream politics in postwar America.
Rebuilding the European core, integrating the periphery, and holding Russia in purgatory were formidable tasks even for a country of awesome
power. They were impossible tasks unless the executive branch had the

consensus support of Congress and the public to provide American policy with necessary laws, dollars, weapons, personnel, and moral approval. The last was the key to all the others. Anything was possible if the government and its foreign policy had the public's blessing of legitimacy. Nothing was ultimately possible without it. So in a real sense, 1946 was the beginning of a battle for legitimacy waged by liberal internationalists against the specter of born-again isolationism. The battle tactics would become clearer a year later, but they were foreshadowed by the creation in late 1946 of the Americans for Democratic Action (ADA). Proclaiming liberal internationalism as the "vital center" of American life, the ADA saw the Truman administration as the embodiment of American pragmatism and political give-and-take, committed to defending that American way against the doctrinaire extremism of both the radical left and the conservative right. Portraying themselves as tough-minded liberals or realists with a heart (a sort of sensitive-macho hybrid), they characterized the right as uncompassionate and the left as utopian. Militantly anticommunist on one hand and pro–New Deal reform on the other, the ADA perfectly embodied what later would be called Cold War liberals. It also anticipated centrist tactics in the battle for legitimacy: use anticommunism to both muzzle the left and co-opt the right. The Cold War with Russia was not the only cold war that began in 1946.

4 | The Crisis of the New Order, 1947–1950

> We are the giant of the economic world. Whether we like it or
> not, the future pattern of economic relations depends upon us.
> The world is waiting and watching to see what we will do. The
> choice is ours. We can lead the nations to economic peace or we
> can plunge them into economic war.
> —*Harry S. Truman, 1947*

On a gloomy, grey, Friday afternoon, February 21, 1947, the British embassy delivered a "blue piece of paper"—an extraordinarily important note—to American Under Secretary of State Dean Acheson. It announced Britain's intentions to end its military and financial support of the Greek monarchy and the Turkish government within the ensuing thirty days. The announcement climaxed seven days that had seen Britain end its three-decade control of Palestine and its centuries-old dominion over India. Three days after receiving the "blue note" and following a weekend of frenetic State Department activity, Acheson mused aloud to a journalist friend on their way to lunch at the Metropolitan Club: "There are only two powers left. The British are finished, they are through. And the trouble is that this hits us too soon, before we are ready for it. We are having a lot of trouble getting money out of Congress."

Ready or not, the denouement of British imperium in the eastern Mediterranean would provoke a rapid and decisive American initiative to fill the void. Its most dramatic manifestation would be the Truman Doctrine. Neither British action nor American reaction, however, was as important as the larger context in which both took place. The crisis of British disengagement was but part of a much larger structural crisis in postwar capitalism, exacerbated by a challenge from the Soviet empire. And the Truman Doctrine was but a stop-gap response to that larger crisis, both less important and less enduring than the revolutionary responses embodied in the Marshall Plan of 1948 and the North Atlantic Treaty Organization in 1949. Even those measures, for all their startling innovativeness, would not remedy capitalism's troubles. Renewed structural crisis and renewed Russian challenge in late 1949 and early 1950 would dictate an even more revolutionary turn in American foreign policy. Its ultimate expression

72

would be National Security Council document paper #68, NSC-68. Its consequence would be a new kind of cold war, one both more militaristic and more Third World oriented.

The Dollar Gap Crisis

From the last fiscal quarter of 1946 through the first fiscal quarter of 1950 the world-system labored with a crisis born of paradox and steeped in irony. World capitalism seemed to require a hegemonic center (at that point, the United States) to insure that the various parts of the system would act in ways that would produce the greatest health of the whole. Because the preponderant economic power of the United States, upon which its hegemony largely rested, so overwhelmed the devastated European economies that commercial imbalance among major trading parts threatened the well-being of the whole, American economic supremacy nearly undermined its hegemonic function. The shorthand expression of this postwar paradox was graphic as well as cryptic; it was called the dollar gap crisis.

The restoration of European productivity and trade required, on the supply side, a seemingly limitless amount of food, raw materials, capital goods, and technology. Only the United States could meet that need in sufficient volume at acceptable prices. Unfortunately, Europe had limited means to pay for these imported factors of production. This was not, of course, a wholly new situation since Europe had run a trade deficit with the United States since 1914 and had continually faced the problem of acquiring sufficient dollars to pay for its deficit. Prior to World War II that problem had been soluble, as Europe generated the dollars out of its own colonial periphery and economic spheres of influence. For example, imports of American machinery ultimately were paid for by exports of raw materials from European colonies to the United States; or, more generally, foreign exchange earned by European investments and manufactured exports to its periphery were converted to dollars and used to balance accounts with the United States. Particularly valuable were the European colonies in South and Southeast Asia, its investment holdings in Latin America, and trade with Eastern Europe.

Now, in the postwar period, Europe's peripheral territories could no longer be counted on as sources of raw materials and dollar-earning profits to balance the books. Political independence movements diminished Europe's economic monopolization of India, Burma, Ceylon, Malaya, Cambodia, Laos, Vietnam, and Indonesia. Russian control of Eastern Europe limited profitmaking there. Most of Europe's Latin American investments had been sold to the Americans to help pay for World War II. In effect, European demands for American imports were expanding dramatically at the very time its means for paying for them were contracting. The resulting shortage in dollars became known as the dollar gap. It stood at $8 billion in 1946 and rose to $12 billion in 1947, with no relief in sight. It had already dampened European imports of American factors of production, and if it soared even higher it might cause a serious contraction of core trade in the world-system.

The American government and big business feared that an unsolved dollar gap crisis would lead to three interconnected catastrophes. First, it might lead Europe down the pathway to economic nationalism. Much of European money remained "soft currencies," not freely convertible to dollars. Most European countries had already experimented with trade restrictions to lessen foreign imports. Many had nationalized basic industries and thus frightened away foreign investors. Perpetuation of the crisis might well incline European countries to expand and make permanent their autarkic economic policies. Second, it might entice Europe to play the Russian card. Communist parties were strong in France and Italy, the British Labor party could move further left, and German Social Democrats might be amenable to political alliance with more radical groups. This leftward drift of Europe, combined with its state capitalist tendencies, might lead it to consider barter deals and political arrangements with the Soviet empire that might further circumscribe American access to Eurasia. Speaking of the world-system and its four industrial cores, the father of the containment policy, George F. Kennan, noted that two of the industrial cores were in Eurasia and that "the greatest danger that could confront the U.S. security would be a combination and working together for purposes hostile to us of the central European and Russian military-industrial potentials."

Finally, the dollar gap might ruin American postwar prosperity and force the United States itself to opt for more statist, self-contained economic approaches. Observing that American exports in 1947 were only 5 percent of the gross national product, compared to 10 percent in the pre-1929 period, economic analysts concluded that American exports to Europe might have doubled the 1947 total of $21 billion if Europe's dollar reserves had not been so strained. Even worse, they projected that American exports to Europe would decline by 40 percent in 1948, down to $13 billion, if some substantial transfusions of dollars were not injected into the European economies. A Europe forced down the nationalist route would not "remain open to American business in the same way that we have known it in the past," warned Secretary of State George Marshall. Echoing the admonition, the Council of Economic Advisers predicted that continuation of the dollar gap and retrenchment in the European market would mean "a drastic readjustment" in the domestic economic system. Free enterprise at home and a free world abroad, those two interdependent variables, were on the line, and that double jeopardy demanded an innovative response to the crisis of 1947 if the security of each was to be protected.

The Truman Doctrine

The dollar gap situation provoked short-, medium-, and long-term American responses: the Truman Doctrine, the Marshall Plan, and NATO. The first grew directly out of the new British crisis in early 1947 (often misleadingly called the Greek and Turkey crisis). Both during and after the war, Great Britain had continued to function as regional policeman to the eastern Mediterranean, spending hundreds of millions of dollars attempting to suppress a radical, antimonarchist rebellion in Greece between 1944 and 1947. That Greek imbroglio, along with British involvements in Egypt, Palestine, Turkey, and Iran terribly exacerbated the British dollar gap problem. Not only did it sidetrack part of a $3.8 billion American loan away from industrial productivity into military dead ends, but an abortive experiment in freer convertibility meant much of the outflow of pounds sterling to the Middle East ultimately was converted to dollars and used to purchase American rather than British goods. So, when the British government formally notified the United States that it would be unable to pick up the $250 million tab for the Greek civil war in the coming year, it implicitly invited the United States to take over the role of regional policeman.

The Truman administration leaped at the opportunity. On March 12, President Truman made an emotional speech to Congress asking for $400 million in military and economic aid, chiefly to pacify Greece. In addition, he incorporated aid to Turkey (still in a diplomatic hassle with Russia over the Dardanelles) and strongly suggested that both Greece and Turkey were victims of Russian or Russian-aided aggression. In universalistic language, he even went beyond the immediate regional context and declared, "It must be the policy of the United States to support free peoples who are resisting attempted subjugation by armed minorities or by outside pressure." Both the tone and content of the speech amounted to a globalization of the Monroe Doctrine, to a declaration that America's proper sphere was not just the New World but the whole world. It was also tacit endorsement of the "containment policy," first articulated a year earlier by Kennan: "a policy of firm containment designed to confront the Russians with unalterable counterforce at every point where they show signs of encroaching upon the interests of a peaceful and stable world."

The Truman Doctrine was a brilliant if disingenuous attempt to do three key things, all of them germane to the dollar gap crisis of 1947. First, taking over the British financial burden would ease the chronic dollar drain of

America's most valued trading partner. Second, succeeding in the task of forcibly ending the Greek revolution would tend to stabilize the whole region and insure that Europe as a whole could continue purchasing its oil from non-dollar sources—that it could get its vital oil without spending scarce dollars buying it from the United States. (As *Time* magazine put it, "The loud talk was all of Greece and Turkey, but the whispers behind the talk were of the ocean of oil to the south.") Lastly, the universalism and anticommunism of the Truman Doctrine would help prepare Congress and the American public for the more concerted effort to solve the dollar gap crisis with the Marshall Plan. By March 1947, administration officials already anticipated that a new venture in foreign economic aid for Europe would be necessary to correct the disequilibrium between the American and European economies. In that context, the Truman Doctrine request for $400 million for Greece and Turkey was also a dress rehearsal for a far larger economic aid solicitation to come for Europe and perhaps elsewhere. (The State Department had already begun a survey of economic aid needs—dollar gap subsidies—for the whole world-system but would not conclude its deliberations until late May.)

President Truman faced a newly elected Republican Congress that he viewed as more nationalistic than internationalistic. Congress, suspicious of an imperial presidency whose power had expanded at its expense through the depression and the war, might prove receptive to the blandishments of a new isolationism. To ask such a Congress for $300 million to finish the British job of crushing an antimonarchist Greek revolution might strike it as an ill-conceived effort to "pull British chestnuts out of the fire." But adding Turkey to the agenda (another $100 million) broadened the focus from one British client-state to the whole region. More importantly, stressing the Russia and communism angle while soft-pedalling the British element appealed to the patriotism and antiradicalism of Congress and avoided its latent Anglophobia.

It would be an overstatement to call the Greek and Turkish crises manufactured, designed to get at the real one, the dollar gap. The Greek civil war was a serious situation and had been so for two and a half years. It is true that Stalin had provided Greek Communists in the rebellion with little aid and that he feared they might be as independent-minded as the Yugoslavian Communists, who gave them significant aid. But even if it was unlikely that Greece would "swing into the Russian orbit," the State Department believed it was very possible that it would "drop out of the United States orbit and try an independent nationalistic policy." Coming in a region already shaken by decolonization, a challenging ideology ("Arab socialism," as a variant of autarky and state capitalism), and Jewish efforts to create an independent Israel, such a development could only be further destabilizing. As for Russian pressure on Turkey, it was less serious than it had been a year earlier; but even in muted form it held some concern for American leaders already committed to using Turkish control of the Dardanelles to put a cork in Russian ambitions for the Middle East.

At another level, however, the Greek and Turkish crises were something of twin tempests in a teapot. Neither situation had changed for the worse by early 1947 and Russian actions in the months preceding the Truman Doctrine had appeared subdued and cautious. Indeed, one of Truman's top aides, George Elsey, acknowledged that "there has been no overt action in the immediate past by the USSR which serves as an adequate pretext for an 'all-out' speech." Yet the hyperbole and grandiloquent rhetoric of Truman's message clearly belied that reality and suggested that what was being managed was less the crisis itself than public reaction to it. That management was intended not simply to pry $400 million out of a Republican Congress but to prepare the proper political climate in which that Congress would be asked, just three months later, to approve a revolutionary economic aid program for Europe that would ultimately cost *forty times that sum.*

As Acheson's biographer, David McLellan, put it, "Acheson knew for some time that aid to Greece and Turkey was only an advance installment on a much larger problem—that of European economic recovery." He recounts that early drafts of Truman's message, prepared by State Department staffers, candidly stressed economic factors. "Two great wars and an intervening world depression," began the first draft, "have weakened the [capitalist] system almost everywhere except in the United States. . . . If, by default, we permit free enterprise to disappear in other countries of the world, the very existence of our democracy will be gravely threatened." Both President Truman and Under Secretary of State Acheson remarked that the draft "made the whole thing sound like an investment prospectus." Accordingly, they redrafted the document to provide its more biting tone and its aura of globalism and anticommunism. The President fancied that he knew his Congress well and the Under Secretary had seen in congressional hearings how well the image of a communist menace worked to provoke reactions from legislators more known for their fiscal prudence than for interest in world affairs. When Secretary of State Marshall was wired a copy of the final message, he was attending a foreign ministers' conference in London where Soviet-American confrontation had left him considerably nettled toward the Russians. Yet even he wondered if the speech might not be "overstating the case a bit." The President's reply spoke reams about crisis-management on the home front: "it was clear that this was the only way in which the measure could be passed." Following the famed advice of Arthur Vandenberg, the President had indeed "scared hell out of the American people." What worked for the Truman Doctrine would prove recyclable for the Marshall Plan as well.

The Marshall Plan

European Recovery Program (ERP), or Marshall Plan, was the medium-term response to the structural crisis symbolized by the dollar gap. It was to supply Europe with the necessary dollars in the short-run, while requiring it to accept America's long-term prescriptions on how to enlarge Europe's home market and become more price-competitive in the world market. Publicly articulated by Marshall and Acheson in late spring of 1947, hammered into concrete form by inter-European negotiations in the summer, and modified and accepted by the Truman administration in the fall, it was formally submitted to Congress on December 9. Passed on March 31, 1948, the ERP committed the United States to spend $17 billion over a four-year period ending in 1952. Bypassing the UN and its new Economic Commission for Europe (UNECE), it created a solely American agency, the Economic Cooperation Administration (ECA) to implement the program. In Marshall's words, it was to be "a cure rather than a palliative."

The Marshall Plan was arguably the most innovative piece of foreign policy in American history. The dollar amount itself was less revolutionary than the uses to which the dollars would be put. (After all, the United States had already funneled some $9 billion into Europe in the preceding two years through the British loan, the German occupation, and various UN relief agencies.) Aiming to correct the postwar imbalance in world capitalism, the Marshall Plan sought to shape Europe's political make-up and its domestic public policy. It attempted to move Europe irrevocably away from nationalism and autarky toward internationalism and free convertibility. It aimed to integrate Germany into a European market large enough to be viable as a domestic market and competitive enough to hold its own in a comparative-advantage world.

American manipulation of European domestic policies would come directly through ERP "counterpart funds." Europe would be required to match American grant dollars in equal amounts of local currencies and to deposit them in counterpart funds. Each country was to draw up plans for employing counterpart currencies, but the ECA had the power to veto programs it deemed inconsistent with Marshall Plan purposes. During the ERP's first year, the ECA often blocked efforts to use counterpart funds for social welfare purposes it viewed as inflationary and therefore counter to the goal of cost-efficiency. Instead, it forced left-of-center governments in Great Britain, France, and Italy to reduce foreign debts, balance budgets, and keep a lid on wages—that is, to deflate as a means of making Europe price-competitive and able to reduce its dollar trading deficit. More indirectly, the Marshall Plan sent a strong message to European voters that American largess depended on their electing governments willing to accept the accompanying rules of multilateral trade and fiscal conservatism. Communists who denounced the ERP as American economic imperialism and socialists who clung to inflationary deficit spending were clearly not fit recipients. It was not coincidence that French and Italian Communists fared less well than expected in 1948 and that the European political balance shifted rightward from socialist-style parties to Christian Democratic-type parties.

At the same time, the Marshall Plan would require Europe to take a giant step toward a European common market. Wedded to the concepts of comparative advantage and economies of scale, Americans believed that a single, integrated, transnational market—relatively free of high tariffs, national trading quotas, and currency controls—would enable each nation to specialize in what it did best and to sell its large-scale production runs to hundreds of millions of European customers rather than to its more limited home market. Moreoever, greater cost-savings would enable individual nations to be competitive with dollar goods, not only in Europe but in the periphery and perhaps North America itself. As John Foster Dulles (then U.S. representative to the UN General Assembly) told the National Publishers' Association in January 1948, "a healthy Europe" could not be "divided into small compartments." It had to be organized into an integrated market "big enough to justify modern methods of cheap production for mass consumption."

Accordingly, the ECA conditioned its grants on European willingness to increase interregional cooperation. In particular, it made the Organization of European Economic Cooperation (OEEC) into a transnational body that annually reviewed each nation's economic policies and requests and used its real though limited powers to coordinate those national programs in ways that promoted multilateral trade and payments. In like vein, the ECA used its say in the use of counterpart funds to stimulate European investment in so-called critical sectors—industries that had immediate prospects of generating markets in the United States (thus decreasing the dollar gap) and had long-term promise of developing significant comparative advantages in world trade. To be sure, these efforts in the late 1940s necessarily fell short of the ideal goal of a common market. France feared that an integrated Europe would be dominated by Germany; Britain feared that a continental union would diminish its special relationship to the sterling bloc; and European labor feared that its interests were being sacrificed to stimulate supply-side investment. These fears forced American leaders to proceed slowly and to make some compromises between ideal goals and political reality. But the direction of change was apparent: the European Payments Union in 1950, the European Coal and Steel Authority in 1951, and finally the Common Market (European Economic Community) in 1958.

Finally, the Marshall Plan provided the ideal opportunity to integrate Germany into the Euro-American core economy. The logic of America's economic internationalism demanded it, for, as Secretary Marshall noted, "the restoration of Europe involved the restoration of Germany. Without a revival of Germany's production there can be no revival of Europe's economy." Europe could never hold its own or compete in the world-system without the productive skills and the consumptive capacity of a reindustrialized Germany. General Motors Corporation chairman Alfred P. Sloan, for example, firmly insisted that "the other countries" of Europe "are just not comparable with Germany in their efficiency," and that without German integration into the European economy, "there is nothing that could convince us in General Motors that it was either sound or desirable or worthwhile to undertake an operation of any consequence in a country like France."

Understandably, the United States made German reindustrialization the primary objective of its foreign policy during the year between presentation of the Truman Doctrine and Congress's final passage of the Marshall Plan. It pushed levels of German industrial productivity ever higher, while forcefully rejecting Russian demands for participation in the management of the industrial Ruhr and while turning a deaf ear to similar proposals by France to put the Ruhr under international control. Faced with the prospect of an autonomous industrial Germany, restrained only by its American connection, France found the alternative prospect of a rebuilt Germany integrated into a general European market far more palatable. Intertwined and interdependent with the rest of Europe, Germany would have neither the reasons nor the means to upset that arrangement by force. Indeed, a revivified Germany might well aid French recovery. As Secretary of Commerce Averell Harriman put it, the "best reparations [France] can obtain is the prompt recovery of Germany."

Russia had no such reason to moderate its policy toward Germany. Any reindustrialized Germany was a potential danger, and an integrated one was not necessarily less threatening than an autonomous one. Indeed, the latter would have more freedom to cut separate deals with the USSR, while the former might be even more formidable as an agent of general capitalist encirclement than it would be if acting simply for German national interests. It was predictable, then, that Russia would react with sharp hostility to the policy announcements in March 1948 that the three western zones in Germany (Trizonia) would be fused into the Federal Republic (West Germany) during the following year and invited to be a sovereign participant in the ERP. When the American-sponsored currency reform for Germany was implemented in June, effectively separating

Trizonia from the Russian zone, the USSR could choose to accept the *fait accompli* or go down fighting. It chose the latter.

On June 24, Russia instituted the famous Berlin blockade. It was a desperate effort to force its former allies to reconsider their German policy and to back away from reindustrialization, West German unification, economic integration, and ultimately (so Russia feared) remilitarization. Lasting almost eleven, crisis-filled months, the blockade only played into American hands. The United States successfully airlifted supplies to beleaguered West Berlin and, in an overt display of atomic diplomacy, dispatched two groups of B-29 strategic bombers to England. The effort to derail America's German policy came to naught, because Russia was unable or unwilling to go to war. Indeed, the United States itself prolonged the Berlin blockade stalemate as an excuse not to discuss German affairs with the Soviet Union. By May 1949, West Germany had become a firmly accomplished fact, and, confronted with it, Russia ended its counterproductive blockade. Four years after the end of World War II, the United States finally won the war. The Ruhr-Rhine industrial core, that object of Western military strategy, had been politically and economically integrated into an American-dominated world-system.

The Marshall Plan at Home

If the formulation of the Marshall Plan was innovative, so too was the selling of it to Congress and the American citizenry. Carefully calculated and organized, the selling of the ERP aimed for an all-out mobilization of the plan's likeliest supporters—large corporations and organized labor—and for the neutralization or co-optation of its likeliest opponents—leftist progressives and nationalist conservatives. Most heavily targeted and wooed was big business. Disappointed at the low volume of postwar world trade and fearful of a drift back to depression, corporate interests were easily persuaded that Europe could not expand its role as America's best customer unless the United States underwrote and subsidized its economic recovery. Some business leaders even shared the worst-case scenario of Will Clayton, under secretary of state for economic affairs, that failure to pass the Marshall Plan would produce a "blackout of the European market" and spell the beginning of the end for "our democratic free enterprise system." On the other hand, big business did have to be persuaded that ERP dollars would not be spent to prop up socialistic governments, support nationalization of industries, or undermine free enterprise in Europe itself.

Government reassurances allayed those fears somewhat, but government actions spoke more audibly. Rather than administer the Marshall Plan through the existing State Department bureaucracy, President Truman created a wholly new economic recovery bureaucracy (the Economic Cooperation Administration—ECA) that was dominated by corporate executives active in world trade. In effect, the private and public sectors were to share power in carrying out the reconstruction of Europe. Paul G. Hoffman, president of Studebaker Corporation, became the chief of the ECA, and he promptly surrounded himself with a staff composed largely of corporate managers. Counselling him was the Public Advisory Board, composed of appointees from organized business, labor, and agriculture. It, in turn, had a whole series of advisory subcommittees on fiscal problems, oil pricing, overseas (periphery) development, and reparations. Each was dominated by prominent business figures from Chase National Bank, First National Bank of New York, New York Life Insurance, the Rockefeller Foundation, General Motors, Standard Oil of New Jersey, Westinghouse, and numerous international law firms and brokerage houses. With substantial power in such hands, big business no longer feared that the Marshall Plan would subvert free enterprise and their private prerogatives. Indeed, big business returned the favor by providing the administration with its chief lobbying support, the Committee for the Marshall Plan, which enthusiastically preached the virtues of the ERP to the American people and pressured Congress to pass it.

Junior partners on that same committee were representatives of organized labor, especially from the conservative American Federation of Labor (AF of L) and the center-right wing of the Congress of Industrial Organizations (CIO). Keenly aware of America's hegemonic power, these union figures accepted the productionist logic that labor's interests were better served through full production for an expanding world market than by redividing the income generated through production for the national market. As the CIO national convention proclaimed in November 1947, "Foreign markets . . . have offered a source of disposal of excess American production greater and more lasting than was expected. This market can continue for years if America is willing to help rehabilitate a stricken world." Such reincarnations of the overproduction theory produced arithmetic assertions that as many as twelve million American jobs depended on passage of the Marshall Plan. Since such views were challenged by radical labor leaders, the government was careful to reinforce their conservative advocates by giving them a significant input into the ECA itself. George Meany of the AF of L and James Carey of the CIO sat on the Public Advisory Board. Labor representatives headed the ECA missions to socialist governments in Scandinavia. Union figures acted as liaison between ECA headquarters and the Trade Union Advisory Committee (TUAC), representing European labor. American unions cooperated with the newly formed Central Intelligence Agency (CIA) to pump laundered money and support into anticommunist, pro-ERP unions, especially in France. The role was a very junior one compared to that of big business, but it was enough to plausibly demonstrate that the interests of the working classes, both European and American, would not be wholly ignored in postwar reconstruction.

If proponents had to be mobilized and rewarded, potential opponents of the Marshall Plan had to be disarmed or delegitimized. Leftist progressives were of particular concern because they were the one group that had successfully resisted the consensus-building of the recent Truman Doctrine. "Wallacite" (after Secretary of Commerce Henry Wallace) internationalists were the easier subgroup to defuse because they basically agreed with the American vision of a multilateral world. What they had abhorred in the Truman Doctrine had been its confrontational style with the Russians, its stress on military aid and military solutions, and its support of reactionary regimes in Greece and Turkey. But the Marshall Plan could be presented to them as wholly different. It aided parliamentary democracies, mainly of a left-of-center political hue, it stressed economic aid and economic solutions, rather than military, and it actually invited the USSR and its Eastern European dependencies to participate in the economic recovery program. To be sure, the invitation was specious since the price of Russian participation was a price that American officials were confident Russia would not pay, i.e., trimming the sails of Russian national planning in deference to ECA and OEEC insistence that recovery be coordinated collectively rather than administered on a country-by-country, case-by-case basis. Nonetheless, an offer had been made, and if Russia chose to regard it as too bad to accept, that was its problem, and its onus. Henry Wallace himself eventually resisted such pitches and castigated the ERP as "the Martial Plan" and an extension of the Truman Doctrine. But many liberals who had wavered between contrary appeals of the PCA-left and the ADA-center were more receptive. Like journalistic pundit, Walter Lippmann, they found as much reason to praise the Marshall Plan as they had found to pan the Truman Doctrine.

Radicals further to the left proved less tractable. Centered mainly in the labor movement, these communists, independent socialists, and radical New Dealers continued to dissent from the international capital solution. Neither did they succumb to the humanitarian plea that support for the Marshall Plan was essential to save a desperate Europe from cold, hunger, and homelessness. No doubt they were moved by such appeals, as presumably were most caring people of all political persuasions. They refused, however, to believe that the ERP, with all its multilateral strings attached, was as effective or disinterested as UN organizations might have been in carrying out that humanitarian injunction. These radicals opposed CIO endorsement of the Marshall Plan and abandoned coalition politics inside the Democratic party to support Henry Wallace and his Progressive party in 1948.

Unable to disarm such radical critics, the administration and its labor allies sought to delegitimize them in the public's eye. The means employed was an in-house purge of the left from the ranks of organized labor, especially from the CIO, where radicals had the greatest presence. It began in January 1947 when the CIO excluded a large number of radical organizations from its list of those deemed fit for CIO support. A year later, the CIO executive board criticized unionists who supported the Wallace movement, alleging that it was communist-dominated and would split the liberal vote in an era of Republican antilabor repression. It also tacitly permitted noncommunist affiliates (those who had signed the loyalty oath affidavits required by the Taft-Hartley Act) to raid noncomplying, leftist affiliates. In November 1948, the national convention transformed that tacit permission into explicit endorsement, and it openly questioned whether being a CIO member and being a communist were compatible. The process would be completed a year later, in 1949, when communists and alleged sympathizers were excluded from the CIO executive board, and the United Electrical Workers (UE) and the Farm Equipment Workers (FE) were expelled for being undemocratic (i.e., communist-dominated). Expulsion hearings were begun against a number of other unions on similar grounds. Eventually eleven unions, representing more than a million workers, were purged from the CIO ranks and nonradical unions in both the AF of L and the CIO attempted to raid them out of existence.

The 1947–49 purge of labor's left wing was not done at the government's bidding or even largely for foreign policy reasons. The motivations were complex and grew out of political fights within the union movement that dated back to the late 1930s. But the government, through both the Labor and Justice departments, did support the purge. Stifling criticism of its foreign policy was one of the government's motives. One of the reasons labor's center-right wing was willing to excise its left wing (which included many who were prominent in the early CIO successes) was a desire to enhance the legitimacy of labor unions in the public's eye. Demonstrations of labor's own anticommunism was one way to prevent more antilabor legislation from the Republican-controlled Congress and to demonstrate that labor was a fit partner for the White House and business internationalists in shouldering the burdens and sharing the rewards of hegemony. But in proving its own bona fides, the trade union movement sustained a tendency already begun by Truman's internal security programs and soon carried to its logical conclusion by McCarthyism: i.e., the definition of dissent as disloyalty and the consequent enshrinement of bipartisan consensus as the political norm in America. In other words, the Cold War demanded unity, even if achieving that oneness required narrowing the range of foreign policy alternatives and diminishing democratic, pluralistic involvement in decisionmaking.

Deflecting the political right—the Fortress America and Pacific Rim regionalists—proved far easier. In the beginning, the administration coupled humanitarian appeals with the material inducement that even national capital could profit from subcontracting arrangements with multinational business. Ultimately, neither humanitarianism nor economic internationalism was sufficient to carry the day with a nationalist-oriented Congress. As the Truman Doctrine had already demonstrated, however, those same nationalist values made the legislature susceptible to anticommunist and national-security appeals. Russian declination of ERP participation made such appeals possible in late 1947, but it was the Czechoslovakian crisis in early 1948 that empowered the administration to repeat its Truman Doctrine gambit of a year earlier.

For nearly three years, Czechoslovakia had attempted a delicate balancing act between East and West—each pressuring it for allegiance—and between communists and noncommunists at home. While the Communist party was the largest single party (38 percent of the vote in 1947), the government attempted to rule through a noncommunist coalition that sought both trade with the West and friendly political ties with East. With Czechoslovakia caught between the proverbial rock and a hard place, external pressures and internal contradictions led to the overthrow of the coalition neutralist government and the triumph of the Communist party on February 25, 1948. Precipitating the takeover was the Czech interest in the Marshall Plan and Russian fears that it would lure Czechoslovakia into the American orbit. The Truman administration, often critical of the government before it fell, now acquired a sudden and belated affection for it. Like Greece, Czechoslovakia became an example of a free people being subverted from within and without in the manner proscribed by the Truman Doctrine.

Skillfully exploiting the Czechoslovakian crisis, President Truman could and did sell the Marshall Plan in the name of anticommunism. In a master stroke of political acumen, he went before Congress on March 17, 1948 (almost exactly a year after his doctrinal speech) and urged it to pass the ERP, lest all of Europe be destabilized and suffer the same fate as Czechoslovakia. Declaring that the "very survival of freedom" depended on its enactment, he shrewdly urged Congress to couple its passage with resumption of the selective service draft and instigation of universal military training, all to contain the "increasing threat" of expanding communism. The Republican leadership had little choice in its response. Having long whipped the Democrats for their Yalta mentality and their alleged insensitivity to the communist menace, they could not turn a deaf ear to Truman's somber invocation of that same menace without jeopardizing their own political credentials. Their own claims to legitimacy demanded their assent to at least one of Truman's tripartite requests. All three proposals were unpopular in Republican circles, but in early 1948 foreign aid was less unpopular than the peacetime draft and universal military training. Within two weeks of Truman's speech, Congress gave him the money for the European Recovery Program. Classically, the President had asked for more than he expected in order to get what he really wanted.

The North Atlantic Treaty Organization

Truman's speech did something else. It presaged what would be the long-term, political-military response to the postwar crisis: the NATO pact. It was hoped that the four-year long Marshall Plan would create the foundation on which European reindustrialization would build, but economic growth depended as much on political environment as on dollars. New Secretary of State Dean Acheson, for example, later recalled the "very strong belief that economic recovery was closely connected with some sort of progress in the security field. It was felt that economic recovery had progressed through what might be called the primitive economic stages. . . . But to go beyond the point where the European countries were in mid-1948 required . . . a greater sense of security before there could be the additional economic development which required their confidence, the return of capital which had taken flight from those countries, new investment in plant through the capital of the countries concerned."

As long as the Russian army resided on Europe's borders and radical unions and parties existed in its midst, an insecure Europe would periodically be tempted to bolt the internationalist track and forge an opening to the east. A Euro-American alliance, however, could assuage lingering European fears about Russian or German aggression and generally make clear that American hegemony would provide not only for Europe's economic recovery but for its physical security as well. Acheson later wrote in his memoirs, "Western Europe and the United States could not contain the Soviet Union and Germany at the same time. Our best hope was to make these former enemies *willing* and *strong* supporters of a free-world structure. Germany should be welcomed into Western Europe, not kept in limbo outside . . . relegated to maneuvering between the Soviet Union and the allies." And he agreed with one senator's assessment that NATO gave Europe "some confidence against a resurgent Germany as well as Russia."

The NATO alliance would provide Europe with a nuclear umbrella of forward air bases within range of Russian targets. It would offer Europe the voluntary hostage of an American army whose presence in Central Europe would insure that American pledges of mutual defense would be honored; and ultimately it would prepare the way for rebuilding the German *Wehrmacht*, but in an integrated way that would blunt German aggression westward while making Germany a useful counterforce against the East.

The North Atlantic Treaty Organization was the product of such considerations, and a logical corollary to the Marshall Plan. It grew out of the Brussels Treaty for collective defense signed by Britain, France, and the so-called Benelux trio (Belgium, the Netherlands, and Luxembourg) in March 1948. It was in part a response to war-scare fueled by the Czechoslovakian crisis. The following June, the Vandenberg Resolution committed the American Senate in principle to an exploration of possible American participation in the Brussels Treaty organization. Six months later, President Truman's inaugural address announced, as point three of his foreign policy principles, his intention to form a North Atlantic pact. ("Point Four" later became a term synonymous with technical assistance programs for underdeveloped areas.) In April 1949, the NATO pact was signed by the United States, the Brussels Treaty nations, and Italy, Portugal, Norway, Denmark, Iceland, and Canada. (Greece, Turkey, and Germany would be added by 1954.)

Domestic resistance as intense as that in 1947 and 1948 failed to materialize. Left-progressives had been disheartened by Wallace's poor showing in the 1948 presidential race, and the post-election repression of the left quickened pace in both organized labor and the Democratic party. The Americans for Democratic Action had apparently won its three-year battle with the Progressive Citizens of America for the hearts and minds of American liberals. Already right-nationalists and regionalists had twice been hoisted on their own petards of anticommunism and concern for national security. Having acquiesced in the Truman Doctrine and the Marshall Plan, they were easily bought off with perfunctory and unpersuasive promises that NATO would not require substantial numbers of American troops in Europe, nor would it require remilitarization of Germany. To be sure, Senator Taft criticized the assumption "that we are a kind of demigod and Santa Claus to solve the problems of the world" and warned once more against slipping "into an attitude of imperialism where war becomes an instrument of public policy rather than its last resort." In the end, however, even he voted for the NATO treaty. Making the administration's task easier was the lengthy Berlin blockade crisis, which continued a month beyond NATO's signing and which made the Russian threat appear real rather than fancied. Consequently, on July 21, 1949, the Senate overwhelmingly ratified the NATO pact by a 6-to-1 margin, and two days later the administration called for the Mutual Defense Assistance Program (MDAP), to provide its new allies with an initial $1.5 billion in military aid.

Renewed Crisis in the World-System

A contemporary television sports program talks about "the thrill of victory and the agony of defeat". From August 1949 until April 1950, American leaders endured the psychic fragmentation of experiencing both feelings at once. On one hand, the United States had weathered the initial structural crisis in world capitalism and responded effectively with the ideological, economic, political, and military innovations of the Truman Doctrine, the Marshall Plan, and NATO. But, like some cosmic dialectic, history repeated and embroidered itself with renewed and deepened crisis in late 1949 and early 1950. The world-system seemed once more threatened from within, this time by the calamitous consequences of the American "reverse course" policy in Japan and by the continued bottlenecks and dollar shortages that plagued the European Recovery Program. (At the same time, this internal crisis was exacerbated from without by Russian acquisition of the atomic bomb and by the triumph of the Chinese communists in the Chinese civil war.)

The near catastrophe of America's Japan policy was more immediately frightening than any other facet of the renewed crisis. Since 1948, the United States had reversed its earlier course of decentralizing and democratizing Japanese economic life. American occupation authorities had ceased efforts to break up large-scale monopoly capital (the *Zaibatsu*) and were exploring strategies of reindustrialization instead. This "reverse course" reflected a number of factors. The U.S. Congress was anxious to make the Japanese occupation self-supporting, able to sustain itself without American subsidies; and the ERP burden of $17 billion only made Congress more eager to put Japan on a pay-as-you-go footing. In addition, American occupation authorities were fearful that earlier attempts at economic decentralization had strengthened the political hand of Japanese communists and socialists. While Japanese radicals preferred nationalization of private industry, they saw competitive capitalism as more acceptable than monopoly capital, because it diminished the power of traditional industrial oligarchs. Finally, the obvious collapse of the Chinese nationalists and the likely triumph of the Chinese communists had killed any notion of China's acting as a regional surrogate for the United States. Only Japan seemed a likely role model to demonstrate to the rest of Asia the advantages of a procapitalist, prointegrationist model of economic development. To play the role effectively, however, Japanese industry had to be organized on the same principles as that in North America and the OEEC countries: large-scale, specialized production for the world market that would reap the higher profits of comparative advantage and economies of scale.

Following the blueprint laid out by Joseph Dodge, a prominent banker and consultant, the American government instituted the Dodge Plan in late 1948 and early 1949. It aimed at reviving Japanese industrial productivity, making export goods competitive in world markets, and putting the economy on a self-sustaining basis. While clearly similar to ERP goals for Europe, the Dodge Plan differed in one fundamental way. European reindustrialization was geared as much to the enlargement of an integrated domestic market as it was to giving European nations a greater share of the world market. Japan's reindustrialization was focused more single-mindedly on production for export, and not until 1960 would the Japanese home market receive equivalent stress. This difference had profound implications for Japanese social and economic policy. Specifically, Japanese workers tended to be viewed largely as cost-factors rather than potential consumers, and this put a greater premium on keeping wage bills as low as possible so Japanese exports could underprice competitors.

Reflecting this difference, the Dodge Plan was even more wedded to austerity measures than was the Marshall Plan. The latter had financed itself from the pocketbooks of both American taxpayers and European workers. The former attempted to finance itself almost entirely out of labor's decreased share of national income. Accordingly, the Dodge Plan called for severe cuts in social services, a sharp reduction of government employees, repression of the more militant labor unions, Draconian measures to outlaw and suppress strikes, reduction of wages to subsistence levels at which three-quarters of income went for food, and a balanced budget to halt inflation and enhance Japan's competitive position in world trade. Intense resistance by Japanese trade unions did soften American policy somewhat, but by and large the Dodge Plan was enacted as envisioned.

Its consequences, however, were far from anticipated. Industrial productivity did increase perceptibly, but buyers for those products did not materialize. The austerity program forcibly repressed domestic demand while various factors continued to inhibit foreign demand. Civil war and revolution severely limited Japan's traditional markets in China, Southeast Asia, and Northeast Asia. Moreover, protective tariffs still restricted access to North America and Europe, and the Americans retained an insuperable advantage in the high-profit product lines that Japan was determined to enter. By late 1949 and early 1950, Japan's trade deficit with the United States (its counterpart of Europe's dollar gap) was rising as fast as the strength of the yen was falling. More than a few Japanese and American observers feared that Japan stood on the precipice of economic catastrophe, in a situation akin to a business teetering on the brink of bankruptcy. One of earth's four great industrial cores was in danger of becoming a dysfunctional part of the world-system and a drag on the whole.

Compounding that systemic problem were parallel shortcomings in the European core. The Marshall Plan at midpassage had hardly closed the dollar gap. Europe still financed a third of its American imports out of grant dollars, while private profits were slow to generate the dollars to take up the slack. Indeed, dollar scarcity in Britain was so severe that even the United States had to accept the necessity of a sharp devaluation of the pound from $4.03 to $2.80 in September 1949. Since the ERP was set to expire in 1952 and Congress was unlikely to extend it, there remained real fear that the persistent dollar gap would yet wreak havoc on American exports and European recovery. Secretary of State Acheson summed up the situation in early 1950: "Put in its simplest terms, the problem is this: as ERP is reduced, and after its termination in 1952, how can Europe and other areas of the world obtain the dollars necessary to pay for a high level of U.S. exports, which is essential both to their own basic needs, and to the well-being of the American economy. This is the problem of the 'dollar gap' in world trade."

Part of Europe's continuing difficulties were supply-side problems of nagging bottlenecks in European productivity. Still, these seemed soluble problems and productivity, for both factory and farm, had generally increased. The greater problem seemed on the demand side. As George Kennan put it in August 1949, "*It is one thing to produce; it is another thing to sell.*" (Emphasis added.) As in Japan, austerity measures had dampened domestic demand, the Cold War had restricted access to the "socialist" markets, and congressional protectionism and a serious American recession in early 1949 had caused the major capitalist market to contract. Nor did the anticipated alternatives materialize as easily as hoped. European integrationism lagged as the ECA focused on the more immediate problem of production snarls, so inter-European trade and the common market movement were stymied until the European Payments Union helped free the course of commerce in 1950.

To make matters worse, the periphery failed to fill the void. Production of primary commodities in Europe's traditional spheres of influence was static and inadequate. Parts of the periphery, especially in Asia, were beset by wars of national liberation against Western colonialism or by civil wars to see who would rule at home once the imperialists were gone. Even relatively tranquil territories were often more interested in developing domestic manufacturing than in increasing raw material production for their core customers. Because primary commodity production grew so slowly in relation to Europe's demand, Europe paid higher prices for its raw materials than did the United States; and the added costs undercut Europe's ability to compete with America in the world market. It also meant that because Europe's periphery made so little money out of its low-volume exports, it lacked the means to pay for significant amounts of European imports. In short, the revival of European industrial productivity had far less positive impact than expected because it was not accompanied by a parallel and complementary revival of primary commodity productivity in the periphery. The Third World (as it was soon to be called) needed to play its role (assigned it by the core powers) as efficient supplier of low-cost raw materials and as efficient supplemental market for finished products from the core.

Renewed Challenge from the External World

This renewed crisis within the world-system was deepened by critical developments in the external world, in both the Russian and the Chinese empires. In two trip-hammer blows that shook the self-confidence of the capitalist world, Russia acquired the atomic bomb and China went communist. The first event broke the half-decade atomic monopoly enjoyed by the United States and provoked a heated debate among American leaders about its implications. Some feared that by 1954, when Russia might have a meaningful weapons stockpile and a delivery system, the USSR would be a serious threat to world peace. Under Secretary of State Robert Lovett, for example, warned, "We are now in a mortal combat. . . . It is not a cold war. It is a hot war." Others disdained that worst-case scenario and were inclined to regard the Russians as inherently cautious and disinclined to take high risks. George Kennan argued that the Soviet A-bomb added "no new fundamental element to the picture," and he saw "little justification for the impression that the 'cold war' . . . has suddenly taken some turn to our disadvantage." Still under his influence, the Policy Planning Staff of the State Department concluded there was little likelihood of a Russian attack on either the United States or its allies, even after 1954.

Both groups, however, agreed that Russian atomic diplomacy might be dangerous even if Russian atomic weaponry was not. However secure some Americans might feel, Europe and Japan were less likely to be sanguine about Russian intentions. Sharing a physical proximity to the USSR, they were apt to be more concerned about the coupling of the Red Army with the atomic bomb. Likewise, both might have been uncertain that America would risk atomic attack on its homeland to defend them against the Russian empire. They might question the credibility of the American military shield to protect the system. Such fears of the Soviets and doubts about the Americans might easily have led other core capitalist powers to waver in their deference to American hegemony and might have tempted them to play the Russian card in ways that would undermine the new world order for which America had fought World War II.

At the same time, the Chinese communists completed their triumph in the civil war as the last substantial nationalist forces fled the mainland to Taiwan. Communist victory heightened the possibility that China would exit the capitalist world-system, and that prospect seemed more certain with the signing of the Sino-Soviet pact of February 1950, creating a bilateral defense commitment, a settlement of historic territorial issues, and a modest Russian economic aid program. This Chinese departure prompted a famous State Department white paper to defend the administration from charges of culpability by "Pacific rim Republicans," but it also stirred an important debate within the executive branch on the nature and importance of the "loss" of China.

Asian specialists among career bureaucrats tended to think that China was not a Russian puppet, notwithstanding the 1950 treaty, and believed that preconditions existed for splitting the two apart and enticing China back into the world-system. Moreover, they dismissed the notion of foreign adventurism by China and assumed that, once Taiwan was captured, China would devote itself to internal affairs and the task of building a new China. Only if provoked would China intervene in Northeast or Southeast Asia. Global thinkers among more highly-placed "ins-and-outers" assumed otherwise: that China already was part of a monolithic external area (international communism) hostile to the American world order and that China would quickly try to export its revolution eastward into Korea and southward into French Indochina.

In one crucial sense, the internal debate was a moot one that made it immaterial which group was right and which was wrong. Whether China was expansionist or not, a Russian lackey or not, the communist revolution had usurped almost all of Northeast Asia from the world-system (North China, Manchuria, North Korea). That area historically had been Japan's most important market and source of raw materials. Given the near bankruptcy of Japan by early 1950, there was real fear among American leaders that beleaguered Japan might be forced to strike a bargain with China. If that occurred, it might spell the beginning of a Japanese drift away from integration with the American-dominated international system and toward an autarkic, regional arrangement with the Asian mainland. Such a direction taken by Japan might well undermine the very goals for which the United States had fought the Pacific war.

The Militarization Option

From 1947 to early 1950, the American foreign policy elite had persisted in its hegemonic pursuit of a unitary, integrated world-system. Confronted with Russian opposition, European reluctance, and popular ambivalence at home, American leaders had addressed the structural imbalance in world capitalism that was the chief legacy of world depression and world war. The Truman Doctrine tried to ease Britain's dollar gap while creating the ideological justification for isolating Russia outside of the world-system. It also provided part of the raison d'être for the Marshall Plan and the more ambitious project of European reconstruction and the integration of a reindustrialized Germany into what they hoped would soon be a common market. In turn, NATO provided the political-military-psychic glue to keep Europe together and in the world-system even when the tenure of the Marshall Plan had elapsed. Then, at the height of the American triumph—with NATO secured, West Germany established, and Russian opposition in the Berlin blockade crushed—some hidden hand seemed to pull the plug. The failure of the Dodge Plan in Japan, the shortcomings of the Marshall Plan in Europe, the Russian termination of America's atomic bomb monopoly, and the loss of China to the world-system—all combined to produce yet another crisis, this one of a magnitude that would not be seen again for thirty years. In short, by late 1949 and early 1950, American policymakers faced the awesome task of getting European and Japanese reindustrialization and reconstruction back on track while keeping Europe from playing the Russian card and Japan from playing the China card. Their response would be a staggering reorientation of American foreign policy that would determine its shape and direction for the next twenty-three years.

The Truman administration confronted three alternative ways to respond to this tripartite crisis of the dollar gap, the Russian A-bomb, and the Chinese revolution. One option was to acknowledge the altered equation of world power and to negotiate with the Soviet Union over nuclear arms, German policy, and the status of China. Save for a small group of careerists in the State Department, headed by George Kennan, that was not an option afforded serious consideration by American leaders. *Any* negotiations with Russia, whatever their results, seemed likely to endow that country with a certain legitimacy and co-equal "super-power" status. Such a move seemed tantamount to an end of containment and a readmission of Russia to the world-system, which in turn would mean a diminution of American hegemony.

Such developments could only erode free world deference to American-style internationalism and facilitate separate arrangements by Europe and Japan with the Russian-dominated external world that seemed now to stretch from the Elbe to the Amur. Moreover, any concrete results of Russo-American negotiations could only make such consequences more probable. For example, mutual agreement to forego development of the H-bomb ("the super") could only diminish America's role as nuclear umbrella and military shield for the world-system. Neutralization of a reunified Germany could only impair the American policy of integrationism and raise the specter that any future shift to the left in German politics would also produce a shift to the east in German foreign policy. Recognition of the People's Republic of China would legitimize any Japanese tendency toward accommodation with mainland Asia.

The second American option was to do more of what it had been doing: concentrate on the internal problem central to the world-system, namely the dollar gap crisis, and elaborate upon the tested tools of economic diplomacy epitomized by the ERP. What that meant in the long haul was a lowering of American tariff walls to make it easier for Europe and Japan to earn dollars directly by selling in the American market or indirectly by having their customers in the periphery earn dollars by exporting primary commodities to the United States. In the interim, what that suggested was an extension of the ERP beyond its 1952 cut-off date and a parallel "Marshall Plan for Asia," a temporary plug to the dollar gap until the demand-stimulus of the American market could effect a permanent seal. This option was initially favored by the Policy Planning Staff of the State Department and endorsed by representatives of international business and chief executives of both the AFL and the CIO.

Two factors, however, made the choice impracticable in the early 1950s. Domestically, foreign aid legislation and tariff liberalization faced insurmountable opposition from a hostile Congress influenced by interest groups seeking to protect domestic jobs and markets, by fiscal conservatives trying to balance the budget, by Pacific regionalists persuaded of a European bias in American economic diplomacy, and by middle-class taxpayers unwilling to subsidize foreign consumption at the expense of their own. But even if that domestic opposition could be overcome, an extension of pre-1950 economic diplomacy could not address other considerations raised by the 1949–50 crisis. It could not assuage the fears of those who anticipated a real Russian military threat to the world-system after the mid-1950s. It could not reassure Europe and Japan of the reliability of the American military shield and thus reinforce their acceptance of American hegemony. It could not discipline unstable parts of the periphery to end their revolutions, forego forced industrialization, and accept their subordinate place in the world economic division of labor.

The third alternative was to opt for massive militarization. Concretely, that came to mean the development of the H-bomb; the quadrupling of the military budget, from $14 billion in 1950 to $53 billion in 1952; the expansion of conventional forces, including six permanent divisions in central Europe; the doubling of the air force to ninety-five groups with new strategic bases in Morocco, Libya, Saudi Arabia, and Spain; the transformation of NATO from a political to a military alliance and the addition to NATO of Turkey and Greece; the rebuilding of a German army and its integration into NATO forces; and finally, the substitution of military aid for economic-technical assistance and the merger of both forms in one program in the Mutual Security Act of 1951.

That militarized option was, in economic terms, less ideal than the option of expanded economic diplomacy. There were some well-grounded fears that governmental military purchases might become a substitute for the export of surplus domestic production and thus diminish the demand for multilateral trade and programs that fostered it. Indeed, foreign aid bills did face even tougher sledding and administration efforts to ratify the International Trade Organization (ITO) charter for trade liberalization never made it out of congressional committee. More importantly, massive military spending raised the possibility—again made real over time—that government subsidization of profits would siphon away funds for technical research and capital investment from the civilian goods sector, leaving it less innovative and undercapitalized and thus less competitive in the world economy. Finally, American rearmament would necessitate at least a measure of the same from Europe, a sign to Congress that American taxpayers would not shoulder the whole burden of militarization. While that burden was modest for most European economies, it was heavy for Great Britain, attempting to maintain its military contributions to NATO, the Commonwealth, the Near East, and the Korean War as well. Certainly, that factor helped cause the sterling crisis of 1951–52 and led to a general loss of British foreign markets to German competition.

Countervailing economic advantages, political imperatives, and diplomatic goals combined, however, to outweigh those material shortcomings of the militarization option. Many of the economic calculations were positive. Military spending, in the short term, would salvage the troubled aviation industry and might generate recovery from the American recession of 1949–50. In the medium term, it could maintain full productivity and employment until multilateralism was in place and world trade revived. It might prove more a technological stimulus than a deterrent, especially in electronics and the new sphere of atomic power. Moreover, military aid and military subcontracts to foreign corporations would provide a way to launder foreign aid dollars—that is, to maintain the financial transfusion to address the dollar gap, but to do it in the name of national security rather than economic internationalism. Not only did those military aid dollars release European and Japanese capital to develop civilian technology and production, they helped make the periphery a better market for their products. In effect, American military spending, with its insatiate demand for raw materials, fueled a world-wide triangular trade in which the periphery exported raw materials to the United States, which in turn exported capital goods and food to Europe and Japan, which exported finished consumer goods to the periphery.

Politically, the militarization choice seemed the only one that could override domestic resistance on the right. Relatively quiescent since 1948, those right-wing elements revived in the congressional election of 1950, which produced a freshman senatorial class headed by Richard Nixon. Tacitly supported and used by mainstream Republicans, the politics of this element took an ominous turn in the McCarthyism and "Red Scare" witch hunts of alleged communists and fellow-travellers in government and in education, the media, and entertainment. However disreputable, McCarthyites and their sympathizers gained credibility from the administration's own internal security programs, from labor union purges of their left-wing opposition, and from business blacklisting of dissidents. That credibility made them a potent source of opposition to administration foreign policy.

Influenced by Pacific regionalists in their midst, many conservatives questioned the "Asia last" policy of the administration (to quote the Republican platform of 1952), echoing General Douglas MacArthur's belief that Europe was "a dying system" and that America's future lay in the western rimlands of the Pacific basin. Not only did the right-wing opposition question policy, it questioned policymakers themselves. Drawing on a constituency of midwestern small businessmen, Sun Belt nouveau riche oil men and land developers, and some Americans of Irish, German, and East European backgrounds, that opposition harbored a steady antagonism to the eastern, Yankee, Protestant patricians that they perceived as making policy. ("Fordham's revenge on Harvard" was used as a characterization of McCarthyism.) In that political context, only the alternative of militarization could keep the rightist opposition inside a Cold War consensus. Only an option couched in anticommunism and national security concerns could demonstrate to political critics that the administration's ideology was as pure as Caesar's wife. What had been expedient in selling the Truman Doctrine and the Marshall Plan in 1947 and 1948 now became an ironic imperative in the early 1950s.

Finally, and most importantly, the militarization choice did address three policy considerations not wholly confronted by economic diplomacy: national security, European integrationism, and Third World development. Its stress on American and European rearmament appealed to those, in and out of government, who took a Russian military threat seriously or who simply thought it prudent, in a nuclear age, to operate on the basis of a worst-case scenario. Its reaffirmation of America's role as military protector of the world-system—especially by the building of the H-bomb and an increased conventional presence in Europe—would reassure other core powers of the reliability and efficacy of that protection and keep them oriented to the American goal of integrated production and a common market for Europe itself. Indeed, the American effort to rearm Germany was a powerful incentive to European economic cooperation; it provided the most likely means to subsume German freedom of action—

including the freedom to do military mischief—within a matrix of economic interdependence. And the stress on military capabilities might provide an important tool to facilitate the systematic development of Third World extractive economies, so they might function more effectively as markets and raw material providers for European and Japanese recovery. Since much of the periphery, especially the Asian rimlands, was destabilized by war and revolution, military pacification and forced stabilization seemed likely prerequisites to rapid and predictable economic growth. So an updated "big stick" became a potential weapon for coercing parts of the periphery to accept the American rules for the international game.

The National Security Council adopted the militarization option in early 1950, and President Truman examined and approved in principle its position document (NSC-68) in April. One of the most pivotal policy documents in American history, NSC-68 began with an historical preamble that sketched the decline of British paramountcy, the twice-attempted German challenge, the disintegration of European empires, and the Cold War competition for hegemony between the United States and the Soviet Union. Picturing the latter as a revolutionary, fanatical power, driven toward domination of the Eurasian land mass and ultimately the world, the document argued that only superior military force could deter it. Formulated chiefly by Secretary of State Acheson and the new Policy Planning Staff chief, Paul Nitze, this characterization of the Soviet Union evoked sharp protests from within that same department by Russian experts and careerists, notably George Kennan and Charles Bohlen. They counterargued that Russian foreign policy was motivated more by limited geopolitical and geoeconomic goals than by limitless revolutionary zeal. Consequently they urged that NSC-68 either be modified or junked altogether and that ERP-style economic diplomacy be reaffirmed.

While acknowledging possible hyperbole in the policy document, both Nitze and Acheson insisted that the militarization alternative was the only one that could be sold to Congress as well as the Bureau of the Budget and the General Accounting Office. Moreover, it was the only choice that dealt with all the exigencies and long-term concerns generated by the crisis of 1949–50. Whatever the merits of the respective arguments, Kennan and Bohlen were out-gunned. Possessing no power base outside the ranks of State Department bureaucracy, they were no match for their in-and-outer opponents, who not only held positions of greater influence within the government but were plugged into outside sources of power in the Democratic party and the world of corporate business and law.

In its final form, NSC-68 called not only for massive military spending but for significant tax increases to fund it, a reduction of social welfare programs and all services not related to military needs, a civil defense program, tighter loyalty programs for internal security, greater media efforts to build a public opinion consensus for Cold War policies, and psychological warfare and propaganda to encourage popular uprisings in Eastern Europe and Russia itself. The last rested on the possibility that a quantum jump in the arms race might distort the Soviet-bloc economies so badly, and so delay consumer gratification of its subjects, that it might spark internal upheaval.

No precise dollar tag was assigned by NSC-68 to the militarization policy, but guesses by staff people ranged from $37 to $50 billion per year—triple the amount originally requested by the Pentagon for 1950. How to get that kind of money from a fiscally conservative Congress, even in the name of anticommunism, presented no small task for the administration. What was required was an international emergency, and since November 1949, Secretary Acheson had been predicting that one would occur sometime in 1950 in the Asian rimlands—in Korea, Vietnam, Taiwan, or all three. Two months after the President examined NSC-68, that crisis happened. Acheson was to say later, "Korea came along and saved us."

5 | Militarization and Third World Integration, 1950–1956

> Important as trade is, there's much more at stake. America's
> major trading partners—among them Japan, the European
> Common Market countries, the Pacific Rim nations, Australia—
> are linked to this country politically and militarily as well. They
> are an integral part of the delicate balance that has kept the
> world from blowing up since the end of World War II.
> —*Mobil Corporation, public affairs announcement*

The Korean War inaugurated a twenty-three year period variously characterized as the second Cold War, the Vietnam era, and the Long Boom. Save
for a brief moment in the mid-1950s, Soviet-American competition took on
a more militaristic flavor, and its heightened focus on the periphery gave
the contest a more global, less Europe-centered context. Nowhere was this
more evident than in America's longest war, which began with President
Truman's support of French control of Vietnam in early 1950 and ended
with President Nixon's acceptance of the Paris peace accords in early 1973.
This Vietnam era, this second Cold War, coincided with and, in some ways
helped produce the most sustained and profitable period of economic
growth in the history of world capitalism. Global industrial output averaged an increase of 5.5 percent per year; capital movements became more
fluid and freer than ever before; and unprecedented degrees of world economic integration and interdependence made it far more difficult for any
nation, core or peripheral, to pursue autarkic policies of state capitalism or
socialism. This economic boom, the Vietnam epoch, and a reshaped Cold
War were all progeny of the same seed: American responses to the crisis of
early 1950 that began at the policy level with NSC-68 and at the implemen-
tational level with the Korean War.

Waged between June 1950 and July 1953, the Korean War was part of a
twenty-year contest for the rimlands of Northeast Asia, Southeast Asia,
and Taiwan. This Rimlands War, if we may call it that, was fought by American leaders for three interconnected reasons. At their most global, American motives reflected the newly-affirmed commitment to integrating the
extractive economies of the Third World into the industrial core and to
using military force if necessary to effect it. Nowhere did that seem more

necessary than in the Asian rimlands. In Korea, civil war and insurrection had left one hundred thousand Koreans dead and a divided nation paralyzed; in Taiwan, the last remnants of the Chinese Nationalists (KMT) awaited the likely and perhaps final confrontation with the People's Republic of China (PRC); and in Indochina, especially Vietnam, the French had been waging a colonial war against radical and nationalist opposition since 1946. Relatedly, and most pressingly, the Rimlands War was fought to keep the Asian periphery open to the Japanese economy and thus insure Japan's retention as a functioning member of the world-system and, conversely, to prevent Japan from drifting into the Sino-Soviet external world. Finally, and more distantly, keeping Japan and the rimlands together as a regional component of the world-system might eventually act as a gravitational magnet to pull China out of the Russian sphere, out of the external world back into the world of American internationalism.

The Korean War and Its Causes

The catalyst for the Korean War was American policy toward Japan. In November 1949, American authorities in both Tokyo and Washington publicly announced their intention to negotiate a final peace treaty with Japan, formally ending World War II in the Pacific. It would be unilaterally negotiated by the United States (the USSR and others could sign or not sign as they chose), and it would include long-term American retention of military bases in Japan. Privately, State Department and National Security Council staffers began studies that culminated in NSC-48, which went several steps further. It encouraged rapprochement between Japan and its wartime victims in Northeast Asia and Southeast Asia. It endorsed all efforts necessary to end instability in the rimlands and to integrate their economies into the Japanese "workshop." It kept open the option of remilitarizing Japan to help the United States police the region. And it speculated on the possibility of a "rollback" strategy in Northeast Asia—that is, "liberate" Korea and Manchuria and make them again accessible to Japan. In April, President Truman appointed John Foster Dulles (future Secretary of State, 1953–59) to negotiate with the Japanese; and in September 1951, the United States signed both a peace treaty and a mutual security pact with its former enemy. To reassure noncommunist Asia that a reborn Japan would be no threat to them, the United States simultaneously negotiated both a mutual security agreement with the Philippines and the ANZUS pact of protection with Australia and New Zealand.

Russian leaders interpreted America's Japan policy as a "forward" strategy to reintroduce a Japanese presence in the Asian mainland and archipelagos. But they also viewed it as simply part of the larger American militarization option, taken in response to the crisis of 1949–50. So global as well as regional considerations conditioned the Russian responses. The former tended to divide Russian strategists. The optimists saw "signs of approaching crisis" that might signal the internal collapse of the capitalist world-system. Its spatial contraction (the loss of China), its economic contraction (the dollar gap and world recession), and the diminution of American hegemony (the Russian A-bomb) all pointed in that direction. It was crucial, however, that the United States be prevented from redirecting that internal crisis against the external Soviet sphere. And that necessitated, in their eyes, a peace offensive—an invitation to "peaceful competition with socialism"—to nullify any American claims of Russian threats or provocations and defeat American efforts to enlist Europe and Japan in support of rearmament and the militarization option. The pessimists, however, argued that the new American strategy had gone too far to be defused by a peace offensive. NATO and the decision to build the H-bomb bore witness to the fact. With or without provocation, they argued, America and the West might embrace the rollback policy to reverse the deteriorating balance of forces. They might, in the desperation born of crisis, even launch military action in North Korea or China or Eastern Europe. That would require, in their view, that Russia also opt for militarization—massive military spending as well as preemptive probes to shore up Russian strength along the line of containment ("encirclement") that divided it from the capitalist world.

By 1951, Stalin had clearly chosen the militarization policy. But in early 1950, evidence suggests, he tried to have it both ways. Towards Western Europe he directed the peace offensive called for by the optimists. Its purposes were to diminish European fears of Russia, fuel European fears of Germany, and negate American efforts to rearm Germany and militarize NATO. Towards Asia, however, Stalin took the more hardline approach. In December 1949, the Soviets began negotiations with China that produced a Sino-Russian pact in February 1950. It included a defensive arrangement aimed specifically at Japan and any nation allied with it. At the same time, Russia stepped up military aid to North Korea, including armor and heavy artillery. Moreover, there is some evidence, albeit much debated, that Stalin acquiesced in or even approved North Korean requests to escalate the Korean civil war to the conventional warfare stage in late summer, provided the international situation seem propitious and chances of any direct Russian involvement negligible.

If that analysis of Russia's Asian policy is correct, then its "hawkish" nature, in contrast with its more "dovish" European policy, can be explained largely by two factors. First, Russia was frozen out of the Japanese occupation and thus was in no position to subvert from within an American policy that would resuscitate the power of the nation that had been Russia's major rival in Asia since the Russo-Japanese War of 1904–5. Only overt Russian action seemed likely to contain Japan. Secondly, if Russia failed to impede Japanese reentry into the Asian power sphere, it was possible that China itself might try to rally the Asian periphery against Japan. The People's Republic owed little to Russia for its revolutionary success and had already demonstrated its independent-mindedness in the tough negotiating that produced the Sino-Russian pact of 1950. Long fixated on the need to subordinate foreign communist parties to the ends of Russian foreign policy, Stalin and other Russian leaders already feared Chinese autonomy and its potential for creating a third camp (Maoism as an "Asiatic form of Marxism") in a world Stalin had long decreed was divided into two camps only. Russian inaction in the face of America's Japan policy might feed and magnify that potentiality.

Neither Russian policy nor American policy, however, preordained that the Rimlands War would begin most vigorously in Korea. What insured that was Korea's internal situation. Historically an independent or semi-independent state, Korea had been a Japanese protectorate and colony since 1905, and it was relentlessly exploited in that role for the subsequent forty years. The Russian rout of the Japanese in August 1945 and the postwar arrival of American troops left Korea temporarily in joint trusteeship. That quickly hardened into a more fixed division between a Russian-occupied north and an American-occupied south. By 1949, the Russians had withdrawn their forces and recognized the Democratic People's Republic of Korea (DPRK, North Korea), largely in the hope of co-opting pro-Chinese groups there and reorienting them toward Moscow. The United States, after an unsuccessful effort to use the United Nations to reunify Korea, also withdrew its troops and recognized the Republic of Korea (ROK, South Korea). In the meantime, this divided Korea was racked by a civil war that flared on-and-off in various forms: antigovernment insurrections in South Korea in 1948 (the Cheju-do Island uprising and the Yosu troop mutiny), coastal bombardments and border incursions initiated by both governments in 1949 (though the ROK probably initiated more, and with more success), and government repression of the South Korean Labor party and its paramilitary arm in early 1950. In effect, what outsiders call the Korea War was but another chapter in their civil war. In that civil war, both parties attempted to manipulate their patron powers ("the tail wagging the dog"). South Korea, under the heavy-handed rule of Syngman Rhee, did less well, largely because American leaders feared that his notorious adventurism might drag them into inappropriate conflicts at the wrong time and wrong place. North Korea fared better, largely because it could capitalize on Russian fears of Chinese influence. Even then, Russian aid was limited in extent and kind, partly because of Russian fears of any direct encounter with the United States, partly because it may have been that North Korea angered the USSR by crossing the 38th parallel prematurely. Rather than moving in August 1950, in tandem with an expected Chinese invasion of Taiwan, North Korea attacked South Korea in June to head off Rhee's attempt to crush southern resistance forces, which were deemed essential to the northern military effort.

Course and Consequences of the Korean War, 1950-1953

The narrative of that three-year war is a familiar one. North Korean forces moved rapidly south of the 38th parallel in pursuit of their goal of national unification. American leaders made an equally rapid military and diplomatic response. They committed American military forces to the Korean peninsula and secured the blessing of and some aid from the UN—a coup made easier by Russia's interesting absence from the Security Council. After halting the North Korean offensive in midsummer, the Americans turned the military tide in mid-September with the amphibious landing at Inchon that trapped many of the DPRK forces and led the rest to withdraw north of the 38th parallel. Two weeks earlier, the National Security Council made one of the most crucial American decisions of the war: to continue allied advances north of the dividing line and to attempt to unify all of Korea under ROK control. The decision was ratified by presidential order on September 27, and American, ROK, and UN forces crossed the 38th parallel, moving toward the Yalu River and North Korea's border with Chinese Manchuria. In effect, American leaders had decided to go beyond containment of the external world. They had decided to experiment with the possibilities of a rollback strategy. The experiment was a failure. In Asia itself, the American strategy so threatened vital Chinese holdings in Manchuria that it prompted the PRC to intervene in force. Within a month, allied forces had made a costly retreat to the 38th parallel. There the battlefield would once again settle and the war would drag on for a seemingly interminable thirty-one months, with no decisive advantage to either side.

In the United States, the failed experiment produced a political crisis as Pacific regionalists in Congress criticized the administration for using insufficient force to make rollback work. They charged that the United States could have bombed Manchuria, aided the Chinese Nationalists on Taiwan to return their civil war to the mainland, or even used atomic bombs. Senator Joseph McCarthy railed that "American boys [were] dying in Korea" because of "a group of untouchables in the State Department" and that "highly placed Red Counselors" in the American government were "far more dangerous than Red machine gunners in Korea." Said his fellow Republican Karl Mundt, "If we are going to ask our boys to die fighting in Korea and other areas, we certainly should protect them from sabotage behind their backs at home." In that political climate, Congress passed the McCarran Internal Security Act in September 1950, and

Republicans sought to use the Korean War as an issue to regain the political ground lost in the 1948 election.

Fueling this political critique were the parallel and publicized views of General Douglas MacArthur, the American commander in Korea. The resulting Truman-MacArthur controversy, the President's firing of the General, and the consequent political furor highlighted numerous differences between two strong personalities, between civilian control and military prerogative, and between continued rollback and reaffirmed containment. This atmosphere sharpened the conflict between the dominant globalism of American foreign policy and regionalist dissent. In the end, Truman had no recourse but to ride out the storm of political criticism. Fearful of direct conflict with Russia and afraid that a major Asian war would leave Europe anxious for its safety and critical of American recklessness, the President accepted a military stand-off (containment) as the proper American goal in Korea. It was not an altogether popular choice, and public frustration with this "limited war" cost Truman's political party dearly in 1952.

More successful was the administration's most important decision about the Korean War—to prolong the war. On June 23, 1951, a year after war began, the Russians proposed an in-place armistice, essentially along the same line the Americans would accept two years later as the demilitarized zone (DMZ) in the final Korean armistice agreement. More importantly, the Russian armistice initiative dropped earlier Sino-Korean demands: American troop evacuation of Korea, acquiescence in the PRC's hoped-for takeover of Taiwan, and the UN's recognition of the PRC as the only legitimate representative of one China.

Had the Soviet offer been pursued, peace might have come two years earlier to beleaguered Korea, on terms comparable to the 1953 armistice accords. But an early peace without victory not only would have made the Truman administration more vulnerable to appeasement charges, it would have constituted a threat to NSC-68 and the militarization policy as well. Ending the war in 1951, on a less than triumphant note, might only reinforce regionalist criticism in Congress and jeopardize appropriations for permanently high levels of military spending, for the rearming of Germany and the rebuilding of Japan, and for the enforced pacification of Southeast Asia and other unstable parts of the periphery. No, the war had to be prolonged to buy time to implement NSC-68, to so institutionalize it that domestic political vagaries could not undo it. On the other hand, the administration could not reject the peace process altogether without alienating its European allies and risking an antiwar movement at home. So while it rejected the Russian-proposed armistice, it did begin peace talks with China and North Korea. The shooting and talking would go on together for another two years. The process, however perverse and frustrating, bought the administration the time it wanted to implement its global policy, while the lowered casualty levels of defensive warfare diminished antiwar potential at home.

The American policy of delay snatched victory from the jaws of stalemate, as the prolonged Korean conflict provided both the time and the rationale to push ahead with the militarization of American foreign policy. The most obvious measure was mushrooming military spending that reached $53 billion annually by the end of the Korean War and remained in the $34–40 billion range for the remainder of the 1950s. The postwar decrease reflected the so-called New Look strategy of the Eisenhower administration, with its emphasis upon strategic and tactical nuclear weaponry ("more bang for the buck"), and its disinclination to risk Korean-style, conventional warfare to repress revolutions in the periphery. It also reflected the President's own embryonic concern about the perils of creating a domestic Frankenstein (the "military-industrial complex," as he later termed it) and pressures from non-Keynesian, fiscal conservatives in his own party to reduce budget deficits. Nonetheless, even the leanest Eisenhower military budget was two and a half times the size of the pre-Korean allocation—testimony to the enduring revolution effected by NSC-68 and its militarization approach.

The political purposes of this massive military spending were to intimidate the USSR, reassure Europe and Japan of American protection, and aid the forces of order in a volatile periphery. The economic purpose was domestic and international pump-priming, or "military Keynesianism." At home, this meant using research subsidies and government purchasing to underwrite higher rates of profit in the short run while targeting aviation, electronics, and other high-tech growth industries for the long haul, thereby blunting existing recessionary tendencies while retaining American comparative advantage in high-profit enterprises. Internationally, military Keynesianism offered a way to continue high levels of foreign aid in a politically palatable form. The most obvious means were military aid programs authorized by the Mutual Security Act. These averaged about $3 billion annually during the Eisenhower years. In addition, the special Offshore Procurement Program made it possible to subcontract a portion of domestic military spending to foreign corporations. Operative throughout the 1950s, this program was at its height during the Korean War. Its major beneficiary was the Japanese economy, especially in targeted industries like auto and truck production in the high-value durable goods sector. For three years, that multibillion-dollar spending paid for the Japanese trade deficit, temporarily solved the Japanese dollar gap, and brought Japan its first postwar taste of prosperity. Some Japanese, hearkening back to the legendary typhoon that had destroyed an invading Chinese armada, dubbed the Korean War (and its military spending in Japan) the "second divine wind."

Rearming Germany, 1950–1954

If the Korean War was the salvation of American foreign policy and militarization its solution, integration remained its overriding goal: the integration of a reindustrialized Germany into a European economic-military unit, the integration of Japan and the Asian rimlands into a regional entity, the integration of the Third World periphery and semiperiphery into the industrial cores, and the integration of all into all. One world, and free! The Korean War helped make it all seem a possibility—the great facilitator, the Korean connection.

Germany, as always, was crucial. Successfully integrated into the world-system, West Germany's industrial production and consumptive capacity could make Europe a viable, competitive unit in the world economy. Unintegrated, West Germany might well entertain notions of détente with Russia and neutralism in the Cold War, provided the rewards were reunification of the two Germanys into a single German state and an economic entrée into Eastern Europe. Such an opening to the East would be especially likely if the German Social Democrats ever triumphed electorally over the Christian Democrats, for the former not only stressed the reunification issue but clearly favored the state capitalist road of planned production and regulated trade.

The incorporation of West Germany into the Marshall Plan had been designed partly to avoid such an eventuality. That economic integration, however, was slow moving and incomplete, and it left Germans with more potential freedom of action than American leaders could accept. Those same leaders, therefore, opted to push for German rearmament and the political-military integration of West Germany into NATO. Such additional ties to the West, coupled with the on-going economic evolution toward a European common market, would make it far more difficult for Germany to initiate any unilateral arrangements with the East. They would restore some sense of German national grandeur, but within a collective framework that would not threaten the security of Western Europe but keep German political-economic leaders committed to the American rules of internationalism. Toward those ends, the Truman administration approved the principle of German rearmament in April 1950, two months before the Korean War. The decision was an integral part of the militarization option chosen in NSC-68.

The Korean War made it politically possible to bring the German rearmament policy out of the closet. Until then, a Russian peace offensive

had played with some success on French fears of revived German militarism, partly by stressing that Russia's peaceful intentions eliminated any
need for using Germany as a vehicle for military containment, partly by
offering the alternative prospect of a reunified but demilitarized German
nation. The Korean War enabled the United States to make a plausible
characterization of the Russian state as militarily aggressive and expansionistic. It made it possible to suggest that communist aggression in Asia
was really a feint to make the United States overcommit in Asia while leaving less defended the main object of Soviet designs, Western Europe itself.
John J. McCoy—president of the World Bank, first high commissioner in
West Germany, chairman of Chase Manhattan Bank, and chairman of the
Council on Foreign Relations—later recalled that "Korea brought Europe
to its feet. The realization that the Soviets were prepared to unleash armed
forces to extend their power aroused Europe and particularly Western
Germany, whose situation presented a parallel unpleasant to contem-
plate." The subsequent militarization of Russian policy (its response to
NSC-68) in 1951–52 only aided American policy more by confronting an
anxious Europe with a 50 percent increase in the Russian military budget,
a doubling of the Red Army to five million, and the testing of a Soviet
H-bomb by January 1, 1953.

In this altered climate, the Americans made their initial proposal for
rearming Germany in a September 1950 meeting of NATO. To defuse anti-
German fears, the United States sweetened the pot with more military aid
money, a public commitment to station four American divisions in Europe,
and the appointment of an American military commander (Eisenhower) to
lead an integrated NATO force. The startled European leaders accepted
the American proposal in principle, but not in any specifics. What ensued in
the next four years was a complex Franco-American search for an acceptable compromise that would spell out the specifics. In the midst of that
search, Russia resumed its pre-Korean strategems for blunting such a
quest. Britain remained ambivalent, torn between its imperial interests in
the periphery and its continental interest in the European core. And France
went through the motions, uncertain whether it wanted *any* compromise
to prevail, even one of its own making.

The game began in earnest in February 1952 when France proposed the
creation of a European Defense Community (EDC) that would include
twelve German divisions. Inclusion/exclusion were key to the EDC concept. Formally separate from the NATO structure, EDC would be an all-
European arrangement that the Americans could not dominate. Its formal
inclusion, however, of Great Britain would provide France with sufficient
support that Germany alone could not run the show. British reluctance to
participate in EDC slowed the process significantly, however, and Russian
diplomacy threatened to stymie it altogether. Beginning in March 1952, the

USSR began to revive variants of its scheme for neutralization of Germany. Stalin even went so far as to propose consideration of a "Germany *with a national army*" (emphasis added), provided that "a unified and independent Germany" would "be neutralized and all foreign troops withdrawn." Following Stalin's death in early 1953, Russian efforts became a full-fledged peace offensive. The Soviets intensified efforts to end the Korean War, eased pressure on Turkey, sought a degree of reconciliation with maverick Yugoslavia, formalized diplomatic relations with Israel and Greece, and made an even more energetic presentation of its German neutralization concept. Returning to its 1950 pre-Korean position, the USSR suggested that détente with the West was possible and therefore remilitarization of Germany was unnecessary and dangerous. Even Russia's one tough action, its suppression of East German strikers, was interpreted by some Europeans as a sign that Russia could be counted upon to keep "its" Germans in line.

The game ended in December 1954. The big winner was the American policy of German rearmament. After prolonged and paralyzing delay, the French National Assembly finally killed its own brainchild, the EDC agreement, in a close and bitter ratification struggle. But it mattered naught. The German economy and the German state were far more important to the United States than were the French, and the American government made clear its intent to have German remilitarization and political integration, whatever its form and whatever its costs. Working through the British, the Eisenhower administration pressured France to accept a new tack: bring Germany directly into the existing political-military structures of the Brussels Pact and its larger offspring, NATO itself. In recognition of French security needs, Britain belatedly made a commitment of four divisions to the continent, and the United States promised to retain its existing forces in place. Germany paid the highest prices of all: a renunciation of force to secure either reunification or boundary alterations and a self-denying pledge to forego nuclear weapons, chemical warfare, and ballistic missiles. Amidst such blandishments, France finally succumbed on December 24, 1954, and accepted Germany, and its born-again military, as a NATO ally—ironically with less French and more American control than the EDC would have afforded five months earlier.

The Geneva Summit and Post-Stalinism, 1955–1956

Germany, rearmed and in NATO, was a disaster for Russian foreign policy, but not a fatal one. The Russian build-up of conventional forces in 1951–52 and the acquisition of the H-bomb in 1953 had gained the USSR a measure of military respectability and had lessened the likelihood of the United States using preemptive hot war to resolve the Cold War. Even the remilitarization of Germany was unlikely to alter that latter situation, provided the Russians took prudent steps to put their own bloc defenses in order and provided they avoided actions that would prompt or excuse a further Western acceleration of the arms race. Moreover, nothing in European history suggested to Russian leaders that German integration into the West had to be a permanent fixture of the international system. No Russo-German détente was likely in the near future, but the continued existence of sizeable European (including German) opposition to America's remilitarization policies suggested to Russian leaders that it was worth maintaining future options for Germany's place in the international scheme. The battle was lost, but the war not yet conceded. Indeed, where Germany was concerned, there would never be any final Russian capitulation. It has remained the one most central and enduring issue of the Cold War since its inception and will to its end.

The USSR now went through the motions of putting its German policy on the international agenda one last time, before the integration of Germany into NATO could harden into place. Since 1953, Winston Churchill and other European leaders had been calling for a summit meeting between Soviet leaders and their Western counterparts—chiefly out of fears induced by the H-bomb's multiplication of nuclear nightmares and out of hopes generated by Stalin's death and his successors' quest for peaceful coexistence. For much of 1954, Russian leaders had joined the summitry movement, intending to use such a meeting to propound their own German policy and bolster European resistance to America's. Predictably, the Eisenhower administration persistently rejected all suggestions of a summit, from friend and foe alike, until the French National Assembly formally approved of German military participation in NATO. That done, it became increasingly difficult for the United States to resist world pressure for a big-power summit. It became impossible to resist when the USSR suddenly signed a peace treaty with Austria that withdrew foreign troops and reunited that country on a neutralized basis similar to Finland's. With that masterful stroke, Russia gave credence to its peace offensive. It demonstrated that the Iron Curtain could go up as well as down; it gave Europe a role model of how a Germanic state might be structured on a nonmilitary, neutral basis; and it left American leaders without any plausible rationale for continued rejection of a summit. Eisenhower later recalled the Austrian treaty: "Well, suddenly the thing was signed one day and [Dulles] came in and he grinned rather ruefully and he said, 'Well, I think we've had it.' "

For five days in July 1955, the United States, Russia, Britain, and France met in Geneva. There was never any possibility that Russia could successfully use that summit to alter the German status quo. It could publicly approve the notion of German unification, as did the United States, but neither power would approve it in a form the other could accept. Secretary of State Dulles scotched any unification that would neutralize or demilitarize a united Germany or "subtract it from NATO," while Russian leaders countenanced no *other* kind of single German nation. All the USSR could hope to accomplish was the maintenance of its German policy as an option for future reconsideration, and the offering of encouragement to those countries which, at the very least, wished to place reasonable limits on German rearmament. In the aftermath of the Geneva summit meeting, Russia did exactly that by recognizing West Germany, turning over control of East Germany's foreign affairs to its own leaders, and bringing East Germany into the Warsaw Pact. Henceforth, the two Germanies would have to deal with each other in international matters, and if they wished ever again to become one Germany, the clear prerequisite trade-off would be for West Germany to leave NATO and East Germany to leave the Warsaw Pact.

While bereft of tangible results, the Geneva summit meeting, as Soviet Premier Nikita Khrushchev boasted, "had established [Russia] as able to hold [its] own in the international arena." In the decade between the Potsdam conference and the Geneva summit, American and Russian heads of state had never dealt directly with each other. That wall of silence had been of enormous symbolic value to American policymakers, facilitating their effort to isolate the Soviet bloc outside the world-system and to exploit fear of Soviet intentions to obtain international and domestic acceptance of America's hegemonic role in world affairs. In a significant way, Russia's very existence on the other side of that new Great Wall, the Iron Curtain, had helped make possible the transformation of the world-system from a multicentered balance of power world to a hegemonic, integrated one. Certainly it made that transformation faster and more complete. Some observers have suggested that the Russian threat was so useful that if it had not existed, it would have had to be invented. Indeed, it was so useful that it was, at least, exaggerated.

The Geneva summit symbolically ended that decade's veil of silence and, in so doing, bestowed upon the USSR a measure of legitimacy denied it since 1946. Talking and dealing with Russian leaders for five days, especially in the high-theater setting of the summit, seriously diminished prior American contentions that the Soviet Union was a nontraditional state operating in a nether zone outside the geographic and ethical boundaries of the world-system. Taken together with the 1954 Geneva conference on Indochina, the 1955 Geneva summit implied a partial recognition of Russia as a traditional state with legitimate interests of its own in the Asian rimlands, Central Europe, and elsewhere inside the world-system. American leaders naturally denied the implication, but there really was no gainsaying that the dawning of the age of summitry conjured up a picture of the world much different from the one those leaders had cultivated during the early Cold War. The new picture granted Russia superpower status in a bipolar world. The balance of power was once more at odds with the tendency toward hegemony.

Six months after the Geneva summit, Russia took advantage of its new legitimacy, in a dramatic way. At the Twentieth Congress of the Russian Communist party, Nikita Khrushchev stunned his listeners and the world by detailing and denouncing the past sins of Stalinism in his nation's history. Designed largely for domestic purposes and domestic consumption, his endorsement of détente and his subsequent abolition of the Cominform (the Soviet-dominated bureau for communist propaganda) also targeted the forces of neutralism in Europe. Both Khrushchev's apology to Tito's Yugoslavia and his declaration that there were many roads to communism, other than the Russian-prescribed one, were aimed at restoring some nationalist credentials to Western communist parties and bolstering neutralist European sentiment for a process soon to be called disengagement. But for all the risk-taking innovation, Khrushchev's stroke still could not erase the continuing reality that Russia's policy of German neutralization failed to deter the American policy of German integration. And that signal triumph for American hegemony owed much to the policy of delay in winding down the Korean War, which purchased time sufficient to transform NSC-68's blueprint for foreign policy militarization into a reality.

The Beginning of America's Involvement in Vietnam, 1950–1954

That prolonged Korean conflict also spurred American integrationism in the Asian part of the world-system. In so doing, it expanded the Rimlands War spatially to encompass Southeast Asia and extended it temporally by an additional two decades. America's longest war, it was misnamed the Vietnam War (it was fought in all of Indochina). America's role in it actually began seven weeks before the Korean outbreak when, on May 1, 1950, President Truman publicly announced that American dollars and military supplies would be used to aid French efforts to end the Indochina revolutions and to stabilize the region. Like its Korean counterpart, this Vietnamese portion of the Rimlands War was fought as part of a general strategy to integrate the periphery more effectively into core economies and part of a specific strategy to sustain Japanese economic recovery, insure its participation in the world-system and keep open the option that China itself might someday be restored to that system and led down a capitalist road. Unlike the war in Korea, however, the Vietnam War would diminish rather than enhance American paramountcy and would raise the more enduring specter that the Age of Hegemony might be on the downhill slide.

Before World War II, Southeast Asia, save for Siam (now Thailand), had been an outpost of Western colonialism and imperialism: the British in Malaya, the French in Indochina, the Dutch in Indonesia, and the Americans in the Philippines. Throughout most of the Pacific war, Japan occupied almost the entire region and governed it directly or indirectly. That wartime occupation politicized and sometimes radicalized many of the region's inhabitants. Especially liberating was the lesson that Western colonialism was not omnipotent. An Asian people, the Japanese, had brought the vast, white, Western imperium to its knees. Especially sobering was the realization that imperialism by any other name (The Greater East Asian Co-Prosperity Sphere) was still imperialism. Japanese rule was not qualitatively different from Western rule, and it was a sorry substitute for true independence and self-rule. As a consequence, most of Southeast Asia emerged from World War II with strong, bitter anti-imperialist sentiments that were at once anti-Western and anti-Japanese. More positively, they emerged with a fervent commitment to their own independence and to various visions of future nation building. Many Western powers attempted to swim against this tide of Southeast Asian nationalism and to reimpose their colonial rule. This was especially true of France. Beset by postwar economic problems and humiliated by its military and political record in World War II, France sought material gain and renewed grandeur through restored empire in Southeast Asia and North Africa, principally Vietnam and Algeria. In the former, France used every means at its disposal: bogus negotiations, political repression, military force, and the puppet government of the emperor, Bao Dai. In short, France waged a colonial war against growing Vietnamese resistance between 1946 and 1954. A war that waxed and waned, its inexorable thrust was toward last-stage, decisive, conventional warfare.

At the same time, much as in Korea, Vietnamese fought among themselves over who would rule at home, once home rule (independence from France) was established. Coexistent, then, with an anticolonial war of national libertion, was a civil war that cut across regional, ethnic, religious, and class lines and that rival ideologies sought to harness and exploit. Among these were Leninists, like Ho Chi Minh, Trotskyists, Social Democrats, independent Buddhist sects, Catholic actionists like Ngo Dinh Diem, or even collaborationists, like Bao Dai, who harbored his own nationalistic sentiments. This internecine competition was intense, its tactics often ruthless, and its relationship to the anti-French war complex. Almost every group found expedient occasion to make temporary accommodations with the French in order to bring disadvantage on their domestic competitors. Like the American revolution and most revolutions, it had its loyalists, its reluctant revolutionaries, its radicals, its share of simple opportunists, and a vast number of folks just trying to make a living and not get killed.

Over time, Ho Chi Minh and the Communist party successfully subverted their adversaries, identified their political agenda with the cause of anti-colonialism and independence, and established a popular front polity (the so-called Vietminh) that gained ascendance in the civil war and leadership of the anticolonial war.

The American role in Indochina was limited and ambivalent until 1950. On one hand, American leaders did favor eventual decolonization of Southeast Asia and the periphery in general. Closed formal empires were the antithesis of internationalism; they impeded the material access and gain of American capital and seemed ill-suited to survival in the face of postwar nationalism in the Third World. The United States favored a policy of informal empire: that is, granting political independence while retaining economic domination, a policy it instituted in the Philippines as World War II ended. On the other hand, European economic recovery required non-dollar sources of raw materials, and colonial regimes seemed more likely to restore that extractive production than nationalist ones with their dreams of industrialization. In France's case, its pivotal position in American plans for a European common market and a European army inhibited any American pressure on French imperial policy. So too did fears that collapse of the French overseas empire would rebound to the political advantage of French Communists. In that context, American policy waffled during the period between 1946 and 1950. The United States urged the French to promise Vietnam independence at some future, indeterminate point, to grant it some interim autonomy over local affairs, and to "Vietnamize" the war by using indigenous forces rather than the Foreign Legion. Yet at the same time, the United States discreetly looked the other way when France siphoned off Marshall Plan money to help finance the French war effort; and Secretary of State Acheson even concluded by 1949 that the French colonial record in Indochina, once so criticized by President Roosevelt, had been a good one overall and quite unjustly maligned. (The British ambassador to the United States, Oliver Frank, referred to Acheson's "paean of praise about French achievements in Indo-China," that the French "had done far more than they had ever let on.")

Ambivalence gave way to commitment in 1950. In midsummer, following Truman's May 1 announcement of American aid to France, the United States sent a military mission to Vietnam. By the administration's end in 1952, America was paying 60 percent of French war expenses in Indochina. By the time of the Geneva conference of 1954, military aid from the new Eisenhower administration accounted for roughly 80 percent of the costs of France's colonial war. French fingers pulled the triggers, but American dollars loaded the guns. Neither met with much success. In 1954, the Vietminh overwhelmed French forces in the decisive battle of Dienbienphu, and the muddy waters of French politics cleared long enough to produce a government willing to proclaim French colonialism in Indo-china *finis*. After considering its own possible intervention, including the use of tactical atomic weapons (dubbed the "Genghis Khan" option), the United States chose not to stand in France's way. Fearful that the Americans might yet change their minds and pressured by Russia and China to settle for less than total victory, the Vietminh also opted for a political solution to the war, already almost a decade old. The result was the Geneva Accords of 1954, highlighted by French renunciation of colonial pretensions, temporary division of Vietnam at the 17th parallel (the Vietminh in the north, a new provisional government in the south), and national elections in 1956, preparatory to the final reunification of north and south into an acknowledged Vietnamese nation.

Causes of America's Involvement in Vietnam, 1950–1954

American commitment during this first, French phase of the Vietnam War was produced by the resounding clash of two realities. One was the American determination to rebuild Japan through a policy of economic regionalism. The other was the potential frustration of that goal by Southeast Asian nationalists, noncommunists and communists alike. As early as 1949, American policy presumed that the Dodge Plan for Japan would work only if Japanese reindustrialization was accorded profitable markets and cheap raw materials in the Asian rimlands, including Southeast Asia. The Korean War reduced some of the urgency of that conviction, but the war's termination restored an almost desperate edge to that American belief. The sharp reduction of the Special Offshore Procurement Program, the rapid reappearance of a Japanese dollar gap, and the apparent incompleteness and unevenness of Japanese recovery all pointed to Japan's pressing need for economic opportunities in non-dollar areas. Japan had to reduce its trade deficit and dollar drain by buying more of its raw materials and food from someplace other than the United States, and it had to find overseas markets to earn foreign exchange with which to pay off the remaining shortage in its dollar account. (To recall Kennan's 1949 comment, "it is one thing to produce; it is another thing to sell.") Historically and logically, Northeast Asia—Korea, Manchuria, and North China—was the best target for Japanese efforts. But the Korean War and the failure of the rollback strategy made that choice both impracticable and unacceptable. What seemed a more achievable target was Southeast Asia, especially the two great archipelagos of the Philippines and Indonesia, the latter with its one hundred million inhabitants and vast natural resources of oil, rubber, and the like.

From 1950 onward, throughout the entire course of the Vietnam War, American leaders sought an integrated Asian regionalism based on a complementary division of economic labor. Southeast Asia would specialize in primary commodity production of food and raw materials, for which it possessed comparative advantage and in which Japan was deficient. Japan would specialize in industrial manufacture, finance, shipping, and insurance. It would be the workshop of Asia, and Southeast Asia would be the principal market for its manufactured surplus and the outlet for its finance capital. If that regionalism succeeded, Japan and the Southeast Asian rimlands would remain within the world-system; and American hope held out that China might someday return to it.

Such refrains ring resoundingly if redundantly throughout American government documents—from the State Department, the National Security Council, the Council of Economic Advisers, the Defense Department, the Joint Chiefs of Staff, and the White House. The NSC captured the sentiments as early as February 1949, declaring that "Japan will either move toward sound friendly relations with non-commie countries or into association with the commie system in Asia. . . . Every effort should be made to develop alternative sources on an economic basis, particularly in areas such as south Asia where a need exists for Japanese exports." And in 1955, when the United States jettisoned the Geneva Accords and reaffirmed its commitment in Vietnam, the Joint Chiefs showed the military's understanding of the reason for that rededication: "[Japan's cooperation with the United States] will be significantly affected by her ability to retain access to her historic markets and sources of food and raw materials in S.E. Asia. Viewed in this context, U.S. objectives with respect to S.E. Asia and U.S. objectives with respect to Japan would appear to be inseparably related. . . . The loss of S.E. Asia to the Western world would inevitably force Japan into an eventual accommodation with the Communist-controlled areas in Asia."

Two facts were both explicit and implicit in the American rationale. First, Vietnam per se had little intrinsic value. It was important only in the context of what came to be called the domino theory: that the loss of Vietnam would produce the loss of all Indochina (Laos and Cambodia), which in turn would result in the loss of the Philippine and Indonesian archipelagos, which would trigger the loss of Japan itself, the ultimate domino. All Asia would be lost to the world-system, and the 1941 nightmare of a closing world would be revived. Second, the United States acted less in its own direct interest than in the interest of Japan and the world-system as a whole. To be sure, American rearmament in the 1950s did enlarge American demand for southeast Asian raw materials; but, compared to other global interests, Southeast Asia was of minimal concern in preserving American well-being. For Japan, however, (and to a lesser degree for Western Europe) Southeast Asia was an area of vital and urgent national interests. It was in behalf of *those* direct interests, rather than its own, that the

United States acted. It performed that surrogate role out of a perception of it as a function of hegemonic power. The underlying premise of American internationalism was that American capitalism could prosper only if its major trading partners, Japan and other core countries, prospered as well. For Japan to prosper, the integration of Asian rimlands like Southeast Asia seemed essential. Therefore, it became America's responsibility, as the dominant capitalist power, to act for the system as a whole. If power had its perks and profits, it also had its burdens, and they would be painfully more heavy than American rulers envisioned in the 1950s.

Fulfillment of that self-appointed responsibility presented American leaders with one major obstacle: Southeast Asian nationalism. Economic development and integration of the region required a hospitable and stable political environment. There was little enthusiasm, however, for the American scheme, even in independent, noncommunist countries like the Philippines, Indonesia, or Thailand. Indeed, American policy seemed to invoke three hate-symbols for Southeast Asian nationalists: Western imperialism, Japanese Pan-Asianism, and economic dependency. By and large, the area still regarded Western imperialism (not communism) as its principal, historic enemy. Initial American policy appeared to prop up French colonialism and, after French withdrawal, to threaten the area with an American neocolonialism. The area still distrusted Japanese ambitions for regional dominance, yet American policy asked them to accept a new Asian Co-Prosperity all over again, to underwrite the recovery of their former enemy and conqueror. Finally, there was objection to the region's assignment as primary commodity producer. The governments wished to pursue more autarkic policies of forced industrialization to open up avenues of higher profitability and income. Southeast Asian nationalists wanted "to build a steel mill" when the doctrine of comparative advantage and American policy dictated, as one State Department official noted, that they "grow a little more food, or rice, or coffee or whatever it might be." The daily Manila *Times* summed up Asian sentiments vividly: "Why should the Philippine republic agree to a deal under which the Japanese will profit and prosper and the Philippines will remain on the old colonial basis of providing basic raw materials to a former enemy in exchange for the modern equivalent of glass beads, brass rings and hand mirrors? Especially when the Philippines can make its own."

If there was little hospitality for American schemes in Southeast Asia, there was little of the prerequisite stability either. Indonesia had been racked by an anticolonial war of independence against the Dutch in the late 1940s, and its new political structure was shaky and badly stressed by geographic, religious, ethnic, class, and ideological differences. The Philippines, though independent, experienced many schisms comparable to Indonesia's, compounded by a communist-led insurgency (the Huks). And, most obviously, Indochina was so awash with revolution and war that political chaos, not stability, had become the norm since 1946. So long as political instability and/or inhospitability remained, the American notion of Southeast Asia as a regional safety-valve for Japan's economic dilemmas would remain little more than a pipe dream.

The goal for American leaders was economic—increasing Southeast Asian extractive production and consumer demand. The means to that end, however, were political stabilization and, if need be, military pacification. In the noncommunist, semistable archipelagos, the United States stressed co-optation: material and moral encouragement for private-sector groups with vested stakes in the remaining plantation or mining economies; economic aid and military assistance programs for government bureaucrats and the army: the conditional promise of some Japanese war reparations, if trade treaties with Japan were negotiated; and the generalized moral preachment that the day of Western imperialism was over and no longer to be feared but that the clear and present danger to national independence came from the new imperialism of international communism.

Co-optation was irrelevant, however, in Vietnam—the first domino. There was some desultory debate among American leaders about the possibility that Ho Chi Minh might be an "Asian Tito" rather than a Russian sychophant and that some political accommodation might be made with him. But Acheson, and Dulles after him, concluded that it was immaterial whether Ho was a Russian lackey, a Chinese dupe, or a Vietnamese nationalist. The whole thrust of his ideology and policy was to withdraw his nation, and perhaps the region, from the world-system and its international division of labor. It mattered not whether Southeast Asia withdrew to a Russian sphere, a Chinese sphere, or a neutral Asian sphere. It would still be lost to the system, and with it probably the hopes of Japanese recovery. Ultimately, then, military pacification seemed the only answer for Indochina. Crush the Vietminh movement and manufacture a political environment at once stable and hospitable to American plans. Thus the four years of American material support for the French colonial war.

France's crushing defeat in 1954, and the subsequent Geneva agreement, left American policymakers in a terrible quandary. To accept the Geneva settlement was unthinkable. Given Ho Chi Minh's popular stature, unification elections in 1956 would probably end with Vietminh sovereignty over a united Vietnam; Laos and Cambodia would perhaps follow suit; and forces of resistance would be emboldened in the Philippines and Indonesia. The regional balance of power would tilt toward autarky and away from internationalism. Moreover, at the global level, failure to pick up the French cudgels might erode the very credibility upon which hegemony rested. The Truman and Eisenhower administrations had made a clear commitment to keep Indochina in the system. If the United States, reneged in this, could its other commitments in the area be trusted: the Japanese Security Treaty, the ANZUS Pact, the Philippine security agreement? Or, for that matter, NATO or the Organization of American States?

At the same time, however, a direct American takeover of the French military effort seemed equally unthinkable. The Korean War had already demonstrated the dangers and frustrations of fighting a war on the containment perimeter, where one always ran the risk of counterintervention from the external camp of China and/or Russia. Moreover, it was difficult to see how an American usurpation of the French role could command respect or acceptance from Third World nationalists certain to see it as a reimposition of Western imperialism, or from European allies bound to regard it as a heavy-handed rejection of their Geneva negotiating, or from an American public likely to view it as another distasteful, Korea-style "limited" war. Finally, an American war in Indochina seemed not only dangerous and unpopular in 1954, but also unaffordable. The Eisenhower administration's New Look military policies committed so much of its reduced budget to strategic nuclear weaponry that it could not fund the conventional forces necessary for such an effort.

Neutralism versus Integrationism in the Periphery

The American effort to solve this conundrum was informed by other related and unnerving developments in the periphery. In Iran, the Shah fled into exile and the left-leaning Mossadegh government nationalized the Anglo-Iranian Oil Company. In Guatemala, the new Arbenz regime confiscated United Fruit Company holdings and promulgated land reforms. In Asia, the Bandung Conference marked the beginning of the Communist China's effort to put itself forward as the regional spokesman for Asian nationalism and anti-imperialism. Worldwide, India's Nehru, Egypt's Nasser, and Yugoslavia's Tito collectively tried to make the periphery neutral in the Russo-American Cold War. They sought a "Third World" (and originated the term) that would be tied to neither side but committed to the primacy of its own development and well-being. At the very moment at which the United States put such great store on stability in the periphery, much of the periphery seemed committed to a rapid, destabilizing alteration of the status quo. At the very point when the top American priority was to integrate the periphery more systematically and systemically into the process of rehabilitating core economies, much of the periphery seemed inclined to withdraw one foot or both from the world-system, or at least wanted to renegotiate the periphery's role within it.

The American response, then, to Vietnam after 1954 was also part of a more general response to the centrality of Third World problems in the world order. The tasks America envisioned were both specific to Southeast Asia and generic to the periphery: how to defuse neutralism, unseat regimes that were deemed inappropriate role models for the periphery, and build new nations that would showcase the merits of internationalism. All this had to be done on a somewhat limited budget and without incurring the charge of renewed imperialism (neocolonialism) for American foreign policy. Those multiple goals and contradictory constraints evoked from the Eisenhower administration a policy that was part grand design and part improvisation.

The focus for American leaders was on the movement toward neutralism, for its whole thrust ran counter to integration of the periphery. Almost without exception, neutralist countries pursued state investment and trade regulation that defied Western modernization theory and plugged for forced industrialization: India's five-year plans, Egypt's Arab socialism, Yugoslavia's mixed economy, Indonesia's fascination with Chinese economic planning, and Iran's nationalization of its oil holdings. Ambitious pursuits, but these capital-intensive industries required imported capital and technology. Turning to the West alone for such imports would assuredly bring insistence that state planning be modified and principles of economic internationalism be accepted. Turning to the Soviet block alone would probably mean too little capital and technology for the tasks at hand, and it might bring Soviet demands for deference inconsistent with the peripheral nations' autonomy. But, turning to both at once, to the capitalist world and the external world, offered a possible way to sustain their ventures in economic autarky, secure necessary economic and technical aid, and yet not become subservient to either American hegemony or Russian pretensions. They could use the heated-up and militarized Cold War to their advantage by playing one world against the other in a bidding war to up the levels of foreign aid.

What made neutralism viable in the mid-1950s was a change in Russian policy. More confident after the 1953 Korean armistice, the 1954 Vietnam denouement, and the Geneva summit, Russian leaders were more inclined to invest energy and money in derailing the American effort to systematize the periphery's relationship to the core. Crucial, too, was the death of Stalin in 1953. The ensuing internecine battles in Russian ruling circles finally produced personal victory for Nikita Khrushchev as party secretary, and later premier. Those battles, however, also produced victory for a Third World policy that abandoned Stalin's two-camp, two-world position, and pronounced Russian willingness to support the periphery in its quest for decolonization and economic autonomy. Indeed, Khrushchev's public attack on Stalin and his past sins in early 1956 was partly an effort to de-Stalinize Russian foreign policy in the eyes of the Third World. It attempted to defuse American charges of Soviet imperialism by stressing tolerance for diversity within the Soviet bloc, and to validate the sincerity of Russian support for bourgeois, noncommunist, nationalist movements in a progressive move to undermine capitalism's international division of labor. Consequently, by the mid-1950s, the USSR had negotiated foreign aid agreements with nearly a score of Third World countries, including substantial arrangements with Indonesia in Southeast Asia, India in South Asia, and Egypt in the Middle East.

To American leaders, it seemed that the triumph of neutralism might well be fatal to the well-being of the world-system, given (as Secretary of State John Foster Dulles noted) "the industrialized nature of the Atlantic Community and its dependence upon broad markets and access to raw materials." To counter that possibility, the Eisenhower administration evolved a two-fold strategy: strengthen *non*-neutralist parts of the periphery through regional alliances and individual nation-building and nullify neutralist regimes through covert action, if they were sufficiently vulnerable, and through co-optation if they were not. The first stratagem would create a series of regional pacts that would place non-neutralist countries under American political-military protection, put them on a steady diet of American military and economic aid, and use them as examples to the rest of the periphery that playing by the rules of American internationalism was rewarding indeed. In the Middle East, the United States sponsored the Baghdad Pact in 1955, which centered around Turkey, Iran, Iraq, and Pakistan, and augmented it with a separate agreement with Saudi Arabia about U.S. air bases and military aid. In Southeast Asia, the United States created and participated in the Southeast Asian Treaty Organization (SEATO) in 1955, which embraced Thailand, the Philippines, Pakistan, the ANZUS bloc, British Malaya, and, by separate protocol, the former French areas in Vietnam, Laos, and Cambodia. Finally, in East Asia, the United States signed a military aid agreement with Taiwan and threatened mainland China with retaliation after several episodes of PRC bombardment of off-shore islands between Taiwan and China (Quemoy and Matsu in 1954, 1955, and 1958).

Within such regional frameworks, the United States began its first ventures in nation-building. Out of fragments of broken colonial empires it sought to create new nations that would be sufficiently autonomous to be credible and yet would be politically stable market economies, integrated into global multilateralism. They would not be dominoes that would fall and vanish behind the boundaries of the nether world. Instead, they were to be showcases to the periphery of the material rewards of development via the world market rather than development by state planning. South Vietnam in the 1950s was, of course, the quintessential example of such nation-building. Beginning cautiously, even skeptically, in 1955, the United States gradually enlarged its effort to create a South Vietnamese nation where none had existed before. Rejecting the Geneva Accords' call for nationwide elections both north and south of the 17th parallel, American leaders provided increasing amounts of military, economic, and technical aid to the Republic of South Vietnam headed by Ngo Dinh Diem. His American-supported army became the chief vehicle for extending centralized authority over local bases of power. Moreover, his deregulation of economic controls, coupled with American capital and confiscated French lands, prompted an initial spurt of infrastructural and industrial development. The consequence was the replacement of an older French-oriented elite with a newly empowered and enriched Vietnamese bourgeoisie centered in the army, the Saigon bureaucracy, and the Diem clan. By 1960, that transformation would dispossess so many economic, ethnic, and religious groups that it would provoke a resumption of the Vietnamese civil war. In the late 1950s, however, the experiment seemed so successful that accolades of "world statesman," "Asia's Churchill," and "Vietnam's George Washington" were bestowed on Diem by prominent Americans.

At the same time, the United States attempted to defuse the neutralist movement by targeting key regimes for either covert overthrow or offers that were too good to refuse. The advantages of covert action were its relative inexpensiveness and its ability to partially mask American involvement. On the other hand, such ventures were not only problematical but, if practiced frequently and indiscriminately, lost both those advantages. They placed a strain on the administration's New Look budget and evoked Third World charges of American imperialism. Consequently, the strategy was reserved for use in nations where the configuration of internal social forces made them susceptible to destabilization and where their neutralism had produced transgressions against international order that were deemed too serious to be accepted. Such sins usually involved contract cancellations and property confiscations directed against foreign capital, compounded by dealings, or rumors of dealings, with the USSR.

Iran and Guatemala were the most obvious examples of successful covert actions. A strategic key to the Persian Gulf and a major oil producer in the world-system, Iran had in 1953 nationalized the Anglo-Iranian Oil Company, forced its young Shah to flee the country, and initiated the neutralist strategy of bidding East against West by exploring the possibility of a Russian loan. In cooperation with British officials and Iranian monarchists, the Central Intelligence Agency (CIA) of the United States provided arms, transport, communications and bribe money to help overthrow the Mohammed Mossadegh government and return the Shah to the Peacock Throne. The new regime reversed the oil nationalization, accorded American oil companies a half-share of the previous British monopoly, embraced a militant anticommunism, and launched an ambitious modernization program heavily dependent on Western capital and markets.

Likewise, in Guatemala in 1954, the elected government of Jacob Arbenz Guzman confiscated nearly four hundred thousand acres owned by the American-controlled United Fruit Company, resisted arbitration over the consequent issue of adequate compensation, and purchased arms from the Soviet bloc when hostile American intent grew more evident. Supported by compliant approval from the Organization of American States (OAS), the United States trained and armed anti-Arbenz *contras* in Honduras and Nicaragua, funneled aid and bribes to dissident officers in the Guatemalan army, employed American labor unions to neutralize radical influences in Guatemalan labor organizations, and used CIA logistical support and small-scale air cover to facilitate the overthrow of the Arbenz government. The new military regime returned United Fruit Company land, jailed or executed its opponents, and, for the next decade, became the major recipient of American military aid in Latin America.

The Suez and Hungarian Crises, 1956

The limited efficacy of such covert coups, however, dictated different tactics in other neutralist countries. The classic and ill-fated example of alternative means came in 1956 with the American effort to reverse Egypt's advocacy of neutralism for the Third World. Led by Gamal Abdel Nasser, Egypt had attempted the time-honored stratagem of bidding West against East in an effort to secure better market terms for its export economy and imported arms for its continuing confrontation with Israel. Declaring American prices too high, Nasser negotiated a barter arrangement of Egyptian cotton for Czech arms in September 1955. The move confronted American policymakers with the unpalatable alternatives of bidding against the Soviet bloc (which would validate Nasser's neutralism) or cutting off all aid to Egypt (which would end American influence in a nation arguably the most important in the Middle East).

Secretary of State Dulles opted for a more ambitious and imaginative response. He proposed that the United States, Britain, and the World Bank fund Egypt's Aswan Dam project, a costly, long-term grand scheme to expand and modernize Egypt's agricultural sector and its electric power infrastructure. Agreed to in principle by Nasser in February 1956, the project was expected to saddle Egypt with such financial obligations that it would have to repudiate the Czech arms deal as unaffordable and plug itself into the internationalist framework of the United States and the World Bank. Unfortunately for Secretary Dulles, the consequences were rather different than anticipated. Attempting to salvage some of his legitimacy as Third World statesman, Nasser recognized the People's Republic of China in May, stalled on any repudiation of the arms barter, and scheduled a much-publicized, neutralist summit with Tito and Nehru in July. Unhappy with these developments, and under pressure from Israeli supporters and American cotton growers at home, Dulles abruptly withdrew American funding for the Aswan Dam. The cancellation, timed for the start of the Nasser-Tito-Nehru summit, clearly aimed to demonstrate that neutralism did not pay. In this it rested on a corollary assumption (which later proved false) that the Soviet Union lacked the means to provide alternative funding for such massive undertakings.

Nasser's response was stunning. He immediately nationalized the British-controlled Suez Canal company with the announced intent of using operating profits from the canal to fund the Aswan project. Stung by Egypt's action and dubious about Nasser's promise to keep the canal open to the flow of Persian Gulf oil, Britain and France joined with Egypt's regional adversary, Israel, to reimpose Western control of the canal. On October 29, 1956, Israeli armies invaded the Sinai peninsula and moved toward the canal zone. As prearranged, British and French air units began bombing Egyptian military forces a day later. The action had been taken without notifying the Americans. It was also taken at a time when the USSR seemed indecisive over how to respond to the mounting crisis in the Eastern bloc unleashed by Khrushchev's pluralistic "many roads to communism" policy. Earlier in the year, the Polish road had taken a decidedly autonomous turn. Now, in a worst-case scenario, the Hungarian road seemed to lead away from socialist economics and out of the Warsaw Pact itself. Encouraged by Western preoccupation with the Suez crisis, Russia resolved the Hungarian one by a swift and bloody suppression of Hungarian dissidents. Having done so, it immediately adopted the posture of Egypt's defender by threatening the West with nuclear-armed missiles.

The Suez and Hungarian crises combined seemed to kick the legs out from under much of American foreign policy. Britain, France, and Israel had revived the specter of Western imperialism at the very moment when America hoped to lay it to rest. In doing so *sub rosa*, without American knowledge, they also undertook the first substantive postwar defiance of American hegemony by its traditional allies. Moreover, Russia's unopposed "pacification" of Hungary belied the empty rhetoric of the American doctrine of liberation for Eastern Europe, while Russia's rhetorical intervention in the Suez crisis enabled it to pose as the defender of Third World self-determination while obscuring its vitiation of that principle in Hungary. Moreover, its effort to involve itself in the Suez controversy threatened to introduce a Russian presence into a part of the world-system that had been off-limits since the Truman Doctrine of 1947. Finally, Egypt (and through it, much of the periphery) saw the crisis as a confirmation of the dangers of revivified gunboat diplomacy by the colonial West and as a validation of the wisdom of using the USSR as a counterweight to Western influence. C. D. Jackson, Eisenhower's special adviser on psychological warfare, captured some of the complex circumstances: "We are in an awkward position of having to cheer for freedom with one side of our mouth and deplore most of the juvenile delinquencies of these new nations with the other side; and if we have any mouthroom left, tell our European allies that it is all a terrible pity and that we are all for them in their efforts toward orderly decolonization."

Confronted with such manifold liabilities, the Eisenhower administration did the one thing it could do to minimize them. It diplomatically and economically intervened in the Suez crisis to cut short the tripartite take-over of the canal. It used the UN General Assembly to call for a truce and then cut off oil exports from the Americas until Britain, France, and Israel complied. By the end of the year, their forces had withdrawn and Egyptian control of the Suez artery restored. In effect, the American intervention reminded its Anglo-French allies of the deference demanded by American hegemony. It also partially blunted the impact of Russia's forward movement in the Middle East and attempted to put the United States on the side of anticolonialism and Third World self-determination. What it could not do was obliterate from the collective memory of the world community that it had been America's heavy-handed manipulation of the Aswan Dam enterprise, first to reward and then to punish Egypt, that had precipitated the untoward train of events in the first place. Nor could it alter the reality that American efforts to derail neutralism in the periphery had failed, and at the very time when American policy had assigned top priority to the integration of the periphery into core economies. The failure of antineutralism and pro-integrationism was to initiate, during the second Eisenhower administration, a searching debate among the American foreign policy elite over the proper means to their agreed-upon ends. Similar in kind if not in degree to the debate over NSC-68 in 1950, this new exchange would produce a reaffirmation of the militarization option, though in forms more geared to the pacification and stabilization of the periphery.

6 | Hegemony at High Tide, 1957–1967

> The great battleground for the defense and expansion of freedom today is the whole southern half of the globe . . . the lands of the rising people.
> —*John F. Kennedy, 1961*

There are tides in the fortunes of nations. High tide for American hegemony came in the late 1950s and in the 1960s, a time encompassing the second Eisenhower administration and the foreshortened presidencies of John F. Kennedy and Lyndon B. Johnson. High tide, however, simultaneously marked the beginning of ebb tide, and that was visible in the same span of years. With the clarity of hindsight, one can now see that the long, slow ebbing of hegemony was the ironic consequence of the very means by which it had been pursued—the militarization of American foreign policy and the forced integration of the world-system. Integration was to facilitate new competition to American economic supremacy. Militarization was to prove a petard upon which the nation hoisted itself in Southeast Asia. Both would raise significant questions in American society about the ledger balance of global suzerainty—whether the rewards produced merited the sacrifices.

The Triumph of American Internationalism

The true measure of hegemony is not power alone. It is a nation's ability to use that power to realize some approximation of its preferred world order. Gauged by that yardstick, 1957–58 marked the juncture when a free world-system truly became more fact than fancy. Until that time, postwar world capitalism remained plagued by the dollar gap, by restrictions on currency convertibility, and by a world trade still characteristically bilateral in nature. In 1957, however, the "Inner Six" continental nations of France, West Germany, Italy, Belgium, the Netherlands, and Luxembourg agreed to the Common Market (the European Economic Community, EEC). As the culmination to the European integration movement begun a decade earlier by the Marshall Plan, the EEC seemed certain to increase the volume of intra-European trading, and correspondingly to decrease purchase of supplies from dollar areas, and to end the postwar dollar gap. To be sure, integration remained incomplete, as Britain failed to negotiate acceptable terms for admission and formed its own Outer Seven free trade bloc with Austria, Switzerland, Portugal, and the Scandinavian nations. Nonetheless, the danger of that schism was substantially reduced in 1958 when the European Payments Union was dissolved and both EEC and the Outer Seven agreed to free currency convertibility. When Japan simultaneously took the same step, the world economy eliminated one of the major impediments to the flow of goods and capital between core countries, and between them and the periphery areas tied to their currencies.

The formation of the EEC, the universalization of free convertibility by capitalist core countries, and the resolution of the dollar gap crisis for Europe and Japan all marked the flowering of postwar internationalism. Yet, even as Eden seemed realizable, new serpents (or the old ones in new skins) appeared, as out of hiding, in the Garden. As we shall see later, the most perilous of these new dangers was a periphery prone to revolution. But a hazard of similar dimension was the renewed possibility that Europe, economically recovered and unified, might yet march down the road to regional autarky. More concretely, the existence and expansion of the EEC posed the possibility that it might restrict American access to European markets in favor of its own regional enterprises. It might make its own separate economic and political arrangements with the Soviet Union, presumably in an effort to multiply profit-making opportunities to the East while minimizing security threats from that quarter. Finally, it might try to perpetuate special economic privileges with its colonies and former colonies and create partially closed core-periphery trading spheres; for example, a Euro-African block that would enjoy a semiautonomous status in the world system.

Those dangers most dramatically revealed themselves in three interconnected areas: (1) U.S.-EEC economic relations and the American effort to insure that the Common Market would not be incompatible with internationalism or the profitability of America's own economy; (2) U.S.-French relations and the attempt to defuse French President Charles de Gaulle's autonomy-minded policies in matters both military and materialistic; and (3) U.S.-German relations and the never-ending American enterprise to resist neutralization schemes for Germany—schemes put forth by some Europeans, a few Americans, and, especially and most forcefully, the Russians.

America and the European Common Market

Continental Europe's formation of the Common Market and its acceptance of free convertibility coincided with the American recession of 1957–58, upon which the recession of 1959–60 piggybacked itself. Partly the product of normal cyclical factors, those twin recessions also reflected two long-term developments: a dollar drain and the first signs of an American trade deficit. Once desperately short of dollars, Europe found itself by the mid-1950s with a growing surplus of that currency—the result of military aid, military spending by American forces in Europe, the in-flow of private American investment, and Europe's improved trading performance. As dollars increasingly drained from the United States and Europe's dollar reserves surpassed necessary levels, many Continental nations began to convert excess reserves into gold, placing a strain on America's gold supply and ultimately upon the value of the dollar itself.

An integral part of that dollar drain was the deterioration of America's trading position in world commerce. While the United States trade balance did rebound from the late 1950s recession, it never again reached the favorable peak of 1957; and by 1968, American trade would produce a deficit now two decades old and growing. Indeed, the export of American consumer goods was already in the red by 1959, and only continued high-volume sales of capital goods would keep the overall balance in the black for another decade. At root, that trade deficit reflected the initial stages of neglect in adequately capitalizing and updating the American industrial machine. That neglect, in turn, was partly the result of American hegemony itself and its dual pursuit of military Keynesianism and global integration. It simply was more profitable for American capitalists to invest in state-subsidized military production or in state-protected multinational enterprises overseas that enjoyed the added advantage of cheaper factors of production. The consequent loser was the civilian economy at home and its capacity to compete abroad.

Economic logic dictated a number of possible responses to the dollar drain, the trade disequilibrium, and the underlying problem of civilian sector neglect. Military spending could be cut, capital exports directly or indirectly controlled, and U.S.-EEC tariff walls negotiated downward. Of that troika, only the last was pursued unequivocally, and continuing protectionist groups in the United States and Europe made even that a slow, laborious process. In 1958, the United States proposed that the General Agreement on Tariffs and Trade (GATT) be resuscitated and reciprocal reductions be negotiated with the Common Market. In 1960–61, the so-called Dillon Round resulted in some tariff reductions, but congressional restrictions limited cuts to 20 percent. Moreover, the tedious item-by-item process was never completed, leaving tariffs on many disputed commodities wholly unchanged. A year later, Congress did pass the Trade Reduction Act, which authorized across-the-board negotiations and cuts up to 50 percent, and the Treasury Department proposed the Kennedy Round of trade talks.

Had that process proceeded with dispatch, it might have produced significant cuts in EEC agricultural and industrial tariffs, providing markets for American agribusiness and making it less necessary for American industrialists to leapfrog EEC tariff walls. Instead of exporting capital to European branch plants and producing American goods overseas, American corporations could have found it as profitable to produce them at home and export them (rather than the capital) abroad. Such was not the case. France's veto of Great Britain's entrance into the Common Market in 1963 initiated a whole series of obstacles to the Kennedy Round. When it finally did come to pass in 1967, events had passed it by. The economic consequences of the escalating Vietnam War so exacerbated the dollar drain, the trade imbalance, and the maladies of the civilian sector that significant tariff cuts ironically did less to help American exports than it did to open the American market to ever-more-competitive capitalists from Germany and Japan.

Capital controls might well have been another way to slow the dollar drain, and perhaps push American capitalists to invest at home those dollars the American government prevented them from investing abroad. Eventually, the Vietnam War would force the imposition of capital controls to slow the frenetic flight of the dollar abroad, though even then controls were seen as temporary stopgaps. But in the late 1950s and early 1960s, proposals for such controls received a collective back-of-the-hand. Pointing to British history a century earlier, many argued that overseas investments helped rather than hurt the balance of payments. A mature creditor nation, allowed to invest abroad unrestricted for a long period of time, would create a capital base so big that its annual returns would outweigh the annual capital outflow. Even if that calculus proved mistaken, they argued, unrestricted capital movements were necessary to keep the American economy from being frozen out of key markets by high tariffs in EEC countries and developing nations in the periphery. Tariffs might prevent the entry of American goods, but they could not prevent American multinational corporations from investing capital directly in branch plant production inside those overseas markets. Indeed, one can posit that the first major wave of U.S. multinational investments was a defensive effort to keep the Common Market from going autarkic and restricting U.S. commercial access, and to prevent Latin American import-substitution policies from reducing traditional American markets. Only with time would American capitalists discover the more enticing virtue that multinational ventures could be made far more profitable than comparable ones in the homeland.

The only remaining major remedy for the dollar drain was to cut military spending. Yet that medicine was never taken. Quite the reverse. A major campaign by influential Americans called for a sharp increase in military expenditures, on both nuclear and conventional systems. Both the

Gaither Report of the Ford Foundation in late 1957 and the Rockefeller Brothers Report of the Rockefeller Foundation in 1958 argued that a Soviet military build-up had established superiority in long-range ballistic missiles (the notorious "missile gap") and that Soviet success in putting the first satellite in orbit (Sputnik in 1957) had created a clear lead in the space race. They concluded, in a manner reminiscent of NSC-68, that the United States ought to up the military budget by 50 percent and initiate a $25 billion fallout shelter program.

This reprise of military Keynesianism was partly the product of purely economic factors, especially the 1957–58 recession and pressure from the military-industrial complex, by then an established feature of American life. It was also, however, the consequence of global strategic-political considerations that transcended short-term economic logic. For some prominent Americans, revolutionary upheaval in the periphery dictated the need for extensive and sophisticated counterinsurgency warfare, especially (as this chapter later discusses) in Southeast Asia and Latin America. Harvard's Henry Kissinger and other academic pundits ("NATO intellectuals," as one critic described them) called for an enlarged and diversified military capable of fighting great varieties of "limited" wars; and three army generals, including Maxwell Taylor of the Joint Chiefs of Staff, resigned to protest Eisenhower's economy-minded emphasis on massive retaliation. But the European core figured as prominently as the Third World in the thinking that produced the Gaither and Rockefeller reports. One time-tested way to deflect the new EEC from the path of autarky, or of separate arrangements with the East, was to heat up the Cold War. Enlarge on the specter of the Soviet threat and use a beefed-up American nuclear shield to insure that Europe would continue to depend on the United States for its protection and security. As ever, the clear *quid pro quo* was fealty to the hegemonic rules of internationalism.

Eisenhower resisted the accelerated militarization of the late 1950s. His party preferred balanced budgets, and he feared "turn[ing] the nation into a garrison state." Moreover, he had certain knowledge, gleaned by high-altitude reconnaisance flights over the USSR, that the "missile gap" was "nothing more than imaginative creations of irresponsibility." Even his administration, however, succumbed to the militarization campaign in some measure. While rejecting the Gaither Report, it did make modest increases in military spending. It also created the National Aeronautics and Space Administration (NASA) and passed the National Defense Education Act (NDEA) to upgrade the nation's technical, scientific, and language skills. At the same time, it tried to slow the dollar drain by pressuring EEC countries to defray some of the costs of keeping an American army in Europe. For example, the Treasury Department tried to secure a commitment from West Germany to make a direct, annual payment of $650 million to that end. While the attempt failed, it did produce an offset agreement that Germany would make prepayments on its debts and military purchases to ease the immediate dollar drain.

The succeeding Kennedy administration offered *no* resistance to the militarization campaign. The new President had endorsed the Gaither Report and made the missile gap a campaign issue in the 1960s election. Aided by a Congress that openly embraced deficit spending economics for the first time ever, the Democratic administration jumped military spending 15 percent in its first year and brought Maxwell Taylor back into the government as the President's personal military adviser. By 1963, the military budget stood at $56 billion (40 percent bigger than Eisenhower's biggest) and ICBM's had more than doubled to nearly five hundred. By the end of the following administration, Lyndon Johnson's, that number had passed one thousand—a redoubling that took place despite the enormous costs of conventional ordnance in the Vietnam War. To be sure, Kennedy had paused in the arms race long enough to negotiate a test ban treaty eliminating above-ground testing of nuclear explosives, and Johnson agreed to a nonproliferation treaty to discourage yet more nations from acquiring nuclear weapons. Yet both agreements reflected standard American tactics of negotiating arms limitations only when a prior binge of military spending permitted it to operate from a clear position of superiority. Moreover, neither agreement seriously hampered U.S. interests. The test ban treaty came after an American switch to smaller warheads and more accurate delivery made atmospheric tests of megabombs unnecessary. The nonproliferation agreement was wholly consistent with the American desire to perpetuate its near monopoly of nuclear weaponry in the world-system.

The United States and De Gaulle's France

American monopoly-mindedness, so characteristic of postwar atomic diplomacy, was at the heart of Franco-American differences—a schism that powerfully reinforced the independent-mindedness of the Common Market and weakened the political-military integration of NATO. Beginning in 1958, the return of Charles de Gaulle to power sparked renewed French resistance to American hegemony. That renewal grew partly out of de Gaulle's grand vision of the EEC as French-led (of course), playing an independent role in world affairs, mediating the East-West conflict, and managing the North-South clash with the Third World. Even more pressing were de Gaulle's suspicions of the United States.

Economically, the French president articulated the pervasive fears in his country that American multinational corporations would soon turn Europe into a dependent economic colony. Bemoaning a "Yankee Peril" (or *The American Challenge*, as one popular book was titled), many French feared that superior technology and managerial skills would enable American branch plants to steal the internal French market away from its own nationals. Militarily, de Gaulle never trusted the reliability of the American nuclear umbrella and its operative premise that America would risk hearth and home to defend Europe from nuclear attack. Conversely, after the Cuban missile crisis of 1962, the French leader came to fear that American recklessness and military adventurism in Latin America or Asia might drag Europe into a nuclear holocaust against its wishes and interests. Those fears of American economic and military power and policy translated into two courses of action for France. France made an effort to keep the EEC a purely European arrangement, rather than an Atlantic community that would come to be dominated by the United States. It made the decision to build its own atomic/hydrogen bombs and bomb-delivery systems, to create an autonomous nuclear force not dependent on America's umbrella.

From 1958 to 1963, the United States sought to frustrate French autonomy in two ways. First, it pushed for British inclusion in the Common Market, to help water down French influence in the EEC, and it sought to use the Dillon and Kennedy Rounds to open the EEC to American goods as well as capital. Secondly, the United States tried to maintain its atomic monopoly, in the guise of a multilateral force (MLF) that would give Europe a sense of participation while retaining de facto American veto power. Specifically, it proposed turning over a portion of America's nuclear deterrent in Europe to collective NATO control—chiefly a missile-firing submarine group manned by a mixed-nationality contingent. The United States sought European approval of MLF by carrot and club alike. For example, it offered American-made Polaris missiles to Great Britain if it would scrap its own missile program, Skybolt, and transfer some of the Polarises to MLF submarines. And it made the same basic offer to France. More coercively, the United States hoped that its own acceleration of the arms race, both in technology and in size, would make it too expensive for France or other European powers to pay full membership fees to the "nuclear club." In that sense, America's military build-up in the 1960s was directed as much at its European allies as it was at the USSR. In effect, American leaders argued for a comparative advantage division of labor even in the military sphere. While America sought to continue its monopoly of high-tech nuclear weaponry (albeit, sharing some through MLF), it urged Europe to do what it could do best and most easily: substantially increase its contribution of conventional forces to NATO.

In the end, de Gaulle would have none of it. In early 1963, he formally vetoed British participation in the EEC, lest it transform the Common Market into "a colossal Atlantic community under American domination and direction." At the same time, he slapped away the very offer America had used to induce the United Kingdom into the MLF, forcefully indicating French determination to create "her own national defense." In justifying both moves to likely American critics, he sardonically noted that "in politics and strategy, as in economics, monopoly naturally appears to him who enjoys it as the best possible system." Three years later, France capped its independent policy by withdrawing from NATO and forcing the military organization to move its headquarters from Paris to Brussels. All in all, de Gaulle's economic and military policies gave Washington a foretaste of growing European power, and perhaps autonomy. The most immediate consequences, however, were to push the United States even closer to Germany and to put an even greater premium on continued German integration and remilitarization.

The Recurring German Crisis

From 1946 on through the Marshall Plan, the Berlin blockade, and the campaign for the European Defense Community, Germany had been the linchpin of American policy in Europe. It was the one economic unit capable of pulling the European economy in locomotive tandem with the American unit. It was the one nation with the military potential to defend the north German plains and entrée to Western Europe. German entrance into NATO and the "economic miracle" of German productivity surges and trade expansion suggested that the postwar American policy of German reindustrialization, remilitarization, and integration had born impressive fruit. But, as the past had already amply demonstrated and the future would bear out, there was a vulnerability in American policy: the ever-present possibility, however remote, that West Germany would be wooed away from its niche in the American world order. French diplomacy tempted Germany with joint dominance of the EEC, and of an independent European initiative in world affairs. Russian diplomacy, in alternating fits of crisis and détente, reincarnated its policy of German neutralization time after time—always with the enticing rewards of German reunification and liberal access to COMECON, the Soviet bloc equivalent of the EEC. Interestingly, such notions even found favor among influential American dissidents, who seemed to regard neutralization as a positive step toward the eventual withdrawal of Russian and American troops from all of Europe and the mutual dismantlement of NATO and the Warsaw Pact.

Between 1957 and the Cuban missile crisis in 1962, Germany's place in the world-system once again occupied center stage in international affairs. The USSR first flipped on the spotlight in early 1957 by using the Polish foreign ministry to float a trial balloon known as the Rapacki Plan, which called for the denuclearization of Central and Eastern Europe. Old hat in some ways, the Rapacki Plan's timing gave it new urgency. Coming only months after the Russian intervention in Hungary, it implicitly suggested that denuclearization would make it strategically possible to pull the Red Army out of Eastern Europe (and the United States Army out of West Germany), and thus eliminate Soviet interventionism as a political fact of Eastern European life.

Dissident American leaders—those who had lost the NSC-68 debate and were refighting it over the Gaither Report—quickly appropriated the Polish proposal. George F. Kennan, with his still immense visibility as the "Father of Containment," predictably led the way. Addressing an audience of European notables in the Reith lectures in late 1957, he proposed anew the notion of disengagement—denuclearization, mutual troop withdrawals from Central and Eastern Europe, and a reunified but neutral Germany. Interestingly, old Kennan colleagues like Dean Acheson sounded the tocsin in attacking his proposals, repeating arguments that neutralization could destroy Germany's integration into the world-system and send Germany— and other European states—careening down their own separate roads, some perhaps leading to bilateral deals with Moscow. Without the means "to monitor the continued integration of Germany into the West," Acheson warned, "we should be continually haunted by the spectre of a sort of new [Nazi-Soviet] Agreement." The Eisenhower administration itself made little comment on that debate. Its sentiments clearly paralleled the Acheson position. But its failure to renounce unequivocally the Rapacki Plan was a way of dampening the recent demands of West German leaders for control of missiles, aircraft, and artillery with nuclear capability, and a means of defusing what seemed an ominous overture to a German finger on the nuclear trigger.

Similarly concerned over apparent German rambunctiousness and disappointed with the official American silence that greeted the Rapacki proposal, the USSR manufactured a crisis to force the West to confront once again the neutralization option. In November 1958, Khrushchev issued an ultimatum: begin East-West talks over Germany within six months or face the *fait accompli* of a Russian-East German peace treaty and the transfer of East Berlin to German control—a transfer he expected would eventuate in the evacuation of *all* troops from Berlin and its establishment as a "free city" (a municipal microcosm of a neutralized German state). Beyond the specifics was the transcendent threat of a permanently divided Germany, a permanently divided Europe (EEC/NATO and COMECON/Warsaw Pact), and the perpetuated presence of North American and Eurasian armies. The optimal goal of Russia's threat was the generation of serious Western interest in the Rapacki and Kennan schemes. Failing that, the Soviets hoped to normalize Berlin's status. They sought to blunt its role as a center of Western espionage, as an apparent example of capitalism's greater affluence, and as an exit door from East to West (three million people had moved through it since the Berlin blockade crisis).

Eisenhower's secretary of state and his army chief of staff both counselled brinkmanship and a military show of force. So did those, in and out of government, who had written the Gaither Report or were at work on the Rockefeller Brothers version. The President, however, succumbed neither to Khrushchev's ultimatum nor his own warhawks. He simply waited and stayed calm. The Soviet premier, hoping not to reinforce the hand of Eisenhower's hardline critics and preferring to take his chances with the chief executive, quietly dropped his six-month deadline while keeping the substance of his threat intact. The result was a year-long odyssey during which the United States and the Soviet Union talked about Germany generally and Berlin specifically but could never locate zones of compromise between the incompatible poles of integration and neutralization. A foreign ministers' conference was convened in May 1959. Khrushchev and Eisenhower carried on conversations at Camp David in September 1959 at the tag end of the Soviet leader's spectacular visit to the United States. And both leaders prepared for a summit in Paris in May 1960. That meeting self-destructed in the furor over the Russian downing of an American U-2 spy plane deep over Soviet territory and Eisenhower's acknowledgment of its photographic reconnaissance mission. But Khrushchev's angry scuttling of the summit only ratified what already was apparent: there was to be no meeting of the minds over the Berlin issue.

One year, one American President, and one summit later, Khrushchev tried his hand one more time. In June 1961, at a summit meeting in Vienna with John F. Kennedy, he reissued his ultimatum, once more with a six-month deadline. Unlike his predecessor, Kennedy did not simply stall and let the hand play itself out. On July 25, in a televised speech to the nation, he gave what one critic called "one of the most alarming speeches by an American President in the whole nerve-wracking course of the Cold War." Kennedy called for sharp increases in the military budget; authority to mobilize the National Guard, to activate reserves, and to extend enlistments; the immediate dispatch of forty thousand additional troops to Europe; and the beginning of a long-term, massive civil defense fall-out shelter program. All of these requests were justified by the Berlin crisis. Two factors motivated the administration's first venture in brinkmanship—aside from the challenge to Kennedy's machismo alleged by many authors. In the aftermath of the Bay of Pigs fiasco two months earlier (to be discussed shortly), the United States needed a quick and ready way to reestablish its credentials as world policeman. Secondly, the new administration's commitment to accelerated militarization required a crisis to justify implementation of that policy. Just as Truman and Acheson had needed a crisis like the Korean War to save NSC-68, so Kennedy needed a crisis like Berlin to save the Gaither Report. Not surprisingly, most of the items called for in Kennedy's speech first had been proposed by the Ford and Rockefeller Foundations. They now became state policy.

After three high-tension weeks, Khrushchev ended the crisis. His diplomacy frustrated and war unthinkable, he did a perversely brilliant thing. He sanctioned the surprise building of the Berlin Wall. Criticized in the West as a symbol of Russian oppression and of communism's failure, the wall nonetheless stemmed the mass exodus of the technicians and professionals so essential to the Soviet bloc. Moreover, it signalled a shift in Soviet policy on the German issue. While accepting the failure of neutralization for the foreseeable future, Russia dramatized the price Germany would pay for that failure. No neutralization meant no reunification. Two Germanies was the admission charge for integration into NATO and the EEC. Thereafter, for a full decade, West and East Germany would largely go their separate ways, more and more integrated into different worlds. Not until 1971 and the eve of Russo-Western détente would the German issue again figure as centrally in the Cold War.

Looking back over the decade since 1957, American leaders took comfort in their relationship with the European core. The perceived perils of European autonomy had been largely avoided and deference to American hegemony maintained. The EEC had not become an exclusive European club but had been significantly transformed into an Atlantic community. American multinational corporate investment and branch plant production inside Europe had made the United States a de facto participant in the EEC. The threat of German neutralization had repeatedly been stayed and West Germany remained firmly anchored in and integrated into NATO and the Common Market. Only de Gaulle's France would continue to pursue its semiautonomous course, but with mixed success and in increasing isolation. Indeed, French diplomacy, rather than pulling Germany toward France, tended to push Germany and the United States together into a special relationship that rivaled or surpassed historic Anglo-American amity. *"Ich bin ein Berliner"* (I am a Berliner), said Kennedy in 1963 in the shadow of the Berlin Wall—not far from the Potsdam meeting ground where Russian, American, and British leaders had met to consider the fate of Nazi Germany less than two decades earlier.

Third Force for the Third World

There could be no sanguineness, however, about America's relationship to the Third World periphery in the decade after the Suez crisis. Since the crisis of 1949–50 that begat NSC-68, the United States had placed high priority on the economic integration of the periphery into core market economies—as investment opportunities, as sources of cost-cutting raw materials, as consumer goods markets. In general, the United States saw Third World economies as important, integral strands in the overlapping triangular trades that were the warp and woof of global multilateralism. As Kennedy put it in 1961, "The great battleground for the defense and expansion of freedom today is the whole southern half of the globe . . . the lands of the rising people." It was a judgment given economic validation by the increasingly important role of the periphery and semiperiphery in the world economy. The periphery had played a key role in the economic revival of Japan and Europe. Especially influential were the primary commodity export economies of Southeast Asia and emerging Africa. Even for the United States, the world's chief capital exporter, the Third World absorbed one-third of overseas investments; and that one-third generated more aggregate profit than the two-thirds invested in Europe, Japan, and Canada.

By the late 1960s, an even more significant trend had become apparent in semiperipheral nations like Brazil, Mexico, South Africa, Taiwan, and South Korea. While core country investments in raw materials slowed down (save for investments in oil), increasing amounts went into manufacturing—initially into semifinished products and light nondurable goods, and later into more finished durable goods. Carried out by wholly-owned core subsidiaries or by joint ventures with the host nation, these industrial enterprises in selected, semideveloped nations represented the beginning of a geographic shift in the manufacturing zones of the world-system. As the German Ruhr, the British north country, and the American northeast quadrant began their slow, long-term decay, Western industries found it more profitable to relocate in the newly industrializing countries (NICs). Indeed, throughout the 1960s, manufacturing grew at only a 1.2 percent annually in core countries, but at 4.2 percent in the NICs of the semiperiphery. As with American investment in the Common Market, that investment-production shift began largely as a defensive measure to overcome tariff barriers imposed by developing nations pursuing so-called import-substitution policies. Ultimately, however, that redivision of international labor was embraced by multinational companies, because it lowered their corporate costs and increased their bottom line profits.

As promising as those economic developments were, political conditions throughout the Third World perpetually threatened the core's capacity to control and profit from complementary economic activity in the outer zones of the world-system. Southeast Asia, so vital to Japanese economic growth, remained as volatile and revolutionary as ever. The oil-rich Middle East—that Achilles heel of European and Japanese industry—

witnessed an upsurge in Nasser's influence after the Suez crisis and a further spread of Pan-Arabism (the United Arab Republic movement) and statist doctrines of "Arab socialism." In Africa, the anti-imperialist independence movement pushed the decolonization of that continent ever faster and ever more southward. The triumph of the Algerian revolution in 1962 ended formal colonialism in Saharan Africa; the 1963 victory of the Mau-Mau movement in Kenya largely completed decolonization in the vast sub-Saharan African waist; and movements had begun that would produce in the 1970s independence for Angola and Mozambique in the lower third and sustained struggle against the South African regime into the 1980s. In Latin America—that traditional sphere of the United States— peasant revolutionary movements developed in periphery countries like Cuba, Bolivia, Guyana, Jamaica, and the Dominican Republic. Urban guerrilla warfare erupted in semiperipheral states like Argentina and Uruguay. Populist-style governments in Brazil, Chile, and Peru experimented with state capitalist alternatives to continued dependence on the world market. Indeed, the UN's Economic Commission for Latin America (ECLA) grew into a major critic of core country exploitation of the Third World and a leading proponent of nonsocialist ways of ending economic dependence and renegotiating the world economic division of labor.

Exacerbating the problem of revolutionary Third World nationalism was the tangible aid and rhetorical incitement given it by the external, non-capitalist world. Not only did the Soviet Union continue its moral and material support, begun in the 1950s, but China intensified its efforts to sponsor Asian wars of national liberation and to expand its ideological influence into Africa, Latin America, and the Middle East. Buoyed by its stalemate of the United States in Korea and by the French collapse in Indochina, the Beijing regime proclaimed the impending defeat of imperialism and its "running-dog" client states in the periphery. Ebullient and self-assertive in its early stages of revolutionary nation building, China called on other parts of the periphery to emulate its "Great Leap Forward" into forced industrialization and collectivized agriculture.

Proclaiming the United States a "paper tiger," China not only publicly disdained American claims to hegemony but challenged Soviet global pretensions as well. By 1958, the beginnings of the Sino-Soviet split were already evident in Soviet criticism of the efficacy of Chinese economic planning and the alleged deviancy of its ideological doctrines. They were also evident in Chinese criticism of Russia's episodic summit diplomacy and peaceful coexistence policies, and the tendency of Russian policy to be what China saw as unduly cautious in the face of American atomic diplomacy. That nascent Sino-Soviet schism compounded the unstable situation in the Third World since those powers were forced to compete with each other for influence in revolutionary situations in order to sustain their respective revolutionary credentials and legitimacy, both at home and abroad. Of these two noncapitalist nations, China seemed, to President Kennedy, to pose the more serious problem, since, he argued, "the Chinese would be perfectly prepared, because of the lower value they attach to human life, to sacrifice hundreds of millions of their own lives if this were necessary to carry out their militant and aggressive policies."

The consequent Third World problem for American policymakers, while no longer new, was unprecedented in scope and intensity. In a global economy, where core prosperity depended in part on integration and dominance of the periphery, how did one secure governments in the Third World that were at once politically stable and largely supportive of economic internationalism? The response—evident during Eisenhower's second administration and even more explicit during the Kennedy years— was to create a dual personality for the United States as world policeman, the classic "tough cop, nice cop" combination. The former made it clear that radical revolution was not an acceptable means for effective change in the world-system; it would be met, if need be, with harsh repression and enforced pacification. On the other hand, the gentler gendarme was ever solicitous of nationalist sensibilities and generous to a fault with humanitarian and economic aid for those who proved their worth as recipients. Perhaps the clearest exemplars of the duality were the Green Berets and the Peace Corps, both youthful elites responding to similar exhortations from the same American President to remake the Third World in America's image. One bore the sword and the other pushed the plow. The former—an unconventional ranger-type military unit—would train and lead indigenous forces in contending with insurgents in the countryside. The latter—a volunteer group of teachers, farmers, technicians, and health care workers—would win "the hearts and minds" of peasants worldwide.

Implicit in this duality was a perpetual search for a "third force" in the periphery. Usually characterized as a middle ground between communism and right-wing dictators, this much sought-after, liberal third way was also a quest for some charismatic leader possessing impeccable nationalist credentials on one hand but tolerant of economic internationalism on the other. The quest was hardly novel. The Marshall mission had sought such a half way house in China in 1946 (as, for that fact, had Woodrow Wilson thirty years earlier in Mexico). But in the late 1950s and early 1960s, the search was given a constancy and centrality it had never before had. Eisenhower, for example, said of Cuba, "Our only hope lay with some kind of non-dictatorial 'third force', neither Castroite nor Batistiano." Or, as Graham Greene's "quiet American," a fictionalized CIA agent, put it in Greene's novel of mid-fifties Vietnam, "what the East needed was a Third Force," prompting his British rival to observe "that fanatic gleam, the quick response to a phrase, the magic sound of figures: Fifth Column, Third Force, Seventh Day."

The Third Force Quest in the Middle East and Africa

Pursuit of that magic figure spanned three continents. In the Middle East, the third force notion proved more semantic than supernatural. Spurred on by the formation of the United Arab Republic in 1958 (Egypt, Syria, and Yemen), the amalgam of nationalism and Arab socialism known as Nasserism threatened other Arab regimes in Iraq, Jordan, Lebanon, and Saudi Arabia. Earlier unrest, in 1957, had already produced the Eisenhower doctrine, giving congressional authorization for aid or even military intervention for nations threatened by international communism, a concept quickly broadened to mean any threat to territorial integrity and independence. Then, in mid-1958, pro-Nasser groups assassinated King Faisal of Iraq and seized control of the government, and vulnerable regimes in Lebanon and Jordan invoked the Eisenhower Doctrine to ask for police protection.

Anglo-American fences having been mended since the 1956 Suez crisis, fourteen thousand American marines waded ashore on the Mediterranean beaches of Lebanon while British paratroopers thumped to earth in Jordan. The interventions saved those regimes, though they did not prevent Iraq from leaving the Baghdad Pact. They also marked a turning point in American foreign aid programs. Whereas once 75 percent of American aid had gone to Europe, hereafter 90 percent would go to the periphery. Moreover, it would increasingly go in the form of military assistance, or in sale of arms to states having the wherewithal to pay, like the oil-producing states of Saudi Arabia and Iran.

Objectively, the Eisenhower Doctrine was no different from the Truman doctrine of a decade earlier. It did involve, however, a semantic switch generated by the third force orientation of American policy. Arab states like Jordan, Saudi Arabia, and pre-coup Iraq had, in the United States, been stereotyped as oppressive feudal monarchies and sheikdoms—the antithesis of democracy and modernity. Now the typecasting changed dramatically. In the mass media, such states were transmogrified into "the *moderate* Arab nations." American social scientists began to characterize such regimes as "traditional modernizers," occupying some middle ground on the continuum between tradition and modernity. In effect, America's quest for a Middle Eastern third force—for a hybrid of political nationalism and economic internationalism—resulted in an invention rather than a discovery. Necessity was indeed the mother of invention, and the consequence was an arbitrary American assignment to moderate Arab states of certain presumably desirable traits: they were westernizing states trying to soften the trauma of breaks from traditional cultures; non-Christian states, to be sure, but devout in their anticommunism and temperate in their Moslemism; anti-Israeli, undeniably, but not irrationally and pathologically so.

The third force pilgrimage in emerging Africa was less a matter of invention than a great roll of the dice. The poorest part of the world-system, portions of sub-Saharan Africa were not without value, for key raw materials or for their strategic-commercial relationship to the Gulf of Aden, the Mozambique Channel, and the Cape of Good Hope. The acceleration of decolonization in the 1960s was complicated by the usual difficulties of early-stage national integration—an integration attenuated by the historic consequences of prolonged European imperialism and racism. It was further compounded by the multiplicity of external states attempting to exploit the vulnerability of African independence movements. Both Russia and China offered material and moral support to a number of revolutionary factions in Africa. They sought to frustrate any long-term American assumption of Europe's primacy in the continent, to demonstrate their own anti-imperialist, antiracist credentials, and to play out the Sino-Soviet rift on yet another stage. Consequently, for hegemonic America, Africa became yet another theater in which the world's policeman could demonstrate that wars of national liberation, especially those supported by the external world of Russia and/or China, were unacceptable.

More concretely threatening to American interests in Africa were the highly active colonial and ex-colonial European powers. This was perhaps less true of the Outer Seven (non-EEC nations) representatives, namely Great Britain and Portugal. The commercial policies of that free trade bloc were less restrictive than those of the competing bloc, and American investment in British banks and multinational companies gave Americans an immediate share of profits and production in British ventures. So the United States officially backed Portugese colonialism (though it hedged its bets by sending CIA aid to "safer" African factions in Angola), and it generally followed the lead of British policy, especially in white enclaves like Southern Rhodesia and South Africa. The EEC representatives in Africa, however, were another matter, especially France and Belgium. By and large, EEC countries employed more discriminatory economic measures in their colonies and spheres, and the fear persisted that an EEC-African economic bloc might facilitate Common Market efforts to achieve some autonomy from America's world order. As a consequence, the United States was less inclined to support colonial endeavors such as France's in Algeria and Belgium's in the Congo (now Zaire).

The quintessential example of all these diverse currents was the Congo in the 1960s. There the internal complexities of region, religion, and ethnicity interacted with external complexities introduced by Russia, China, the United States, Britain, Belgium and France, and by independent African states like Ghana—and then there was the UN, using and being used by all parties. There, after formal independence from Belgium was attained in 1960, a whole series of attempted regional secessions and central government coups and countercoups turned the Congo into a turbulent and tragic land from 1960 until 1967. Amidst all, the United States continued the search for its third force, "its man" in Stanleyville. The central government head, Patrice Lumumba, was too leftist and pro-Soviet for the part. The leader of the secessionist movement in mineral-rich Katanga province, Moise Tshombe, was too connected to EEC-based copper and cobalt interests. So the United States backed a UN effort to suppress the Katangan secession movement, while approving opposition efforts to kill Lumumba. By 1963, Kantanga was reintegrated, Lumumba was dead, and the new central government was oriented toward Washington rather than Antwerp or Moscow. In 1964, however, a substantial radical rebellion broke out again, with support from two new players, China and Ghana. Incongruously, ex-secessionist Tshombe emerged to put down the violent upheaval, aided by white mercenaries and finally by a joint Belgian-American airborne intervention to free European and American hostages and crush the insurrection. The United States, uneasy with Tshombe's Belgian connection, was not unhappy with his subsequent overthrow. From 1965 onward, American foreign policy proclaimed—belatedly—discovery of its third force leader in General Joseph Mobutu. Unhappily, he hardly met Eisenhower's earlier definition as a type somewhere between a Castro and a Batista, for he was indistinguishable in genre from the latter.

The Cuban Revolution and the Alliance for Progress

It was in Latin America and Southeast Asia that the quest for the third force grail shattered into shards, on the hard rocks of revolution in Cuba and Vietnam. In Latin America, the fortunes of the hemisphere and the fortunes of Cuba were inextricably linked in the late 1950s and early 1960s. The relationship, however, was not one to one. Even without the Cuban revolution, developments in Latin America as a whole conceivably moved American policy toward accommodations with a middle ground between the entrenched oligarchies and pluralistic pressures for change. Throughout the 1950s, a strong residue of anti-Americanism remained, half-hidden in the shadows of history. It showed itself in the Caribbean periphery's hostility toward past American interventionism and the racism and cultural arrogance that accompanied it, in the South American semiperiphery's resentment of American regional hegemony in an area where some nations, like Brazil, entertained such pretensions themselves, and in the whole hemisphere's sensitivity to the reality of its economic dependence on the North American colossus. The depth of that dependency was dramatized by the American recession of 1957–58, which had a disastrous impact on Latin American export income, which persuaded some states to push ahead with import-substitution programs of economic nationalism, to diminish *dependencia*. That determination took form in urban riots and the harrassment of Vice President Richard Nixon during his 1958 visit to Montevideo, Lima, and Caracas.

The American response attempted to channel Latin American developmental efforts into modernization dependent on foreign finance and profitable to American interests. It both predated the Cuban revolution and anticipated the Alliance for Progress. First, the Eisenhower administration eased loan repayment to the Export-Import Bank by switching from hard currency to soft currency loans. Latin America could now repay loans in their own currencies rather than in dollars or gold. Secondly, the United States joined with the Organization of American States in creating an Inter-American Development Bank capitalized at $1 billion, half of it subscribed to by the United States. The bank was conceptualized and approved in 1958, formalized in 1959, and its general purposes were articulated in the 1960 Act of Bogota. They committed the bank to infrastructural loans that would complement private investment and help establish a floor for economic development. Though the loans were opposed by the secretary of the treasury as risky, Dulles successfully promoted them on the grounds that "it might be good banking to put South America through the wringer. But," he warned, "it will come out red." Soon thereafter, the revolution in Cuba proved that unorthodox banking might not have prevented the same result.

Fidel Castro's "July 26th movement" came to power in Cuba on New Year's Day, 1959, about six years after its desultory beginnings. Much debate has raged around the nature of that revolution. Was it Marxist-Leninist from its inception or was it an indigenous revolution pushed toward communism and the Soviet orbit by inflexible American policy? Important at one level, the question is immaterial at another. However one characterizes *Fidelismo* (and the Cuban leader's own versions have altered repeatedly), the fact is clear that Castro and most of the "July 26ers" were committed to altering Cuba's dependence on the United States and launching a semiautonomous course of agricultural diversification and industrial development. The effort to carry out that commitment inevitably brought Cuba into conflict with vested American interests there. Even more importantly, the Cuban enterprise flew in the face of American prescriptions for the proper place of the periphery in the world order. Far more modest ventures in a far less important country had been deemed unacceptable in Guatemala just five years earlier. Not surprisingly, American leaders now drove home the same harsh proposition: the system *might* reward those who abided by the internationalist rules of the game, but *never* those who broke them. Castro's 1959 visit to the United States received a cool official reception, and the American-dominated World Bank rebuffed his overtures for a long-term developmental loan. A clear signal of yet tougher responses to come; Castro was on notice to make a choice: to fish or cut bait, where his revolution was concerned. He was unwilling to junk the revolution, and, not willing to accommodate international capital on its own terms, he chose to press ahead without it. The events of 1960 flowed logically from that choice. In February, Cuba made a deal with the USSR to exchange Cuban sugar, at pegged prices, for Soviet petroleum, producer goods, and technical assistance; in July, the United States radically cut its sugar quota for Cuba; and finally, in January 1961, the Eisenhower administration broke diplomatic relations with the Castro regime.

The new Kennedy administration addressed the Cuban-American impasse in two ways in 1961. It sought to nullify the spread of Castroism elsewhere in the hemisphere and to behead the movement at its source. In short, the Cuban-American impasse led to both the Alliance for Progress and the Bay of Pigs. The former was an enlargement and extension of Eisenhower's economic diplomacy. Pledging $20 billion in aid over the coming "developmental decade," the United States asked Latin American countries not only to commit their own funds but to promise socioeconomic reforms in land holding, tax burdens, housing, and public health. Like the Marshall Plan, the American aid program was a joint public-private undertaking. While the bulk of the funding was public, state-sanctioned private groups contributed dollars, facilities, and personnel to the Alliance for Progress. A perfect illustration was the American Institute for Free Labor Development. Headed by George Meany of the AFL-CIO and Peter Grace of W. R. Grace and Co., this labor-capital partnership engaged in such diverse activities as building public housing for Latin American workers, training Latin American labor leaders in the dangers of communism and in the advantages of productionism over redistributive strategies, and working with the CIA against left-leaning governments.

Also as the Marshall Plan did, the Alliance rested on certain American assumptions about the proper road to development. For the peripheral parts of Latin America, the first and necessary stage of modernization was the commercialization of agriculture on a more large-scale, mechanized basis. Land reform was to be geared more to that goal than to any break-up of the *haciendas* and redistribution of land to the peasantry. For the semi-peripheral parts of Latin America, the next and necessary stage was development of semifinished manufacturing and light industry. Tax reform, for example, was geared to alleviating burdens on an infant, urban bourgeoisie whose consumption and investment potentials were essential to that goal's realization. Realization of those diverse goals for all of the region would help attract the private capital of profit-seeking multinational corporations and, in turn, help keep the region firmly integrated in the world market economy.

The Bay of Pigs, the Cuban Missile Crisis, and Beyond

While the Alliance for Progress pursued its goals of dependent development and counterrevolution in subtle ways, the Bay of Pigs covert operation went right for the revolutionary jugular. Conceived and approved in Eisenhower's last year, the CIA-organized enterprise was to be a Guatemalan replay. The United States would arm and train anti-Castro Cuban émigrés, arrange their logistical support, and provide a modicum of symbolic air cover. Done in the right combination at the right place at the right time, the total effect, it was hoped, would be to frighten Cuban revolutionaries while emboldening Cuban counterrevolutionaries to rise up and join in the fray. To that end, fifteen hundred Cuban *contras* (ironically, trained in Nicaragua) disembarked on the shores of Cochinos Bay on April 17, 1961. Much criticized for its ineptitude, the Bay of Pigs invasion failed to generate either panic in its adversaries or uprising among its presumed sympathizers. The resulting debacle burdened hegemonic America with the very epithet that the operation was supposed to demolish, "paper tiger": a global policeman without real clout on its own neighborhood beat. One adviser reassured Kennedy that he would have "ample opportunity . . . in Berlin, Southeast Asia, and elsewhere" to prove that the United States was not a paper tiger. But the administration's concern was not so easily assuaged, and it redoubled its anti-Castro efforts. For the next eighteen months it would continue nonrecognition, economic warfare, aid to the *contras*, attempts to mobilize OAS and NATO policy support, assassination plots—and, so it was rumored, plans for a more full-fledged military intervention down the line.

The Cuban missile crisis in the fall of 1962 killed any prospect of another American intervention, but not before it threatened to kill much of humankind in a Russo-American nuclear exchange. In mid-October, American aerial reconnaissance confirmed that the USSR was installing medium-range missiles in Cuba. Soviet reasons for that step remain a matter of conjecture. Many explanations have been offered, some or even all may be true, but none can be absolutely verified. Certainly the resolution of the crisis did secure an American promise not to invade Cuba, and that consequence may have been intended from the beginning. Certainly Soviet security had declined in the face of Kennedy's remilitarization program, and the missiles may have been conceived as a quick-fix to Russian inferiority in intercontinental ballistic missiles (ICBMs). The Soviets certainly retained a lingering hope of reviving the German neutralization strategy, even after the 1961 Berlin crisis, and maybe the Cuban missiles were meant to give Russian power sufficient credibility to reopen that issue. And certainly Khrushchev was under political attack both at home and in Beijing for his domestic economic shortfalls and for the failure of his coexistence diplomacy to produce concrete results for either European disengagement or Third World revolution, so perhaps a triumph for Russian atomic diplomacy would have disarmed his political foes and salvaged his position of authority.

There are ample accounts of the American response to the Russian initiative. Most have focused on the process of decision making centered in the specially created, eleven-person executive committee of the NSC, pondering which members favored a land invasion, an air strike, a naval blockade; how the blockade option emerged as the policy choice. But more striking than the tactical differences within the executive committee was its unanimity that negotiations were out of the question and that force of some sort was in order. All agreed on the reasons why. The Bay of Pigs incident had already raised questions about the efficacy of America's police power, and the United States could not permit a resurgence of those questions. Even more emphatically, the question of credibility could not be tolerated when the issue once again was Cuba, when so little time had passed since the 1961 fiasco, when Soviet actions were so blatant, and when the challenge came in an area widely regarded as an "American lake" since 1905, when the British had bowed to the Monroe Doctrine and withdrawn their West Indies squadron. At stake was not Kennedy's own macho manliness. Were that an issue, the 1961 Berlin crisis would have settled it. The substantive issue, well understood by the executive committee, was whether the United States could maintain any serious pretense at global hegemony if it was unable or unwilling to exercise hegemony in a region of the globe that was geographically proximate and historically had been alleged to be an American sphere of control.

The thirteen-day crisis was resolved by Russo-American agreement on October 28. Responding to a letter of October 26 from Khrushchev, Kennedy accepted a proposal that Russia withdraw its missiles in return for an American pledge to respect Cuban territorial integrity: that is, a no-invasion pledge. A second Khrushchev letter on October 27 escalated Russian demands to include America's withdrawal of its missiles in Turkey. Presumably this was to mollify Khrushchev's internal critics by demonstrating that his high-risk adventurism had won gains for Russia's security as well as Cuba's. Formally, the Kennedy administration evaded the second letter simply by ignoring it and answering only the first. But informally and privately, the President's brother, Attorney General Robert Kennedy, told the Soviet ambassador that "President Kennedy had been anxious to remove those missiles from Turkey and Italy for a long period of time . . . and it was our judgment that, within a short time after this crisis was over, those missiles would be gone." One day later Khrushchev accepted the deal. Russian missiles would leave Cuba; America would not invade Cuba.

The Russo-American exercise in reciprocal adventurism and brinkmanship had multiple consequences. It renewed a frightened world's interest in arms limitations, while it paradoxically stimulated a Soviet arms build-up to insure that Russia would never again be so humiliated by superior American power. It hurt Khrushchev's political position in the Soviet bloc, where his diplomacy was viewed by many as risking much, gaining little, and ending up full circle, embracing peaceful coexistence. It reinforced the Kennedy administration's penchant for risk taking elsewhere in the world (including Southeast Asia), since it seemed apparent that Russia would not directly challenge the United States outside the USSR's own sphere of influence. It led some American allies to question whether the United States could be trusted to use its vast power in prudent, rational ways. But it also did something else. It killed the third force paradigm in U.S. Latin American policy, sending the Alliance for Progress to an early grave. From its inception, the Alliance had been beset by mismanagement, corruption, the limitations of its own developmental vision, the wariness of private American investors, and Latin American suspicions of North American motivations. Now, with revolutionary Cuba safely secured from the threat of American overthrow, there seemed little likelihood that the Alliance for Progress alone could stay the spread of insurgency and autarky in the southern half of the Americas.

So persuaded, American leaders moved rapidly from the subtler ways of alliance to the harsher means of social control, especially during the administration of Lyndon Johnson. By 1967, the Alliance itself had largely devolved from a developmental program to simple boosterism for American exports, requiring that Alliance funds be spent only on American products rather than lower-priced alternatives. Meanwhile, the CIA and private American agencies cooperated with British covert groups in an effort to destabilize an elected leftist government in the former British colony of Guyana. The CIA and AID (Agency for International Development) worked with Brazilian military, police, and business interests in effecting the overthrow of the Goulart government in 1964. The new regime replaced Brazil's import-substitution policies with a domestic austerity program designed to make its exports competitive in the world market—economic internationalism exchanged for economic nationalism.

The interventionist tendency of Johnson's Latin American policy climaxed in April 1965 when twenty-five thousand American troops invaded the Dominican Republic. Their goal was to put down a revolutionary effort to return Juan Bosch to power. Only three years earlier, American leaders had hailed Bosch as a third force savior who would find a middle ground between the reactionary supporters of slain dictator Rafael Trujillo and the forces of Castroism. By 1963, when he was deposed, Bosch and his third way were being dismissed as ineffectual by those same American leaders. Seeing three possibilities in the Dominican Republic—"a decent democratic regime, a continuation of the Trujillo regime, or a Castro regime"—Kennedy concluded, "We ought to aim at the first, but we can't renounce the second until we are sure that we avoid the third." By early 1965, Johnson came to regard Bosch as merely a dupe for more radical elements. It was on this premise of alleged communist and Castroist influence that the United States intervened a year later to crush the insurrection and return the Dominican Republic to conservative hands. Behind that premise was an even larger one made clear by President Johnson in early May, namely, that *all* revolutions were dangerous because they were open-ended phenomena whose direction and resolution could not be predicted or controlled. Not only would the United States no longer tolerate another Cuba in the hemisphere, it would not tolerate even the *possibility* of another Cuba, however remote the chance. The old Wilsonian distinction between good revolutions and bad revolutions was a thing of the past. The only good revolution was a dead revolution.

Escalating the Vietnam War

The third force approach to Latin America had been preceded to the grave by its twin in Southeast Asia. Since 1954, Ngo Dinh Diem had been the embodiment of that middle way. A devout Catholic and staunch anticommunist, he was also a nationalist, who had opposed French colonialism and the Bao Dai puppet government. For all his apparent early success in nation building, his regime generated increasing opposition by its unkept promises of land reform, its police-state jailings of dissidents by the tens of thousands, and its corrupt nepotism on a larger-than-life scale. By 1960, the process seemed less like nation building than self-aggrandizement; only the army, the Saigon bureaucracy, and the Diem clan shared in the power and profits. Episodic resistance to the Diem government had begun in 1957, carried out by the many former Vietminh who had remained in the south after the Geneva Accords and then been largely abandoned to their own fate while Ho Chi Minh tended to his socialist version of nation building in the north. Beginning with assassinations of selected government representatives in the countryside, the resistance had escalated to outright formal rebellion by 1960 and the insurgents' formation of the National Liberation Front (NLF). Vietminh dominated it, but noncommunists joined as well, prompted by Diem's arrest of a score of his most prominent, noncommunist opponents.

Faced with a *fait accompli*, the Ho regime in the north had to abandon its more parochial concerns or forfeit any claim to revolutionary leadership for a unified Vietnam. So, in September 1960, North Vietnam formally recognized the NLF and committed itself to the overthrow of Diem, the ouster of the United States, and the unification of a single Vietnamese nation. Aid from the north, largely small-scale and volunteer in 1960, became larger and more systematic from 1961 onward. The battlelines, once dissolved after the 1954 Geneva agreements, had reformed by 1961, but with the French now departed and the Americans front and center. Moreover, the battle lines went beyond Vietnam to neighboring Laos where a parallel, though less clearly-defined, civil war embroiled shifting factions of the left, right, and center. Indeed, it was Laos that drew Kennedy into his first Soviet-American conflict in early 1961, a crisis only temporarily resolved by a 1962 agreement that settled upon a centrist coalition government with more leftist participation than American political toleration could comfortably or long accept. In short, the Vietnam conflict was an Indochinese regional conflict from the very inception of the Kennedy-Johnson military escalation.

Early American responses to the Vietnamese civil war were conditioned by ideas of the national interest both old and new. Most prominent among the old was the continuing commitment to economic integration within Asia and the important role of Southeast Asian raw materials, food, markets, and investment opportunities for sustaining Japanese economic growth. Related to it was Southeast Asia's strategic importance in guarding the trade routes for Persian Gulf oil bound for Japanese ports. The latter would grow in importance as Japan increasingly shifted from coal and water power to petroleum, and the former would remain almost as important in the 1960s as it had been in the 1950s. Not until the Kennedy Round began to open the American market in the late 1960s would Japan have a major supplemental market beyond the Pacific rim.

Nearly as important as economic regionalism and Japanese growth, and clearly related to it, was the notion of American credibility. Having defied the spirit of the 1954 Geneva Accords, having made a clear regional commitment in SEATO and related bilateral pacts, and having backed the Diem regime for a half-dozen years in third force nation building, the United States could not easily keep the sword sheathed without calling into question its sincerity, its "word" as hegemonic power and global policeman. It might have been able to had the commitments been less firm or the area less important, had it been Central Asia perhaps, or Central Africa. But the commitments were firm, and even conspicuously advertised throughout Asia. Moreover, the area was vital to Japan and the world economy, and the threat that the "dominoes" would fall seemed real. American leaders sensed the danger not only in Indochina's civil wars but in Indonesia's leftward drift under Sukarno, in Korea's uneasy armistice and division, in Taiwan's military vulnerability, and in the regional magnetic lure of China's Third Worldism, its conviction that the "East Wind [was] prevailing over the West Wind."

Asian regionalism and American credibility were augmented by yet another idea of what was in the national interest, an old yet new idea. Fifteen years earlier, France's postwar commitment in Vietnam had been made partly on the basis of the "Ten Pin theory." The notion was that the fall of one piece of the French empire (even one of marginal importance like Vietnam) might threaten to tumble other parts of the empire, even those quite distant from Vietnam and more important than it (for example, Algeria)—like a bowling ball striking the headpin and one by one knocking over the rest, until the final tenpin fell. By the early 1960s, American leaders had come to the same conclusion. Not only could the dominoes of the Pacific rim topple but so could the tenpins of America's informal yet global empire—the Caribbean basin, Central America, Micronesia, and Liberia. Empires were of a piece, and the loss of one member affected the organic health of the whole. In other words, the famed falling dominoes theory really was two theories. The most obvious concerned the Asian geopolitical region only and aligned the dominoes in a proximate geographic line: Vietnam to Indochina to the Southeast Asian archipelagos to Japan and the whole Pacific rim. The second variation, however, concerned the informal worldwide American empire and aligned them not on the basis of geography but on the basis of their common relationship to American dominance and their common instincts to resist it. Sensitivity to this connectedness was not new in American leaders, but the Cuban revolution and that nation's secession from the American sphere gave that sensitivity a sharpness not present before. The Cuban exit, if coupled with a similar departure by Indochina, had potential relevance for the likes of Liberia and the Panama Canal zone. The 1960s protest chant of "one, two, three Vietnams" was one American leaders had already confronted on their own. They concluded that while one could be accepted and even two endured, the possibility of a third might bring down the whole edifice.

Fears notwithstanding, the Kennedy administration greeted the expanding civil war in Vietnam with some degree of confidence, even anticipation. The new President had been strongly influenced by army dissidents like Maxwell Taylor and James Gavin who had opposed Eisenhower's New Look strategy and stressed the need for flexible responses to limited wars, including peasant-supported insurgencies in the periphery. One such response that evolved was the theory of counterinsurgency warfare, "a wholly new kind of strategy," as Kennedy described it. Political and military in nature, counterinsurgency stressed the need to win "the hearts and minds" of Third World peasants away from the insurgents, through diverse means of technical assistance, village-level community organizing, and controlled economic modernization. In turn, rapidly mobile small-group units, like the Green Berets, would train local units for village self-protection while themselves attacking insurgents, who had been cut off and alienated from their village support. The army dissidents persuaded Kennedy of the military feasibility of counter insurgency, while his social science advisers from the university-corporate-foundation world persuaded him that America had the social engineering skills to make it politically feasible.

"The best and the brightest," as David Halberstam dubbed them, these part-time émigrés from the likes of Harvard, M.I.T., Ford Motor Company, the Rockefeller Foundation, and the Council on Foreign Relations were the direct descendents of Bruce Catton's "War Lords of Washington" in the early 1940s—only younger, less burdened with a past in the Great Depression, when America "couldn't do," and more imbued with a "can do" optimism that Senator William Fulbright called "the arrogance of power." These second generation War Lords, while fearful of developments in Vietnam, still saw in that revolution an opportunity to demonstrate the efficacy of counterinsurgency techniques, to themselves and the world—especially the Third World. In the process, they would save the day for Asian regionalism, American credibility, and the republic's informal empire. As Under Secretary of State George Ball later acknowledged, "Hubris was endemic in Washington." There were few, least of all the President, ready to listen to Charles de Gaulle's prediction to Kennedy: "You will sink step by step into a bottomless military and political quagmire, however much you spend in men and money."

Within this context of perceived national interests, Kennedy dispatched Lyndon Johnson to Vietnam in the spring of 1961, followed by Maxwell Taylor and Walt Rostow in the fall. Dismissing criticism that Diem was not a viable middle-ground representative, the Vice President's typically earthy rejoinder captured the essential negativism of the third force notion: "Shit, man, he's the only boy we got out here." On not dissimilar premises, Taylor and Rostow urged increased military assistance for Diem, including American counterinsurgency units. Numbering over three thousand by the end of 1961, America's misnamed "advisers" totaled nearly seventeen thousand when Johnson succeeded Kennedy to the presidency. In the interim, the actuality of revolution transformed the lofty hearts and minds rhetoric of counterinsurgency into the grim reality of Diem's "strategic hamlet" program. In the name of village protection, the program separated rebels from their potential peasant support in a manner reminiscent of nineteenth-century Indian removal and reservation resettlement. The Diem government removed peasant families and even whole villages from traditional lands and resettled them in larger, more defendable arrangements sometimes little better than concentration camps.

The backlash came in the Buddhist crisis of early 1963. Buddhist political sects had a much more nationalistic agenda, which was trivialized by some as merely Buddhist reactions to Catholic privileges under Diem. These sects attempted to head off the escalating civil conflict before it could result in a general bloodbath, permanent national disunity, recolonization—or all three. Disturbed at increasing violence by the National Liberation Front, repression by the Diem government, and the increasing presence of American military and political power, Buddhist groups were bent on exploring a negotiated political settlement with the NLF before it was too late, either by pressuring Diem to move in that direction (there is some suggestion that he might have been doing so before his murder) or by overthrowing him and taking on the task themselves. Dramatically staged for world viewing in mass demonstrations and gripping scenes of individual suicide by immolations, the Buddhist protest garnered a harsh response. Government forces fired into crowds, attacked the leading Buddhist pagoda, and arrested more and more critics of the government. But the futility of such repression, and U.S. fear that Diem himself might yet swing toward negotiations, increasingly led American leaders to question whether Diem was either viable or trustworthy to continue as America's "only boy" in Saigon. After much waffling, they gave their final answer in late 1963, when the American government essentially stood aside and gave its blessings to a military coup that climaxed in the assassination of Diem and his brother, just weeks before Kennedy himself met a similar fate.

Diem's end also marked the end for third force policy in Vietnam. A desultory search for a third force leader would continue among military politicos, like Khanh, Ky, and, ultimately, Thieu. The search was now guided less by some ideal criterion of hybrid pro-Americanism/anticommunism/Vietnamese nationalism than by the simpler expedient of who could keep order and who could take orders. From late 1963 onward, the United States would take increasingly direct control of "enforced pacification." As early as December 1963, President Johnson ruled out a Buddhist-style political settlement, declaring that "neutralization of South Vietnam would only be another name for a Communist takeover."

In a reaffirmation of his position of two years earlier he declared, "The basic decision in Southeast Asia is here. We must decide whether to help these countries to the best of our ability or throw in the towel in the area and pull back to our defenses to San Francisco and a 'Fortress America' concept." On the diplomatic front, the United States rejected a tripartite call by France, Russia, and North Vietnam for a reconvening of the Geneva conference and an effort at negotiated settlement. On the military front, it encouraged South Vietnam to strike back at the North through ranger-type raids, while in neighboring Laos the United States overturned its 1962 agreement by pushing the centrist government to the right and by launching secret air attacks on Vietminh supply routes. By mid-1964, however, the government of South Vietnam was no more secure than the year before. Its own internal fabric was shredded by constant turnover at the top (seven different military governments in 1963 alone), and in the field its army (ARVN) fared poorly against the NLF, despite Green Beret "advisers" and the Laotian air war. Clearly, counterinsurgency was as dead as its third force progenitor, and the only remaining options were negotiation or escalation of direct American military involvement.

Publicly, the choice of options seemed open for debate. Politically, Johnson and the Democrats campaigned in the 1964 election as the party of peace against a Republican party still heavily influenced by Pacific regionalism and a willingness to use extreme force to maintain American access to the Asian rimlands. In the embryonic antiwar movement in the United States, there was a popular misconception that a large Johnson victory would free the President from the ghostly baggage of Kennedy's Vietnam commitment and lead to negotiations. Many accepted at face value the President's assertion that the United States would not "send American boys nine or ten thousand miles away from home to do what Asian boys ought to be doing for themselves." Even the Gulf of Tonkin crisis in August 1964 was viewed by many as simply a political ploy to defuse Republican criticism of irresoluteness in dealing with Asian communism. Some perceived it as a public pose of Democratic tough-mindedness and willingness to use force while privately keeping open the path to political settlement. In fact, there was no such public-private dichotomy in the August crisis. The administration was already leaning irreversibly toward escalation by then and was selecting its future bombing targets in North Vietnam before Americans went to the polls in the fall. It did, however, need congressional support, upon which to base its likely escalation. What better time to get it than before an election when even doubting Thomases in one's party would sublimate their own concerns for the sake of party unity, and what better way to get it than to have a peace candidate call for warlike action, to the applause of future doves and future hawks alike.

So in early August 1964, after two reported attacks by North Vietnamese torpedo boats upon American destroyers in the Gulf of Tonkin, the Johnson administration ordered immediate retaliatory air attacks on North Vietnamese ports; and it requested a congressional resolution implicitly sanctioning its action and giving blanket approval for "all necessary steps" to repel future hostile acts. Even more grandly, it sought approval to respond to invitations for protection from any nation in the SEATO regional sphere. Retrospectively, it is clear that the American destroyers were operating in a strategically sensitive area (the Gulf of Tonkin is bordered by North Vietnam, China, and the Chinese island of Hainan), probably in support of South Vietnamese commando or spying operations. Moreover, there is considerable likelihood that the second attack never took place. Nonetheless, the administration seized upon the incidents, adroitly orchestrated congressional and public reaction, and secured landslide passage of the Gulf of Tonkin resolution—unanimously in the House and with but two nays in the Senate.

Six months later Johnson cashed Congress's blank check. He accepted his advisers' view that the United States had three courses of action—"cut our losses and withdraw, . . . continue at about the present level, . . . expand promptly and substantially." He also accepted their collective counsel to choose the third option. Exploiting an NLF attack on an American airfield, the President initiated aerial bombing of North Vietnam in early February. By March, operation "Rolling Thunder" intensified and systematized that bombing while simultaneously matching that effort in the South against suspected NLF positions. Actually decided upon in December 1964, the operation began an eight-year aerial bombardment unparalleled in history. It would drop more bombs by its end than were dropped in World War I, World War II, and the Korean War combined—all on a single country (North and South Vietnam combined) slightly larger than the state of New Mexico. Based upon the failed World War II notion of strategic bombing, the air power strategy failed once again in Indochina. It achieved none of its objectives—demoralizing North Vietnam and the NLF, firming up the fighting resolve of ARVN, and minimizing American casualties. To be sure, the air war would remain a major weapon in the American arsenal in Indochina. Moreover, its periodic but always temporary stoppage was a useful device to reassure the American citizenry and overseas allies that negotiations were not inconceivable. On the other hand, its invariable resumption was an obvious way to signal renewed American resolve, and a new round of escalation, to America's adversaries. In the last analysis, however, the Vietnamese civil war could not be ended by force without a substantial infusion of American infantrymen. By the end of 1965, American military personnel in South Vietnam numbered 185,000. A year later the number reached 385,000, and by the end of 1967 the number stood at 535,000. Patrolling had been subsumed into search-and-destroy operations, and they, in turn, into full-fledged campaigns.

The combined land and air war killed thousands of civilians, made refugees of one-quarter of the peasantry, chemically traumatized the ecological environment—created enormous hostility toward America in the very client-state it sought to salvage. Like the French in their failed war in Algeria, the Americans were winning all the military battles and losing the political war that ultimately was determinant. Moreover, the failure was but a microcosm of what had happened generally to American policy in the periphery during the decade beginning in 1957. It had begun as a political search for a third force, partly to avoid widespread American interventionism that could only overtax American power while compromising its stated anticolonialism. The futility of that quest had resulted—in both Asia and Latin America, Vietnam and the Dominican Republic—in the very interventionism and seeming imperialism it had sought to sidestep. As when Britain was on the downhill side of hegemony in the 1880s, informal empire seemed to be mutating toward formal empire as America sought to control a world perhaps beyond its power of control.

7 | Dissent, Détente, and Decline, 1968–1976

> You may be right in African terms, but I'm thinking globally.
> —*Henry Kissinger, 1976*

> Compared to people who thought they could run the universe, I
> *am* a neo-isolationist and proud of it.
> —*Walter Lippmann, 1971*

In the near-decade between Johnson's last year in the White House and the American bicentennial in 1976, the United States came to bear a striking resemblance to Great Britain nearly a century earlier. Still indisputably and overwhelmingly the most powerful nation in the world, the United States nonetheless showed clear evidence of decline in its capacity to perform its functions as center for the world-system. The age of hegemony, now nearly a quarter-century old, seemed to be winding down, though it remained to be seen whether America would accept that decline and accommodate to it or attempt to recapture the strength and the strategy to reverse the process. For the moment, however, the sheer weight of hegemony seemed to grind down and crumble the very pillars upon which it had necessarily rested. Substantial domestic dissent raised fundamental questions about the efficacy and desirability of America's role as world policeman. Economic supremacy and the worldwide boom it had fueled for two decades gave way to diminished American competitiveness, the collapse of the postwar monetary system, and a prolonged slump of repetitive recessions. Russia's final emergence as a truly global power, and America's inability to prevent its re-entry into the world-system, helped produce détente and a measure of legitimacy heretofore denied the Soviets. And the American political defeat in Vietnam led not only to an abortive effort to "Vietnamize" that war but to a general strategy of limiting direct American intervention in the periphery and a choice to work instead through surrogate regional powers in Asia, Africa, the Middle East, and Latin America. In sum, the late 1960s and early 1970s saw the United States lose a measure of the legitimacy, economic dominance, exclusivity, and self-confidence that were requisite to the prolongation of the age of hegemony.

Domestic Dissent in the Vietnam Era

Since American entry into World War II, American internationalism had rested upon a broad base of domestic support. Elite leaders—the "war lords of Washington," "the best and the brightest," the "ins-and-outers," "the wise men"—might shape and make policy, but they could not execute it successfully over time without pervasive approval from the American citizenry and the Congress that more or less represented it. The tax dollars and bond subscriptions of the American public largely funded the state's global role, and its older adolescents filled the ranks of the world's most powerful police force. Acting for that diverse, pluralist constituency, Congress retained the crucial appropriations power to raise taxes, authorize borrowing, and expend monies for the military machine and foreign aid, as well as the constitutional power to declare war. Acting within such pluralist contraints, the foreign policy oligarchy, which was centered in the executive branch, had to find ways to maintain a long-term public consensus that approved and supported the republic's hegemonic role in world affairs. The American elites had to fight the Cold War much as they had World War II, in ways that minimized the material and human sacrifices of the American public while maximizing its economic and psychic rewards. Hegemony on the cheap!

From the mid-1940s to the mid-1960s, American internationalists had fared superbly in their effort. During the 1950s, leftist dissent was crushed in an anticommunist crusade. During the 1960s, rightwing dissent was temporarily so discredited that its sacrificial 1964 presidential candidate, Barry Goldwater, suffered a devastating defeat—in part because the right's version of global policing, with its casual references to nuclear confrontation, frightened the American public with a trade-off of greater costs and fewer gains for acting as free world leader. Centrist moderates in both parties, however, had a better deal for the middle-American public, one that avoided the "welfarism" of the left and the "warfarism" of the right and that might touch middle-class purse strings and heart strings alike. Committing themselves to fulfill *The Promise of American Life* (as Herbert Croly, founder of the *New Republic,* titled one of his books), centrist elites persuasively argued that world power and internationalism offered no threat to the American dream. On the contrary, they offered the only way to make it come true. Not only could one have both "guns and butter," as Lyndon Johnson put it, but one could have butter (wealth) in sufficient abundance *only* if guns (global policing) were employed to keep the world free and prosperous. In essence, bipartisan centrists promised to fulfill middle-class dreams through a growth strategy of global trade and capital expansion. It was the classic productionist strategy of enlarging the overall economic pie while keeping the relative shares the same. At the same time, however, a portion of the economic surplus generated would be targeted for social programs designed to defuse potential discontent among recent rural migrants, inhabitants of depressed regions like Appalachia, workers in declining industries such as textiles, elderly citizens on fixed incomes, and the Black underclass. Truman's Fair Deal and Kennedy's New Frontier—each stressing a rise in the minimum wage, Social Security extension, manpower training, and Appalachian revitalization—embodied what Truman called "the way of progress" midway "between the reactionaries of the extreme left" and "the reactionaries of the extreme right."

Productionism had worked wonderfully well in the 1961–67 period. Despite early signs of erosion and the revival of international competitors, the American economy remained the envy of the world. Rocketing ahead with a growth rate in excess of 6 percent annually, the American gross national product (GNP) was so large that just *one part* of it—the overseas part generated by American-led multinational corporations—was larger than the *total* GNP of either Germany or Japan in 1967. Deriving 22 percent of its profits from overseas economic activities, America's direct foreign investment was larger than the direct foreign investment of all the rest of the world combined. In a sense, however, the Long Boom of American and global capitalism between 1950 and 1973, worked almost too well. While productionism handsomely rewarded the American upper and middle classes, its surplus distribution did not commensurately aid the disadvantaged classes, *The Other America*, as Michael Harrington's book dubbed the nation's poor. The modest reforms of liberal social programs did not significantly alter that fact.

Of that other America, it was the large Black underclass, both urban and rural, that was most economically marginalized and the small Black bourgeoisie that was most excluded from non-economic forms of power. Ironically, it was the resulting Black revolution of the 1960s, the civil rights movement, that led to the deterioration of the domestic Cold War consensus. Barred from high quality education, politically disenfranchised, socially segregated, and denied a fair share of productionism's profits, Blacks protested, in a movement that rocked American society with boycotts, sit-ins, "freedom rides," marches, and mass demonstrations. Black protest drew from such diverse ideologies as Marxism and Black capitalism and used such diverse approaches as civil suits in the courts and civil disobedience in the streets. It was at its most alarming for America in the urban riots of 1965 (Watts), 1967 (Detroit), and 1968 (Washington), and in Black militant action across the nation's campuses.

All this had relevance for the Cold War consensus in two instrumental ways. First, the civil rights revolt encouraged and frightened the state into targeting significantly more dollars for social programs. That became especially so when other groups, like migrant farm workers, public school teachers, women, and the elderly, began to emulate Black tactics in pushing their own claims for empowerment and economic rewards. The result was Johnson's Great Society program, which existed between 1965 and 1968: Medicare and Medicaid, VISTA (Volunteers in Service to America), federal aid to secondary and higher education, the Job Corps, Head Start, the Department of Housing and Urban Development (HUD), and the War on Poverty. This upscale social program, coupled with the huge costs of militarization, generally and in Vietnam specifically, created (as some critics named it) a "warfare-welfare state" that hurt the middle class dearly. Only higher taxes or more borrowing or increased runs of the government printing presses could fund both the war in Vietnam and the war on poverty, and each of those means would cost middle America. The state attempted to mask that fact by keeping the lid on taxes, in an effort to sustain the notion that guns and butter were indeed possible. The extra money printing and the borrowing, however, pushed prices and interest rates in an inflationary spiral that would reach double-digit annual levels by the mid-1970s. The result, in economist James O'Connor's phrase, was a "fiscal crisis of the state." Hegemony abroad and social control at home demanded continued high levels of military and social spending, but the higher taxes and/or inflation necessary to finance them cut into middle-class purchasing power. That, in turn, dampened demand and reinforced the recessionary tendencies of the early 1970s. The consequent "stagflation"—high unemployment and high inflation strangely bedding down together—dramatized the enormous economic cost of global dominance, just as the Vietnam casualty rates underlined the high human cost. Hegemony on the not-so-cheap!

The second way that Black protest dented middle-class support for global hegemony was in its stimulus to the campus-based, New Left antiwar movement. Powerfully pricking the moral conscience of the nation, the civil rights movement drew thousands of idealistic white youths into its midst. There they acquired and honed skills for political organizing, heightened their sensitivity to racism and repression, and rubbed shoulders with Black militants, some brandishing radical critiques of core exploitation of Third World peoples. They had already been exposed to the 1950s' radicalism of C. Wright Mills, Herbert Marcuse, and William A. Williams. Now the coupling of academic analysis with hands-on experience in the civil rights fight helped produce a student-dominated New Left that easily projected the war at home into the war in Vietnam. They saw in Southeast Asia a conflict that embodied the same racism, repression, and economic exploitation that they were challenging in America, and against which they could employ their new expertise in political activism. Fueling the movement even further was their collective guilt about being white, middle-class, and privileged: able to realize the American dream when the

Black underclass could not; able, if they chose, to largely escape the Selective Service military draft when poor Blacks could not (who instead often joined the military as their only avenue of mobility); able to enjoy the fruits of productionism and global expansionism while much of the Third World, it was argued, paid for them through continued economic dependence and diminished political autonomy.

From the founding of Students for a Democratic Society (SDS) in 1963 through the university teach-ins and demonstrations of 1965–68, even to the extent of bombings of banks, corporate offices, and university buildings, rebellious middle-class students occupied center stage in a movement that condemned not only the Vietnam War but the general impropriety of America's role as world policeman. While most students were not actively antiwar, and most opponents of the war were not students at all (they were often the older blue-collar workers who were paying much of the economic and human costs of the war), the high visibility of student protestors raised an issue of profound relevance for American hegemony. Could the American system continue to flourish at home and abroad if a whole generation of middle class youth opted out ("turned on, tuned out" as the saying went) and failed to give that system its expected two-score years of service as engineers, lawyers, public servants, managers, and technocrats? Some elites ignored the question and answered youthful rebellion with state repression, as in the Ohio National Guard killing of Kent State demonstrators in 1970 or the political trials, like the "Chicago 8" conspiracy trial in 1969. Other elites, however, saw such measures as counterproductive and wondered increasingly, in a cost-benefit way, if the war in Southeast Asia merited the possible "loss" through alienation of a generation.

Such concern, compounded by many others, led some elite leaders themselves to voice dissent from the Vietnam War effort and, more broadly, to question the proper relationship of means to ends in fulfilling America's hegemonic role. The erosion of domestic support, the concern of American allies that too many eggs were going into the Vietnam basket to the neglect of other responsibilities, the incredible and unanticipated will to persevere shown by North Vietnam and the NLF, the deleterious impact of the war on the health of the economy, the alleged demoralization of American military forces in Southeast Asia: all led to an agonizing reappraisal by many American leaders. At the more rarefied upper reaches of the foreign policy elite, the soul searching was an exclusive, in-house affair conducted according to prescribed rules. In the Council on Foreign Relations George Ball and McGeorge Bundy did polite battle over the immediate issue of whether or not to remain in Vietnam. At the middle-echelon level of the foreign policy establishment, especially among staffers in the State Department, CIA, and Pentagon, the reappraisal broke the bonds of such gentlemanly discourse and spilled over into the public domain. Persuaded that the White House would never liquidate the Vietnam commitment without public pressure, some began to leak embarrassing information to Congress and the press. The most spectacular of these was the 1971 *New York Times* publication of the "Pentagon Papers," leaked by Daniel Ellsberg, a former Defense Department official. This classified internal history of American involvement in Southeast Asia contained many secret documents that portrayed a foreign policy process that neglected opportunities to negotiate, mindlessly pursued only battlefield solutions, covered up military operations likely to incur public disapproval, and lied about the sincerity of peace efforts.

From 1968 onward, elite dissent became increasingly respectable. The Senior Advisory Group on Vietnam ("the Notables") counselled President Johnson to turn the war over to South Vietnam and initiate a long, phased withdrawal designed to salvage as much honor and credibility as possible. Former secretary of state Dean Acheson spoke for the majority when he told Johnson that the United States could "no longer do the job we set out to do in the time we have left and we must begin to take steps to disengage." At the same time, Senators Eugene McCarthy and Robert F. Kennedy, running on antiwar platforms, challenged Johnson for the party's nomination in 1968; and after Johnson's decision to stand down from the race, they challenged his hand-picked successor, Hubert Humphrey. Print-media representatives of the business community, like the *Wall Street Journal,* increasingly questioned the wisdom of the war in Indochina. And Congress, subject to elite and pluralist pressure alike, rescinded the bipartisan blank check it had given the White House in the Gulf of Tonkin resolution, suspended appropriations for the expanded war in Cambodia in 1970, instructed the President to cease all Indochinese military operations in mid-1973, and climactically passed the War Powers Act later that year, placing restraints on the chief executive's capacity to wage undeclared wars like those in Korea and Vietnam.

The cumulative impact of domestic dissent—born of fiscal crisis, student rebellion, and elite disunity—was to isolate the imperial presidency from its traditional bases of support. Especially galling to Johnson was his assessment that "the establishments have bailed out." The President had been dismayed at defense secretary Robert McNamara's defection in 1967 and thunderstruck by the policy reversal of his Senior Advisory Group in 1968. Similarly, Nixon was furious at the Pentagon Papers publication and the numerous other leaks he attributed to dissidents in the executive branch itself. As Henry Kissinger, his National Security Adviser, put it: "What the hell is an establishment for, if it's not to support the President?" Nixon particularly, given his California roots and the Pacific regionalism of many of his early backers, had never felt fully accepted by the Eisenhower-

Rockefeller wing of his party, even though he came to embrace its internationalism. By 1970, his long-term ambivalence gave way to a "siege mentality," in which he increasingly distrusted the elite-dominated bureaucracies in the State Department, Department of Defense, and CIA. More and more, he attempted to bypass the bureaucracy and concentrate foreign policy formation in his own hands and those directly accountable to him. Increasingly, policy was not only formulated but implemented by the President's National Security Adviser and by his loyalists on the NSC staff—a process that reached a troubling climax in the Iran-*contra* scandal of 1986–87.

At the same time, the President created the notorious "plumbers" group to fix leaks from the bureaucracy to the news media or the Democratic Party. Their methods included wiretaps of journalists and public officials and breaking into Daniel Ellsberg's psychiatrist's office and into Democratic headquarters at the Watergate hotel. The ensuing attempt to cover up the plumbers' operation produced the Watergate scandal of 1973 and brought Nixon to the brink of impeachment and finally to resignation in 1974. In effect, the beleaguered imperial presidency had moved tentatively but clearly toward authoritarianism, secret government and government by fiat at home. But its colossal failure and disgrace ironically diminished the perceived legitimacy of the chief executive and, in turn, the legitimacy of the hegemonic strategies so intimately connected with half a dozen presidents over three decades of war and cold war. In sum, domestic dissent, and the inability of the President to negate or sidestep it, helped produce by the early 1970s the so-called "Vietnam syndrome": skepticism that complex world problems lent themselves to simplistic military solutions and a related uneasiness about whether America had the moral right or even the requisite power to play global policeman. That skepticism and uneasiness would inhibit the military exercise of hegemony in the 1970s and even, in the case of Central America, in the 1980s. President Nixon expressed his view of the situation when he told a 1971 convention of the Veterans of Foreign Wars that "the history of civilizations is strewn with the wreckage of nations that were rich and that fell before people that were less rich and considered to be inferior to them intellectually and in every other way, because the rich nations, in their maturity, lost their drive, lost their desire, lost their dynamism, lost their vitality."

American Economic Decline

If domestic dissent and its policy restraints raised doubts about continued American hegemony, so too did the quickening decline of American economic supremacy. It had been that dominance that had given the United States a vested stake in economic internationalism since the early 1940s. It also had provided the leverage to force other capitalist nations to accede to its economic principles and the wherewithal to reward them handsomely for their deference, witness the Long Boom from 1950 onward that fueled world capitalist prosperity with American dollars, equipment, and markets! But in a lengthening period of declining American productivity and profitability, would the vested stake in internationalism not be compromised by growing protectionist efforts to safeguard vulnerable industries? Would the United States still have sufficient leverage to influence the fiscal and commercial policies of emerging capitalist competitors like Japan and the EEC? And, the bottom line, would the American promises of material rewards have sufficient plausibility in an era of repeated and deepening recessions (1971–72, 1974–75, 1979–80, 1981–82) that cumulatively constituted the greatest economic slow-down since the 1930s Great Depression and seemed strongly reminiscent of the Long Depression of 1870–1900?

By 1968, the American balance of payments problem (the dollar drain) had mutated from a pronounced tendency to a full-blown crisis. Military spending, overseas investments, and a commercial trade deficit produced an unfavorable balance of payments that generated a European-Japanese run on gold and a demand for a new international monetary standard. For a decade, the capitalist world had operated on an international gold standard. The price of the dollar, the one universal reserve currency, was fixed at 35:1 ($35 = 1 ounce of gold). All other currencies, their value also determined by their relationship to gold, were freely convertible into dollars. By 1968, as we have seen, the dollar drain had created a glut in Europe that so far exceeded its reserve needs that it increasingly began to convert dollars into gold, cashing in on the American promise to redeem all dollars in gold in return for the dollar's privileged position as the fixed norm around which all other currencies rotated.

There was a limit, however, to that dollars-to-gold conversion process. Pushed too far it could deplete American gold reserves and force the United States to devalue the dollar to protect those reserves. In turn, that might require Europe and Japan to devalue their currencies, lest their markets be flooded with cheaply priced American goods. The total result might well be a competitive round of currency devaluations reminiscent of the 1930s, which could destroy the stable system of exchange rates necessary for doing global business on a predictable basis. On the other hand, Europe and Japan were reluctant to continue accepting unlimited amounts of dollars, because they strongly believed the dollar was already overvalued. Sustained high levels of American military spending, augmented by more recent increases in social outlays, had fueled a rapid price-wage inflationary spiral. Moreover, the American government had refused to slow it through higher taxes and interest rates lest the economic costs of the Vietnam War and global policing be too obvious. So while the real value of the dollar (in terms of purchasing power) declined, the international fixed value remained the same. In effect. European and Japanese exports to the United States were paid for in "cheap" dollars, while American exports to those countries were paid for in "dear" currencies.

In theory there was a traditional solution to this problem, one the United States itself had forced on Europe in the Marshall Plan, on Japan in the Dodge Plan, and on the Third World in Export-Import and World Bank loans. That solution was deflation. If the United States had followed its own rules of economic behavior, it would have deflated its economy through spending decreases, tax increases, tighter interest, wage cuts, layoffs, and the like. Nonetheless, one of the perks of global power and hegemony is that one can break the rules as well as make them. Aside from an income tax surcharge and voluntary controls on overseas investments, neither tactic very effective, the United States declined its own medicine. It could not massively cut military spending without abandoning its hegemonic role nor accept higher unemployment without killing domestic support for that role—or so American leaders believed in the late 1960s. So the United States attempted to pass the buck to Europe and Japan. Either they learned to live with the status quo or corrected it themselves through revaluations upward of their own currencies. The latter might give them full value for their exports to the United States, but it would also make American goods more competitive in their own markets (which is what American leaders sought) and would perhaps eventually force them to confront the politically thorny option of deflation that American leaders were trying to evade. In effect, the United States chose to do nothing and to let other trading nations pay the price of exchange readjustments.

The American policy of benign neglect succeeded only in part. It did force Germany and other European countries to revalue upward, but the revaluation was less than the United States had hoped for. Moreover, Japan adamantly rejected any readjustment whatsoever. So, in late summer 1971, the administration attempted to *force* Japan and Europe to negotiate a revamped system of new fixed rates. The United States unilaterally devalued the dollar and suspended its convertibility into gold. At the same time, it imposed a 10 percent surcharge on all foreign imports (threatening Europe and Japan with a trade war), while imposing domestic wage and price controls (seducing Europe and Japan with an apparent commitment to slow American inflation). The combination of coercion and conciliation resulted in the Smithsonian Agreement in December 1971. In it, other core nations agreed to revalue their currencies in exchange for removal of the American surcharge and the resumption of dollar convertibility to gold. Unfortunately, setting new fixed rates in the volatile world of the early 1970s was like threading a moving needle. The dollar simply would not stay put. The removal of wage-price controls renewed inflation, and the American trade deficit, structually rooted in long-term neglect of civilian industry, failed to respond to the devaluation initiative. The United States did try the expedient of devaluation and new negotiations for fixed rates again in 1973, but stabilization remained as elusive as ever. In the end, it was Germany and the EEC that resolved the problem their own way. They agreed that they would set fixed rates only among themselves, letting the composite EEC currency float against the dollar. In short, they would let global demand, rather than political agreement, determine the true purchasing power of the dollar in the world market.

The resolution was symptomatic of the new economic power enjoyed by Germany and the Common Market countries. Its acceptance by the United States—reluctantly at first, positively by 1975—was symptomatic of something just as significant. The United States had, for the time, given up on efforts to stop the dollar drain. Indeed, its 1974 abandonment of all capital controls virtually invited American capitalists to invest overseas. Like Great Britain a century earlier, the United States seemed to be relinquishing its industrial primacy and its demand for foreign commodity markets. Instead, it appeared to be accepting its transformation into a *rentier* nation, living off the income of its rents—that is to say, its direct and indirect overseas investments.

Interestingly, the "oil shocks" administered by OPEC (the Organization of Petroleum Exporting Countries) actually reinforced that *rentier* tendency. The temporary oil embargo of 1973, and subsequent OPEC price hikes, sent the annual cost of oil imported by the United States skyrocketing from $5 billion in 1972 to $48 billion in 1975. One consequence of that energy crisis was stimulation of civilian industrial investment in the search for alternative energy sources, be they nuclear, coal, shale oil, wind, or solar energy. That stimulus to productive investment, however, proved to be short-lived in some cases and unsuccessful in others. In a more major and enduring consequence, the oil shocks provided New York *rentier* capitalists with a much enlarged pot of gold to invest throughout the world-system. Not only did the United States pay for its higher-priced oil in dollars, but Europe and Japan, even better OPEC customers, paid for them out of their dollar glut reserves. Surfeited with those "petrodollars," Saudi Arabia, Iran, and other OPEC nations pumped many of them into New York (and London) financial institutions, where they were reinvested wherever the best profits were to be had.

But where? In what? And how was the United States to use those dollars to revive the aggregate rate of profit and reinvigorate a slump-ridden economy? Core countries were only spottily attractive. The German and Japanese economies had certainly fared better than the American, but the 1974–75 recession, and those of the late 1970s and early 1980s, were truly worldwide downturns. Collectively, the GNPs of all core nations declined 13 percent in 1974 and offered American capitalists profit-making opportunities only marginally better than those found in civilian industry at home. The less developed countries (LDCs) of the periphery attracted ephemeral attention in the boomlet of 1972 that heightened global demand for their raw materials. The brutal downturn in 1974, however, virtually killed the world market for all primary commodities save food and oil. That collapsed demand, coupled with its own increased oil bills, made the periphery the least attractive venue for profit-seeking investors. There was an out, however. There was one zone in the world-system still capable of sustaining economic growth, one last frontier of the many forged since Columbus, da Gama, and Magellan had pioneered the first: the semiperiphery.

The Semiperiphery as Last Frontier

Semiperipheral nations characteristically had possessed a fair degree of political integration, as well as ambitions for regional influence outside their own boundaries and a commitment to industrialization and modernization at home. In the early 1970s, there were two camps of semiperipheral nations. One consisted of parts of the socialist external world: China and the Soviet-dominated COMECON—Eastern Europe, North Korea, North Vietnam, and Cuba. The other and far larger was the intermediate zone of the capitalist world-system: Brazil, Mexico, Argentina, and Venezuela in Latin America; Portugal, Spain, Italy, Greece, Norway, and Finland in Europe's outer rim; Egypt, Saudi Arabia, Israel, Iran, and Turkey in the Middle East; Algeria, Nigeria, and Zaire in Africa; India, Indonesia, South Korea, South Vietnam, Taiwan, and the Philippines in Asia; and Canada, Australia, New Zealand, and South Africa in the old British Empire.

Since the 1960s, many nations in the capitalist semiperiphery had pursued policies of import substitution. They employed trade regulation to regain part of the home market for indigenous industry, and they exported their industrial surplus into neighboring parts of the periphery in exchange for raw materials. Since those policies clearly threatened traditional core country markets, the multinational corporations of those nations evaded those trade regulations by investing directly in branch plant production inside the semiperiphery producing consumer goods, steel, vehicles, and durables. They also discovered and honed the profit-making advantages of multinational enterprise of integrated production involving two or more countries. On one hand, they enjoyed the benefits of mobilizing local capitalists to help finance their ventures and provide them with political protection, and enjoyed the cost savings of cheaper factors of production, especially wage bills for workers and managers. On the other hand, they profited from the opportunities created by internal trading. The branch plants bought most of their machinery, licensed technology, and raw materials from their own parent companies in the core, while selling most of their products back to the core in return—either for consumption in the core country or for re-export elsewhere in the world market. Not only did that internal trading generate considerable business at both ends, it permitted parent and progeny to exploit inventive pricing and bookkeeping to hide profits and evade taxes in both the core and the semiperiphery.

By the 1970s, the rate of profit created by such multinational ventures by the semiperiphery was impressively high, and had already attracted significant investment from the United States, Europe, and Japan. By then, the declining rate of profit in the core, and the prolonged recessionary contraction that it produced, was adding zest, even desperation, to core efforts to find profits in the semiperiphery. As a result, unprecedented amounts of investment capital, bank loans, engineering, and capital goods flowed from the United States and other core countries into that intermediate zone. Overall, the rate of profit was twice as high for capital invested in the semiperiphery (especially the Asian rimlands) as it was in core economies. Nowhere was this more true than in large international banks. Citibank Corporation, for example, by 1976 earned three-quarters of its profits abroad. As the new world redressed the balance of the old, the semiperiphery had come to redress the profits of the core. Unfortunately, the rescue effort was not without its perils and pitfalls. While industrialization in the semiperiphery created greater possibilities for economic integration, it also created a working class where none had existed before. Often better organized and more cohesive than the urban middle class, it possessed a potential for power disproportionately greater than its actual numbers—including a potential for rebellion that was soon demonstrated in Chile, Portugal, and South Africa, and would be seen again by decade's end in Iran, Poland, the Philippines, and South Korea.

Revelation of the profit-making *realities* of the capitalist semiperiphery also alerted the United States to the profit-making *potential* of the noncapitalist semiperiphery. China, for example, had been stunned by the failure of its Great Leap Forward—its up-by-the-bootstraps program in forced industrialization. Persuaded that more capital-intensive methods were necessary for success, China acknowledged an increasing need to turn outside its borders for technology, engineering skills, and capital. Even in the best of times, the Soviet Union lacked the capability to meet those needs alone. And in what was then the worst of times—with the Sino-Russian split growing and hostile armies congregated on their mutual boundaries, the Soviet Union lacked the will and intent as well. Predictably, perhaps, China began to explore the possibilities of easing relations with the United States and Japan and fostering joint ventures for Chinese infrastructural development.

At the same time, the Eastern European semiperiphery grew increasingly restive under Soviet control. Part of that restlessness grew out of the Russian tendency to place limits on Eastern European development (Soviet-style *dependencia*) and to impose "command" economies (planned rather than market determined), the efficiency of which was widely criticized. Russia, for its part, found its formal empire in Eastern Europe to be an economic burden that depleted its own ability to deliver on material promises to the Russian people. Indeed, some Western economists estimated that Russia spent an average of $8 billion annually subsidizing Eastern European economies. Seeking ways to put the area on a more self-sustaining, pay-your-own-way basis, and of defusing indigenous discontent at the same time, the Soviets in the late 1960s moved to experiments in economic liberalization and mixed command-market strategies. The experiments, however, threatened existing bureaucracies, both Russian and Eastern European. They also stimulated a political liberalization that did not sit well with old Stalinists, and ultimately raised questions about the loyalty of the Eastern bloc to Soviet foreign policy and its security needs. These contending tendencies came in 1968 to center upon Czechoslovakia, where the economic and political experimentation was the most extensive and most imaginative. Unhappily, the "Prague spring" (the 1968 precursor of mid-1980s "openness") gave way to a "Prague summer" of Thermidorian reaction and Russian military intervention to restore the status quo in Czechoslovakia.

Détente and Triangular Diplomacy

The evolution of the semiperiphery as the new frontier in global capitalism helped to produce American détente with Russia and China in the early 1970s. "A relaxation of tensions," the literal meaning of the French word, came to characterize those relations. The origins of détente, to be sure, preceded the recessionary contraction of the 1970s, and noneconomic factors played important and often primary roles in détente's unfolding. Nonetheless, the global economic crisis that began with the monetary crisis of 1971 played a powerful and often overlooked role in promoting peaceful coexistence. As Kissinger told the United Nations in 1975, "the global order of colonial power that lasted through the centuries has now disappeared . . . The cold war division of the world into two rigid blocs has also broken down and major changes have taken place in the international economy . . . Therefore it is time to go beyond the doctrines left over from a previous century that are made obsolete by modern reality . . . The world is a single global system of trade and monetary relations." Within that single system, détente with China was indispensible if that nation was to be buttressed in its new inclination to look outside for modernization help. Without the normalization of Sino-American relations, there could be no joint developmental ventures, no technology transfers, no scholar exchange programs, no training of Chinese engineers in American universities—no Chinese market, as the West had fantasized since the days of Marco Polo.

Similarly, détente with Russia was essential if that nation was to feel secure enough to abandon its repression in Eastern Europe and to open the economies of that semiperipheral area to Western capital and technology. Few American businessmen and policymakers expected détente to open vast new markets in Russia itself; though in fact, détente would lead to the doubling of American exports to Russia, mammoth grain sales, and a relaxation of American strategic controls on the sale of technology and capital goods. The general American assumption, however, was that the fifty-year Russian commitment to command economics and national autarky, and the entrenched bureaucracy that depended on their perpetuation, would make Russia a rather limited economic frontier. Possibilities in Eastern Europe, however, seemed far more expansive. Most of Russia's Warsaw Pact allies yearned, in varying degrees, to resume their earlier experiments in mixed economies, and they looked to the West for the capital investments, bank loans, joint-stock manufacturing ventures, and subcontracting arrangements to make those experiments viable.

In purely economic terms, Russia was not hostile to an enlarged Western role in Eastern European economies. Its 1968 intervention in Czechoslovakia could not erase the continued reality that Eastern Europe wanted to end its dependence on the Soviet Union and promote its own economic modernization. Russia, for its part, certainly was not averse to reducing the enormous economic drain that its COMECON "colonies" made on it. Moreover, Soviet economic analysts believed that Western economic inputs could make Eastern European economies more efficient and self-supporting. They believed that experiments in market economies could not succeed so long as they were restricted to the small national markets of each COMECON country. Mirroring American thought, they concluded that only large-scale, specialized production for a world market could bring true efficiency to Eastern Europe. The solution, therefore, was to open COMECON to Western trade financed by Western banks. The import of engineering and capital goods would upgrade Eastern bloc industry, while the necessity of exporting to pay for the imports and loans would force greater efficiency on state managers and workers.

The sticking point was political and military. Russia feared that Western economic penetration would also eventuate in a political penetration that would reorient Eastern Europe from its Russian alliance to a connection with the West. Already insecure in the face of America's forward base system (FBS) in Central Europe, if Russia lost Eastern Europe as a security buffer its insecurity would rise to intolerable levels. Reflecting that perspective, the Soviet Union had affirmed the Brezhnev Doctrine, in the aftermath of the 1968 invasion of Czechoslovakia. In it, Russia reserved the right of intervention to "save" any Eastern bloc country from "world imperialism," whether it wished to be saved or not.

Détente resolved the sticking point. In effect, it constituted a de facto acceptance of the Brezhnev Doctrine and an American acknowledgment that the USSR was the undisputed military-political policeman in Eastern Europe. That American acquiescence in Russian regional hegemony was the necessary price for economic entrée to Eastern Europe. It was an uncomfortable fee to pay, particularly since it generated some political backlash among some voters of Eastern European heritage in the United States. On the other hand, paying that price was not without its material benefit to the United States and the West. If capitalist investments, bank loans, and joint-stock ventures were to be significant in Eastern Europe, a regional power with the will and capacity to protect them and enforce adherence to contractual agreements would be needed. As corporations rely on unions to enforce work agreements on their own rank and file, the West needed Russia to enforce economic discipline on these client-states. In effect, the United States did what Britain had done at the turn of the century in acknowledging the Monroe Doctrine in the Caribbean basin and trusting the United States to protect British interests there as well as its own. It paid its obeisance to Russia's Monroe-style doctrine for Eastern Europe. The results were not unimpressive. By 1976, one-third of COMECON's trade was determined by world market prices, leading one Hungarian analyst to comment that Hungary's economy was "a socialist planned economy under the control of the market." Eastern Europe had been partially reintegrated into the world economy, and not even the renewed Cold War of the Carter and Reagan years could obliterate that fact.

In and of itself, the effort to penetrate the COMECON and Chinese economies would never have produced détente. American motivation was insufficiently strong to act as sole causation. It was the fortuitous conjuncture of that motive with other equally powerful factors, and the unique manner in which they combined to reinforce each other, that brought détente into being. Of those other factors, three were most significant: Russian military parity, the Sino-Soviet split, and independent initiatives by Europe. All would be modified and molded by the economic realities of American commercial decline, German and Japanese ascent, and the general economic contraction engendered by the collapse of the world monetary system, the OPEC oil shocks, and the deepening cycle of business recessions.

By 1970 nearly a decade of Russian military rearmament had brought that country to a station of near parity with American nuclear and strategic power. The American nuclear umbrella, for twenty-five years a crucial lever in gaining European and Japanese deference to American leadership, seemed far less serviceable, since now any American nuclear declaration almost certainly would reap a retaliatory Russian rebuttal. The Americans had two choices. They could up the level of military spending and technology to restore their superiority and first-strike capabilities. Alternatively, they could accept the new status quo, mutual assured destruction (MAD)—the ability of either superpower to survive a first strike and still respond with a rain of fire upon the other's great cities. "Let's put it in plain words," Nixon told the NATO Council in April 1969, "the West does not today have the massive nuclear predominance that it once had, and any sort of broad-based arms agreement with the Soviets would codify the present balance."

American leaders chose the second option because economic reality allowed no other. Massive military spending would only feed the domestic inflation that already had led middle-class America to question the Vietnam War and had perhaps further diminished the popular legitimacy of American hegemony. Moreover, it would only worsen the American balance of payments problem and the overseas dollar glut, and perhaps step up the European attack on the overvalued dollar and its privileged position as the global reserve currency. The choice of mutual deterrence was to make it possible for Nixon to reduce the armed forces from 3.5 million in 1968 to 2.3 million in 1973, and to end the draft in the latter year. The formal "codify[ing] of the present balance" resulted in the 1972 SALT I agreement (Strategic Arms Limitation Treaty), which restricted development of antiballistic missile systems (ABMs) and froze the numbers of intercontinental ballistic missiles (ICBMs) and submarine-launched ballistic missiles (SLBMs) more or less in place. Subsequently, the ill-fated SALT II negotiations of 1972–77 sought an absolute mutual limit on the number and types of delivery systems. SALT I failed to limit development of new offensive weapons systems and the SALT II's sought-for limit actually exceeded the real level already in place. So neither SALT I nor SALT II represented a reduction in the scale of nuclear weaponry. They did, however, represent American acceptance of sufficiency (parity) rather than superiority.

Facilitating the American acceptance of Russian military parity was the growing rift between the Soviet Union and the People's Republic of China. By 1969, the schism had resulted in major military encounters along their lengthy border, and sporadic rumors circulated of a possible preemptive nuclear strike by Russia against China. Internationally, China challenged Russia's dominance of the noncapitalist bloc by effecting a détente with Tito's Yugoslavia, praising Romania's efforts to follow an autonomous foreign policy, condemning Russia's invasion of Czechoslovakia, and supporting the increasingly independent political position of European communism, especially that of the Communist parties in Italy and France. Russia countered by making a treaty of trade and amity with India, perhaps China's staunchest Asian rival. Similarly, it sought to negotiate a peace treaty with Japan in the hopes that Russo-Japanese détente would check Chinese power in Asia, though that attempt in the early 1970s floundered over the Sakhalin territorial issue. Eventually, the 1970s would see Russia and China clash at least indirectly in the India-Pakistan war in 1971, the Angolan civil war in 1975–76, and the Vietnam-China border war in 1979.

The Sino-Soviet split was tailor-made for what came to be called "triangular diplomacy"—"the calculated management of policy on mutual relations between and among the United States, the Soviet Union, and China." Formulation of that "calculated management" began in 1969, during the Nixon administration's first year, with a series of national security study memoranda by the NSC (NSSM-14, -35, and -68). They began with a general reassessment of American alternatives for its China policy, proceeded to explore the future of trade with Communist China, and then, only after divining the trade possibilities, examined Sino-Soviet relations. That American rethinking climaxed three years later in February 1972 with Nixon's surprise trip to Beijing. It began a process that would climax by the decade's end in the full normalization of Sino-American relations. It was a process, as Kissinger described it, that would "send enormous shock waves around the world." That initial Nixon visit ended in a joint communiqué that stated in its conclusion, "Neither should seek hegemony in the Asia-Pacific region and each is opposed to efforts by any other country or group of countries to establish such hegemony."

The 1972 communiqué was the first substantive fruit of triangular diplomacy. Essentially it was an American effort to exploit the hostility between China and the Soviet Union. The key, however, was to keep the exploitation subtle enough that it did not drive the two former allies back together again. In Kissinger's judgment that meant doing three interrelated things. First, the United States should resist the temptation to force events that would widen the chasm between Russia and China. Instead, it should rely on "the dynamics of events" that evolved naturally from Sino-Soviet differences. Second, it should maintain an aura of uncertainty so neither Russia nor China could be sure in which, if any, direction America leaned. "The President," said Kissinger, "is in the position of the lovely maiden courted by two ardent swains, each of whom is aware of the other but each of whom is uncertain of what happens when the young lady is alone with his rival." Finally, and perhaps most importantly in a triangular relationship, it "served [American] purposes best if we maintained closer relations with each side than they did with each other."

President Nixon and National Security Adviser Kissinger maintained the public posture "that we are not colluding with, or accommodating, one at the expense of the other." Accordingly, they avoided overt political alignment, military aid, or even full diplomatic recognition of China in an effort not to provoke Russian hostility to levels that would damage other facets of détente. Tacitly, however, the Nixon administration always tilted toward China at Russia's expense. The United States and China quickly developed a tacit cooperation in the contested terrain of the Third World. For example, the American "tilt" in favor of Pakistan in its 1971 war with India was in fact a tilt toward China. Kissinger, quite erroneously, interpreted that war as "a sort of Sino-Soviet clash by proxy," with India acting as Russia's proxy and Pakistan as China's. The American dispatch of the Seventh Fleet to the Indian Ocean, and its implied though never intended threat to intervene in Pakistan's behalf, was in large part an effort to send the correct signal that would steady the resolve of "all our Allies, China, and the forces for restraint in other volatile areas of the world." Similarly, the United States and China backed the same factions in the Angolan civil war, the Front for the National Liberation of Angola (FNLA) and the National Union for the Total Independence of Angola (UNITA). Their shared purpose was to head off any successes by the Russian and Cuban-supported Popular Movement for the Liberation of Angola (MPLA). The United States would continue its support into the 1980s, while China withdrew support from Angola in late 1975 after UNITA began collaboration with South Africa and China began to fear for its revolutionary credentials with other Black republics in Africa. Nonetheless, for a two-year period, during the most crucial part of Angola's violent birth, China and the United States shared the same "proxies" in an obvious effort to diminish Russian influence.

Anti-Russian collaboration by the United States and China, however informal and indirect its forms might have been, obviously complicated détente between the Soviet Union and the United States. In other ways, however, that collaboration actually facilitated that relaxation of tensions. For the United States, the Sino-Soviet split made détente *possible*. Without it, the United States could not have afforded to cut military manpower in favor of more long-term, high-tech weapons development. Given Russian nuclear parity and conventional force superiority, such cuts would have severely damaged American credibility as protector of the First World and enforcer in the Third. The Russo-Chinese schism, however, kept such enormous amounts of Russian conventional and nuclear forces tied up in northern Asia that it significantly diminished Russia's capability for making war in Europe or aiding revolution in the periphery. For Russia, the Sino-Soviet split made détente *necessary*. Détente made it possible to concentrate a maximum of its resources on the Chinese challenge without jeopardizing Russian security in Europe. It also became the means of preventing a full-fledged Sino-American alliance. If the Cold War once more became the norm, Russia might confront a Sino-American "encirclement" more powerful and more extensive than anything since the German-Japanese anti-Comintern pact of the 1930s. On the other hand, so long as détente remained the designated standard, the United States was likely to keep its support of China more limited and tacit, and thus less threatening to the Soviet Union.

Finally, one more major factor drove both the United States and Russia toward détente. It was the independent initiatives of Europe to draw Russia into transnational regional arrangements that would promote economic interdependence, cross-cultural interactions, and reciprocal security. Reflecting the increasing economic and political clout of the EEC as well as America's declining hegemony, these autonomous ventures presented Russia with an offer too good to refuse and the United States with a *fait accompli* it could only accept.

Germany was the key European actor. During the 1960s the percentage increase in European East-West trade had been phenomenal, and the dynamic German economy was the major beneficiary. Germany and other EEC countries saw enormous possibilities for expanding the absolute volume of that trade in the 1970s—indeed far sooner than American business perceived such opportunities. "European countries look on us as suckers," said Senator Charles Percy of the Foreign Relations Committee. "When they see restrictions by the U.S. government on our doing business with Eastern European countries . . . they are amazed that we have such blinders on. In our ideological battle, what we forget is that what we lack is gold, and what we need is trade."

Two factors persuaded Germans and other Europeans that significant further trade expansion could not occur without a full-scale restructuring of European-Russian security and political relations. One was the Czechoslovakian suppression in 1968 and the subsequent Brezhnev Doctrine that made abundantly clear that Russia feared that increased East-West economic ties might diminish Russian security in Eastern Europe. The other related factor was continued Russian fear of latent German expansionism and the possibility that Germany might "go nuclear." Powerfully reinforcing these perceptions was the decisive factor of German politics. In 1969, the Social Democratic party (SDP), under the leadership of Willy Brandt, came to power in West Germany. Brandt and the SDP had long made German reunification their primary goal and had favored *Ostpolitik* ("Eastern policy", closer relations with Russia and COMECON) as the means to secure it.

Germany commenced to play the Russian card in 1969. It signed a nuclear nonproliferation treaty in January, thus easing Russian fears of Germany joining the "nuclear club." *Ostpolitik* shifted into high gear the following year. After numerous meetings between Brandt and Soviet Foreign

Minister Andrei Gromyko, West Germany and Russia signed a nonaggression pact in August 1970. Germany implicitly recognized the realities of Russian-imposed postwar boundaries. Four months later, in December 1970, Germany made its recognition explicit in a treaty with Poland that accepted the territorial gains Poland had made in 1945 at Germany's expense. Two years later, after complex negotiations, Brandt climaxed his opening up to the East by signing a treaty with East Germany in which each party diplomatically recognized the other. Brandt's hope was that the dynamic of equal Germanies dealing with each other would be more likely to produce eventual reunification than the dynamic of equal superpowers deciding Germany's fate for it.

Germany's initiative took place in the context of a larger European initiative, and it acted as a catalyst to accelerate the latter. Since 1966, the Warsaw Pact had sought a general conference on European security, while NATO since 1968 had requested talks on mutual balanced force reductions (MBFR) in the European theater. The Czechoslovakian crisis of 1968 had slowed initiatives on both sides, but Germany's *Ostpolitik* revived lost momentum. So too did the American Senate's consideration of the Mansfield resolution in 1971 calling for a substantial unilateral reduction of American troops in Europe. It alarmed American policymakers, who feared such a move would damage American credibility in Europe and elsewhere. It alarmed Russian leaders, who saw a continued American military presence as a useful counterweight to German influence in NATO and a barrier to any German reconsideration of the nuclear option. It alarmed Western European decisionmakers, who feared American withdrawal would make them potentially more vulnerable to a variety of challenges from Russia and Germany.

All these variables finally combined to create the Conference on Security and Cooperation in Europe (CSCE) in 1973. Its study groups and negotiating teams worked for two years, on the neutral ground of Finland, and finally produced the Helsinki Accords in July 1975. The Helsinki Accords were the high-water mark of détente. Their three major parts focused on security, economic cooperation, and humanitarian issues. The first amounted to a generalized nonaggression pact and confidence-building measures such as agreement to give advance notice of military exercises. The second part committed East and West to promoting freer transnational trade, joint manufacturing ventures, technology transfers, transportation, tourism, and labor migration. The last pledged greater educational and cultural exchange, including freer access to print and electronic media and more liberal regulation of transnational marital unions, visits by relatives, and reuniting of families.

The Helsinki agreements offered Russia an opportunity too inviting to decline. To be sure, the USSR feared that section three would unduly promote Western culture and lifestyles in COMECON countries, and later, in the 1970s, Russia would have second thoughts about sections on security and economics. In 1975, however, those provisions seemed to serve Russian interests well by implicitly validating Russia's suzerainty in Eastern Europe and by facilitating the Western financial and technical assistance that would be necessary if Eastern Europe were to be modernized and Russia's economic burden reduced. As a consequence, Brezhnev praised CSCE achievements lavishly, though not unreservedly, at the Twenty-fifth Party Congress in 1976.

For the United States, the 1975 agreement was a fact of life it had to accept, but it had serious misgivings. In the late 1960s, the United States had been unenthusiastic about the possibility of NATO-Warsaw pact negotiations. Projected over time, such a process might reunite Eastern and Western Europe into an autonomous whole, might undermine America's hegemonic position as free world leader, or might create separate Euro-Russian accords on security and trade. That fear eased substantially in 1972 when the United States insisted on, and Russia accepted, American participation in the CSCE talks. Even with on-going American input, however, the final agreement evoked mixed American feelings. Certainly sections two and three fit well with American interests in promoting cultural pluralism and market economics in Eastern Europe. On the other hand, the first section's tacit acceptance of a Russian sphere in Eastern Europe was certain to spark domestic political criticism in the United States. Indeed, Democratic Senator Henry Jackson of Washington called the Helsinki venture "misguided and empty" and Republican Governor Ronald Reagan of California said of the final agreement, "I think all Americans should be against it."

More fundamentally and enduringly, the Helsinki Accords raised fears among American leaders that Europe would be so euphoric about the spirit of Helsinki that it would pursue across-the-board reduction of military forces in Europe. The end result might seriously erode the American military presence and role as Europe's protector and further diminish American hegemony. In the context of 1975, such fears were not academic. Revolution in Portugal seemed to portend a communist triumph and Portugal's exit from NATO. In Italy, the government teetered on the brink and finally fell from power in early 1976, raising the possibility of communist participation in a coalition government. French and Italian communists pledged themselves to a "democratic path to socialism" and carved out positions increasingly independent of Moscow's—a development known as Eurocommunism. Collectively, these developments presented the possibility of a Europe both more leftist and more autonomous. That such a leftist Europe might also be independent of Russian domination made it seem no less a threat to the continued integration of Europe into a larger, trans-Atlantic community. In a revealing statement, Kissinger told American ambassadors overseas, "the extent to which such a [Eurocommunist] party follows the Moscow line is *unimportant* [emphasis added]. Even if Portugal had followed the Italian model, we would still have been opposed. . . . [The] impact of an Italian Communist Party that seemed to be governing effectively would be devastating—on France, and on NATO, too."

In time, Eurocommunism would fade as a political force in Europe. Nonetheless, America's fears of European autonomy, a constant since de Gaulle's empowerment in the early 1960s, would remain a constant into the 1980s. In the mid-1970s, however, American leaders had to shunt that fear aside and accept the fact that Russian-American détente had been transformed and broadened into a general East-West détente. To do otherwise might have prompted a European backlash and might have damaged America's own "relaxation of tensions" with Russia, which was so important to America's own economic need, military security, and experiments in triangular diplomacy.

Détente and the American Public

By the presidential election of 1976, détente was a non-word in American politics. Neither candidate, Republican Gerald Ford or Democrat Jimmy Carter, could invoke the term without risking political damage. That political reality was a barometer of the strains and contradictions from which détente had begun to suffer. As established policy for both Russia and the United States, for both the East and West, détente would remain at least partially intact until early 1979. Signs of erosion, however, were increasingly evident by 1976. The causes were to be found in the denouement in Vietnam, in a realigned domestic opinion decidedly hostile to détente, in a Eurocommunism equally threatening to both the USSR and the United States, and in differences between Russia and America over the relationship of their détente to the periphery and semiperiphery.

Vietnam was the first wound in the heart of détente. After the 1968 Tet offensive and Johnson's withdrawal from the presidential race, American policy waffled between continued war-making on one hand and tentative peace talks and scaled-down bombing raids on the other. Richard Nixon came to the presidency in 1969 with a "secret plan" to end that policy drift and the war itself. His surprise offering was the Nixon Doctrine and so-called Vietnamization. While acknowledging the limits of American power and the failure of military escalation, Nixon reaffirmed the fifteen-year-old American commitment to make South Vietnam a viable nation-state and, in addition, a stabilizing force for the whole Indochina region. In essence, he stated that the United States could help Third World peoples, but in the last analysis, they had to save themselves. In the future, therefore, the United States would avoid opting for unilateral military intervention—for more Vietnam Wars—but instead give others the economic and military wherewithal to fight their own battles. (The American ambassador in Saigon called it "changing the color of the corpses.")

Making South Vietnam into a viable country had even less chance of success in 1969 than it had in the late 1950s when Eisenhower had first tried his nation-building enterprise. Both Nixon and Kissinger privately understood that fact. "I've come to the conclusion that there's no way to win the war," the President told several aides. "But we can't say that, of course." In private conversations on the eve of his formal appointment as National Security Adviser, Kissinger repeatedly told associates at Harvard the same thing. Advocating a policy of "decent interval," he hoped for a delay of two to three years between American withdrawal and South Vietnam's surrender that would avoid the appearance of a direct defeat for the United States.

Nixon initially hoped that the "decent interval" could begin by early 1970. He apparently based this optimism on his self-confident ability to use the carrot and stick to get an acceptable settlement with North Vietnam and the NLF. The stick would be a replay of the atomic diplomacy that Eisenhower allegedly used to end the Korean War. He *would* use the threat of nuclear weapons, he told one adviser. The carrot would be Russian intercession with North Vietnam, since the new President "believe[d] the Soviet Union would like to use what influence it could appropriately to help bring the war to a conclusion." Atomic diplomacy, however, was never credible, since the political fallout at home and abroad would certainly have been catastrophic. Moreover, the notion of Russian intercession rested upon a debatable assumption about Russian intent and an exaggerated assumption about the extent of Russian control over North Vietnam.

When his optimism proved misplaced, Nixon chose to put Indochina through the meatgrinder of Vietnamization for four long, bloody years. While gradually withdrawing American troops and finally ending the draft, the administration poured money into an effort to make the ARVN into a bigger and better fighting force. It also stepped up bombings raids, including secret B-52 attacks on Cambodia. Eventually, it expanded the land war into both Cambodia (1970) and Laos (1971), in an effort to interdict North Vietnamese supplies, to create a buffer along South Vietnam's lengthy western frontier, and to replace Cambodia's neutralist government with a right-wing military regime allied to the United States. However, the ARVN's ineptness and North Vietnam's expanded military operations in early 1972 laid bare the futility of Vietnamization. Only massive

American bombing of North Vietnam and the mining of its harbors staved off total disaster in 1972. But the United States could not go on playing Linebacker (as the seven-month-long bombing operation was called), forever plugging holes in the ARVN's line to stop the on-rushing opponent. The clarity of that fact finally forced the Nixon administration into serious negotiations in late 1972.

Peace seemed at hand in October when North Vietnam and the United States agreed to a ceasefire, to a staged withdrawal of American troops, an exchange of POWs, and to political arrangements, including elections, to settle Vietnam's future. South Vietnam, however, balked at the retention of North Vietnamese troops in the south during the interim period. Despite American promises of continued support, it refused to sign the agreement. In an effort to demonstrate the intensity of sustained American commitment, Nixon unleashed the long war's most violent bombing of the North: Linebacker II, the so-called "Christmas bombings." North Vietnam paid the price, but the offensive's major objective was to impress South Vietnam with American resolve. Still reluctant, the south nonetheless succumbed to American pressure and signed an agreement in early 1973 that was substantially the same as the one it had rejected in late 1972—but with a secret addendum pledging American support if North Vietnam violated the accord. Untenable on the face of it, the ceasefire did indeed collapse as each side used force to position itself more securely for any political settlement. Lacking either the unity or the sense of purpose of its battlefield adversary, the Army of the Republic of South Vietnam fared poorly in 1974 and finally dissolved in ignominious defeat in 1975. At the same time, Khmer Rouge revolutionaries were capturing Cambodia's capital city and the Laotian coalition government was collapsing and giving way to a communist regime. Nation building had come to Indochina with a vengeance, but not in the manner or with the results envisioned by America two decades earlier.

The shockingly sudden collapse of Saigon and the rest of Indochina seemed to much of the public an "indecent interval" and made it impossible to mask the reality of American defeat. The United States seemed, to many, like the "pitiful, helpless giant" Nixon had warned against in 1970. Gerald Ford, succeeding to the presidency after Nixon's Watergate-induced resignation, attempted to give the lie to the image by raiding Cambodian territory to free thirty-eight merchant seamen confined by Cambodia after its navy seized the American cargo ship *Mayaguez*. Supported by majority public opinion that America had demonstrated it was no paper tiger, Ford's venture in gunboat diplomacy provided at best modest, short-term therapy for the national image. Moreover, the ineptitude of the raid's timing and execution was disquieting to a nation coming to grips with the loss of its omnipotence. Cambodia had actually released the crew hours before the raid, and the attack itself cost forty American lives.

The confidence-shattering loss of Indochina in 1975, combined with an on-going realignment of domestic political opinion, offered a very serious challenge to the policy of détente with Russia. Seasoned cold warriors had always opposed détente and peaceful coexistence, either on the grounds that the Soviets were wholly untrustworthy or that it was bad for the profits of the American defense industry. Since the mid-1960s, however, another component of anti-détente opinion had increasingly emerged. Its common denominator was its concern for Israel's survival as a nation-state. Its common fear was the possibility that détente would lull the United States into reducing its moral and material commitment to Israel, while Russia would maintain or enlarge its own commitment to the Arab enemies of Israel. Most such proponents were Jewish, often liberals mutating into conservatives (neoconservatives), and sometimes prominent in opinion-influencing fields. Their number included, for example, Irving Kristol, editor of *Policy Review*, Martin Peretz, editor of the *New Republic*, Norman Podhoretz, editor of *Commentary*, and Ben Wattenberg of the American Enterprise Institute. Others were not Jewish but led economic and political constituencies with important Jewish participation: for example, George Meany and Lane Kirkland, both of the AFL-CIO, and Senator Patrick Moynihan of New York and Adlai Stevenson III of Illinois.

The Yom Kippur or October War of 1973 seemed to confirm the worst fears of such Israel supporters. In a surprise war engineered by Anwar Sadat of Egypt, Israel initially suffered alarmingly high losses, then rallied to repulse its Arab opponents, and eventually crossed the Suez Canal and threatened to trap the Egyptian Third Army in the Sinai Desert. In a stress-filled period stretching over many weeks, America's resupply of the Israeli military was crucial to its resurgence, and the Nixon administration did call a worldwide alert of American military forces when Russia threatened to intervene unilaterally if the United States failed to join it in enforcing a UN cease-fire on Israel. In the eyes of pro-Israeli Americans, however, this American support of Israel was more than offset by two disturbing developments. First, the United States joined the USSR in cosponsoring the UN resolution that demanded a cease-fire before Israel could complete its encirclement of the Egyptian army. Second, the United States sternly threatened to end its resupply operation if Israel did not end its violations of the cease-fire and agree to a truce.

The lesson drawn by Israel's supporters from these developments was not that détente had failed; that they would have welcomed. On the contrary, despite the Soviet-American tension during the American military alert, détente by and large worked. It worked, however, in ways contrary to

Israel's long-term desire to maximize its freedom to pursue its own security. Détente in operation had demonstrated that the two superpowers might collude in ways inimical to chosen Israeli policy. It also demonstrated increased sensitivity by American leaders to the economic clout manifested in the OPEC oil embargo during the war. Taken together, Russian-American détente and OPEC solidarity seemed to pro-Israelis to pose a situation far different and far less satisfactory than the earlier epoch (the 1967 Six Days' War, for example) when they could count on simple, uncompromisingly pro-Israeli, anti-Soviet policy by the United States.

The political effect of the October War was to intensify and enlarge the coalition of anticommunist ideologues, military-industrial politicos, and American supporters of Israel. Most prominent in its leadership was Senator Henry Jackson of Washington. A long-time anticommunist, supporter of Israel, and defender of the defense industry ("the senator from Boeing," said some derisively), Jackson also had strong presidential ambitions. Identifying himself with the attack on détente therefore became a means by which he hoped to broaden his political base, tapping into the wide ideological diversity present in the curious-bedfellows coalition of conservatives and liberals.

The major consequence of these political developments was to change and complicate the concept of "linkage" that American leaders had brought to détente. The original notion conceived a linkage between economic benefits for the USSR and acceptable Soviet foreign policy. If the Russians played by the American rules of the international game they would be rewarded with most-favored-nation (MFN) trade status and with generous access to credits from the Export-Import Bank. Such was the intent of the trade reform bill introduced in 1973 by the Nixon administration as an integral part of détente. In October 1973, however, Jackson coauthored the Jackson-Vanik amendment to that trade bill, which would have denied MFN status to Russia unless it liberalized emigration for its Jewish citizens. Although annual Jewish emigration from the Soviet Union had recently increased from fifteen thousand to thirty-five thousand, it fell significantly short of the sixty thousand that Jackson publicly demanded. A year later, in 1974 Adlai Stevenson III introduced his own amendment, which would have limited Export-Import Bank credits for the USSR to a total of $300 million over a four-year span, a sum far less than Russia already enjoyed without the trade reform legislation. Taken together, the Jackson-Vanik amendment and the Stevenson amendment killed MFN status and export-import credits for Russia and gutted the economic component of détente. More importantly, it transformed the meaning of linkage. Détente would depend on proper Soviet behavior not only in its foreign policy, but also in its internal policies toward Jews and toward dissidents in general. By 1976, Secretary of State Kissinger had concluded that "the principal danger we face is our own domestic divisions."

Détente, Europe, and the Third World

The secretary's assessment was perhaps overstated—he had made similar judgments at times about the primacy of external dangers. The two most prominent concerned the inability of détente to assimilate Eurocommunism and a similar, more serious inability of détente to transcend Russian-American competition in the Third World periphery. Eurocommunism was threatening to the USSR and the United States alike. As we have seen, American leaders strongly feared that Europe was moving rapidly to the left, under the influence of Eurocommunism. If it journeyed very far in that direction the result might be the destruction of NATO and the transformation of the Common Market into an independent European venture, less integrated into a trans-Atlantic economy. Not only did American policymakers worry about Portugal's leftist revolution and Italy's political chaos, they were anxious about Spain's political future after Franco's death in 1975, about Greece's political polarization, and about that country's clash with Turkey over control of Cyprus. In effect, the whole southern rim of Europe, the Mediterranean world, seemed to be sliding away from its North Atlantic moorings. In two respects, this independent European left was more threatening to American interests than European communist parties dominated by Moscow would have been. The latter would probably have been less popular since their nationalist credentials would have been suspect. Moreover, the latter could be expected to respond to Soviet discipline and direction. Eurocommunist parties, however, were not only popular and legitimate but unresponsive to Soviet discipline. In effect, détente could not be used to contain the European left and keep it from unsettling the status quo.

Eurocommunism was equally threatening to the Soviet Union. Not only did it not automatically function as an external arm of Russian foreign policy, its withdrawal of obeisance to the Soviet Union damaged that nation's long-cultivated image as the fountainhead of revolutionary change in the world. Principal offenders, in Soviet eyes, were the Italian and Spanish Communist parties, who led the way in condemning the 1968 intervention in Czechoslovakia. French communists joined that list of transgressors in 1975 by casting their lot with the Eurocommunist movement.

Even more alarming to the Soviets was the spillover of Eurocommunism's influence into Eastern Europe. By mid-decade, both Romania and Yugoslavia had begun to take public policy positions closer to those of the Italian and French communists than to those of Russia. Moreover, Poland joined Romania and Yugoslavia in promoting Western economic ties at a pace uncomfortably fast for the Soviets. By 1976, Polish industrial strife was offering intimations of Solidarity's future formation, and one Polish leader affirmed that "Polish Communists have an ambition to play an important role in Europe, creating a mode of socialism acceptable to everyone, including our comrades in both directions"—east and west. By 1976, Russia's leading ideologist was attacking Eurocommunists as "enemies of Marxism" and of Russia's "real socialism"; and the head of the Bulgarian Communist party, Moscow's closet ally, condemned their "anti-Sovietism" and "subversion against proletarian internationalism." In an earlier Cold War context, when those parties were confronted with a common capitalist foe, such words would have carried sledge-hammer impact. In the looser atmosphere of détente, they were more stinging than crushing. In effect, détente made it as difficult for Russia to control the European left as for America to contain it.

Détente's inability to digest Eurocommunism was compounded by its inability to deter Russo-American conflict in the Third World. At the root of the failure were fundamental differences between the Soviet Union and the United States over the very meaning of détente. From the Soviet perspective, détente denoted "a changing world, one no longer marked by American predominance but by a political parity of the Soviet Union with the United States that matched their military parity." That notion of political parity implied two things for the Third World. First, the USSR would collaboratively share political dominance in areas where both had substantial national interests, like the Middle East. Second, the United States would accept the political legitimacy of competition between capitalism and socialism in those parts of the periphery, like Africa and Latin America, where Russian interests were less direct and developed.

From the American perspective, however, détente never meant political parity with the Soviets. It meant military parity, as SALT I had confirmed. It also meant, as Nixon acknowledged, that Russia was one of "the five great economic superpowers," along with America, Japan, the EEC, and China, who would "determine the course of the economic future." Acknowledging political parity, however, would have been tantamount to relinquishing American hegemony, and that the United States was not prepared to do in the early 1970s. Indeed, American leaders viewed détente as a way to sustain that hegemony. It was to be the means by which a still dominant America could "manage" Russia's re-entry into the world-system in ways that would insure its acceptance of the American rules of the game or codes of conduct. Similar to the policy of economic appeasement in the 1930s, détente was to persuade Russia that operating inside the world-system and playing by its internationalist rules was both safer and more profitable than staying outside that system and confronting it across a Cold War chasm. "By acquiring a stake in this network of relationships with the West," Kissinger declared, "the Soviet Union may become more conscious of what it has to lose by a return to confrontation."

Contrary to Russian expectations, America's rules and codes did not accept Russian co-suzerainty in the Middle East or the legitimacy of "the socialist road" elsewhere in the periphery, even when that road was peaceful and democratic. In the Middle East, a principal purpose of American policy was "to reduce the role and influence of the Soviet Union," and détente, as Kissinger affirmed, was simply a different strategy to achieve that goal. Indeed, the strategy worked well in the early 1970s. In the aftermath of the Six Days' War in 1967, Russia had strongly supported Egypt with military and technical aid to rebuild its defeated army, while the United States upped the technological level and dollar value of its military aid to victorious Israel ($1.2 billion in 1971–73). After the death of the Egyptian president, Nasser, in 1970, Russia began to retrench its aid and refused requests from Anwar Sadat, Nasser's successor, to accelerate its help in preparing Egypt to recoup its 1967 territorial losses. Sadat interpreted the Russian rebuffs as proof that the USSR valued its developing détente with the United States more than its political support in the Arab world. Reassessing his options, the Egyptian leader broke his Soviet connection, expelling twenty thousand Russian advisers and technicians in 1972, and sought a new tie-up with the United States. In March 1973, Egypt's chief national security adviser met with Kissinger and requested American political pressure on Israel to force it to return the Sinai to Egypt. Contemptuous of Egyptian power, especially after the Soviet expulsion, Kissinger admitted that "in my heart I laughed and laughed" at Egyptian warnings that "if there wasn't some agreement then there would be war. . . . A war? Egypt? I regarded it as empty talk, a boast empty of content." With Russia neutralized, Israel armed, and Egypt an idle threat, the United States ignored the Egyptian initiative and opted for "standstill diplomacy" in 1973.

That do-nothing policy served détente well before the October War. In the absence of any likely Middle East crisis, the United States could afford to give Russia a token role in the region. Soviet-American summit meetings in the early 1970s often included joint declarations of agreed-upon principles for solving the Israeli-Arab conflict. The vague statements gave Russia a sense of co-participation in the region, while the misleadingly stable situation made concrete actions unnecessary. The Yom Kippur War, however, struck a sharp blow to Russian illusions about sharing the policeman role in the region. While the USSR and the United States cooperated in fashioning the initial cease-fire, Israeli reluctance to carry out its terms made Russia suspicious that Israeli behavior had tacit American support. In an effort to determine the direction of American policy, Russia proposed a joint Soviet-American intervention to force Israeli compliance. It ended its proposal with an admonition that the USSR would have to act alone if the United States did not join it as a partner, and it readied some fifty thousand Russian troops for possible airlift to Egypt. The immediate American response was, as Kissinger later described it, "our *deliberate* overreaction." The United States announced a worldwide alert of its military forces, warned the Soviets against unilateral intervention, and made clear it would not support Soviet troops as part of any UN peacekeeping force to enforce the truce in the Sinai.

The American overreaction dissolved any Russian illusions that détente meant a share of police power in the Middle East. Kissinger's subsequent "shuttle diplomacy" between 1973 and 1976 drove the point home. Foreign Minister Gromyko made the Russian awareness clear when he told President Ford at Helsinki in 1975, "We understood that you were going to include us in the [Middle East] peace process and that our two countries would work together. Here you are, going off on a tangent. This is contrary to the spirit of détente, and it's upsetting us." Ignoring those Russian sentiments, Kissinger pursued his own unilateral course. Aware of his underestimation of Egyptian power and now convinced that American interests could not long be maintained in an Arab region while operating only through a non-Arab ally, Israel, the secretary of state jetted between the United States and the Middle East, and between Cairo and Tel Aviv, in an effort to wean Egypt into the American camp and to normalize Egyptian-Israeli relations. The latter goal floundered temporarily on the complexities of the Palestinian refugee question and the role of the Palestine Liberation Organization (PLO). Nonetheless, Israel did agree in 1975 to withdraw from the Sinai and agreed with Egypt, to accept a UN-policed buffer zone. By 1976, Egypt had finished with the last vestiges of Russian military assistance, began receipt of substantial American aid in its place, and symbolically stood by while Israel invaded Lebanon against Egypt's former Syrian ally. As Sadat put it, "ninety-nine percent of the cards in the game are in American hands whether the Soviet Union likes it or not." Egypt and Israel were now both part of the American network—and well on the road to the Camp David accords of 1978.

The October War followed by less than a month the overthrow of Salvador Allende's government in Chile, and the latter disabused the Soviets of another notion about the meaning of détente. Once an economic dependency of Great Britain, Chile had drifted into the American economic orbit after World War I. By the post-World War II period, its raw materials and communications infrastructure were largely controlled by American corporate giants like Kendicott and ITT. But in the 1960s, Chilean centrists had begun experiments with "Chileanization"—the requirement that foreign enterprises become joint ventures with 51 percent Chilean control to insure some profit reinvestment in Chile itself rather than profit repatriation back to New York. In 1970, the Chilean people went one step further, electing a socialist to the presidency. Salvador Allende, a long-time Marxist spokesman in the Chilean Senate, became Chile's chief executive pledged to go beyond Chileanization to the outright expropriation of foreign holdings and to the planned development of Chilean industrialization. He aimed to use wealth redistribution to build up the internal market for industry, rather than use austerity measures to become competitive in the world market.

Unable to block Allende's election in 1970 (though it tried), the United States launched a sustained effort to destabilize his government and bring it down. Using a combined "insider, outsider" strategy, the United States targeted anti-Allende forces in Chile for American support, while trying to isolate the nation from external economic and diplomatic support. Support went to conservative trade unionists, many trained by the American Institute for Free Labor Development, in Front Royal, Virginia, to Chilean army officers, many trained at Fort Benning or in the Panama Canal Zone, and to anti-Allende politicos, many of whom were recipients of CIA money. All were encouraged in the counterrevolutionary role they already aspired to. The American government spent $6–8 million on its destabilization efforts inside Chile, and American corporations and trade unions expended a further, undeterminable amount. Externally, the United States cut off economic aid (save that to the friendly Chilean army) and penalized Chilean exports. It used its influence with the World Bank and private American banks to deny long-term lending and encouraged European and Latin American nations to follow similar courses of action. "Make the economy scream!" President Nixon exhorted his subordinates. Scream, it did. Buffeted by rampant inflation and fears about their property rights, Chile's middle class turned to the pro-American military to oust Allende forcibly, after the 1973 congressional elections failed to diminish his political strength. The end result was the overthrow and murder of Allende in 1973 and his replacement by a repressive miltiary regime, whose austere economic policies mirrored the advice of "the Chicago boys" (Chilean disciples of University of Chicago economist Milton Friedman) on the best ways to modernize.

The Chilean coup, coupled with the October War, would sharply modify and limit the meaning of détente. Russia had hoped détente would mean the legitimization of free competition between capitalism and socialism in the Third World, especially when it took place at the ballot box. The United States, however, assumed détente would mean Russian acceptance of the status quo in the periphery and a commitment not to rock the boat by encouraging radical actions. In the case of Chile, Russia's involvement with the Allende government was minimal, and its indirect advice to Allende was to curb his more radical followers and to proceed cautiously. Even so, the United States would not accept the electoral validation of a noncapitalist road. "I don't see why we need stand by," said Kissinger, "and watch a country go communist due to the irresponsibility of its own government."

Allende's overthrow made clear the unbridgeable gap between Russian and American conceptions of détente's relationship to the Third World. Any implication that it involved a diminution of America's hegemonic policeman role in the periphery was clearly invalid. The peaceful, democratic route to socialism was no more acceptable than the violent, revolutionary one. Both violated "the rules of the game," "the codes" of economic internationalism, and both were subject to possible American intervention, however covert its form might be. Faced with this reality, and the parallel reality of its exclusion from the Middle East, the Soviet Union seemed to confront two stark choices. It could abandon the Third World, the necessary price for continued and still useful détente with the United States and with Western Europe, or it could abandon détente in order to uphold its ideological legitimacy and revolutionary credentials, both at home and abroad. Instead, it opted for a middle way, sometimes known as "sub-imperialism." At the same time, and for somewhat similar reasons, the United States embraced the same option.

Sub-Imperialism and Modified Détente

Sub-imperialism means the use of substitutes, or proxies, to act on behalf of a given core power. Such surrogates were peripheral or semiperipheral nations whose own regional interests largely dovetailed with those of their core patron. Often newly industrializing countries that were far advanced in political integration, they presumably had the ability to absorb large amounts of high-tech military assistance and, if need be, put it to effective use either through force or through the threat of force. Cold War use of such proxies certainly began before the 1970s, but developments early in the seventies rapidly widened their use.

One such development was the increased self-questioning about America's capacity and will to act unilaterally as world policeman. The overextension of American power in Vietnam, the decline of the American economy, and the domestic backlash against military intervention abroad posed anew the perennial problem of any hegemonic power: while its interests were virtually limitless, its means clearly were not. Yet, in the 1970s, American elites continued to see the need for global policing if the world-system was to be a single, integrated, free world, playing by one set of internationalist rules. Suasion and rewards might well serve to secure the adherence of most to those rules, but there would always be those whose ideologies and interests would produce deviation from those norms. For them, coercion—military or economic, overt or covert—was the only answer that came readily to the minds of American leaders. If, however, American power was too constrained to be universally and unilaterally applied, then there was one obvious solution. The United States could turn to trusted regional allies in the semiperiphery and enlist their aid in maintaining the status quo in their part of the world-system.

That same device offered the obvious solution to the Russian-American tensions over détente's relationship to the Third World. By 1974, it was obvious to both the Americans and the Soviets that their different conceptions of détente's implementation in the periphery were quite irreconcilable. Détente might codify the nuclear status quo, enlarge economic intercourse, and enhance ties between the two halves of Europe. It would not, however, end Soviet-American competition in the outer zones of the world-system. Nonetheless, acting out that competition through surrogates offered a way to minimize Soviet-American friction and to keep great power rivalry in the periphery from undermining the entire edifice of détente. This sub-imperialism had its own danger—that unilateral actions by proxies might drag the great powers into open conflict, against their interests and judgment. In other words, the tail might wag the dog. Taken on balance, however, the strategy seemed a way to make Soviet-American competition in the Third World indirect and once-removed and, hopefully, less dangerous to world peace. In effect, both the United States and Russia globalized the Nixon Doctrine of supplying regional clients with guns and money, but little manpower, to help them fight or foster revolution, as the case might be. Nowhere was this better exemplified than in the Middle East and in southern Africa.

In the Middle East, Israel remained the principal American surrogate; but Egypt was assuming nearly equal importance, as it completed its reverse course from the Russian to the American orbit. Stung by that reversal and by its exclusion from the regional peace process, Russia retaliated by intensifying its aid to Syria and Iraq. The United States, however, more than offset that development by transforming Shah Pahlavi's Iran into an important military power. Iran's tasks were to check radical Iraq, block Soviet overland access to the region, and police the oil-rich Persian Gulf. Nixon's state visit to Teheran in 1972 resulted in an open-ended invitation for the Shah to spend unlimited amounts of his petrodollars on high-tech arms purchases from the United States. During the next half-decade, before his overthrow, the Shah purchased a staggering $20 billion in arms from the United States—"like a drunk using a credit card in a liquor store," ventured one American critic. At the same time, the American army and the CIA developed close, symbiotic relations with the Iranian military and with SAVAK, Iran's infamous secret police. While the Shah used his military might more for internal repression than external policing, American politicos and academics continued in the mid-1970s to give him high

marks for his alleged benevolence in guiding his traditional culture into the
bright sunlight of modernity. "An island of stability," said Jimmy Carter,
after his election to the presidency in 1976.

The United States used the Republic of South Africa, a continent's
length south of Suez, as another regional surrogate. To be sure, it did so in a
less open, more equivocating fashion than it used Iran, partly because of
domestic American criticism of that regime's racist social policy of apartheid. Nonetheless, Kissinger's "tar baby" report of 1969 and NSC memoranda of 1970 clearly dismissed Black insurgent movements as not "realistic and supportable," and concluded that "the whites are here to stay and
the only way that constructive change can come about is through them."
Accordingly, the United States relaxed its arms embargo against South
Africa in 1970 and facilitated military shipments to that country, while encouraging other surrogates, like Israel and Iran, to do the same. Relatedly,
the United States defied a UN economic boycott and began purchases of
raw materials from Rhodesia'a white minority government, knowing they
would foster that country's purchasing powers in the international arms
market.

The utility of that South African connection was put to the test in the
mid-1970s, and came up suspect. Beginning in 1974, an Angolan revolution, led by the Popular Movement for the Liberation of Angola and supported by Soviet aid, challenged Portuguese colonial rule and finally
toppled it in 1975. But, as in Zaire's ouster of Belgian colonialism a decade
earlier, Angolan independence merely mutated into a civil war over who
would rule now that home rule had been secured. The CIA had given clan-
destine aid to UNITA and FNLA, anti-MPLA forces, even before independence. Now the United States stepped up that effort and, more especially,
encouraged South Africa to do the same. In early August 1975, South
Africa began a limited military incursion into southern Angola; and in October, three thousand South African regulars (the number later doubled)
joined with UNITA forces in a major offensive. In turn, the USSR escalated
its aid and, in particular, encouraged Cuba to do likewise, acting as the
Russian surrogate while also acting out its own ambitions to lead a Pan-
African liberation movement in the Caribbean and West Africa.

In 1976, the Cuban and Russian-backed MPLA won out over the South
African and American-backed opposition. Still, the internal conflict lin-
gered in desultory fashion into the 1980s. Despite Angolan efforts to work
out profitable arrangements with American oil companies and to invite
Western capital and technology, the United States would persist in its efforts to destabilize that country from within. In that pursuit, it collaborated
with South Africa, notwithstanding the latter's own political, economic,
and racial crises in the mid-1970s and again in the mid-1980s. Clearly, the

short-run profits of specific American business interests took a back seat to the global concerns of the state. As Henry Kissinger put it: "You may be right in African terms, but I'm thinking globally." Not until the late 1980s, with renewed détente apparently in the making, would America's global thinking find merit in pursuing a negotiated withdrawal of both Cuban and South African troops and a political settlement for Angola.

In 1976, America commemorated its bicentennial. More than a celebration of two hundred years of American independence, it was also a therapeutic binge to help America forget about the previous decade of turmoil and decline. The years between 1968 and 1977 had witnessed unparalleled domestic division of opinion over the benevolence of the imperial presidency and the efficacy and propriety of America's global policing. Public dissent was less sharply focused by 1976 than it had been during the Vietnam War, and it competed with a counter yearning to resume a more assertive role in world affairs. Yet the divisions remained strong, and the frustrations over the inability to resolve them would play an important role in the loss of confidence that President Jimmy Carter in 1979 called a "national malaise."

Externally, the decline of American economic power, its inability to use its leadership to deflect worldwide recession, and the emergence of vigorous capitalist competition from its old World War II enemies, Germany and Japan, all meant that America could no longer call the economic shots in the world-system. The dollar was devalued; the gold standard was junked; and international economic decisionmaking partially collectivized in the annual economic summits of core country heads of state, more frequent and important meetings of their central bank directors, and in the on-going study groups of quasi-private organizations like the Trilateral Commission. And yet none of these changes stayed the decline of American manufacturing, the geometric increases in its trade deficit, its transformation toward *rentier* status, or the consequent price in domestic stagflation paid so dearly by a divided American people.

During the same time, American leaders had been forced to accept the legitimacy of Russia's status as a superpower and to modify their rhetoric and behavior toward America's Cold War adversary of twenty-five years' standing. This acceptance of détente meant the formal acknowledgment of Russian hegemony in Eastern Europe. To be sure, by 1976 détente became a non-word, in the aftermath of Saigon's fall and Russo-Cuban involvement in African revolutionary movements. Nonetheless, détente's rhetorical demise did not necessarily mean its end as policy. Whether American leaders liked it or not, economic access to the noncapitalist parts of the semiperiphery remained important to their hopes of renewed growth for American capitalism and world capitalism. The partial re-entry of COMECON and China into the world-system seemed a fixture of the future, one that had to be taken into account, whether the United States pursued the "world order" politics of early in the Carter administration or the "Third Cold War" stratagems of the late Carter and early Reagan years.

8 | The Carter Cold War, 1977–1980

> There can be no going back to a time when we thought there
> could be American solutions to every problem.
> —*Cyrus Vance, 1979*
>
> We have it in our power to begin the world over again.
> —*Ronald Reagan, 1980*

The decline of modern hegemonic powers resembles the decline of more ancient empires. The process is politically and economically earthshaking. Within the contours of the world-system, decentering and recentering produce new divisions of labor and responsibility and reapportion the shares of wealth and power among the individual nations. Within the hegemon's own society, a parallel realignment of power occurs, as those sectors and groups still able to compete internationally continue to prosper and grow while those unable to do so either suffer the consequences or try to use the power of the state to evade them. This mix of global and domestic transformation inevitably produces a great debate abroad and at home. Other nations—friend and foe, core and periphery—must calculate the character and the rate of decline of the hegemon and determine how best to minimize its dangers and exploit its opportunities for themselves. Domestically, the objective reality of decline creates its own agenda of pressing questions: How real is the decline? How extensive? Is it reversible? Does it matter? If it does, what is the best response? The answers get filtered through contending subjective realities that are the products of different interest-group needs, competing ideologies, and even contrasting lessons drawn from history or collective memory. So it was with the United States in the late 1970s and early 1980s.

America's World Transformed

The transformation of American society manifested itself in sectoral, regional, and class changes. In the immediate post–World War II period, American economic supremacy had rested on heavy industry, like the steel industry, being integrated into its own sources of primary materials and

191

employing large numbers of semiskilled, often unionized laborers in mass production processes. By the 1970s and 1980s, deindustrialization had transformed those economic stalwarts into "rust belt" or "sunset" enterprises, victims of resurgent foreign competition and the reorientation of American investment into military and space industries domestically and multinational ventures overseas. Concurrent with this decline of traditional, mass-production, heavy industry was the rapid growth of service industries like health care, fast foods, and high-tech "sunrise" industries like computers, robotics, and fiberoptics. This sectoral shift coincided with a regional shift, as both labor and capital moved increasingly from the northeast and midwest to the south and southwest. Indeed, by the mid-1970s, the Sunbelt's economy grew at twice the rate of the northeast's. The trend reflected the former's lure of lower energy costs, real estate prices, wage bills, and taxes for welfare and education. It also resulted, however, from Sunbelt dominance of key congressional committees and a consequent upsurge of federal subsidies to the region in the form of oil depletion allowances, farm credits, highway and public power projects, and, most importantly, military spending.

Finally, both the sectoral and the regional shifts accelerated the class transformation of American society. On one hand, the traditional blue-collar laboring class declined in numbers, their unions lost strength, and they found it increasingly difficult to realize the American dream of home ownership and college education for their children. On the other hand, two other classes grew startlingly in number. One was a sort of underclass—disproportionately female, young, and non-white—who performed low-wage functions in service and clerical jobs. The other and the more dynamic was a highly-paid professional-managerial class in sunrise industries, law, health care, banking, real estate, and marketing. Proportionately far larger than its European and Japanese counterparts, this class, nicknamed "Yuppies" (young, upwardly mobile professionals) greatly expanded America's consumption of new luxury amenities, often from abroad. Along with institutional investors, it also helped fuel bullish stock and money markets, so much so that an increasingly *rentier* nation derived more than one-third of its income from interest alone by 1983. That same new middle class also enlarged its share of power and material rewards by spearheading the conservative political revolt of the Reagan years, which was characterized by a redistribution of wealth upward through banking and real estate deregulation, aid to private education, reduced health and safety standards, the virtual elimination of corporate taxes, and greatly increased military spending.

This transformation of American society was an integral part of the continuing transformation of the global economy. Simplistically stated, the American economy produced less but consumed more, while the rest of the world-system produced more but consumed less. While retaining its leading role in armaments, aviation, agriculture, and raw materials, the United States did a decreasing share of the world's manufacturing and even of its banking. Japan and Europe, especially Germany, expanded their share of expensive, high-value manufacturing while the former played an ever larger role in world banking and finance. The semiperiphery continued to expand its share of world manufacturing, especially in low- to medium-value product lines. In the case of the "four tigers" of the Asian rim (South Korea, Taiwan, Hong Kong, and Singapore), it even began to compete with core countries in more high-tech, high-value undertakings. Even parts of the periphery stagnating amidst low world prices for their primary commodities attempted to gain a share of low-value manufacturing, such as the garment trades, through sweatshop labor.

This redivision of world production was not matched, however, by a redivision of world consumption. The growth of the Japanese internal market did not keep pace with its export expansion, as an inordinate amount of disposable Japanese income went for high-priced food, housing, and services or, alternatively, for supra-savings deposits. Likewise, in Europe, labor-supported entitlement programs made it impossible to raise wages significantly without generating domestic inflationary spirals that individual nations, especially Germany, had historically so much feared. In semiperipheral countries, the escalating debt trap of the 1970s produced both wage-cutting, deflationary programs at home and additional borrowing, at yet higher interest rates, abroad—all to the detriment of domestic consumption. Even in the expansive Asian rimlands, political authoritarianism and regressive income distribution not only dampened domestic demand but created explosive political conditions in nations like South Korea and the Philippines. Finally, in the periphery of Africa and the Caribbean, the combination of sweatshop wages and low raw material export prices made those nations so impoverished that only migration and starvation kept some at even a subsistence level.

One nation did expand its share of world consumption. Despite its declining productivity and comparative advantage, the American market for goods, services, and dollars proved to be the tugboat that pulled core and semiperipheral economies along in its wake. The mass market for smaller automobiles and nondurable consumer goods and the Yuppie market for luxury cars and upscale electronic gadgetry made the domestic American market a major demand stimulus for world manufacturing. Similarly, the massive American military presence throughout the globe was a great spur to local goods and services provided by its allied hosts. Finally, funding of the enormous American budget deficit, largely the product of military spending, required such massive sales of Treasury notes that the resulting high interest rates made the United States one of the most profitable arenas of investment for capitalists worldwide. In some ways, 1977 was the flip side of 1947. Japan, Europe, and parts of the semiperiphery depended for their prosperity on having access to an American market. Yet the American economy, increasingly unable to compete in world markets, could not generate sufficient exports to pay for its imports. The European and Japanese dollar gaps of the postwar period had been replaced by the American yen-mark gap of the post-Vietnam era, and it became European and Japanese investments in the United States that financed both of America's skyrocketing deficits, in foreign trade and in the federal budget. A sort of private Marshall Plan in reverse! Indeed by 1987, the United States had not only become a debtor nation, but the largest debtor nation in the world-system.

The arrangement could not long endure. Left unattended, it could result only in further erosion of the American industrial base—a process certain to fuel protectionist resistance from affected business and labor groups, threaten the nation's ability to defend itself in any prolonged military struggle, and diminish the economic dominance that historically had been the underpinning of American hegemony. On the other hand, short-run efforts to correct the status quo could also be destabilizing to the precarious equilibrium of American overconsumption/underproduction and European and Japanese underconsumption/overproduction. Inflating the American economy through deficit spending, low interest rates, and a cheapened dollar might dampen Yuppie demands for luxury imports and make American T-notes less attractive to foreign investors. Deflating the American economy through spending cuts, high interest rates, and a strengthened dollar might well initiate an American recession that would drag down other economies dependent on a high-volume United States market. Either route could adversely affect a world-system inordinately dependent on the American market for global well-being.

Reflecting that hard truth, the American government oscillated between inflationary and deflationary tactics, often attempting a hybrid of spending, interest-rate, and monetary policies that tended in both directions simultaneously. Meanwhile, at the supranational level, the annual economic summits of core country leaders met with indifferent success in coordinating their respective financial-economic policies. Only the more frequent trilateral meetings of central bank directors provided a measure of short-term predictability, by deciding to either let the value of the dollar float or to stabilize it through dollar purchases by European and Japanese banks. Such measures could be useful palliatives, but any long-run solution had to produce a restoration of American productivity and profitabil-

ity and an increase of purchasing power for Europe, Japan, the Asian rimlands, and other parts of the world-system.

Competing Tendencies: Left, Center, Right

The American decline produced a welter of contending judgments on the
nature of America's maladies and the proper remedy for them. Competing
tendencies or intellectual currents confronted one another over what lessons America ought to take from its experiences of the Vietnam War,
Russo-American détente and triangular diplomacy, the repetitive OPEC oil
shocks, economic stagflation, mounting trade deficits, the emergence of
competing power centers, and Third World demands for a new world
order "bargain," a more equitable division of economic labor and rewards.
Chiefly, these competing currents divided approximately into center- and
right-tendencies, though a weak, amorphous left-tendency did exist, largely among radical and libertarian academics. Never hard categories, the
tendencies changed composition often, as ambivalent individuals leaned
first one way and then another. Moreover, the tendencies themselves
shifted ground as the political climate lurched to the right in the late 1970s.
Many centrists who had favored Russo-American coexistence in the mid-
1970s switched to containment by decade's end, while many rightists who
had earlier supported containment opted for outright confrontation later.

As of 1977, the center-tendency embraced what came to be called
"world order politics." It implicitly assumed that the Cold War was over
and American hegemony with it. In its stead was a multipolar world in
which American power was limited and would have to be wielded selec-
tively and often indirectly. Centrists saw the world's major problems as
essentially economic in nature and too complex for simplistic military solutions. Viewing Russia as a declining power and no longer a major source
of global instability, they believed that the Soviet Union could be controlled
through the economic rewards of détente and the Sino-American pressures of triangular diplomacy. Anxious about competition from Europe
and Japan and committed to an American response of reindustrialization,
the center-tendency nonetheless conceded greater autonomy to other
core capitalist powers and sought their collaboration rather than their
obeisance—"leadership without hegemony," some termed it.

Above all else, centrists attached greater value to North-South relations
than to those between East and West. Particularly important was the semiperiphery and its contribution to global profitability. Praising modernization on both sides of the Iron Curtain, centrist advocates promised bank
loans to finance that process through infrastructural development, new
energy sources, and manufacturing enterprises. Similarly, the center-

tendency urged transformation of peripheral economies into more mechanized, large-scale, high-volume producers of food and raw materials, seeing this as essential to an increasingly industrial world order in the core and semiperiphery alike. Center-tendency proponents even seemed willing to tolerate peasant revolutions as a necessary step in the breakdown of traditional cultures and inefficient oligarchic production. Left alone and not pushed into Soviet arms, such revolutions would eventually turn to the West for markets, money, and machinery if they were to deliver on the material promises to their people.

The right-tendency was certain that the Cold War was far from over and determined that American hegemony was not dead. Its adherents believed the world order still required a paramount policeman. They felt that economic and social problems, notwithstanding their complexity, often could not be addressed effectively until military solutions had first imposed political stability. Moreover, rightists believed that America still had the power and the responsibility to play that role and needed only to regain the will to wield that power. As a consequence, they committed themselves to the remilitarization of American foreign policy and to more formal strategic entente with China. In effect, the conservative policy current envisioned restoration of American global leadership to a level comparable to the late 1940s and early 1950s.

The American military shield, refurbished and rebuilt, would contain the expansion of Russia's "evil empire," which they viewed as the fountainhead of revolution, terrorism, and all things unseemly in the world. It would also force Europe and Japan, wielders of growing economic power and yearners after greater political autonomy, to look still to America for protection and leadership. Similarly, American military might could underwrite the stability of authoritarian regimes in the semiperiphery, insuring that their modernization took place both profitably and predictably. Finally it would counter peasant revolutions in the periphery, especially if those revolutions occurred in strategically sensitive areas like the Persian Gulf, the horn of Africa, or the Central American isthmus.

Two factors influenced the fluid composition of these competing tendencies: ideologically derived lessons from the Vietnam War and economic self-interest. The center-tendency consisted of social democrats, like Senator George McGovern, and business internationalists, like Cyrus Vance, Carter's first secretary of state. Both, in quite different ways, worried primarily about the health of domestic American society and the deleterious effect that global policing had upon it. The social democrats had come, by 1967, to oppose the Vietnam War because they believed it had undermined the material and moral commitment to Johnson's Great Society programs and frustrated their own hopes of social reform, civil rights progress, and labor-capital collaboration. The business internationalists, in turn, had come, by 1968, to oppose the war because they believed it had distorted and inflated the American domestic economy, nearly alienated a whole new generation in the professional-managerial class, and destroyed the domestic consensus upon which postwar American hegemony had rested. Out of the former's concern for social progress and the latter's concern for social order there emerged a consensus to avoid open-ended, Vietnam-style commitments in the future. The United States should set priorities among its international interests, it should take risks only to protect the most important of them, and should generally manage a better balance between means and ends. In the meantime, its major tasks would be to restore social order and harmony at home, reconstruct the distorted economy to make it competitive abroad, and discover what kind of new consensus could be put together in the aftermath of the Vietnam War.

Ideologically, the right-tendency consisted of two pairs of subgroups, Cold War liberals and neoconservatives on one hand and the radical right and Moral Majority on the other. The first pair was the more powerful and important of the two and dominated the Committee on the Present Danger, which lobbied against détente and for remilitarization. Cold War liberals, like Senator Henry Jackson and presidential adviser Paul Nitze, had believed, since the end of World War II, that the promise of American life, of social progress and material well-being, could best be realized through a growth strategy of international economic expansion rather than a redistributive program of domestic reforms. Unlike Vance and other business internationalists, however, they argued that an American military shield was necessary to prevent foes from obstructing that internationalism or friends from deserting it. Neoconservatives, like think tank director Ben Wattenburg and editor Norman Podhoretz, often began as social democrats, stressing a balance of New Deal–type reforms at home and internationalist policy abroad. Détente's danger to Israel's security after the Yom Kippur War of 1973 had led them to shelve their domestic reformism and to make common cause with Cold War liberals. Neither of the pair saw the Vietnam War as a defeat. In the short-run, it was an unhappy stalemate produced by unseemly dissent at home and an undue concern for détente abroad. In the long-run, it was a time-buying victory that stabilized the Pacific rim and kept it safe for democracy and capitalism. Contemptuous of the center-tendency's Vietnam syndrome, they argued that America could continue playing the role of global policeman both properly and profitably, provided it did not get traduced by Soviet détente or domestic appeasers. At issue, they said, was not America's power, but its will to use it.

The other right-tendency faction shared most of the same premises, but was perhaps even more rigidly militaristic. Both the Radical Right and the Moral Majority saw the war as neither stalemate nor victory but as a humiliating defeat. They blamed it, however, not simply on détente and dissent, but on American policy itself. Containment and gradual escalation were failures that denied America the military victory it merited. Either the war should have been won early with a crushing application of American power or the escalation should have proceeded more quickly and logically to larger troop commitments, an invasion of North Vietnam (the Korean War "rollback" strategy) or the bombing and flooding of North Vietnam's dikes. Even worse than the denial of victory were the perceived consequences of defeat. Fiercely committed to a free market ideology, the radical right, many of them former followers of Senator Barry Goldwater, argued that American abandonment of global policing gave a free hand to anticapitalist revolutions, while détente proposed to accord most-favored-nation status to capitalism's avowed enemies in Moscow and Beijing.

Moral Majority advocates, like evangelists Jerry Falwell and Pat Robertson, put greater stress upon their concerns for social purity. For them, the women's liberation, civil rights, and student protest movements of the Vietnam War era had unleashed forces that threatened their notion of the proper moral order. Moreover, the "national malaise" that followed the Vietnam defeat served to sustain those forces of social anarchy. What was required was a new moral crusade to regenerate a sense of national purpose and validate their presumptive right to set the moral standards for the rest of society. Invoking God, country, and the traditional family, the Moral Majority sought that crusade at home in symbolic attacks on the Equal Rights Amendment (ERA), abortion, public education, and the welfare system and abroad in a renewed, remilitarized Cold War with the Soviet Union. Indeed, the overt confrontationism of this subgroup set them somewhat apart from the containment orientation of Cold War liberals and neoconservatives, and worlds apart from the coexistence leanings of the center-tendency.

If ideology was the subjective prism through which factions interpreted post-Vietnam reality, then economic self-interest was the objective fact that fixed those views in place. Roughly correlated, the center-tendency groups had their base of power in eastern banks and insurance companies and in traditional mass production industries, like the automobile industry. Hurt by declining domestic profits, both had self-interest in a foreign policy that relieved the political tensions that might disrupt the freedom and fluidity of capital movements throughout the world-system. Lending institutions in the late 1970s saw bank loans to the semiperiphery (including the COMECON bloc) as their most attractive opportunity. Mass production industries could remain competitive only by subcontracting parts production to semiperipheral countries, like Brazil and Mexico, or by exploring joint-venture possibilities with their core competitors.

Both constituted the *rentier* sector of the American economy. Finance capitalists lived off the rents of their investments and loans overseas, while traditional industrial capitalists rented out whole product lines like sub-compact autos for foreign manufacture. Interested in maximal capital fluidity and persuaded that Vietnam-style military adventurism was counterproductive in promoting it, they looked instead to détente with the socialist bloc and a new world order bargain with the Third World to help realize that end.

The right-tendency had its base of power in the military-industrial complex, in Sunbelt boosters and land developers tied to that complex, and in oil companies concerned about the potential volatility of the Middle East and the unpredictability of OPEC. Hurt by détente and the less frenetic pace of military-space spending, they had a self-interest in a foreign policy that exacerbated political tensions and that rationalized the need for far higher levels of military spending at home and rapid deployment forces abroad to protect vulnerable energy sources.

In the context of America's sectoral and regional transformation, these groups constituted the dynamic growth portion of the American economy. Possessing comparative advantage in military-space industries and still competitive with Europe and Japan in other high-tech lines, these sunrise industries were far less sanguine than the *rentier* sector about giving up the ghost of hegemony and the profits that went with it. Indeed, many entrepreneurial leaders of this sector were nouveau riche capitalists, just now getting their chance at big money and operating by a more free-wheeling, on-the-make standard of conduct than old money capitalists, who had long ago arrived and had accumulated portfolios to prove it. Such *arriviste* types were more inclined to make empires than to relinquish them.

At the center of this profound, intra-elite debate stood a new President, Jimmy Carter, whose inconsistent and ill-formed world view made his favor a continuing object of contention between center and right. A governor of Georgia, little known prior to 1976, he had been seen by some Establishment leaders as a possible antidote to the more frightening candidacy of George Wallace, with its southern populism and northern blue-collar support. As such, he was recruited by David Rockefeller and Zbigniew Brzezinski into the Trilateral Commission of core country leaders and given a crash course on how the world-system worked. Given the preexisting schisms among American elite figures, however, the mixed signals given the trainee perhaps made the experience more confusing than educational. Reflecting that ambivalence, the first two years of the Carter administration, 1977–78, manifested contradictory tendencies. The dominant one followed the centrist orientation advocated by Secretary of State Vance. The subordinate one was the right-tendency urged by National Security Adviser Brzezinski.

From the beginning, the Carter administration was a house divided against itself, and it did not stand. A ruling coalition of subgroups within the same tendency might have been possible, as the later Reagan years were to demonstrate, but the coupling of two contending tendencies was not viable. Vance and other centrists, clustered in the State Department, counseled the President to stabilize the arms race, to refrain from "play-[ing] China against the Soviets," and to resist the impulse "to link Soviet behavior in the Third World to issues in which we have so fundamental an interest as SALT." Dismissing the importance of East-West competition as a game in which the United States already "held most of the cards," Secretary Vance stressed the primacy of restructuring the world order of international capitalism, especially the North-South relations between the core and its outer zones.

Brzezinski and other right-tendency advocates, centered in the NSC and the Defense Department, advised the President to take the Soviet threat seriously and to make clear to the Soviets that "the costs of disruptive behavior in the world" might include the derailment of SALT II negotiations and the forging of closer Sino-American ties. Torn between confrontation or cooperation, Carter concluded by mid-1978 that "the United States is adequately prepared to meet either choice," yet he seemed unable to decide which one the country should pursue. Commenting on a particularly confusing presidential address to the United States Naval Academy in June, the *New York Times* observed: "The White House Lions and the State Department Beavers have struggled to a draw. If we heard him right in his address on the Russians yesterday, President Carter told the Lions to keep on roaring about Soviet behavior in Africa and he told the Beavers to keep on building a structure of arms control agreements. And he told the Russians he must govern a nation of both lions and beavers."

Initially, in 1977, Carter tilted toward the center-tendency. Save in the SALT II talks, the United States attempted to ignore the Soviet Union and to concentrate on improving its relations with the Third World, in both the socialist and the capitalist spheres. In the former, the administration targeted Poland and Yugoslavia, the two Eastern European countries most tied to Western bank loans. Vice President Walter Mondale and Secretary of Defense George Brown visited Belgrade on separate occasions in 1977 and President Carter himself visited Warsaw in December of that year. Similarly, the American government sought to improve relations with two non-European COMECON countries, Vietnam and Cuba. Unofficially, it opened talks with Vietnam over the issue of Americans missing in action (MIAs) from the Vietnam War, while formally, in Paris, it initiated a dialogue over possible American economic assistance and general means of improving bilateral relations. While continuing to press Cuba for troop withdrawal from Angola, the administration dropped that withdrawal as a condition for improving Cuban-American relations. Accordingly, it proceeded to establish limited relations with Cuba through the reciprocal establishment of diplomatic interest sections in Havana and Washington. In addition, the United States lifted restrictions on Americans traveling to both Vietnam and Cuba, as well as North Korea and Cambodia.

In the capitalist portion of the Third World, the early Carter administration focused on Latin America and Africa. There the United States had to confront the unhappy legacy of the Vietnam War, one that suggested that America did not respect Third World nationalism, that it supported right-wing military dictatorships and was contemptuous of non-white races.

In Latin America, the failure of the Alliance for Progress in the 1960s and America's part in Allende's violent overthrow compounded that legacy. Carter responded with a neo–good neighbor policy to improve America's image and to improve its position for North-South negotiations over core-periphery economic relations, which he expected to be the major issue of the 1970s and 1980s. Keys to the new policy were the Panama Canal Treaty and human rights diplomacy. The 1978 agreement with Panama promised to restore the canal and its zone to Panama by the year 2000 and increased Panama's immediate share of canal receipts, but it retained the American right of intervention should the canal's neutrality be threatened. Prompted by the potential of Panamanian revolution, the treaty also aimed at a larger regional audience to demonstrate U.S. respect for Latin American sovereignty and national integrity. So important was the treaty in administration eyes that it cashed an inordinate number of political chits to insure its safe passage over opposition from part of the right-tendency.

At the same time, the early Carter government trumpeted American support for free elections and the right to dissent and its opposition to press censorship, torture, political murder, and other tactics of authoritarian regimes. Human rights diplomacy, designed to restore lost moral leadership and global respect for American ideals as well as power, focused especially on Latin America, where its application was less selective and inconsistent than in other parts of the world. In varying degrees, Argentina, Brazil, Chile, Haiti, the Dominican Republic, and Paraguay drew public American criticism for human rights violations. Guatemala and Bolivia even suffered cuts or cancellations of American military and economic assistance.

In Africa, the legacy of Vietnam combined with that of Kissinger's "tar baby option" of the early 1970s to produce an image of America as a white, racist, quasi-colonial power. The corrective Carter response was a policy of "African solutions for African problems." That suggested, first, that the United States ought to deal with Africa on its own terms rather than as part of global Soviet-American struggle. For example, in early 1977, Katanganese, operating out of Angola, invaded their former homeland province (renamed Shaba) in southern Zaire. Despite close American ties to the

Mobutu regime in Zaire, the Carter administration ignored rumors, later proved false, that Cuban troops were part of the invading force. On Vance's advice, Carter chose instead to "deal with the Shaba invasion as an African—not an East-West—problem."

The second facet of this Africa for Africans approach was the selective application of Carter's human rights policy. The chief target was South Africa with its white supremacist apartheid regime, where the United States endorsed the "Sullivan Principles," calling for American companies in South Africa to practice nondiscrimination in hiring and firing. Criticism of human rights abuses by Black African governments, however, was generally more muted, lest the United States appear in the role of white master preaching moral proprieties to its plantation hands. Indeed, the Carter administration further sought to avoid the stigma of white paternalism by making Andrew Young its chief spokesman on African affairs. A Black American and long-time civil rights activist, Young used his important position as Ambassador to the United Nations to cultivate ties with UN delegates from newly independent African nations. In turn, they used him to press Carter for a stronger antiapartheid stand and to strengthen the President's earlier inclination to deal with Africa outside the context of Russo-American competition.

From the very beginning, Carter's "world order politics" developed fissures. The effort to devalue Russo-American relations and concentrate on the Third World per se did not work. Had no immediate East-West issues been on the agenda, that center-tendency approach might have been viable. Such was not the case. Carter inherited the SALT II negotiations from the Nixon-Ford administration. They had come so close to successful conclusion by 1976 that Carter could not abandon them without destroying the remnants of détente and alienating popular American and European sentiment to further limit strategic nuclear weapons. At the same time, if he pushed ahead with the nearly completed talks, the resultant treaty was certain to face strong opposition from right-tendency advocates within and without his administration. Talks with Brzezinski, Senator Jackson, and Paul Nitze of the Committee on the Present Danger had made that abundantly clear.

The President tried to finesse his way out of this dilemma by proposing to the USSR that the previous negotiations be junked and SALT II started over from scratch. He hoped that his promise to broaden the scope of the treaty would bring centrists to his side, while his promise to take a tougher negotiating stance with the Russians would win over the right. The Soviets, however, derailed Carter's gambit. Condemning his proposal as an indication that the United States was "not serious" about limiting nuclear arms, the Russians warned that abandoning earlier progress would force the

Russians to put new items of their own on the agenda. Prominent among them was long-standing concern by the Russian military about the American forward base system (FBS) in central Europe that threatened the Soviet heartland. Unwilling to risk any alteration in FBS, Carter had to abandon his venture and resume talks on the previous basis.

Continuing SALT II talks kept Russo-American relations in the forefront of policy considerations instead of on the back burner where Carter had wanted them. Not completed until 1979, the SALT II talks produced a treaty that was marginally better than Carter could have had in 1977 had he followed through on Ford negotiations. It established parity, upper limits, and technical verification for all strategic delivery vehicles, and prohibited the use of multiple warheads (MIRVs) on more than half the total launchers. In the two-year negotiating interim, however, the SALT II process became a domestic political lightning rod, less important for its substance than for its political symbolism. The domestic fight over SALT II made it a political metaphor for the choice between coexistence and containment, between the center- and right-tendencies.

The latter made good use of the long delay to hoist coexistence on the petard of Carter's own human rights policy. Intended primarily to distance the United States from Third World dictators, that policy became a convenient tool for anti-détente groups to link coexistence to acceptable Soviet behavior in its domestic as well as its foreign policies. They insisted that Carter apply human rights policies against the USSR for its suppression of dissent, its violations of the Helsinki Accords, and especially its treatment of Soviet Jews. In apparent response, Russia began to offer political dissidents emigration as an alternative to prison and by 1978 had upped the number of Jewish emigrants to thirty thousand annually (the highest level since 1974) and to fifty-one thousand by 1979 (nearly the figure Henry Jackson had demanded in 1973). But Russian concessions, however numerous, seemed unlikely to satisfy the right-tendency, and they continued to push Carter to maintain his criticism of Soviet domestic affairs. Requiring conservative votes for his Panama Canal treaty, the President did so, only to find later that Republicans might vote for the canal treaty *or* SALT II, but not both. By 1978, Soviet Premier Brezhnev publicly blamed increasing Russian-American discord on domestic American "forces interested in the arms race" and opposed to "the relaxation of international tensions in general."

Beginnings of the Carter Cold War

Ironically, Brezhnev's own policies in the Third World and in Europe provided useful fuel for his American critics. Since détente's first days, the

United States and the USSR had sharply differed over détente's application to the Third World. American insistence on Russian respect for the
status quo vied with Soviet insistence on its continued right to support
revolutionary nationalist movements. Events in Angola had already demonstrated the extent of the Soviet-American chasm and would continue to
do so. New Soviet involvement, however, in Southwest Asia and Northeast
Africa, made it possible for anti-détente forces to argue plausibly that the
gap was unbridgeable. In an "arc of crisis" (as Brzezinski termed it), extending from Afghanistan to the horn of Africa, a series of coups and countercoups in 1978 produced Marxist governments in Ethiopia, South Yemen,
and Afghanistan, all of which enjoyed Soviet support—in Ethiopia's case,
Cuba's support as well. Somalia and the Sudan had earlier received Russian aid, but they now turned to the West in retaliation for Soviet-Cuban
support of their more imposing Ethiopian neighbor.

Retrospectively, it seems clear that Soviet policies were largely a series
of opportunistic, ad hoc reactions to crises that were indigenous in nature.
At a more regional level, however, they were also a response to America's
success in freezing Russia out of any Middle Eastern political settlement,
detaching Egypt from the Russian camp, and encouraging a move toward
Egyptian-Israeli détente. The last began in September 1977 when Egyptian
leader Anwar Sadat made his startling, unprecedented visit to Israel to
meet Prime Minister Menachem Begin. The process ended a year later in
September 1978 with the Camp David agreement, which formally made
peace between Egypt and Israel, restored the Sinai to Egyptian control,
and, hopefully, set the stage for a Middle East peace settlement independent of any Russian participation.

Anticipating the Camp David agreement, Russia stepped up its activities
in the horn of Africa from early 1978 onward. Its probable motive was to
offset Egypt's final defection and transform that Arab power into an American Achilles' heel instead. Both Yemen and Ethiopia, after all, derived their
chief strategic value from their positions astride the southern bottleneck
of the Red Sea, which in turn funneled into Egypt's vital Suez Canal. Similarly, Russia sought to punish Egypt and disperse its power by supplying
arms to Egypt's western neighbor, the hostile and volatile Libyan government of Muammar al-Qaddafi. Whatever Russia's motives, Brzezinski interpreted its actions as "a serious setback in our attempts to develop with
the Soviets some rules of the game in dealing with the turbulence in the
Third World."

Concurrently in Europe, the Soviet Union continued to implement its
1976 decision to introduce SS-20 missiles into the European theatre. More
mobile and more accurate than the antiquated S-4s and S-5s they replaced, the SS-20 was part of a long-overdue modernization effort by the

Russians to counter America's forward base system and its potential first-strike capabilities. Now twenty years old, the S-4 and S-5 missiles were an inadequate deterrent to the F-111 squadrons in Europe or the Polaris-Poseidon submarine bases in Scotland and Spain. German officials and other European leaders, however, saw the Russian move as more political than military in nature, and their fears provided grist for the rightist mill in America. While Europeans were supportive of détente generally, some feared that European acceptance of Russian-American parity over American supremacy might make Europe susceptible to Russian intimidation. They worried aloud whether the United States would risk hearth and home without the margin of safety provided by its previous supremacy. SALT II's impending limitations on cruise missiles and Carter's indecision over proposals to build a neutron bomb combined with the Russian introduction of SS-20s to heighten those fears.

As European "defense intellectuals" conveyed those anxieties to their American counterparts, right-tendency proponents like Brzezinski picked up their arguments and used them to pressure Carter for a concerted recommitment to NATO and its remilitarization. Such steps would renew European dependence on American military protection, negate Russian efforts to detach Europe from the larger North Atlantic community, and put the Soviet Union under the gun of an enhanced first-strike capability for FBS. As a consequence, NATO did agree in 1977 to a 3 percent annual increase in each member's military spending, and the United States doubled its F-111s in Europe to 164 and increased the warheads in its Europe-based submarine fleet five-fold to four hundred by introducing new MIRVs and additional vessels. Still, Vance and other centrists dissuaded the President for the moment from any firm American commitment to a full-blown theater nuclear force (TNF) of Pershing-II and cruise missiles.

By late May of 1978, the altered political climate at home and international circumstances abroad made it possible for the National Security Adviser to persuade Carter to take two key steps. He played the China card and he promoted the remilitarization of NATO. It can now be seen that both acts were decisive in the final move from residual détente to renewed Cold War, though it is unclear whether the President himself understood the implications of these acts.

Playing the China card was a direct response to Brzezinski's geopolitical analysis of events in the arc of crisis. The national security adviser had long wished to transform triangular diplomacy, with its double-détente, into an overt anti-Soviet alliance between China and the United States. Vance had stymied that goal in 1977, urging Carter instead to maintain a more even-handed approach to Russia and China and to avoid any military-strategic ties to the latter lest they threaten SALT II talks with the Soviets. In early 1978, however, Brzezinski argued that the China card was the only viable trump to Russian expansionism in the horn of Africa and in Afghanistan. Hoping to mollify his right-wing critics, Carter ignored Vance's counsel and dispatched Brzezinski to China in May 1978. Telling Chinese leaders that *"The United States had made up its mind,"* the national security adviser negotiated with them an agreement to establish formal diplomatic relations, an extensive educational and cultural exchange program, transfer of technology procedures (including some with strategic implications), and procedures for sharing military intelligence about the Soviet Union. In the midst of his talks, Brzezinski found time to visit the Great Wall, challenging his Chinese hosts to a foot race, with the exhortation, "last one to the top fights the Russians in Ethiopia." The Chinese approvingly dubbed him "the polar bear tamer." More forebodingly, a Soviet spokesman warned, "For China to become some sort of [anti-Soviet] military ally to the West, even an informal ally, . . . then there is no place for détente."

On May 30th and 31st, the Carter administration fired the other barrel in its détente-killing salvo. At a NATO summit meeting in Washington, it promoted and secured long-term commitment to the modernization and expansion of the alliance's military forces. Cool to German calls for a long-range theater nuclear force in 1977, the United States took the lead in 1978 in promoting TNF as part of NATO's arsenal. Carter himself had foreshadowed the American initiative in an address in March at Wake Forest University. In a speech drafted by Brzezinski, the President denounced the "ominous inclination on the part of the Soviet Union to use its military power—to intervene in local conflicts, . . . as we can observe today in Africa." Moreover, he warned, "We will match . . . any threatening power. . . . We will not allow any other nation to gain military superiority over us." Ten weeks later the NATO summit tentatively endorsed TNF, including an "evolutionary upward adjustment" providing the capability to strike the Soviet Union itself. After a three-month NSC review, the United States made its endorsement final in September 1978. It did so not for military reasons, for it considered the existing forward base system and its nuclear submarines adequate to defend Europe. Rather it did so almost entirely for political reasons, to reassure Europe of continued protection under America's nuclear umbrella and to reinforce its dependence on the United States. A year later, in December 1979, in an almost inexorable outcome of its earlier decisions, the United States began to deploy 108 Pershing-II missiles and 464 GLCMs (ground-launched cruise missiles) in Europe. Retrospectively, the seven days in May that produced the 1978 NATO summit, as well as Brzezinski's China initiative, constituted the watershed break between the era of détente and that of renewed Cold War.

The Carter Cold War and the Third World

Considerations of credibility and profitability drove the final nails into the coffin of coexistence and ushered in a renewed era of containment and even confrontation. The Russian ventures in Africa and its decision to deploy SS-20 missiles in Europe, coupled with the American initiative in China and its choice of TNF in Europe, certainly made revivified Cold War a strong possibility. What made it a foregone conclusion were the 1979–80 global recession and the collapse of Russo-American proxies both in the Persian Gulf and in their special spheres of influence, in Eastern Europe and the Caribbean basin respectively.

Throughout the détente era both the United States and Russia had used Third World surrogates to protect their interests in the long arc that curved from Afghanistan to South Africa. The results for both sides had been mixed. The clients were often unstable and unreliable, frequently changing governments and switching sides in East-West competition. Egypt, Ethiopia, Sudan, Somalia, and Afghanistan had all shifted their loyalties, variously from East to West, from West to East, or from neutralism to one or the other. Moreover, the indirect application of Russo-American power through proxies did not prevent superpower competition in the Third World from reaching ominous levels by 1978 in the arc of crisis. Still, that use of substitutes (sub-imperialism) was a less costly and less risky mode of operation than the direct interjection of American or Soviet power into the region.

Revolutionary Moslem fundamentalism in Iran and Afghanistan destroyed the basis for sub-imperialism and prompted both the United States and the Soviet Union to act unilaterally and directly. In the Iran of the 1970s, the United States had become the trainer and adviser of both the Iranian army and its notorious secret police (SAVAK); it also sold more arms to Iran (for petrodollars) than to any other nation in the world, educated tens of thousands of Iranian students at American universities, and was the Shah's biggest cheerleader. In return, Iran under the Shah acted as a demonstrator model for the Moslem world, earning the rewards of pro-capitalist modernization while containing Russian expansion, keeping Iraq in line, and generally policing the Persian Gulf.

Despite major squabbles over Iran's role in OPEC oil pricing or America's price tag for its arms, the Iranian connection was as solid as ever when revolution abruptly severed it in 1979. The revolution's vanguard was an unstable coalition of Moslem fundamentalists hostile to culturally disruptive modernization, a lumpenproletariat marginalized and impoverished by forced and distorted modernization, and a radical intelligentsia anxious to reshape modernization along more socialist lines. The revolution moved first to force the Shah from power and then to prevent any possible American action to return him to power. The Moslem fundamentalist faction, led by Ayatollah Ruhollah Khomeini, adroitly manipulated anti-American sentiment to consolidate its control of the revolution over both its bourgeois and radical competitors. On November 4, 1979, revolutionary Iran took a decisive step: it seized the American embassy and took fifty-eight American hostages. Searing itself across the collective American psyche, the fifteen-month-long hostage crisis and its imposed sense of impotence created a nationalistic, xenophobic backlash that helped Ronald Reagan oust Carter from the White House and speeded up the very militarization process Carter himself had begun.

At the same time, Russia faced incipient revolution in Afghanistan. A nineteenth-century pivot between the British, Russian, Chinese, and Ottoman empires, it retained potential strategic importance for its Khyber Pass, an entry to the Indian subcontinent, and for the proximity of its mountainous southwestern border to the Persian Gulf. In 1978, a military coup toppled a neutralist regime and replaced it with a Marxist government. From the beginning, however, the government was not to Russia's liking. Its dominant personality, Hafzullah Amin, attempted to force his socialist version of modernization upon the unready and unwilling population of Moslem peasants and herdsmen. Particularly galling to those patriarchal people were his efforts to establish social and political rights for women. His reward was a fragmented but fundamentalist-dominated uprising that began in March 1979 with a massacre of Soviet advisers and their families. Fearful that his failures would prompt Soviet reprisals, Amin apparently tried to emulate Sadat's gambit of deserting the Russians and opting for the West. Long rumored to be a CIA mole, Amin certainly acted the part in seeking aid from China, Pakistan, Saudi Arabia, Libya, and the Shah's Iran. Afraid that it was about to lose an important buffer, Russia had to determine, in the Central Committee's words, how best to prevent the establishment of "a pro-imperialist bridgehead of military aggression on the southern borders of the USSR."

By 1979, both the United States and the Soviet Union faced the possible loss of prized surrogates in a strategically important part of the globe. Moreover, they both faced a new phenomenon that defied classification by the usual Cold War categories—a wild card in the international system that threatened Russia and America alike. In Iran, Khomeini's groups crushed both supporters of the Shah and anti-Shah radicals and created a theocratic, fundamentalist Moslem state that seemed at once anticommunist and anticapitalist, anti-Russian and anti-American, opposed to modernization in any form. In Afghanistan, bonds of religion and geography, of traditionalism and antimodernism, made Moslem resistance groups there likely emulators of Iran's theocratic revolution.

Of the two superpowers, the Soviet Union seemed to understand the tide of Moslem fundamentalism better. Possessing a large and rapidly growing Moslem population of its own in the Central Asian republics, the USSR understood that Iran and Afghanistan posed a long-term threat that went far beyond conventional geopolitical considerations. The status of Russia's ethnic and religious minorities constituted an explosive social problem, akin to that of race in America. Should Afghanistan go the way of Iran, the cumulative example might well rend the very fabric of a Soviet society already worn thin by a host of other socioeconomic problems. Moving preemptively to defuse the Afghan situation, the Russians attempted a political settlement that would have replaced the Amin government with a broader coalition and would have slowed the radical assault on traditional culture. When both Amin and his fundamentalist foes obstructed that political move, the Soviets replaced the carrot with the stick.

On December 27, 1979, the Soviet military invaded Afghanistan, ousted and executed Amin, installed a Marxist regime more to its liking, and occupied the country with more than one hundred thousand troops. As in America's intervention in Vietnam, however, the action only provoked full-scale resistance by indigenous groups and enticed Russia's enemies (the United States, China, Egypt, Saudi Arabia, and Pakistan) to supply the Afghan rebels with military and economic assistance. It trapped Russia in its own Asian quagmire. It would be nine years before the USSR would finally acknowledge the futility of military repression and agree to end its occupation, by 1989, in return for an end to Western military aid to the Afghans. Even then it sought Western aid in thwarting a fundamentalist takeover and in assuring a secular, neutralist regime that would serve the interests of East and West alike.

In the United States, neither the Vance nor the Brzezinski factions understood the unique phenomenon of religious fundamentalism. To Vance, the 1978 revolution in Iran was simply a conventional Third World revolution that the United States could eventually co-opt and reintegrate if it exercised patience and quietly supported moderate elements in the revolution. To Brzezinski, it was a radical revolution that, along with the coup in Afghanistan, threatened the strategic security of the oil-laden Persian Gulf. As such it demanded a stern, tough response. The hostage crisis in November 1979 and the Russian invsion of Afghanistan seven weeks later resolved the ambivalence in favor of the right-tendency analysis.

Brzezinski welcomed the Afghan invasion for its seeming validation of his express concern for "the consequences of Soviet presence so much closer to the Persian Gulf." Though considerable evidence suggested that

Soviet motives were local and defensive rather than global and expansive, the national security adviser warned the Soviets that the Afghan invasion meant that "SALT was now in jeopardy" and "the scope of our relationship with China would be affected." Thereafter, the United States withdrew SALT II from Senate consideration and "open[ed] the doors to a U.S.-Chinese defense relationship." China, which had been strongly critical of the invasion of Afghanistan as "a direct threat to the security of China," began to supply covert aid to Afghan rebels and dispatched a military mission to the United States to consult with American military leaders. The United States, for its part, extended most-favored-nation trading status to China and granted it export licenses for some four hundred items in the area of advanced technology in military support equipment. Brzezinski's triumph was capped by President Carter's pronouncement in January 1980 of the so-called Carter Doctrine, vowing American military intervention, if necessary, to defend the Persian Gulf. The doctrine was imparted credibility by the American naval build-up in the Near East; the completion of negotiations over bases in Somalia, Kenya, Oman, and Egypt; and a renewed American call for a rapid deployment force to extinguish brush-fire crises in the region. Ecstatic over the Carter Doctrine, Brzezinski declared, "For me it was a particularly gratifying moment because for more than a year I had been seeking within the U.S. government the adoption of such a policy."

Ironically, Carter's "terrific overreaction" to the crisis in Afghanistan carried even beyond the bounds his security adviser thought prudent. Angered by the Russians and made vulnerable to his right-wing critics, the President invoked a shopping list of sanctions against the Soviet Union: an embargo on grain and high technology, a boycott of the 1980 Moscow Olympic games, restrictions on Russian fishing in American waters, and the postponement of new Russian consulates in the United States. Since all sanctions were to stay in place until Russia evacuated Afghanistan, the effect was to hold the totality of Soviet-American relations hostage to that one issue. The new result was a de facto freeze in relations during Carter's last year in office, one that carried over into Reagan's first administration.

If the collapse of regional surrogates in the Near East raised the odds of direct American-Russian confrontation, then developments in Nicaragua and Poland, each power's sphere of greatest influence, further fueled the impulse toward renewed cold war. Befitting their historical and strategic primacy, both the United States and the USSR invoked sacrosanct doctrines, Monroe's and Brezhnev's, to rationalize their dominance in their spheres. In both cases the assertion served to warn off other core powers from attempting intrusions and to reserve the right of unilateral intervention to maintain the integrity of the given sphere. Both rationalizations also rested on the assumption that the inability to prevent outside intrusion or internal defection in one's sphere would inevitably and seriously damage the credibility and legitimacy of a dominating power. Could American pretense to global hegemony be taken seriously if it could not maintain its unquestioned suzerainty in the Caribbean basin? ("El Salvador itself doesn't matter—we have to establish credibility," said one White House official.) Could Russia's pretense to superpower status be deemed plausible if it could not keep Eastern Europe in line?

In the Caribbean islands and rimlands, Nicaragua ranked in importance only behind alienated Cuba in American eyes. Since 1936 it had been ruled by the nepotistic Somoza family, much in the fashion of the Diem family in South Vietnam and the Marcos clan in the Philippines. Closely tied to Sunbelt congressmen on the armed services committees, Somoza's Nicaragua had provided the training bases for American-sponsored interventions in Guatemala in 1954 and Cuba in 1961 and had sent its own troops to join those of the United States in the Dominican Republic in 1965. Despite Carter's human rights diplomacy, the connection between the United States and the Somoza government remained intact until the end of the 1970s.

What forcibly ended it was the escalating Sandinista revolution in mid-1979, led by Marxist students and proletarianized peasants but supported by angry middle class groups disempowered by the Somoza regime. The internally divided Carter administration, faced with the loss of a trusted puppet and fearful that the Sandinistas might follow the Cuban road, lurched back and forth in its responses. Efforts to use collective or indirect force failed when the Organization of American States rejected an American overture for joint intervention and, in turn, the Nicaraguan national guard collapsed as an instrument of internal repression. Subsequent American efforts at political mediation failed either to create a provisional government (Somozismo without Somoza) or to force the Sandinistan revolutionaries to broaden and moderate their political base. Unable to prevent the Sandinista revolution or its subsequent move to the left, the Carter administration finally moved to suspend all forms of aid to Nicaragua, including humanitarian aid. Confronting the prospective loss of a prized surrogate and the possible spread of revolution elsewhere in the Caribbean basin, the options of remilitarization, Big Stick diplomacy, and renewed Cold War held strong attraction for American leaders seeking to maintain the global credibility of American hegemony.

In like vein, Russia faced a prospective revolutionary development in Poland and the possible spread of revolution throughout its Eastern European sphere. Poland had led the way among Warsaw Pact nations in seeking Western bank loans and technology in the 1970s era of détente. High wage bills, however, and inadequate economies of scale made it difficult for Polish industry to generate sufficient receipts to service its huge foreign debt, especially when global recession in 1979–80 reduced foreign demand for Polish products even further. Left with no other recourse, Poland resorted to another round of borrowing from foreign banks in order to fund its external debt. By the end of 1980, that debt stood at $27 billion—the third largest in the world.

This period of rapid, unbalanced, and not very successful industrialization created the necessary preconditions for organization of the Polish working class, who sought some influence in the economic process. Recession spawned austerity measures, which in turn produced the sufficient conditions for spawning the Solidarity trade union movement. Shutdowns of inefficient industrial works, acceleration of production lines in those that remained operative, and a sharp decline in real income combined to ignite an intense trade union resistance movement that increasingly resorted to industrial strikes and mass demonstrations and to political manipulation that attempted to play Church and State against each other. Solidarity received much praise and encouragement—and it was rumored, covert financial aid as well—from the other side of the Iron Curtain. The prospective alienation of Russia's most prized client state and the possible spread effects to all of Eastern Europe made Big Stick diplomacy and renewed Cold War strongly attractive to Russian leaders as well, as they sought to maintain the credibility of Russia's superpower status. The behavior of Brezhnev and his polyglot successors would shortly demonstrate this.

The Carter Cold War and Global Recession

In April 1980, Vance resigned as secretary of state. His departure symbolized the death of détente and the reascendancy of containment over coexistence. Concern for American credibility in both the core and the periphery, the tensions of East-West competition in the arc of crisis, and the complications of domestic politics had had a weighty and cumulative impact. All pointed toward the remilitarization of American foreign policy and the need to reassert American hegemony and global policing after nearly a decade of post-Vietnam retrenchment.

Finally tipping the scales to the right-tendency position was the global recession of 1979–80 (the Carter recession). It made the remilitarization of American policy seem not merely useful strategically and psychologically, but imperative economically. The Carter recession was but a continuation of the Nixon recession of 1974–75. The intervening half-decade had hardly been a model of economic boom. Inflation averaged 9 percent annually (it was 14 percent by 1979) and unemployment 6.5 percent, while the rates of GNP growth and productivity increases declined to 65 percent and 30 percent respectively, of their 1960s levels. What measure of prosperity did exist between 1974 and 1979 was owed largely to the semiperiphery. Save for the military-industrial complex, low profits and disinvestment continued to characterize American domestic enterprises. It was only bank loans and multinational corporate ventures in the Pacific rim, Eastern Europe, South Africa, Mexico, and the South American cone that kept the aggregate rate of profit on American capital acceptably high. By 1979, however, the semiperiphery could no longer function as savior of the system. Victims of an insidious "debt trap" and of the extraordinary burden of its servicing, most of the semiperipheral nations stalled in mid-development and deteriorated as avenues of profitable investment. (Only Asia's Four Tigers, aided by sounder Japanese financing and nearly duty-free access to the American market, partly defied that trend.) Moreover, there was some anxiety that debt traps might turn into debt bombs if several major debtors were to default simultaneously. If that happened, global economic interdependence—that crowning glory of American hegemony—might turn into a nightmare of falling financial dominoes.

Deprived of its semiperipheral crutch, the American economy had to come to grips with the dampened profits and the distortions generated by long-term disinvestment in the civilian industrial sector and overinvestment in military production and overseas enterprises. America had to do for itself what it had helped other core countries do three decades earlier. It had to identify and implement a long-term strategy for reviving American productivity and making American goods cost-competitive at home and in world markets. Any such strategy, to be successful, had to mobilize the maximum possible amount of capital and target its investment into high-growth, high-profit sectors where the United States might regain comparative advantages vis-à-vis its Japanese and German competitors.

During the Carter administration, the ill-defined and never-implemented inclination was to copy the competition. ("If you can't beat 'em, join 'em!") Amidst hand wringing about "national malaise" and "zero-sum games," occasional and more positive calls for reindustrialization began to surface. While a bit vague, what they seemed to suggest was some form of corporatism: that is, capital, labor, and the state collaborating (as parts of one body) in some mutual sacrifices (for example, cuts for both labor and management) and in planning investment strategies. Some exponents of reindustrialization favored the Japanese model of using a state institution (in Japan the MITI, Ministry of International Trade and Industry) as the vehicle for that collaboration. For example, there was some talk of reviving the 1930s Reconstruction Finance Corporation (RFC) and making it into an American-style MITI. Others favored the German model of less institutionalized and more informal cooperation between existing state agencies, business associations, and trade unions. Whatever the form, it was assumed that conscious planning was needed to target investment into sunrise industries while training and relocating workers and managers in dying, sunset, industries.

However, this neo-New Deal concept never made it to the action stage. Since the end of World War II, the notion of state economic planning and deficit financing (Keynesianism) had been an ideological anathema to the American business community and to a fiscally conservative Congress. Deficit spending for military goods and research, of course, had always been an exception to that ideological maxim. Predictably, the beneficiary of that *military* Keynesianism, the military-industrial complex, had sought to protect its near monopoly of state dollars by adding its not-very-principled voice to the opposition of deficit spending for *non*military purposes. Given ideological hostility and military-industrial opposition, it was quickly evident that corporatist investment strategies were not politically feasible.

With no viable alternative, the Carter administration fell back upon the Cold War economic formula of stepped-up military spending at home to foster employment of workers and capital, and stepped-up military commitments abroad to protect and expand America's share of global economic opportunities. Carter sharply increased budgetary appropriations for the military, especially for high-tech weapons systems research and development. The administration upgraded the hardened-silo construction for Minuteman-III missiles, accelerated the Trident nuclear submarine program, and announced its "deceptive mode" scheme for deployment of the projected MX missiles. The last, an extravagantly expensive plan, would have crisscrossed the American West with a matrix of underground railroads that could transfer MXs secretly from one mobile launch site to another. Similarly, in Europe, the United States pressed forward enthusiastically with the theater nuclear force development. Indeed, in June 1980, Carter even sent an "astonishing" letter to German Chancellor Helmut Schmidt—the originator of the TNF concept—warning him not to negotiate TNF's status during a state visit to Moscow. The American government took these steps within the context of an aggressive new strategic doctrine, Presidential Directive-59 (PD-59), secretly signed by Carter on July 25, 1980. Its general outlines, deliberately leaked, seemed to suggest that America had abandoned parity and mutual assured deterrence for a position of strength that would make it possible to wage and win "a prolonged, limited nuclear war."

Economic need as well as strategic considerations prompted this wave of military spending. For example, the mammoth MX underground railroad grid might do for the construction industry in the 1980s what Eisenhower's interstate highway system had done for it in the 1950s. The Carter administration, however, never candidly acknowledged such growth considerations. Instead, it justified American military spending solely as a response to massive, prolonged Russian military spending that threatened to replace superpower parity with Russian superiority. Echoing Kennedy's missile gap rhetoric of the early 1960s and previewing Reagan's "window of vulnerability" message of the early 1980s, Carter administration spokesmen produced statistics to demonstrate that Russian military spending had increased "steadily and significantly by an average of four to five percent a year," and that "this Soviet trend has continued, even as the rate of growth in Soviet GNP has declined." Secretary of Defense Harold Brown, claiming that there could be "no doubt about the steady increase in the Soviet defense effort each year for more than 15 years," expressed particular concern over the Russian emphasis on investment and procurement in new weapons systems.

In reality the figures were exaggerated and the judgments inaccurate. Later, CIA analysis would demonstrate that Soviet military spending increased by no more than 2 percent annually from 1976 to 1978 and then leveled off; that development of new weapons investment had been stagnant, showing zero percent annual increases; and that procurement of planes, missiles, and ships had actually slowed. Similar conservative estimates were available to the Carter administration in 1980, as they were to the succeeding Reagan administration in 1981. Both, however, chose to publicize and act on the less plausible but higher numbers in order to justify spending well in excess of any reasonable security needs. The spending was perhaps not in excess of the economic need to jump-start a stalled American economy, the political need to defuse conservative critics, or the hegemonic need to revive Third World respect for American military power and European and Japanese dependence on it.

9 | The Reagan Cold War and Détente Revisited, 1981–1988

> Peace requires hegemony or balance of power. We have neither
> the resources nor the stomach for the former. The only question
> is how much we have to suffer before we realize this.
> —*Henry Kissinger, 1988*

The term *Catch-22* might have been invented to describe the quandary of a hegemonic power in decline. If that nation sustains the high-level military spending necessary to carry out its global policing, it neglects civilian research and development, distorts the general economy, and reduces its ability to compete with others in world markets. On the other hand, if it cuts military spending to restore civilian productivity and trade competitiveness, it diminishes its role as global protector for a capitalist free world. It becomes less effective in containing or confronting the system's enemies, or in forcing its friends to depend on its protection and therefore defer to its rules of the game. Hegemony necessarily rests upon both military and economic power, and the dilemma facing a maturing hegemon is that it cannot sustain both. Such is the nature of world-system dynamics.

Reagan and the Hegemonic Dilemma

The first Reagan administration, in the early 1980s, attempted to repeal the laws of history and perpetuate American hegemony ad infinitum. Its words and deeds were reminiscent of Britain's desperate effort at this century's beginning to have its cake and eat it too. Not only did the Reagan administration seek to expand America's military role in the world, it sought to restore its economic efficiency through "managed recession" and "supply-side economics."

The militaristic aspect of this double agenda was perhaps predictable, given the political make-up of the administration's inner circle. In this administration, unlike the divided Carter administration, one tendency—the right—monopolized power, though it did split somewhat over the virtues of containment versus those of outright confrontation with the Soviet Union.

The radical and evangelical right, absolute in its condemnation of Russia's "evil empire," favored confrontation and hoped that an expensive Cold War would so warp an already distorted Russian economy that it would provoke antigovernment social upheaval within the Soviet Union. Cold War liberals and neoconservatives, more pragmatic and issue-oriented, pushed the more conventional and less risky option of containment. The President himself, absolutist of heart but pragmatic of mind, drifted between the two inclinations within the right-tendency. Despite these differences, both groups favored the remilitarization of American foreign policy. That consensus reflected in part the enormous power wielded by corporate representatives of the military-industrial complex, like Secretary of State George Schultz and Secretary of Defense Casper Weinberger, and by professional military men, like Secretary of State Alexander Haig and National Security Advisers Robert McFarlane, John Poindexter, and Colin Powell.

The first Reagan administration carried the remilitarization begun by Carter to its apogee. The new President called for $1.5 trillion in military spending over the 1981–85 period—a staggering sum that represented 8 percent of America's GNP (compared to 3.5 percent of Germany's and less than 1 percent of Japan's). Significantly, a greatly increased proportion of that military spending shifted from the operation of existing equipment to research and development of new weapons systems. In 1980, 64 percent of America's military budget was for operating expenses and 36 percent for new investment. By 1986, the latter had surpassed the former by a 51-49 percent margin. This high-tech upscaling of the American military was to produce an expanded and modernized strategic force of B-1 bombers and MX missiles, an augmented theater nuclear force in Europe, a navy with fifteen battle groups, and a rapid deployment force. The total package was to be capable of fighting three Vietnam-type wars at once, of fulfilling Carter's PD-59 goal of protracted, limited nuclear war capability, and of closing the "window of vulnerability" that allegedly exposed American land-based missiles to a Russian first strike. The political consequences were perhaps more important. This late-century version of gunboat diplomacy would reinforce reliance by the Euro-Japanese core on the American military shield, deter revolution and facilitate stabilization in the periphery and semiperiphery, and counter any Soviet military intimidation of the capitalist world-system.

The Reagan militarization program created problems for the administration's economic goal of reviving the profitability of American industry and its ability to hold its own in both domestic and foreign markets. To be sure, massive military expenditures acted partly as a Keynesian pump-primer. Deficit defense spending constituted a direct state subsidy that underwrote high profits for major and minor contractors. Moreover, the military sector's increasing proportion of research investment was supposed to spin off new product lines and more rationalized production techniques, which could be used to aid the faltering civilian sector. On the other hand, the noncompetitive, cost-overrun contracts for the defense industry inflated prices for the whole economy, making civilian goods less cost-competitive with those of trading rivals. The guaranteed, state-subsidized high profits of the military-industrial complex magnetically pulled capital into its orbit from the underinvested civilian industrial sphere. The huge federal budget deficit, boosted relentlessly by military spending, required such high-interest borrowing by the state that it diminished the pool of credit available to the private sector. In short, the two symbols of American economic decline, the budget deficit and the foreign trade deficit, seemed even less eradicable as a consequence of such military spending.

While aware of these problems, the Reagan administration thought there was a way to continue state subsidization of the military sector and still attract vital capital to the civilian sector. Viewing the budget and trade deficits as symptoms rather than sources of economic ills, the new government argued that the root of the problem was a declining rate of profit in domestic industry that discouraged new investment. The solution, therefore, was to make civilian industry so much more cost-efficient that the resulting higher profits would attract the additional capital needed to sustain innovation and to hone competitiveness in world markets. The American economic snowball, on a downhill run since 1971, could be stopped and pushed back uphill to the summit again.

The means employed were recession and deregulation. Unconventional in the 1980s, they would have been ordinary in the 1880s. The first order of business, in this drive for efficiency, was to put the American economy and its people through the terrible wringer of recession. It had to happen fast so it would be well over by the 1984 elections, and it had to happen hard if it was to squeeze inefficiencies out of the American economy. Initiated by the central bank's tight money, high interest rate policies, the recession began in late 1981 and lasted through 1982. Throughout the economic downturn, the administration tried to manipulate it to bring the Carter administration's double-digit inflation to near-zero levels. It sought also to eliminate inefficient producers or force them into mergers with more competitive ones and to reduce labor costs and the power of the unions that sustained them. The presumed savings from deflated prices, lowered wages, and rationalized management would make American products more competitive in both the American and world markets. While the Reagan recession was the most severe economic plunge since 1937, its timing, middle-class approval of its anti-inflationary success, and the President's own personal popularity meant that the hand that turned the economic wringer in 1982 paid no political penalties in 1984.

Deregulation was the other means to economic efficiency, and it began concurrently with the recession and continued on track thereafter. Like its recessionary partner, deregulation sought to eliminate inefficient producers and facilitate capital accumulation for the rationalized survivors of competition in the marketplace. The "hidden hand" of the market, rather than state or corporatist economic planning, would choose America's targets for investment and reindustrialization. This free enterprise solution sought to restore competition between capitalists by deregulating airline fares, ending AT&T's monopoloy of the telephone industry while freeing it to compete in other forms of telecommunications, and generally reducing barriers to mergers and takeovers in the private sector. For the survivors in this social Darwinian arena, the administration made easier the task of profitmaking and capital accumulation. It sharply cut corporate taxes in 1981, greatly eliminated costly health and safety regulations for industry, and gave business a free hand to cut wages and fringe benefits through union-busting and "take-back" contracts. (Indeed, the Reagan administration legitimized the latter process itself when it broke the Professional Air Traffic Controllers Union in a 1981 strike, even though PATCO had supported Reagan's election.) Freed from governmental controls and fattened by savings-induced profits, the private sector would presumably make its own assessment of which "demand" could most profitably be "supplied," of what industries and which product lines to target.

In the long run, as we shall see, "Reaganomics" failed to deter America's competitive slide in the world of international business. In the short run, however, it produced a stunning success that peaked in 1984, when that year's 5.5 percent increase in GNP rivaled boom year figures from the 1950s. The costs, to be sure, were extraordinarily high. The Black underclass, female-headed, single-parent families, and other marginalized groups suffered severely as the result of sharp spending cuts in social welfare, a sphere that did not enjoy the Pentagon's untouchable status. Likewise, the ecology of the whole society fared poorly as the result of loosened environmental controls, reduced health and safety standards, and a general unresponsiveness to heightened concern over acid rain, toxic poisoning, and waste disposal. Nonetheless, white America, especially its middle and upper stratas, did well indeed. Moreover, the apparent Reagan "economic miracle" had incredible impact abroad. Europe especially was so impressed with the American economic comeback that both its capitalist and noncapitalist halves, the EEC, and COMECON, increasingly agreed that the flexibility and adaptability of the free market made it superior to command economics in promoting innovation and growth. Indeed, Reaganomics may have made more intellectual conquests east of the Iron Curtain than west of it.

The Reagan Cold War

"Riding tall in the saddle," its self-confidence temporarily resuscitated by massive militarization and the economic miracle, the first Reagan administration carried forth the Cold War banner first unfurled by Carter in 1979. Except for its "Caribbean basin initiative", the new American foreign policy differed little from its predecessor. The Reagan approaches to the theater nuclear force issue in Europe and to the arc of crisis in Southwest Asia and Northeast Africa tended to elaborate on Carter policies rather than depart from them in any innovative manner.

The short-term propellent for the Caribbean basin initiative was a determination to restore eroded American credibility. Its premise was that one had to be feared before one could be respected. The long-term stimulus was a nagging anxiety that the dominant regional power, Mexico, ultimately ran the risk of a social upheaval, born of recent economic chaos and declining political legitimacy. Any regional destabilization, any Caribbean version of falling dominoes, might only heighten Mexico's potential for self-destruction. Confronted with the reality of revolution in Nicaragua and the potential success of revolution in El Salvador, the Reagan administration tried to destroy the one and thwart the other.

It introduced helicopter gunships to El Salvador, increased the number of American military advisers there, buoyed the regime of Napolean Duarte with economic aid (more than $300 million per year by 1985), and tried to enhance Duarte's legitimacy at home and abroad by staging demonstration elections in 1982 and again, more successfully, in 1984. Similarly, in Nicaragua, the United States attempted to destabilize and oust the Sandinista government by tactics that seemed a composite of those used in Guatemala in 1954 and Chile in 1973: economic pressure, managed subversion and the threat of American military intervention. Cutting off its own aid, the American government encouraged private investors, foreign governments and multinational banking institutions to do the same. At the same time, it trained, organized, and financed a counterrevolutionary army (the *contras*) of former Somozista national guardsmen and other disaffected émigrés to launch military raids into Nicaragua from neighboring Honduras and Costa Rica. It was hoped that the Sandinistas' inability to provide public security or to deliver on the economic promises of the revolution would create the basis for an internal overthrow of the regime. If that hope proved vain, the United States held in reserve the possibility of its own military intervention. It graphically displayed its capabilities in that option by engaging in massive military maneuvers in Honduras, sizeable naval deployments off both Nicaraguan coasts, and by covertly mining Nicaraguan harbors. To further dramatize the point, the United States invaded and occupied Grenada in late 1983, to demonstrate, somewhat ineptly, American willingness and ability to use force in the Caribbean basin against alleged Cuban-Soviet agents of regional destabilization.

Taken on balance, the Caribbean basin initiative not only failed, but it undermined the very dominance it sought to extend. American aid to El Salvador and the 1984 demonstration election did sustain Duarte in office against the opposition of peasant revolutionary groups and right-wing death squads. Nonetheless, any political settlement remained remote—a future oligarchic triumph at the polls was possible and a reescalation of the revolution probable. In Nicaragua, America's unrelenting seven-year effort to overthrow the Sandinista government managed, instead, to produce an anti-interventionist movement in the United States, a modest amount of anti-American criticism in Western Europe, and compromise political proposals from Latin American governments. In the United States, a loose coalition of center-tendency elites, reform elements in the Roman Catholic Church, and student groups invoked "the Vietnam syndrome" to pressure Congress to bar aid to the *contras* in 1984, cut it to smaller sums in later years, and limit it to humanitarian forms in 1988. Abroad, European social democrats, in and out of government, extended moral support and some financial aid to the Sandinistas.

More importantly, Caribbean basin nations themselves snatched the initiative from the United States out of fear that America's counterrevolutionary tactics would inadvertently promote the spread of revolution instead. They were particularly fearful that the American conversion of Honduras into a garrison-state proxy might destabilize that country in the same way that comparable tactics had done a decade earlier in Cambodia. Mediating initiatives by Mexico and Venezuela in the early 1980s bore little fruit. More successful was a plan by President Arias of Costa Rica, delivered unannounced in 1987, in which the five Central American republics called for a cease-fire, a negotiated political settlement, elections, and liquidation of any foreign military presence. While its ultimate success remained problematic in late 1988, the Arias plan did suggest that American regional suzerainty be modified to accept a measure of autonomy for its smaller and weaker neighbors. Though still committed to its Caribbean basin initiative, the Reagan administration was forced to grant at least rhetorical support to the Arias plan. Moreover, the Committee for Santa Fe, an ad hoc study group with close ties to George Bush, argued in its "Strategy for Latin America in the Nineties" that "OAS peacekeeping operations in

Central America are vastly preferable to the non-aligned or hostile efforts that would be mounted by the UN in this sensitive area."

In the volatile arc of crisis, the Reagan administration perpetuated its predecessor's analysis and policy. It viewed in the shifting crisis spots a coordinated pattern of Soviet expansion, and it affirmed its intention to implement the Carter Doctrine's vow to use American or allied forces to protect that strategic region. American aid to Afghan rebels, coupled with similar support from China and several Arab states, escalated the level of Soviet-Afghan conflict and helped sustain the Afghanistan War for nearly a decade. Proponents of American policy have argued that American pressure was crucial in the 1988 Soviet decision to evacuate Afghanistan and effect a political settlement. On the other hand, the political settlement envisioned was essentially the same kind Russia had sought since 1979, so American policy might well have sustained the war and postponed peace unnecessarily. Moreover, American covert intervention in Russia's geographic sphere provided the Soviets with a tit-for-tat rationale for aiding Nicaragua's Sandinistas in America's sphere.

More overt were American efforts to safeguard and support its Egyptian and Israeli allies. Egypt's major security concerns were Libya and Ethiopia. The United States effectively isolated the latter through completion of its regional base network and solidification of its ties with Somalia and Sudan. Horribly burdened by drought-driven starvation and political-military strife, Ethiopia became a costly commitment to Russia and Cuba rather than a geopolitical asset. As for Libya, the United States effectively used Qadaffi's alleged support of international terrorism to question his legitimacy and thus justify economic pressures, gunboat diplomacy, and finally a 1986 air attack (assassination attempt) on Qadaffi's living quarters. The results were a much lower international profile for the Libyan government during Reagan's last two years in office.

On the other side of the Suez, American support of Israel was less effective. After the Camp David agreement with Egypt, Syria became Israel's chief security concern. Most stressful to Israel was Syria's involvement in the severe chronic political turmoil of Lebanon, a nation which, by its proximity and by welcoming Palestine Liberation Organization (PLO) bases, was a perpetual source of Israeli anxiety. When Israel intervened in the Lebanese civil war in 1982, hoping to check Syria and crush the PLO, it trapped itself in Lebanon's political quagmire and opened itself to public censure for its harsh tactics. The United States, attempting to extricate its ally, negotiated a mutual PLO-Israeli withdrawal from Beirut. It then landed two thousand American marines to help enforce a cease-fire.

The short-term result was a debacle of epic proportions. The American occupation, ineffectual from the beginning, staggered under the impact of a Lebanese suicide attack that killed 241 marines in their compound. It ultimately ended in ignominious withdrawal, despite the President's earlier assertion that peace and American credibility required it to continue. In the long run, the Lebanese imbroglio only compounded Israeli security problems. With the PLO's withdrawal from Lebanon and dispersal into other Arab states, the remaining Palestinian masses had to generate their own agenda and resources. Those living in Israel itself opted for demonstrations and street riots, compared by some to civil resistance in South Africa. Israel's increasingly harsh repression of these demonstrations not only produced worldwide opprobrium but set the stage for the pivotal, yet ultimately inconclusive, 1988 Israeli election. More than ever before, America's chief Middle Eastern ally fissured over the best means to preserve its security: whether to trade "territory for peace" with its Arab neighbors or annex additional territory as buffers against those same neighbors.

In the strategic pivot of the arc of crisis, the United States sought to implement the Carter Doctrine to keep open the Persian Gulf and its flow of oil to Japan and Europe. Through its tenure, the Reagan regime exploited the Iran-Iraq War (1981–88) to maintain the status quo and a regional balance of power in the Gulf. Claiming neutrality, the United States aided both warring parties and helped prolong the war. The extended military stalemate not only drained the resources of Khomeini's fundamentalist theocracy in Iran but diminished Iraq's potential to act as a Soviet surrogate. With Israeli complicity, the United States covertly sold arms to Iran in 1985, while it simultaneously and covertly promoted an Iraqi oil pipeline to the Gulf of Aqaba. Public disclosure of the former occurred in 1987 during congressional investigation of the Iran-*contra* scandal, charges that the Iran arms sale was part of an exchange for American hostages and that its inflated proceeds illegally funded Nicaraguan counterrevolutionaries at a time when Congress had prohibited all *contra* aid.

By 1987, the Iran-Iraq War had taken a dangerous turn. Military successes by Iran threatened the balance of power, and its use of mines, gunboats, and missiles threatened oil tankers in the Persian Gulf. The disequilibrium forced the United States to tilt toward Iraq, despite long-range American hopes that, after Khomeini's death (he was in his eighties and rumored to be in poor health), an Iranian-American rapprochement could be consummated. The United States intervened directly in the Persian Gulf, using its expanding naval-air armada to keep open the oil lanes to the markets of the world. The move provoked public criticism from American centrists that it violated the War Powers Act and risked expanding the Iran-Iraq conflict into a regional conflict involving the United States and potentially even Russia.

The Persian Gulf intervention also engendered right-tendency criticism, however. Brzezinski, for example, thought the administration was missing a great opportunity both to demonstrate the vitality of American hegemony and to punish Iran militarily. He urged that the American task force expand its protection of American and American-flagged Kuwaiti tankers to cover all oil shippers of whatever nationality. He also criticized the Reagan administration for not ordering more aggressive naval-air actions in the gulf, actions that would provoke a rash Iranian response and give the United States an excuse to launch a substantive air campaign that would show Iran and the world that the American bite was as bad as its bark. Ironically, the Reagan presidency now found itself, like its predecessor, an object of contention between center- and right-tendencies. Moreover, it did so at a time when the Iran-*contra* scandal was producing charges from diverse political perspectives that the President was either weak or lying. Either he was not running his own foreign policy and was leaving it to NSC subordinates or he was running it duplicitously, without regard for law and without congressional advice.

If the Reagan administration let the Carter Doctrine guide its actions in the arc of crisis, it also carried Carter's belated enthusiasm for a theater nuclear force in Europe to its logical conclusion. First, it pushed ahead with deployment of intermediate range ballistic missiles (IRBMs) and introduced land-based cruise missiles into Germany and Britain. It did so despite strong public opposition from a Euro-American "nuclear freeze" movement that demanded a moratorium on all missile deployment and mutual, negotiated reductions. Public opinion did force Soviet and American leaders to carry on desultory talks between 1981 and 1983, but Russia broke them off completely in 1984, and their renewal in 1985 led nowhere until the INF treaty breakthrough in 1987.

In those talks, the United States insisted on a "zero sum" solution—the withdrawal of *all* Russian and American intermediate missiles from the European theater. It would not, however, consider Russian demands that French and British missile forces or the American submarine component of its forward base system be counted in that zero sum equation. The Soviets could either accept the American proposal or both sides could keep matching missiles. The first choice would demonstrate the effectiveness of American atomic diplomacy. The second would perpetuate European dependence on American protection and put Russian cities minutes away from American IRBMs. It seemed a no-lose situation for American policy, unless Russia interpreted TNF as a first-strike threat and took some precipitous action. For Europe, however, the choices constituted a life-or-death affair. If Washington and Moscow found no basis for reduction or withdrawal, Europe ran the risk that a future nuclear war might be a limited theater war, rather than a global confrontation, using Europe as its graveyard battlefield.

The Semiperiphery and the Limits of Militarization

The Caribbean basin initiative, confrontationism in the arc of crisis, and TNF missile diplomacy in Europe constituted the core of the Reagan Cold War policy. While its effectiveness was open to considerable debate, the fatal flaw of militarization and confrontation was its irrelevance. Enhanced American military power might or might not be effective in putting down peasant revolutions in Central America, or negating Russian involvement in Southwest Asia, or introducing missiles into Europe to keep it from being pressured out of its North Atlantic orientation. It was a powerless giant, however, when it had to confront the unraveled skein of social upheaval that had spread throughout the semiperiphery of five continents and whose enormity was such that it defied any militarily imposed solution. Throughout the 1970s, the amazing increases in industrial productivity in the semiperiphery had rested upon the massive displacement of its peasantry and the high rate of exploitation of its industrial working class. The consequent economic crisis of internal underconsumption and external debt trap, magnified by culture shock, family disruption, and other forms of social trauma, created the preconditions for widespread popular unrest. Moreover, the repressive behavior of the authoritarian regimes that often governed those societies provided the unwitting catalysts for transforming unrest into rebellion.

In South Africa, the continent's only industrialized country, the emergence of a permanent, urban-based Black proletariat made the antigovernment strikes and uprisings of the mid-1980s a far more serious challenge to ruling-class legitimacy than had been similar upheavals of the 1960s and 1970s, led only by students and the peasant-based African National Congress (ANC). In the Philippines, high unemployment in the industrial sector, coupled with spiraling inflation and the martial law measures of the Marcos clan, led to the heightened violence and mass demonstrations that ultimately forced Marcos into exile in 1986 and installed Corozon Aquino as his shaky successor. Likewise, in South Korea, the strategic alliance of traditional student protestors with increasingly militant and organized workers demanded greater participation and rewards from the rapid growth of Korean steel, auto, and shipbuilding industries. By the end of 1987, the cumulative impact of industrial strikes, mass demonstrations, and violent clashes with government forces finally forced the suspension of martial law and the holding of public elections—though the indecisiveness of the electoral results left the legitimacy of the ruling government still in doubt in early 1988. In Poland, the working-class organization, Solidarity, climaxed a year of strikes and demonstrations in 1981 with calls for a national referendum on the government and its economic policies. Government imposition of martial law late in the year and the arrests of Solidarity leaders quelled the crisis (and perhaps avoided Soviet intervention). Nonetheless, the increased social power of the Polish working class, and its anger at both the nature of state economic planning and the lack of working-class input, made Solidarity a specter that would not go away; it continued to haunt the Polish government (and its Russian patron) into the late 1980s.

These revolts in the semiperiphery affected American national interests in very direct ways. The United States had strategic interests in virtually all of the more volatile countries. South Korea, with its American army presence, and the Philippines, with American air and naval facilities at Clark Field and Subic Bay, possessed the most obvious significance. South Africa and Poland occupied space that had geopolitical value in the world-system. Similarly, the United States held vast numbers of loan notes to these nations and often large investments as well, in multinational industry. Beyond direct American interests, however, was the larger interest for the capitalist world-system as a whole—the danger of one or more of these semiperipheral nations defaulting on debt obligations. Either continued instability or radical revolution would sharply increase the probability of that development.

In defense of national and systemic interests, Reagan's militarized foreign policy was helpless. It came up against the same reality that had produced the Vietnam syndrome in the 1970s—the limits of American power relative to the number and enormity of global problems to be confronted. This was especially evident in the semiperiphery, whose countries could never be the likes of Guatemala in 1954 or the Dominican Republic in 1965 or Grenada in 1983. They were endowed with larger areas and populations and higher degrees of economic development, national consciousness, and military capabilities. Any one of them might well prove more impervious than even Vietnam to external military solutions. More than one would be an epic nightmare and would make a mockery of the Reagan goal to create a military force with three-war capability. The only recourse for the administration was to continue aiding authoritarian regimes so long as they seemed viable, to prod them towards reforms and a broadened political base when their control grew too tenuous, and when their legitimacy was lost, to abandon them and seek to fill the political void with a compromise regime that might yet safeguard American interests. It was a reformulation of the Eisenhower-Kennedy third force strategem—but only as a policy of last resort.

In South Africa, the administration modified its constructive engagement policies. It imposed a prohibition on bank loans and restrictions on sales of computers and nuclear equipment to the South African government, while simultaneously holding secret, exploratory talks with its ANC adversary. Although the Reagan regime still opposed the stock divestiture strategy of anti-apartheid protestors, it apparently had determined by 1985 that South Africa needed prodding. By 1986 it had concluded the same thing about South Korea. Convinced that the cycle of repression and resistance was dangerously out of control, the United States reinforced those Korean leaders who believed that only public elections could defuse domestic discontent, recoup the lost legitimacy of the ruling class, and restore some semblance of stability. Finally, in the Philippines, the Reagan administration—with palpable reluctance—concluded that the Marcos regime had exhausted its legitimacy when rioting citizens refused to accept the honesty and validity of his "demonstration" reelection in October 1985. So, in early 1986, it urged his exodus, though it did provide him with a degree of sanctuary for himself, his entourage, and his wealth.

Militarization, Reaganomics, and Star Wars

If militarized foreign policy seemed irrelevant to the situation in much of the world-system's intermediate zones, its economic consequences were a decided liability for the administration's free market reindustrialization efforts. The sternest indicators of this remained the twin deficits in foreign trade and the national budget. Reaganomics had posited that both deficits would automatically disappear when deregulation and market incentives produced such large-scale growth that cost-efficient American exports would tip the trade balance America's way and increased profits would expand the nation's tax revenues. Instead, both deficits grew by giant jumps. The American trade deficit, which stood at about $30 billion when Reagan entered office, had reached $130 billion (and was still growing) when he was inaugurated a second time four years later. Even allowing the dollar to depreciate against Japanese and German currencies after 1985 did not counter the trend. Likewise, the federal budget deficit skyrocketed from $59.6 billion in 1980 to $202.8 billion in 1985. Much of that increase grew out of the government's military Keynesianism—deficit funding (borrowing) to pay for military research, goods, and services.

The trade and budget deficits were symptoms of a more fundamental imbalance between aggregate profitability and civilian sector productivity. The overall rate of profit remained high for American capital after the 1984 economic upsurge. Indeed, the earnings yielded between 1985 and 1987 fueled one of the longest, most impressive bull markets in Wall Street's history, especially during the last year before the stock market crash of October 1987. On the other hand, growth in real GNP declined by half from its 1984 peak, averaging about 2.8 percent annually from 1985 to 1988 (about the same rate as economic growth under Carter prior to the 1979 recession). Moreover, annual real growth in nonmilitary production averaged even less.

This disjuncture between profits and productivity flowed from one central weakness in Reaganomics: simply putting money into capitalists' hands did not automatically insure that they would invest it in the right places. Instead of targeting their investments largely in new technologies, industries, and product lines, they tended to invest in spheres that offered surer, short-term profits requiring less long-term risk. Some capital stayed in the bond market, emulating European and Japanese purchases of the high-interest Treasury notes used to finance the huge national debt. Far more went into "paper entrepreneurship"—the rearrangement of industrial assets in the hope of short-term gains. In a merger mania akin to that of the 1920s, capitalists increased their profits less by new production investment than by corporate takeovers, often hostile, of other companies. Financed with "junk bonds" promising high dividends, these "leveraged buy-outs" (LBOs) not only introduced financial notes of dubious value into the economy but failed to address the fundamental need for massive new investment into civilian sector production.

Finally, all too much capital actually shifted *away* from the civilian sector to the military. Lured by the military spending pot-of-gold, traditional defense corporations, like Lockheed, General Dynamics, and McDonnell Douglas, became even more dependent on military spending, while largely civilian producers, like Ford, General Motors, Bendix-Autolite, and General Tire, shifted appreciably into the Pentagon sector. The end result not only prolonged the crisis of underinvestment in the civilian sector, but it perpetuated American competitive inefficiency as well. In the crazy-quilt world of Pentagon capitalism (cost overrun contracts and rigged bidding in which even the loser got rewarded by the winner with subcontracts) efficiency had always been less important than state subsidization of high profits. Indeed, some critics have estimated that American taxpayers got only $3 in value for every $10 in taxes that their government invested for them in military spending. In the meantime, German and especially Japanese capitalists, far less burdened by the collective and draining underwriting of an inefficient military sector, continued to innovate and invest in civilian product lines, where the discipline of the world market demanded they be efficient or be unable to compete. In sum, military Keynesianism and domestic deregulation had failed to meet the pressing need to channel new investments, labor, and entrepreneurial energies into industries that could revive America's competitive standing in world trade.

The Reagan administration's solution to its own economic conundrum began as a military program but evolved over time into an economic one as well. It was the Strategic Defense Initiative (SDI), or "Star Wars," first promoted publicly by the President in early 1983. It was the President's "dream" of a foolproof antiballistic missile system that could destroy enemy missiles in space before they reached American targets. SDI received its impetus from two factors, one internal, one external. First, the administration grew increasingly concerned that the American public would not support an escalating nuclear arms race for an indefinite period of time. The psychic burden of an intensified "balance of terror" and the economic burden of a budget deficit out of control seemed more than they would bear for very long. Even by 1983, public criticism made deployment of the MX missile a fit subject for scorn, and mass viewing and discussion of a television fictionalization of World War III, "The Day After," revealed a stratum of anxiety waiting to be tapped. In response, SDI offered assurance that America could continue its global policing role without jeopardizing the safety of its own citizens, while simultaneously reducing the budget for offensive weapons.

Second, Russia's own continued military build-up made it questionable that America could ever regain the balance of power superiority that the administration deemed essential to America's hegemonic role. SDI, however, offered a way to side-step the balance in offensive weapons by securing an American monopoly on a perfect defensive system. If it worked, SDI would turn Russian over-reliance on heavy throw-weight ICBMs into a Soviet liability and leave the strategic balance heavily in favor of America's more diversified nuclear force of submarines, bombers, and cruise missiles. Moreover, even if it failed as a defensive system, the technological innovations in lasers, optics, supercomputers, and telecommunications might have very practical "offensive capabilities" in destroying conventional Soviet tanks, planes, and vehicles in a European-theater war. Even if it could not negate Russian ICBMs, it could negate the Red Army.

Although SDI may have been, as author Strobe Talbott put it, "the ultimate example of advertising an imaginary product," it had some unimagined consequences. Despite the considerable public ridicule directed at it and the sizeable attack on its viability by much of the scientific community, the movement for SDI snowballed from 1983 to 1987. In large part, it did so because much of the economic community came to see it not simply as a military program but also as an economic strategy. It might or might not work as the former, but that might not matter if it worked as the latter. If it did, it could provide the ideal means for investing $1 trillion (as many estimated its cost to be) into research and development that would restore America's technological edge over Japan and Germany in futuristic product lines and sunrise industries. Malcolm Browne, science editor of the

New York Times, caught some of the ebullience of such hopes when he quoted government predictions that Star Wars would generate between $20 and $25 trillion in *civilian* sector goods and services.

This was Keynesian pump-priming with a venegeance. In concept it was no different from corporatist schemes to create a New Deal-style Reconstruction Finance Corporation to perform the same targeted investing. It had two potential advantages going for it, however. First, it had a greater chance of securing congressional appropriations, since Congress had always been more moved by security arguments than economic ones in doling out tax dollars. Second, it created a mechanism for rationing the transfer of technology to industrial competitors. Formulated as a defense program, it could use classified information categorization to monopolize the more profitable high-tech research results for itself and restrict their movement elsewhere. (It was like the World War II atomic bomb project in that respect.) Awareness of that fact put Germany and Japan in quite a bind. When the United States offered to negotiate SDI subcontracting with them, they were caught between the obvious desire to buy into that high-tech system, lest they be frozen out altogether, and the fear that the United States would still use security classification to shut them out of the "right stuff." Ultimately, both bought in, but with trepidation and crossed fingers.

In 1986 in Reykjavik, Iceland, a summit meeting between Soviet and American heads of state made clear how non-negotiable SDI had become to President Reagan. His Russian counterpart was Mikhail Gorbachev, who had brought greater youth and dynamism to Soviet leadership after nearly a decade of stagnation produced by Brezhnev's long illness and marked by his death in 1982 and the subsequent deaths of his successors, Andropov in 1984 and Chernenko in 1985. Part of a new generation and a new breed, Gorbachev believed, according to one oft-repeated story, that his country was "in danger of becoming Upper Volta with missiles." While it had made awesome strides in military and space production and in the steel, concrete, coal, and oil industries, its ability to deliver on the material promises of the revolution to the Soviet peoples had been profoundly deficient. The Russian failures in agriculture, consumer goods, and high technology put the Russian economy far behind Western core nations. Indeed, in many respects it lagged behind even semiperipheral countries, like South Korea and Taiwan, in efficient use of resources. Attendant to those economic ills was a host of social maladies that threatened the stability of Soviet society, but none could be effectively addressed without coming to terms with the distortions in the Soviet economy. One way would be to confront the entrenched economic bureaucracy and introduce some market mechanisms into the economy, including the legalization and absorption of much of the flourishing black market capitalism that had long existed.

As pressing, however, was the need to liquidate the excesses of Cold War military spending that had misshaped the Russian economy even more than they had America's. To that end, Gorbachev took to Reykjavik the stunning, surprise proposal that the two superpowers cut all nuclear weapons by 50 percent within five years, in exchange for the de facto scuttling of SDI. Acceptance would significantly lessen Russia's economic burden and release money, people, and research for upgrading the civilian economy. It was a bold, shrewd move that sought to mobilize those in the Reagan administration, like arms negotiator Paul Nitze, who wanted to use SDI as a strategic bargaining chip, while it sought to neutralize those in the Russian military not enthused about any agreement that scaled down their ICBM force.

Surprised by the Gorbachev initiative, Reagan and his small group of advisers could not ignore it without abandoning the prodisarmament high ground they had assumed for 1986 congressional elections. Moreover, Reagan himself favored the 50 percent comprehensive cuts in nuclear weaponry, since it would free up money for Star Wars without further exacerbating the critical budget crisis. Consequently, the American delegation joined its Russian counterpart in one long, sleepless yet ultimately "lost weekend." SDI was the sticking point. The American delegation itself was split between those who defined SDI as inviolate and those who saw it as just a negotiating lever. In the end, Reagan himself made the choice. More personally involved with the Star Wars initiative than perhaps any other piece of policy during his two administrations, he would not abandon it nor his optimism that it was the ideal solution to America's future security and economic needs. An exhausted and disappointed Nitze could only mutter: "We tried, we tried. By God, we tried. And we almost did it."

If Reagan's commitment to SDI torpedoed Strategic Arms Reduction Talks (START) in 1986, it could not prevent a successful IMF (Intermediate-Range Missile Force) treaty in late 1987. At a Washington summit in December, Reagan and Gorbachev signed a "double zero option" agreement to eliminate *both* short-range and medium-range missiles from the European theater. Its wholesale elimination of an entire category of weapons and its unprecedented on-site verification procedures made the IMF treaty a ground-breaking pact. While the pact had only marginal significance for overall strategic relationships, it did have great political significance. For the Americans, it seemed to document their claim that the American military shield continued to work well in reducing Europe's vulnerability to external intimidation. Most Europeans could now rest easier in the knowledge that the superpowers would not use their continent as a neutral atomic battlefield. Only in Germany was there some resurgent fear that IMF actually heightened the possibility of a conventional war fought on the north German plains.

For the Russians, INF may have been even more significant. It conceivably signaled the end of the USSR's four-decade quest to detach Europe from its North Atlantic moorings. Indeed, there were suggestions in Soviet writings that Gorbachev's efforts to restructure the Soviet economy and society would not be affordable or successful unless Russia abandoned its postwar effort to play the superpower role. One Soviet leader told an American acquaintance: "We are about to do a terrible thing to you. We are going to deprive you of an enemy." Calling to mind Reagan's fondness for the aphorism "it takes two to tango," the Russian remark raised an interesting issue. Could Cold War between two superpowers be waged if one power refused to participate?

What made INF possible was Gorbachev's ability to hurdle the SDI stumbling block. Democratic victories in the 1986 congressional elections, and an accompanying resurgence of center-tendency opinion, seemed to erode political support for SDI in Congress. Oppressed by the awful weight of the federal deficit, the legislature showed decreased enthusiasm for spending large amounts on research and development, or on early deployment of SDI's initial stages. While this political shift was not decisive, it was sufficient for Gorbachev to take a calculated gamble. He wagered that the radical right would fail in its intense campaign for early deployment of SDI, so that, as Attorney General Edwin Meese hoped, it would "be in place and not tampered with by future administrations." If Gorbachev's guess was correct, then the clock would be on his side. Any Reagan successor, after all, was unlikely to share his fanciful obsession with Star Wars. Budget constraints and skepticism about SDI's practicality might not destroy SDI, but they were likely to scale it down to more modest dimensions and perhaps transform it from a partly strategic program aimed at Russia to a solely economic program aimed at Japan and Germany. Based on that calculation, Gorbachev proposed in early 1987 that Russia and the United States conclude "without delay" a separate agreement on medium range missiles in Europe, without linking it either to SDI's future or to the larger issue of START.

Despite opposition from other Soviet leaders, Gorbachev went through with his gamble in December 1987. By then, two developments had made his bet close to a sure thing. First, a variety of considerations, some of them personal, had led Casper Weinberger and Richard Perle to resign the number one and two positions in the Department of Defense. Both had been in the forefront of the early deployment campaign for SDI. The new secretary of defense, Frank Carlucci, leaned instead toward the Nitze position of bargaining away SDI for a more comprehensive START treaty. Second, and more importantly, the astounding crash of the Wall Street stock market on October 19, 1987, so traumatized American business and government leaders that it seemed certain they would oppose any substantial

SDI investment that would enlarge the budget deficit. As a consequence, the final IMF protocol treated SDI simply as an issue upon which the United States and the USSR had agreed to disagree. As Max Kampelman, the chief American negotiator put it about Star Wars, we merely "kicked the can down the road."

The New Détente

The IMF treaty ushered in a stunning series of events during Reagan's last year in office. Almost all were initiated by the Soviet Union, but they required active American participation. Each party began the process of dismantling and destroying its European missiles, under the watchful scrutiny of the other. In Afghanistan, Russia began the liquidation of its nine-year war by agreeing to a phased troop withdrawal in exchange for a similar withdrawal of American aid to Afghan rebels. In Angola, the United States, Russia, Cuba, and finally South Africa accepted an Angolan plan for the gradual evacuation of all foreign troops, chiefly Cuban and South African, and a political effort to settle that nation's fifteen-year-long civil war. In the Middle East, the United States and the Soviet Union supported a UN-initiated cease-fire in the eight year Iran-Iraq War and the beginnings of formal peace talks. In tacit return, the United States began to cut back its naval convoying operation in the Persian Gulf. Despite confrontation over the shooting down of an Iranian civilian passenger plane by an American frigate, behind-the-scenes overtures continued the problematic search for some basis for Iranian-American rapprochement.

All of these developments constituted détente, in fact, though American leaders did not describe it so in policy statements. Indeed, the détente of the late 1980s transcended that of the early 1970s in the extent and variety of open exchange between America and Russia. American journalists visiting a secret, top-security radar station in the Soviet Union, Russian generals observing first hand an American underground nuclear test explosion, military personnel on both sides visually verifying IMF implementation: all these would have been nearly inconceivable a decade and a half earlier. Intrinsically stunning, these developments seemed even more mind-boggling when contrasted with the militarized, Cold War confrontationism of the first Reagan administration.

Republicans in the 1988 presidential election argued that improved Soviet-American relations were a consequence of, rather than a contradiction to, the early Reagan crusade against the "evil empire." The rebuilding of American military power and the will to use it, they affirmed, had caused the Soviets to back down in Afghanistan, Angola, and Europe. It was a replay of the old "Munich syndrome" argument that weakness only whetted the imperial appetites of totalitarian powers (like Nazi Germany or communist Russia), while strength and resolve were the only things such nations understood and respected. Democrats never seriously challenged that analysis, and their presidential candidate promised to sustain the Soviet-American initiatives begun by the second Reagan administration.

The more fundamental reasons for détente, however, were more structural than political. In essence, neither nation could any longer afford the Cold War. Their economies were distorted by forty years of global jousting, and both Russia and America desperately needed a respite from the Cold War in order to pursue their internal strategies of economic reform and restructuring. *Glasnost* (openness) and *perestroika* (restructuring) were not possible for Russia so long as a military-industrial bureaucracy obstructed the former and a militarized economy prevented the latter. Reindustrialization and a favorable trade balance were not feasible for America so long as a parallel complex of military leaders, defense contractors, and "defense intellectuals" possessed the power to have their private needs determine public agendas.

In the American case, the stock market crash of October 1987 was crucial in driving home the point. Until that juncture, the prolonged and impressive bull market promoted the illusion that soaring profits would eventually translate into productivity growth and a gradual diminution of the budget and trade deficits. The jolting severity of the crash, however, not only unmasked the artificiality of inflated profits, it suggested to many observers that a recession was an inevitable part of a realistic readjustment of profits vis-à-vis production. For those so persuaded, the only real question was whether it was better to wring out the American economy at once in 1988, or to postpone the recession until 1989 or 1990.

Those favoring the latter option advised the administration to let the dollar continue to weaken against Japanese and German currencies, thus driving up the cost of foreign imports and ultimately turning around the trade balance. Nonetheless, they realized that a declining dollar would make T-notes less attractive to foreign investors, who ran the risk of purchasing those notes in current dollars but getting repaid later in cheaper dollars. Any consequent decline in foreign lending would force the government to confront the budget crisis with tax increases that would dampen domestic demand and produce a recession two or three years down the line. Those inclined to bite the economic bullet immediately were also those inclined to believe that high interest rates were essential to compensate foreign investors for the dollar's decline. While that would sustain foreign underwriting of the budget deficit, it ran the risk of confronting recent Wall Street losers with a credit market so tight that their compounded ruination would precipitate an immediate recession. The resulting decline in tax revenues could only intensify the budget crisis.

Economic calculations and the political need to avoid an election-year recession led the Reagan administration to choose the first option and thus postpone the day of reckoning. However, whether the overvalued American economy paid the piper now or later, the likely consequence would be a further expansion of the budget deficit at a time when many economic leaders had concluded that America could not continue to fund the prosperity of the present by borrowing against that of the future. Clearly, spending had to be cut and/or revenues enhanced—soon and significantly. Taxes could be raised to increase government revenue, but the deflation of disposable consumer income could generate its own economic slide. Social welfare for the poor could be cut, but earlier Reagan slashes in that sphere had left little more than bare bones to trim. The Social Security system could be reduced and its funds detoured into general revenue, but only at the risk of serious disruption to a system already faced with the inherent demographic problems of a rapidly growing elderly population.

Given the limited alternatives, it seemed clear that a freeze or even a reduction in military spending was necessary, provided it did not jeopardize national security. Realistically, there was not much danger of the latter. The Reagan militarization program had been based upon an inflated estimate of Russian military power and an improbable worst-case scenario of Russian intentions. In practical terms, therefore, there had always been room for military cuts. Moreover, any doubts about that proposition vanished with Gorbachev's top-priority commitment to domestic *glasnost* and *perestroika* and the consequent deemphasis on Soviet external involvement in Europe, Southwest Asia, and the horn of Africa. Just as the Great Crash of 1929 had led core powers to reduce their international involvements and concentrate on domestic recovery, so the more subtle, long-term decline of the distorted Russian and American economies had finally produced a conjuncture where both, more or less simultaneously, saw the need to set the Cold War aside and confront their own internal economic and social ills.

By 1988 even the right-tendency coalition in the Reagan administration had reluctantly accepted the need to relieve the Pentagon budget of its sacrosanct status. The new secretary of defense, Frank Carlucci, ordered the military services to cut their 1989 budget proposals across the board. At the same time, the administration pressured its European allies to take greater responsibility for their own defense, in the aftermath of the IMF liquidation of short-and medium-range American missiles. As it did so, it did not deign to deny rampant rumors in Europe that the withdrawal of American missiles might well be followed by a retrenchment in other forms of American military presence. Not surprisingly, Europe sought to fill the expected void by cooperative ventures of its own. France and Great Britain announced plans to build a "European" super-fighter aircraft, and

Germany and France set in motion efforts to create experimental Franco-German fighting units drawn from their respective armies. Even less surprising was the lack of American opposition to these moves. Getting Europe to shoulder more of its defense burden could only relieve America's economic burden while letting its NATO allies cope with the competitive distortions of increased military spending.

10 | The End of the Cold War and the Future of Hegemony

> The emperors, kings, prime ministers and presidents of great
> powers have always preferred the heady world of diplomacy,
> war and international affairs to the unglamorous realm of
> fiscal reform, educational change, and domestic renewal. . . .
> It is left to later generations to pay the price.
> — *Paul Kennedy, historian, 1990*

> By God, we've kicked the Vietnam syndrome once and for all.
> — *George Bush, 1991*

As the hourglass emptied on the twentieth century, the modern world-system stood at a moment of crisis similar to another such moment one century earlier. That prior crisis had led directly to two world wars sandwiched around the greatest world depression in the history of modern capitalism. The similarity of the two crises, a hundred years apart, raised the obvious question. Would this new crisis be resolved more satisfactorily, in ways that might prevent the calamities of the early twentieth century from being visited upon the twenty-first?

Most observers of the 1990s' predicament focused on the revolutionary rush of events unleashed by the surprising end of the Cold War, and on the conflicting responses of euphoria and anxiety in the West. On one hand, the overthrow of communism in Eastern Europe, the reunification of Germany, and the collapse of the Soviet Union all produced an initial cacophony of self-congratulation that America had won the Cold War and, in the process, validated its own system of free enterprise capitalism. "The End of History" had been reached, announced one former State Department official triumphally, and market democracies prevailed everywhere on the planet Earth. On the other hand, trepidation followed hard on the heels of that ecstatic boosterism. Its causes were obvious—the world recession, the shortfalls in Western European integration, the unexpectedly rocky road of Eastern Europe to capitalism, the traumatizing civil wars in Yugoslavia and the former Soviet Union, uncertainty about the future direction of Germany and Japan, America's vacillation over its role in a post–Cold War world, the revival of Pan-Russianism, the inept search for a new world order and the UN's place in it, and uncertainty over GATT and the hydra-headed emergence of trading blocs.

The crisis, however, was even more than it appeared. What seemed cause was often consequence, and what seemed startlingly sudden often had been a long time in the making. Myopically focused on the short-term crisis after 1988, most analysts failed to perceive that it, in turn, was the spectacular capstone to a far longer and deeper crisis stretching back some twenty years. The problem was not merely that of adjusting to post–Cold War realities. The problem was also that of addressing the longer-term decay of the world-system occasioned by political decentering and economic slowdown. In short, the revolution, evident to all in the early 1990s, was the product of a devolution, evident only to a few, that had originated in the early 1970s.

That devolution undermined the two factors essential to the peace and prosperity of the world-system. First, prolonged economic growth in gross world product (GWP) was necessary to lift all ships of state and thus act as a disincentive to war. Contrarily, prolonged economic slowdown or catastrophic contraction would tempt more disadvantaged nations to resort to war as a means of redistributing limited material rewards. Second, some center of power was necessary to maintain the peace and to enforce the rules of market liberalism against dissident nations. Contrarily, a diffusion and decentering of power tended to destabilize the world-system and run the risk of trade wars and real wars alike. Such were the lessons of a century ago, when the Long Depression of 1873–97 and the decline of British hegemony had undermined those two prerequisites and propelled the world-system into a nearly fatal epoch. Would the long slump of 1973–93 and the decline of American hegemony lead to a similar state of affairs?

The Quiet Depression

The twenty-year long slump (or "Quiet Depression") entailed a marked slowdown in GWP growth in the world-system as a whole and a sharp economic redistribution both between and within zones of that system. Overall, GWP grew at half the pace of the two decades before 1973, and its recessionary episodes of zero growth became ever more intractable and worldwide. The periphery became increasingly pauperized, the core witnessed an actual decline in manufacturing, and only the semiperiphery of newly industrializing nations remained dynamic and expansive. Within zones, America lost some of its competitive edge in world markets to core rivals, Germany and Japan (running an immense trade deficit with the latter), while the Pacific rim nations of South Korea, Taiwan, Hong Kong, and Singapore (with Thailand, Malaysia, and Indonesia waiting in the wings) demonstrated a sustained growth that was not replicated by the semiperiphery of South America or the oil-producing states in the Middle East.

Capping those long-term trends was the global recession of the early 1990s, which began in America and rippled around the world. It was a recession less disturbing for its length or severity than it was for the structural deformities that underlay it. The initiating American recession had been inevitable since late 1987, but short-term fixes had served to postpone it until after the 1988 presidential election. Increases in productivity ground to a standstill in the first fiscal quarter of 1989, and recession officially began fifteen months later, in July 1990. Misinterpreting the crisis as simply a psychological one "rooted in fear," mainstream opinion predicted that it would "not be as severe" as preceding ones, only to see that prediction repeatedly squashed by the false hopes of recovery in the consecutive springtimes of 1991 and 1992.

In reality, the 1990s recession was a classic case of chickens come home to roost—the climax to twenty years of "eroded productivity growth and decayed infrastructure," the payback for "so many years of stagnant income." Those two cornerstones of American hegemony—massive military spending and massive overseas investment—had combined to underfund and undermine the very American Dream they alleged to protect. The *New York Times* reported that American family incomes, which had risen more than 100 percent between 1950 and 1973, rose less than one-tenth that amount after 1973, and even that small increase was almost entirely "attributable to the entry of middle-class housewives into the paid labor force." Moreover, the inequitable redistribution of income upward meant that "only the wealthiest 20 percent of American families . . . gained ground over inflation" between 1973 and 1993. The result was a structural crisis rooted not merely in fear but in the reality of domestic underconsumption. American middle-class and working-class families still yearned for the dream of owning a home, a new car, of having leisure time and educational mobility, but they possessed decreased means by which to secure these goals. In sum, if the consequence of the Cold War had been that "the Soviet economy just happened to go over the cliff first," then the American economy hovered on the brink of its own precipice. And it did so at a time when its financial institutions, weakened by bad loans in the real estate bubble of the 1980s, offered little by way of a safety net.

The international consequences of the American recession proved disastrous. Given the pivotal place of the United States in an interdependent world market, America's recession eventually became a global one. World economic growth that had stood at a healthy 4.3 percent in 1988 steadily deteriorated until it stagnated at zero in 1991. Even Japan and Germany, whose fortunes had risen as those of the United States had declined, fell victim to economic malaise. The recession forced Japan to deemphasize its dependence on the American market and to reorient its trade and investment, toward its Asian neighbors—South Korea and the so-called "Greater China" community of mainland China, Taiwan, Singapore, and Hong Kong, as well as the Southeast Asian countries of Thailand, Malaysia, Indonesia, and Australia. Similarly, the recession in Germany tended to dilute its leadership role in the creation of a European Union in 1992. Instead Germany concentrated on its own internal problems of integrating the former East Germany and forming a single national economy; and the fiscal policies pursued in behalf of that goal tended to undermine the larger European goals of a single European currency and coordinated fiscal policies.

In the end, all of Europe suffered Germany's fate, as the economic dominoes generated by the American recession continued to topple around the planet. Strong and euphoric in 1989, Western Europe had looked forward to a post-1992 epoch in which the unified European economy would hold its own and compete on equal terms abroad with Japan and the United States; in which it would play the pivotal and so very profitable role of financial and technological angel in the reconstruction and reintegration of the Russian empire and Eastern Europe into a larger all-Europe framework; and in which it would play an ever more important and autonomous role in keeping the peace worldwide.

By 1993, pessimism reigned supreme in Europe. The Maastricht Treaty of European Union had barely managed ratification in the face of revived nationalist sentiment. The collapse of the exchange rate mechanism (ERM) had made the goal of a single currency seem a distant dream and had manifested a disturbing tendency for each nation to go its own way in moments of crisis. Unemployment, much of it structural rather than ephemeral, had reached double-digit levels, and forecasters bleakly predicted that European unemployment would remain around 10 percent even after economic recovery had taken place. Given the wages and welfare costs of its labor—significantly higher than those in America and Japan—Europe found it difficult to be cost-effective in competing in the world market. As a consequence, Europe began to edge away from its historic commitment to workers' rights and social welfare and looked increasingly at the model of "hire and fire" that had deregulated the American and British labor markets and marginalized unions in the Reagan-Thatcher decade. The European compact of social partners that existed between capital, labor, and the state began to fray around the edges, and the possibility of intensified class conflict greatly tarnished the once giddy prospects of 1989.

The twenty-year economic slide that climaxed in the early 1990s unleashed centrifugal forces that threatened to scuttle the post–World War II order of multilateralism and internationalism. A gathering army of special interests began to challenge the orthodox American premise that prosperity and peace were best served by a world whose economy was interdependent and a culture that was homogenized—an unregulated, global market serving a universalistic global village. *American workers* organized against GATT and the North American Free Trade Agreement (NAFTA) for failure to protect their jobs against the impersonal movement of whole factories ("runaway shops") in search of cheaper labor and higher profits abroad. *German ultranationalists* terrorized foreign workers competing for German jobs and prodded the German government to restrict its postwar openness to immigration. *Yugoslavian ethnic groups,* no longer assuaged by the material rewards of multicultural collaboration, fell apart in a civil war blood-bath of "ethnic cleansing." *Religious nationalists,* from Iran to Algeria, sought to reclaim some of the cultural identity long denied and denigrated by the homogenizing forces of the westernized global village. And *environmentalists* worldwide, once tolerated or even respected in more prosperous decades, now gravitated to more militant methods as the imperatives of hard times placed a greater premium on promoting productivity than on protecting against pollution and destruction.

In short, increasing numbers of historical actors no longer accepted uncritically the notion that an international growth strategy could raise all ships on its ascending tide. As ships foundered instead in a receding current, those actors turned to narrower, more self-centered activity to sustain and defend their interests, be they those of class, nation, ethnic community, religion, or ecology. In an age previously dominated by internationalist thought and action, each tended to define problems and solutions increasingly in nationalist terms. Only environmentalists waffled, promoting multilateral solutions to problems of global warming and acid rain but opposing international trade agreements that marginalized environmental issues. For the others, however, the boundaries of their worldviews ended at their nation's borders.

The End of the Cold War Stability

In this struggle between internationalism and born-again nationalism, two developments made it ever more difficult for the centripetal tendencies of the former to triumph over the centrifugal character of the latter. They were the end of the Cold War and the end of American hegemony. Each, after a fashion, had been a source of systemic stability, and the passing of each put that stability at risk.

In the quarter-century following World War II, the Cold War had evolved into a de facto system, a stable system in which the American and Soviet antagonists ironically became symbiotic allies of a kind. While their Cold War policies aimed to check each other's expansion, they also served a more important purpose of keeping their allies and clients, as well as their own citizens, safely in line. Exploiting the ubiquitous need for protection in a high-risk nuclear world, each had used the mutual fear of the "other" to maintain the integrity of their respective camps against nationalist fragmentation. By the early 1960s, in the aftermath of the Cuban missile crisis, each came to tacitly accept the other's hegemony in its respective system. And the national security managers of each came to experience a kind of kinship and admiration for their counterparts, who were, after all, engaged in the same pursuit of fostering integration and fighting disintegration in their own world. In an ironic way, the American and Soviet adversaries needed each other—needed the Cold War—to further their own hegemonic ambitions. The failure of détente in the 1970s and the renewal of their cold war in the 1980s seemed to validate that proposition.

By 1988, however, Gorbachev and the Soviets had rejected that theorem and opted out of the Cold War system. That radical step reflected an equally radical recognition—that both the Soviet Union and the United States had lost the Cold War and that the old Axis powers of Germany and Japan had been its major beneficiaries. While Soviet-American jousts in Europe, Afghanistan, and Africa had been diminishing the economies of each while adding to the security of neither, Japan had been leading a dynamic Pacific rim toward economic superiority, and Germany was leading a determined Europe toward 1992 unity and renewed global competitiveness. With Soviet cold warriors discredited by the Afghan quagmire and the failure of missile diplomacy in Europe, Gorbachev sought to end the costly Cold War symbiosis with the United States and to cast the lot of the Russian empire with its old wartime adversaries. In particular, he sought rapprochement with Germany and Soviet participation in an enlarged European union of east and west, while he also explored new openings to Japanese finance and technology. If the détente of the 1970s had failed to secure American aid and an end to Soviet backwardness, perhaps an updated venture would fare better if it looked chiefly to Germany and Japan instead.

Gorbachev's bold gamble required the Soviet Union to do two things. If it was to be part of a larger Europe, it first had to obliterate the Iron Curtain that divided Europe from itself and demonstrate that the cold War was truly over. It had to give Western Europe a long-term sense of security in return for long-term Soviet access to its economic support. In short, disengagement had to follow on the heels of nuclear disarmament. Second, the Soviet Union had to restructure its internal economy in ways that would make it attractive to foreign economic interests. While retaining its socialist infrastructure, it would have to open more of its economy to privatization, profit incentives, and the discipline of the competitive market. And that, in turn, would require making some room in the political process for a new entrepreneurial class, almost certainly at the expense of state managers, Communist party bureaucrats, and the military professionals.

The ironic consequence of those two steps was the disintegration of the Russian empire at home and abroad. Gorbachev had gone for a ride on the back of a tiger, and the beast first unseated him and then devoured him. In Eastern Europe, Gorbachev knowingly initiated the process by acknowledging the legality of Poland's Solidarity movement and by renouncing the Brezhnev Doctrine, thus setting aside the Soviet role as regional policeman in Eastern Europe. Now unfettered by "Red Army socialism," the USSR's former satellites overthrew or voted out Communist governments. Less than a year separated Solidarity's triumph in Poland in 1989 and the fall of the Berlin Wall in East Germany; between these events, other pro-Soviet regimes fell like the proverbial dominoes— Czechoslovakia's passing being the most peaceful and democratic, Romania's the most violent and authoritarian. In a twinkling, the Russian empire lost all that it had gained in World War II.

The Soviet empire had been a vast, sprawling, multicultural empire held together by the fear of foreign aggression and by the internal power of the Red Army and the Communist party. With the fear vanished and the power diminished, the long-sublimated forces of race, religion, ethnicity, and region found their historic moment. Beginning with the tense secession of the Baltic republics in 1989, the disintegration climaxed in 1992 with the further secession of the Ukraine, Belorus, and Georgia. Only a nine-republic Russian Federation remained at the core of the old Soviet Union. Along the way, Gorbachev had fallen from power and had been replaced by his old nemesis, Boris Yeltsin—a political transfer that took place in the midst of violent civil wars on the periphery of Russia and two aborted but traumatic right-wing coups in its very center. Feeding that political crisis, and being fed by it, was a paralyzing collapse of the Russian economy, as free marketeers, black marketeers, and state managers competed to expedite, exploit, or prevent the move from communism to free enterprise. The economic anarchy that ensued was stagflation with a vengeance, nearly fulfilling the CIA prediction that "the decline would eventually equal or exceed the 30 percent drop in G.N.P. and the 25 percent unemployment rate experienced in the United States during the Great Depression of 1930–1933."

The twin collapse of the Russian empire and of communism resulted from many complex causes. At its root, however, was the erroneous assumption that Western inputs of technology, money, and expertise would be sufficiently large to see the Russian empire through the difficult but heady process of *glasnost* and *perestroika*. Such was decidedly not the case. Instead, hopes of capitalist largess foundered on the rocks of global recession, German nationalism, doctrinaire American ideology, and Japanese resistance. The worldwide recession of 1990–94 meant that capitalist coffers were relatively bare; so even if the developed core wished to rescue Russia and revitalize Eastern Europe, there was, as one American official said off the record, "not enough money in the West to finance" it. More concretely, West Germany's pell-mell effort to incorporate East Germany proved so extraordinarily expensive that it seriously diminished the stock of available German assistance to the Soviet Union. Gorbachev had expected German reunification to be a slow, incremental process that would leave West Germany free to function as his country's major patron. When that expectation proved false, Gorbachev tried to blackmail the West into slowing the process by insisting that any reunified Germany had to withdraw from NATO. Fearful itself of an autonomous, unified Germany, the United States happily cooperated in the effort to retard reunification; but its exertions were too ineffectual to stop the determined efforts of West Germany to unify as rapidly as possible, whatever the costs. Only when that reunification was nearly a fait accompli did Gorbachev reverse positions and urge the United States to keep Germany in NATO, as a means to check any future German ambitions for European hegemony.

Inadequately aided by Germany, the Soviets looked to Japan and the United States as alternate sources of funding and technology. Both proved resistant. Preoccupied with the Pacific rim, Japan was more concerned with China than with the Russian empire. Mainland China had enjoyed astounding economic growth and had cultivated extensive and intimate ties with overseas Chinese communities in Taiwan, Hong Kong, and Singapore. While a long-term threat to Japanese influence, this "Greater China" also offered a short-term money-making opportunity for Japanese investment and technology transfers. Its political stability, sustained by suppression of dissident opinion, made it even more inviting. By comparison, the depressed and unstable Russian empire held little attraction for practical-minded Japanese investors.

For its part, the United States actually complicated Gorbachev's gamble on Western aid. On one hand, the United States unstintingly supported Gorbachev as the only leader capable of holding the Soviet Union together in its transitional phase. Maintaining political order and territorial integrity for the Soviet empire was, indeed, the major thrust of American policy during the administration of George Bush. It reflected the American desire to carry forth the stability of Soviet-American symbiosis, forged first in cold war, into the new era beyond. But it also reflected the American belief that "movements on the economic front depend on political stability." Without political order, "it would be pouring money down the proverbial rat hole," as one American leader remarked informally. Consequently, while they were less seized by "Gorbymania" than some European counterparts, American policymakers spared few efforts to support Gorbachev's retention of political power. Indeed, they not only held his chief rival and eventual successor, Boris Yeltsin, at arm's length, they even inferred that his unseemly behavior made him unfit to lead the Soviet Union.

On the other hand, America's economic policy undermined its program of political stabilization. The United States wanted to retain Gorbachev but not the economic model he embodied, and it could not have it both ways. Gorbachev sought a " 'third way,' some hybrid of socialism and capitalism that would ease the Soviet Union's entry into the world economy." But American leaders would have none of it. Encouraged by a bevy of American economists and former "defense intellectuals" reborn as instant economic experts, the Bush administration insisted on "shock therapy" for the Soviet Union, and later for the Russian Federation that followed. Dismissive of halfway measures and "third ways," they urged Gorbachev, and later Yeltsin, to throw caution to the wind and embrace the free market instantly and unequivocally. The shock therapy proposed reflected the laissez-faire free market ideology that had emerged triumphant in the United States (and Great Britain) during the Reagan (Thatcher) era of the 1980s. It also represented the hard-nosed conviction that only a Soviet embrace of unregulated free enterprise would persuade Congress to support a Marshall Plan–style aid program for the Soviet Union (and even then, the recession and the American budget deficit might dissuade it).

Unable to convert Gorbachev into a free marketeer, America's doctrinaire economic ideology only undermined its political desire to keep Gorbachev in power. Bereft of American support, his "third way" economic policies failed badly and provoked demands from free market supporters of Boris Yeltsin that he embrace the shock therapy or resign. At the same time, his liquidation of the Russian empire abroad and its disintegration at home, compounded by its loss of status as a global superpower, provoked demands from old communists and the military that he end political and economic liberalization, or resign. Repeatedly tacking left and right between those hostile poles, Gorbachev's pragmatic shifts kept him temporarily in power; but each swing further undermined the centrist ground on which he stood. By late 1991, he had barely survived a right-wing military coup, only to be forced out by the Yeltsin forces that had seemingly saved him. Two years later, Yeltsin himself would barely survive a similar move, and by early 1994, he seemed to turn rightward in response to an electoral upsurge of Russian nationalism and neocommunism. Retrenchment on free market reforms coincided with Pan-Russian efforts abroad to influence the course of the Yugoslav civil war and at home to reintegrate the old Soviet empire. For the United States, it was the worst of all possible worlds. A Russian empire that was now too weak to be a credible and useful threat in sustaining American hegemony; a Russian empire too anarchistic and stagnant to be the new frontier that could revive global economic growth. Instead, a Russian empire that was a problem of monumental dimensions. How to salvage it economically and politically, and how to fit it into any post–Cold War order?

The Gulf War and the End of American Hegemony

The end of the Cold War hurried the end of American hegemony, though not before a "last hurrah" in the Gulf War against Iraq. The demise of American global preponderance, coupled with the collapse of its symbiotic Soviet rival, raised anew the prospect that decentering of the world-system also meant its destabilization.

The end of the Cold War initially gave a stimulus to the long-dormant center-tendency that a decade earlier had called for the diminution of America's global policing and for intensified efforts to revive America's economy. From Congress, the General Accounting Office, high-powered ad hoc committees like the American Agenda group, and even the pages of *Foreign Affairs* came calls to confront the long-neglected budget and trade deficits, to make substantive cuts in military spending and use the consequent "peace dividend" to address America's educational and infrastructural weaknesses, to define the solutions to world problems in economic rather than military terms, and to accept the end of American hegemony and the need for more collective approaches through the UN or the G-7 group of industrial nations. Even when the Persian Gulf crisis erupted in 1990 with Iraq's invasion of Kuwait, that center-tendency still packed considerable clout. In the evolving debate over the efficacy of military versus economic sanctions, centrists produced impressive advocates of the latter before congressional committees—including former secretaries of defense Robert McNamara and James Schlesinger. They argued that economic sanctions alone would force Iraq out of Kuwait, and if they did not, the intervening time could be used to transform any eventual intervention into a UN enterprise rather than a largely American one. The force of their argument was reflected in the narrow margin by which Congress approved the option of military action in January 1991, a margin generated chiefly by southern votes from areas highly dependent on military contracts.

The Bush administration, however, never faltered in its right-tendency belief that the end of the Cold War in no way diminished the need for American hegemony. Committed to free enterprise at home and free trade abroad, it continued to see America's future wholly in terms of a global multilateralism that would be promoted and protected by American military might. For all of the President's calls for a "new world order," it was the perpetuation of the old order of Pax Americana that remained his purpose. Amid the clamor for peace dividends, his administration envisioned only a 10 percent reduction in military spending over a five-year period, most of that in personnel rather than in weapons development. Meanwhile, the administration actively sought new rationales for American intervention, now that the old rationale of Soviet expansionism was no longer viable. International terrorism had earlier served such purpose in 1986 with the Reagan administration's air strike against Libya. In December 1989, international drug trafficking helped to justify an American invasion of Panama that climaxed in the capture, arrest, and subsequent trial of General Manuel Noriega. And on the eve of the Gulf crisis in August 1990, the Pentagon announced its new "blueprint for United States military strategy in the 1990s," directed not at East-West threats but at North-South dangers in the Third World, occasioned, it said, by the "growth of regional powers," especially "in the Middle East."

Given its military predilections, the Bush administration speedily seized upon Iraq's invasion of Kuwait on August 2, 1990, to put its "new battle plan" into action. Quickly moving beyond the minimalist position of economic sanctions against Iraq, it embraced the military option of expelling the Iraqi army from Kuwait. By early September, the administration had already leaked precise and prescient details of its military plans. In late September, Brent Scowcroft, Bush's national security adviser, indicated that economic sanctions were probably too slow-acting, and Les Aspin, chair of the House Armed Services Committee, concluded that the administration was "looking more and more favorably upon the war option." In October and November, the United States transformed its military deployment in Saudi Arabia from a defensive to an offensive posture, doubling the troop levels and announcing the end of troop rotation until the crisis was resolved. Finally, in January 1991, on the eve of the Gulf War itself, the President, sparing no political muscle, secured congressional approval for his impending military action; he also flexed his diplomatic muscle to abort a last-minute Soviet diplomatic intervention that might have obviated military action.

Both short-term and long-term considerations underlay the American tilt towards war in the Persian Gulf. Of the former, Bush's own political ambitions probably were an important factor. Kevin Phillips, famed political analyst, noted in November, as the administration moved publicly to the "war option," that "George Bush's re-election in 1992 is developing uncertainties." With the President already down in the opinion polls following his inept handling of the budget crisis, and with the recession clearly under way, Phillips concluded, "a deep slump—which is looking increasingly likely—would insure a bitter 1992 campaign." On the other hand, a quick, decisive, victorious stint as warrior president in the Persian Gulf might do for President Bush what the Falklands War had done a decade earlier for Prime Minister Margaret Thatcher in Great Britain. Battlefield glory in a foreign war might dull or even erase public concern about the domestic economy and turn a nondescript leader, described as a "wimp" by some critics, into a national hero.

Relatedly, short-term concern over the American and global economies also inclined the United States to decisive intervention. Oil was predictably the key to such worries. Iraq's conquest of Kuwait's oil production, and its threat to Saudi Arabia's, left that Middle Eastern power in a position to profoundly alter the structure of world oil prices. Indeed, Saddam Hussein, in the month before he authored Iraq's invasion of Kuwait, warned that he would "use force against" Kuwait and Saudi Arabia "if they did not curb their excess production," which he said had weakened oil prices and hurt the Iraqi economy. With that warning now acted upon, American leaders feared that Iraqi use of the oil weapon might send the price of oil ($16.40 a barrel prior to the war) soaring to $65 a barrel, according to one World Bank study, and to $100 or more, according to some oil experts. One *New York Times* writer warned that the high costs of that new "oil shock" would deepen the American recession and speed its global spread, probably putting the difficult GATT negotiations under intolerable protectionist pressures and dealing "a severe blow to world trade." Moreover, "the harsh economic consequences" of higher oil prices "for the industrialized West would have undermined [Soviet] reforms, which depend heavily on Western support and trade," a consideration that also helped to explain Gorbachev's acquiescence to American interventionism in the Gulf.

While such short-term political and economic factors were undoubtedly important in prompting American military action, they pale in significance alongside the administration's long-term desire to perpetuate the credibility of American hegemony and to continue with its ongoing hegemonic project. Notwithstanding the end of the Cold War, the American government believed that the structural imperatives of global capitalism required a hegemonic center to make and enforce the international rules of liberal capitalism. Moreover, it continued to believe that only the United States had the power to play that role—both the "soft power" of ideas and the "hard power" of military might.

Within weeks of the Iraqi invasion and America's initial response, the pages of leading newspapers and journals overflowed with quotes from leaders at home and abroad to that effect: "There is still only one superpower in the world, and it is the United States"; "The realities are American power and leadership . . . there is often absolutely no substitute"; "[American] military men see a chance to show they are needed after all, even if the Soviet bear has curled up in his den"; "The crisis showed that the Soviet Union's decline as a superpower has not diminished the value of America's military card"; "The bipolar, cold war world has given way not to 'multipolarity' but to 'unipolarity,' with the U.S. as the only pole left." Such was the rush of hegemonic reaffirmations. Some of the rhetoric bordered on triumphalism and seemed to suggest that American could once again play the same role it had in the 1950s and 1960s. Some of it was more restrained and noted that American military superiority was no longer matched by economic supremacy as it had been in that earlier epoch. But most speakers on the subject disputed the position of "declensionists" that America, like other great powers before it, had passed its prime and was on a slippery downhill slope.

The stunning American-led victory over Iraq in early 1991 further emboldened such hegemonic pretensions. "By God, we've kicked the Vietnam syndrome once and for all," said a triumphant George Bush, a sentiment echoed by many others in and out of government. "We have emerged from the morass of self-doubt and found that we are truly a great power," said a political science professor at a major American university. "The most important" change wrought by the war, said the lead financial writer for the *New York Times*, "is the new perception of American power, with the American image changing from a declining to an ascending force in the world." The chorus of call-and-response ended with the American President's assessment that "out of all this will be a new-found—let's put it this way: a re-established credibility for the United States of America." For right-tendency advocates, the lessons about the moral and material limits of American power, derived from the Vietnam War, had at last been unlearned, and America could now resume its appointed task.

That task, which dated back to the end of World War II, was to carry out America's hegemonic project. Part of the task, of course, had been the containment and management of the Soviet Union, but that had been only one part of the hegemonic project, and not always its most pressing. So too had been co-opting Britain into a "special relationship" that offered the former hegemon some pride and profits in compensation for the absorption of the Commonwealth and the old empire into the American free world. So too had been managing Germany and Japan in a manner that contained recidivism while promoting them as the economic locomotives of European and Asian growth. So too had been the containing of revolutionary Third World nationalism by the carrot-and-stick of economic assistance and military interventionism. And so too had been the aborting of any revitalized American isolationism that might have deprived American internationalism of its material support and moral authority at home. Notwithstanding the collapse of communism and the Soviet Union, those other tasks of America's hegemonic project continued to require U.S. attention.

In that context, the Gulf War offered golden opportunities too tempting to forgo. First, it reaffirmed Britain's "special relationship" with the United States, by providing Britain with both a share of the battlefield glory and the assurance that Kuwait and Saudi petrodollars would continue to flow uninterrupted into City of London banks. Second, it reestablished German and Japanese dependence on U.S. protection—not protection against Soviet security threats but protection of their access to key raw materials and resources. (A "resource war" to replace a "cold war," said some observers, though in fact it was partly the same old war with a new rationale.) Third, it put Third World countries on notice that the end of the cold War did not give them license to play by their own rules of the game. Other justifications for intervention might fill the void left by the collapse of Soviet communism, and America retained the power to act upon them. Indeed, the end of the Cold War actually left the United States in a stronger position vis-à-vis the periphery. No longer would the United States have to contend with Third World countries exploiting the Cold War to play the two superpowers against each other. No longer would the interventionist option be blunted by fear of military confrontation with the Soviet Union. Fourth, the Gulf War recreated the circumstances for renewed public support at home for American hegemony abroad. Its high-tech massacre of a retreating Iraqi army, accomplished with light U.S. casualties, suggested that America could go back to the pre–Vietnam War days of hegemony-on-the-cheap, that the Gulf War was a prototype of "mid-intensity" wars of the future, in which American technology and fire-power would provide quick, decisive victories at small public sacrifice.

Despite those apparent advantages, the Gulf War failed to achieve its goals on any lasting basis. Anglo-American entente, predicated on close personal and ideological ties between Reagan and Thatcher and later Bush and John Major, quickly unraveled in the aftermath of Bush's failure to be reelected in 1992 (a reelection actively supported by Britain's ruling Conservative party). Within a year of Bill Clinton's elevation to the presidency, these two Gulf War allies found themselves at odds over the Yugoslavian civil war, Northern Ireland's "troubles," the pace of European political integration, and the character of Europe's social charter for labor and welfare. Personal dislike and ideological discord between the British Prime Minister and the new American President further fired those differences.

American efforts to perpetuate German and Japanese dependence on American protection carried their own high costs. Not since the American Revolution had the United States solicited financial contributions from other countries to pay for a war, and Germany and Japan were the major core countries targeted. No longer able to fund its own global policing, the United States rented out its hegemonic services. Germany ($6.6 billion) and Japan ($10.7 billion) collectively pledged to pay a third of the war's projected $50 billion price tag.

That hired-gun character of America's relationship to the former Axis powers raised several troubling issues for Germany and Japan. Was "the American war," (as it was often described in Europe) really necessary, or could it have been avoided through continued economic sanctions or through the last-minute Soviet diplomatic initiative? If it was unnecessary, was it "an American plot to justify U.S. hegemony . . . by force and long-term domination of the world's oil supply?" A gambit to "guarantee American superpower status well into the twenty-first century, despite declining economic strength?" Such notions, characterized here by the *New York Times*, became popular first among Palestinians and eventually surfaced in Europe and Japan as well. Finally, even if the war was necessary, were the long-term interests of Germany and Japan better served by acting through the United States or by acting on their own? Fueled by mounting nationalism in both countries, the issue was especially keen in Japan, where the public sharply divided over the efficacy of their military forces being sent to the Persian Gulf to show solidarity and whether those troops ought to be armed or limited to noncombatant roles? Fearful of their country's past aggressive tendencies, most Japanese continued to favor cooperation with the United States. But the one million purchasers of Shintaro Ishihara's *The Japan That Can Say No* demonstrated some support for its author's view that "Japan should provide for its own defenses and follow its own strategic interests."

American intervention did not deter the forces of Third World fragmentation and particularism. It did not subsequently prevent the genocidal self-destruction of the Yugoslavian civil war, the warlordism and famine of Somalia, the descent of Haiti into anarchy and repression, the nuclear proliferation evident in North Korea's military policies, or the threat of interracial and intraracial war in South Africa. Caught between its public support of self-determination and its private longing for systemic order and stability, post–Cold War America could only waffle and oftentimes fail.

Even the immediate and tragic consequences of the Gulf War make the point. Anxious to bring down the Iraqi regime of Saddam Hussein, the United States was, however, not anxious to see the Iraqi nation threatened from within by Kurdish and Shiite dissidents, whose respective northern and southern rebellions had been tacitly encouraged by the United States during the war. The prospect of an independent Kurdistan was anathema to two wartime allies, Turkey and Syria, and any increase in Shiite influence in Iraq would likely rebound to the regional benefit of hostile Iran. In that context, the United States tried to solve its conundrum by encouraging a military coup against Saddam Hussein. Had it succeeded, it would have rid Iraq of the war's arch villain while still preserving the integrity of the secular state he had served. Iraqi unity, sans Hussein, took precedence over the self-determination of Kurds and Shiites, both of whom were implicitly left to their own inadequate defenses. "America Deserts the Rebels Cynically," cried one American headline. "What have we wrought?" asked a prominent journalist, who compared America's policies toward Iraqi rebels to the Soviet policy of inaction during the Warsaw rebellion of 1944.

The public euphoria over the Gulf War victory did not last, and it did not translate into renewed popular support for American global hegemony. Instead, the great American middle-class rebellion of 1992 quickly shifted political attention from battlefield maps to economic pie charts. Burdened by decades of economic slowdown, heavy tax loads, income redistribution upward, structural unemployment, and a triple-dip recession that would not disappear, American workers, professionals, and small business people demanded that economic well-being take clear top billing over issues of global geopolitics. After decades of political apathy, the astonishing election of 1992 ousted George Bush from the White House less than eighteen months after his personal triumph in the Gulf War. The results gave nearly one-fifth of the popular vote to the right-of-center populism of first-time candidate Ross Perot, despite his third party status and his inconsistent, on-again-off-again performance. Voters elevated Bill Clinton to the presidency despite his scandal-prone persona and his limited background—reminiscent of Jimmy Carter—as governor of a small southern state. Focusing almost entirely on economic issues, Perot and Clinton cumulatively garnered two-thirds of the national vote. If America had to choose between policing the world and restoring its economic edge, there was little doubt of the contemporary preference.

The Future of the World-System in the Next Quarter-Century

The Gulf War's failure to jump-start America's hegemonic project raised once more the issue of how global rules would be made and enforced in the post–Cold War era. On a vertical continuum ranging downward from integration to disintegration, five possible directions emerge for the future of the world-system over the next quarter-century: American neo-hegemony, Japanese-American co-hegemony, a collective concert of powers, bipolarity, and multipolarity.

While renewed American hegemony is clearly a possibility, it is quite unlikely, unless several things happen. First, it would require that Germany and Japan continue to defer to American global leadership. Given Japan's tendency to resist that leadership, and given recent German independence in its foreign policy and its monetary schemes, such long-term deference may be in doubt—especially when both nations become permanent members of the UN Security Council. Second, since hegemony rests on economic as much as military power, the United States would have to regain its competitive edge in the world economy. Doing so, however, might require America to sacrifice some of its global policing, a choice apparently favored in the political climate of the mid-1990s. Third, mid-intensity wars would have to occur so regularly that they would perpetuate the world-system's dependence on U.S. military protection. But circumstances like the Persian Gulf War are likely to be rare—circumstances where there is a consensus in the United Nations between core and periphery, where the resource at stake is crucial to almost all national economies (as was Persian Gulf oil), where the area is of undoubted strategic importance to most nations' security (as was the Middle East, where the Suez Canal acts as a bridge between three continents), and where the terrain would make it possible to fight a NATO-style war, using NATO forces, NATO technology, and NATO tactics (designed originally for the/North German Plains).

The rarity of such favorable preconditions has been evident in America's inability to respond to the tragic civil war in Yugoslavia that began in early 1991 and still remains mired in its brutal end-game three years later. Accurately predicted by the CIA in 1990, the civil war chiefly pitted Croatian and Bosnian efforts at secession against Pan-Serbian determination to retain control over the former Yugoslavian federation of six republics. The year 1991 witnessed a protracted war between Croatia and Serb-dominated Yugoslavia, while Bosnia's secession in 1992 shifted focus to that beleaguered land. The atrocity-filled war that has often been described as genocidal ethnic cleansing.

Over the course of the war's first three years, the West dithered and debated the merits of watchful waiting, diplomatic mediation, economic sanctions, limited military intervention, and all-out military intervention. All save the last were tried, always inconclusively. At the same time, the West dithered and debated whether the European Union (successor to the European Community after 1993), the American-dominated NATO, or the United Nations should lead the chosen responses. Each seemed to take a turn, always ineffectually.

Largely absent in the Yugoslavian crisis were the circumstances that had made the decisive Gulf War action possible. Political conditions and geographical terrain were unsuited to a NATO-style war; no common resource like oil was at stake nor any agreed-upon strategic importance at risk; and the global economic recession minimized the amount of military funding and popular support available for any bold action from either Europe or the United States.

Worse yet, there was no unity of interests among the great powers vis-à-vis Yugoslavia. Germany, for example, had a long historic association with Croatia, and its unilateral recognition of Croatia's independence in December 1991 forced the European Community and the United States to reluctantly follow suit. That key action, in turn, emboldened Bosnia to declare its independence and insured that Serbian Yugoslavia would do everything to prevent it, thus initiating the second, even bloodier stage of the civil war. Similarly, Russia had a historic association with Serbia, and its unilateral dispatch of token forces to Bosnia in early 1994 effectively forestalled impending NATO air strikes against Bosnian Serbs. Caught between the German rock and the Russian hard place, the United States initially favored the principle of Yugoslavian unity and integrity over the principle of ethnic self-determination; but the failure of that policy, and growing global outrage over ethnic cleansing, finally pushed the United States toward a more anti-Serbian posture. The movement, however, was halting and unsure, and, for the moment, still ineffective.

Japanese-American co-hegemony is the next most integrationist direction. Considered more seriously in Japan than in the United States, it is nonetheless a possibility. There are certainly historical precedents in which a hegemon prolonged its role by forging a kind of tacit co-hegemony with its chief commercial competitor. In each instance, the declining hegemon started out as senior partner in the shared arrangement but eventually devolved into the more junior of the two. Anglo-American relations in the first half of this century are an obvious case in point.

While Japanese-American co-hegemony is possible, it is also quite problematic. Clearly it will not happen if four fundamental preconditions are not met. First, the two nations would have to overcome some real chasms created by their linguistic and cultural differences. While it is true that culture, over time, is plastic and malleable, and that new traditions can be manufactured to replace old ones, such things do not alter over night. Second, Japan and the United States must each best post-1992 Europe and maintain commanding leads in the new technologies of genetic engineering, microprocessing, alternative energy production, and the like. As of 1994, those leads were indeed significant, but the European Union's "White Paper on Growth, Competitiveness and Employment" indicated a determined if tardy effort to close the gap. Third, Japan would have to open its economy more reciprocally to American trade and investment and would have to relieve some of America's military burden, without "going nuclear" and without reviving fears among other Asians of Japanese imperialism. Fourth, the United States would have to downgrade its traditional Euro-centricism and give top priority to Asia. By late 1993, fearful Europeans saw in the public pronouncements of President Clinton and Secretary of State Warren Christopher abundant evidence that this had already happened.

A "new world order" is the direction perhaps most currently discussed in the United States. Its prospects depend largely on a positive answer to one question. Did American hegemony build such sound international institutions that they will survive the end of that hegemony and continue to act as centers for the world-system? If it did, an unstable balance of power might be avoided and a concert of core powers might collectively do what the United States once did alone. In economic terms, core power collaboration would build on long-established institutions like the International Monetary Fund, the General Agreement on Tariffs and Trade, and the G-7 economic summits of heads of state and of central bank directors. These institutions, some argue, have successfully thwarted tendencies toward protectionism and monetary instability in the 1970s and 1980s and maintained global commitment to multilateralism. Moreover, the GATT and NAFTA agreements of late 1993 suggest the continued vitality of liberal capitalism worldwide.

There is less consensus on who will play the role of global policeman in the new world order, when that role is required. Some argue that NATO could do it, if it devolved from its status as an American protectorate into an alliance of equals and if it expanded its membership and its responsibilities geographically. Others argue that the United Nations could do the job, if the United States and the UN Secretariat could negotiate a phased transfer of global policing from America to that international organization. Neither NATO nor the UN, however, demonstrated much efficacy in recent crises in Yugoslavia and Somalia, and the United States itself waffled considerably in its attitudes toward both organizations during the Clinton administration's first year.

Prospects for such a new world order looked very bright eighteen months ago. The Cold War had ended, communism had collapsed, and the march of market forces swept everything before it. On the other hand, more recent developments seem to belie that optimism, and a whirlwind of nationalism, ethnocentrism, nativism, and fundamentalism threatens to undo the triumph of multilateralism. Moreover, the ratification of NAFTA might yet prove a step away from free trade and toward regional trading blocs. Such was the opinion of economists and central bank officials from various countries expressed at an elite 1991 conference, when they predicted that the current GATT round would be its last, and that regional trading blocs would be "as good as we are going to get."

Of all the future trajectories of the world-system, bipolarity is the possibility least discussed. Its prospects for success depend on four preconditions: American decline proves irreversible; the absence of a supra-state makes a new world order impossible; Japan and the United States, despite a close partnership, fail to generate the material conditions necessary for co-hegemony; and Europe is reasonably successful in furthering its own economic and political unification and in integrating the former Soviet empire into a larger Europe.

If these conditions obtain, then it is possible to imagine the world dividing into two great power blocs. One half of this bipolar world might be a Euro-Russian bloc—probably dominated by Germany or some larger condominium—integrated into the peripheral and semiperipheral zones of Africa, the Middle East, and South Asia. The other half might be an Amerasian bloc dominated by the United States, Japan, and greater China, integrated into the peripheral and semiperipheral zones of the Caribbean, South America, and the Pacific Rimlands. It would be organized around intensive and extensive cooperation between NAFTA and an Asian counterpart, like that loosely envisioned at the Asian Pacific Economic Cooperation summit in late 1993.

Since the power base of each bloc would be comparable, the disincentives to military confrontation and trade wars might provide the basis for a relatively durable equilibrium. Like the Cold War, bipolarity might evolve into a stable *system*, one marked by peaceful coexistence and a loosely regulated exchange of goods between competitive equals.

Multipolarity or polycentrism is the final possibility for the future of the world-system. It is possible to argue that the decline of hegemony always tends to destabilize the world-system. If the essential dynamic of the world-system (as Fernand Braudel argues) is that of centering, decentering, and recentering, then it is the decentering stage that is the most dangerous. The process of reorganizing political power is so volatile and contestable that no clear, stable replacement emerges—no neo-hegemony, co-hegemony, concert of powers, or bipolarity.

In such a polycentric world, there is no single, universal set of rules by which all the world plays, and there is uneven power to enforce those contradictory rules that do exist. Such polycentrism is likely if the effort at U.S.-Japanese partnership fails badly and degenerates into mutual recriminations and economic warfare and if Europe proves unable to carry off its own unification and the integration of the old Soviet bloc.

The end result of such developments might be a world of five competing power centers integrated into their regional hinterlands: the United States, Western Europe, Japan, the Russian empire, and greater China—or perhaps only the first three with the old external empires of Russia and China becoming objects of imperialist competition rather than major players in their own right. Driven by the requirements of economic viability, each core power might be inclined to resort to protectionism or other forms of regulated trade. Each might be likely to increase the exploitation of its periphery, increasing the likelihood of Third World revolutions similar to those of the 1960s and 1970s. Each power might be inclined to risk war to secure access to scarce resources. If so, it is possible that the ulti-

mate consequence of such polycentrism might be another unstable balance of power that would finally self-destruct as did those of 1914 and
1939, producing "continuous war between changing partners," with most
of the participants being nuclear powers, should proliferation continue.
And such conflagration might produce either whole social anarchy or a
radical redistribution of power, out of which might emerge another hegemon, a new center for the world-system, though at human price too awful
to imagine.

In the coming quarter-century, any one of these outcomes is theo-
retically possible, and each rests on historical precedent. Hegemony, co-
hegemony, concert of powers, bipolar systems, and balances of power
have all had their moments during the last two hundred years. One can,
however, risk at least one rough generalization. Some variant of integrationism (hegemony, co-hegemony, or new world order) will likely prevail
if three important conditions come to pass. If they prove otherwise, then
some variant of disintegrationism (bipolarity or polycentrism) will come
to dominate.

First, the extent of global interdependency must prove to be markedly
greater than it was a century ago. Pax Britannica presided over a remark-
able degree of economic integration during the nineteenth century, especially in the internationalization of trade and finance, but it proved insufficient to prevent the neomercantilist wars of the early twentieth century.
Pax Americana has furthered economic interdependence, especially
through the internationalization of production; but it remains to be seen
just how thoroughgoing that internationalization has been and whether it
can prevent a comparable process of global fragmentation.

Second, the world economy must prove to be at the beginning of an
expansionist period rather than at the tag-end of a contractionist one. In
the long waves of boom and stagnation in the world economy, the coin-
ciding of the latter with decentering is especially threatening to integration. The Long Depression of 1873–97 helped to destroy the European
concert of powers, and the Great Depression of the 1930s did the same for
Anglo-American co-hegemony. In the contemporary period, it remains to
be seen whether the long slump since 1973 has played itself out. If it has
and the world economy stands poised on the brink of a new global boom,
then the prospect of some integrationist direction is much enhanced. If it
has not and the world economy suffers through continued or even deeper
malaise, then such a prospect is much dimmed.

Third, the former Soviet Union must be stabilized and its descent into
political chaos halted. If stabilization and amelioration occur, then the
former Soviet bloc might well offer the world capitalist market a new frontier for spatial expansion capable of fueling the next long wave of economic boom. If it proves otherwise, then the constituent states of the

former Soviet Union may be the undoing of the capitalist world, draining its financial reserves or perhaps confronting it once more with the threat of Pan-Russian expansionism. It would be the ultimate irony if the collapse of the Cold War had destroyed a stable system within which global capitalism had flourished, while, in turn, the attempted conversion of the Russian empire to the principles of that self-same capitalism caused it to founder.

Bibliographical Essay

Historical literature on the Cold War era is voluminous. The publications noted here represent only a fraction of that vast body, chiefly those works most useful in the preparation of this volume. For a more exhaustive listing of the books and articles published through 1980, see Richard Dean Burns' fine annotated bibliography, *A Guide to American Foreign Relations since 1770* (1982). It should be supplemented with J. L. Black, *Origins, Evolution, and Nature of the Cold War: An Annotated Bibliography* (1985). Thomas G. Patterson, et al. *American Foreign Policy, A History*, vol. 2 (1988), and Walter LaFeber, *The American Age: United States Foreign Policy at Home and Abroad since 1750* (1989), the two best textbooks in American diplomatic history, also contain selective yet extensive reading suggestions. Gerald K. Haines and J. Samuel Walker, *American Foreign Relations, A Historiographical Review* (1981), discusses the major works in the field and places them in their historiographical context.

General Works

In addition to this volume there are numerous surveys of American foreign relations since 1945. The most thorough, thoughtful, and judicious remains Walter LaFeber, *America, Russia, and the Cold War, 1945–1984* (1985). Stephen E. Ambrose, *Rise to Globalism: American Foreign Policy since 1938* (1985), is especially good on military affairs and on the 1950s. Ralph Levering, *The Cold War* (1982), is strong on public opinion, while T. E. Vadney, *The World since 1945* (1987), is especially informative on the Third World. John Spanier, *American Foreign Policy since World War II* (1968), offers a more orthodox account while John Lewis Gaddis's collection of essays, *The Long Peace* (1987), contains several provocative pieces by a leading historian. Norman and Emily Rosenberg, *In Our Times: America since World War II* (1987), provides a helpful survey of both domestic and foreign policy.

Anthologies

Collections of essays often expedite the reader's introduction to a diverse range of topics and interpretations. Among the more general anthologies, two are outstanding. David Horowitz, *Corporations and the Cold War* (1969), contains two classic articles by David W. Eakins and G. William Domhoff as well as fine syntheses by William A. Williams and Lloyd Gardner. Lynn H. Miller and Ronald W. Pruessen, *Reflections on the Cold War* (1974), has uniformly fine essays, including Pruessen's own on American objectives in the Cold War. Two excellent collections survey America's bilateral relations with two great powers: William Roger Louis and Hedley Bull, eds., *The Special Relationship: Anglo-American Relations since 1945* (1986), and Alexander L. George, et al., *Managing U.S.-Soviet Rivalry: Problems in Crisis* (1982). Other helpful anthologies are more focused in time: Barton Bernstein, ed., *Politics and Policies of the Truman Administration* (1970); Robert A. Divine, ed., *Exploring the Johnson Years* (1981); Richard A. Melanson and David Mayers, eds., *Reevaluating Eisenhower: American Foreign Policy in the Fifties* (1987); Holly Sklar, ed., *Trilateralism* (1985), especially good on the Carter years; Thomas Ferguson and Joel Rogers, eds., *The Hidden Election* (1981), excellent on the links between domestic and foreign policy; Sanford J. Ungar, ed., *Estrangement: America and the World* (1986), on the contemporary period; Robert M. Stern, ed., *Perspectives on a U.S.-Canadian Free Trade Agreement* (1987), important for its treatment of a truly momentous development; and Peter M. Dunn and Bruce W. Watson, eds., *American Intervention in Grenada* (1985).

Biographies

While this volume often stresses structures and forces more than individuals, historical actors remain the ones who survey options and make policy choices. Biographies are often useful in underlining that fact. Among the presidential biographies, Robert J. Donovan's two-volume treatment of Harry S. Truman is a good point of departure: *Conflict and Crisis* (1977), and *The Tumultuous Years* (1983). Dwight D. Eisenhower has received considerable attention. Stephen E. Ambrose, *Eisenhower: The President* (1984), is the standard account; Fred J. Greenstein, *The Hidden-Hand Presidency: Eisenhower as Leader* (1980), was one of the early books to reassess Eisenhower's leadership powers in the presidency; and Robert A. Divine, *Eisenhower and the Cold War* (1981), focuses more sharply on foreign policy issues. Other helpful biographies of the Cold War presidents include Herbert S. Parmet, *JFK: The Presidency of John F. Kennedy* (1983); Ronnie Dugger, *Politician: The Life and Times of Lyndon Johnson* (1982); Stephen E. Ambrose, *Nixon: The Education of a Politician, 1913–1962* (1987), the first in a multivolume project; Betty Glad, *Carter* (1980); and Robert Dalleck, *Ronald Reagan: The Politics of Symbolism* (1984).

More impressive as a group are the many fine biographies of American secretaries of state since 1945. Robert L. Messer, *The End of an Alliance* (1982), is not only a fine biography of James F. Byrnes but an important account of the origins of the Cold War. Forrest Pogue, *George C. Marshall: Statesman, 1945–1959* (1987), is volume four in this magisterial biography of the American warrior-administrator. Gaddis Smith, *Dean Acheson* (1972), and David S. McLellan, *Dean Acheson* (1976), are solid, informative studies of America's most important postwar foreign minister. Acheson's controversial successor, John Foster Dulles, is the subject of two important biographies: Ronald Pruessen, *John Foster Dulles* (1982), the more indispensible of the two, and Mark G. Toulouse, *The Transformation of John Foster Dulles* (1985), crucial for understanding Calvinism in Dulles' personality and world view. Warren I. Cohen, *Dean Rusk* (1980), is a thoughtful inquiry into a complex and illusive figure, while David S. McLellan, *Cyrus Vance* (1985), is a useful initial venture into understanding Carter's first secretary of state.

The thought and actions of other major figures also shed considerable light on American foreign relations since the end of World War II. Ronald Steele, *Walter Lippmann and the American Century* (1980), is an excellent, sometimes brilliant, rendering of this century's most important political essayist. William C. Berman, *William Fulbright and the Vietnam War* (1988), is an important, well-researched account of the figure who for a long time dominated the Senate Foreign Relations Committee. Barton Gellman, *Contending with Kennan* (1984), is important in understanding the complex personality that both fathered the containment policy and then became one of the most articulate critics of its implementation. Michael T. Ruddy, *The Cautious Diplomat: Charles E. Bohlen and the Soviet Union* (1986), is a helpful analysis of a diplomat second only to George F. Kennan as a Russian area expert and in behind-the-scenes policy battles in the early Cold War. John H. Backer, *Winds of History: The German Years of Lucius D. Clay* (1984), is important in understanding the pivotal role of Germany in the origins of the Cold War.

Several single-volume collected biographies are invaluable introductions to important facets of postwar foreign policy. In a class by itself is Lloyd C. Gardner, *Architects of Illusion: Men and Ideas in American Foreign Policy, 1941–1949* (1970), a brilliant collection of biographical essays on ten key policymakers (Roosevelt, Truman, Byrnes, Marshall, Acheson, Clay, Baruch, and Forrestal, and the less visible William Bullitt and Will Clayton). Walter Isaacson and Evan Thomas, *The Wise Men: Six Friends and the World They Made* (1986), while uneven in its analysis, has rigorously unearthed some wonderful information on Acheson, Bohlen, Kennan, Harriman, Lovett, and McCloy. Frank J. Merli and Theodore A. Wilson, eds., *Makers of American Diplomacy* (1974), includes some fine essays on key policymakers, especially Thomas G. Paterson's on Kennan.

Chapter 1

The world-system analysis used in this volume draws its initial inspiration from Fernand Braudel's monumental three-volume opus on *Material Civilization and Capitalism, Fifteenth to Eighteenth Centuries*, especially his concluding volume, *The Perspective of the World*, English translation (1984). Braudel brilliantly distilled the analytical essence of his epic labor in his 1976 Haberman lectures for the Johns Hopkins University, published as *Afterthoughts on Material Civilization and Capitalism* (1977). Elaborating, extending, and popularizing Braudel's framework is the provocative and controversial work of Immanuel Wallerstein, commencing with *The Modern World-System* (1974). Wallerstein has written and edited numerous volumes since then that explore world-system analysis, and many of those explorations have taken him and his associates into the more contemporary period. Three of his books were particularly useful to this volume: *World Inequality* (1975), *The Capitalist World-Economy* (1976), and *Politics of the World-Economy* (1984).

The literature on the domestic sources of decisionmaking is surveyed in

Thomas McCormick, "Drift or Mastery? A Corporatist Synthesis for American Diplomatic History," in Stanley I. Kutler, ed., *The Promise of American History* (1983). Evidence for the crucial role of "ins-and-outers" is to be found in Robert D. Schulzinger, *The Wise Men of Foreign Affairs: The History of the Council on Foreign Relations* (1984), a solid, judicious work; Lawrence Shoup and William Minter, *The Imperial Brain Trust* (1977), which offers a more radical critique of the same organization; Thomas R. Dye, *Who's Running America?*, 4th ed. (1986), which contains good biographical data; G. William Domhoff, *Who Rules America?* (1967); and the earlier classic work by C. Wright Mills, *The Power Elite* (1956).

At a more general level, other major works influenced the analytical framework of this book. William A. Williams, *The Tragedy of American Diplomacy* (1959, 1988) remains the most widely-read and influential exposition of the Open Door paradigm—that is, the imperative of American access to an open, unitary free world economy. Emily S. Rosenberg, *Spreading the American Dream: American Economic and Cultural Expansion, 1890–1945* (1982), integrates that paradigm into a more explicit model of dependency theory and adds a more systematic cultural dimension. Michael H. Hunt, *Ideology and Foreign Policy* (1987), is important for its additional focus upon race and racism. Lloyd C. Gardner, *A Covenant with Power* (1984), brilliantly analyzes the uneasy covenant between liberal ideology and power realities from Woodrow Wilson through Ronald Reagan.

Paul Kennedy's vastly popular *The Rise and Fall of Great Powers: Economic Change and Military Conflict from 1500 to 2000* (1987), appeared after the first draft of this volume was complete. While it did not directly influence the conceptual context of this volume, it did tend to provide welcomed reinforcement as well as some useful supporting evidence for later drafts.

Chapter 2

America's emergence as a core power in the late nineteenth and early twentieth centuries, especially its economic and intellectual roots, is well analyzed in Walter LaFeber's prize-winning *The New Empire* (1963). Thomas McCormick, *China Market: America'a Quest for Informal Empire, 1893–1901* (1967), stresses the role of class conflict and the lure of the Pacific rim. Ernest R. May, *Imperial Democracy* (1961), is strong on the influence of the external Europe-dominated world. David Healy, *U.S. Expansionism: The Imperialist Urge in the 1890s* (1970), is a well-written collection of biographical essays, while Howard K. Beale, *Theodore Roosevelt and the Rise of America to World Power* (1956), centers on America's first "imperial president." Mira Wilkins, *The Emergence of Multi-National Enterprise: American Business Abroad from the Colonial Era to 1914* (1970), provides some of the concrete economic context.

America's maturation as a core power in the 1910s is best captured in Lloyd C. Gardner's ambitious *Safe for Democracy: The Anglo-American Response to Revolution, 1913–1923* (1984), which focuses on three great revolutions, in Mexico, Russia, and China. Frederich Katz, *The Secret War in Mexico: Europe, the United States and the Mexican Revolution* (1981), is a sophisticated and knowledgeable comparison of American, British, and German reactions, and is an impressive blend of social, economic, and diplomatic history. Akira Iriye, *Pacific Estrangement: Japanese and American Expansion, 1897–1911* (1972), presages later Japanese-American conflict over the Pacific rim, while Jerry Israel, *Progressivism and the Open Door: America and China, 1905–1921* (1971), analyzes the relationship between progressive reform movements in America and the continuing effort to keep China open to American influence. Ernest R. May, *The World War and American Isolation, 1914–1917* (1959), remains the best researched account of American entry into World War I, especially in its use of both European and American archives. Arno Mayer's epic *Politics and the Diplomacy of Peacemaking* (1967), is still the standard account of the effort to reorder the postwar world. N. Gordon Levin, *Woodrow Wilson and World Politics* (1968), much influenced by Mayer, stresses the competition between American liberal internationalism, Russian radical internationalism, and German autarkic regionalism.

The literature on the 1920s is exceptionally good. Carl Parrini, *Heir to Empire: United States Economic Diplomacy, 1916–1923* (1969), and Michael J. Hogan, *Informal Entente: The Private Structure of Cooperation in Anglo-American Economic Diplomacy* (1977), are both superb accounts of the uneven transference of economic power from a declining hegemon to an emerging one. Melvyn Leffler, *The Elusive Quest: America's Pursuit of European Stability and French Security, 1919–1933* (1979) adds a military-strategic dimension, as well as an insightful analysis of Herbert Hoover's world view. Robert F. Smith, *The United States and Revolutionary Nationalism in Mexico, 1916–1932* (1972), offers the most innovative example of America's interaction with Latin American resistance to the international division of labor, while Akira Iriye, *After Imperialism* (1969) recounts in detail the frustrations of the great powers in imposing their will on China. Frank Costigliola, *Awkward Dominion: American Political, Economic, and Cultural Relations with Europe, 1919–1933* (1984), is especially strong on cultural affairs, while Warren I. Cohen, *Empires without Tears: American Foreign Relations, 1921–1933* (1987), provides a useful synthesis of the whole decade.

The most provocative and exciting new analysis of the 1930s is Patrick Hearden, *Roosevelt Confronts Hitler: American Entry into World War II* (1987). It builds upon Lloyd C. Gardner's earlier but still important *Economic Aspects of New Deal Diplomacy* (1964). A more orthodox but valuable narrative is Robert Dalleck, *Franklin D. Roosevelt and American Foreign Policy, 1932–1945* (1979). David Green, *The Containment of Latin America* (1971), is a good starting point on the Good Neighbor policy. John A. DeNovo, *American Interests and Politics in the Middle East, 1919–1939* (1963), is an excellent piece of research on a very significant topic. Douglas Little, *Malevolent Neutrality* (1985) challenges older more benign interpretations of American policy in the Spanish civil war. David Reynolds, *The Creation of the Anglo-American Alliance, 1937–1941* (1982), is a polished and persuasive analysis of the Anglo-American "special relationship" in the making. While conventional in its interpretation, William L. Langer and S. Everett Gleason, *The Challenge to Isolation, 1937–1940* (1952), still is a standard empirical point of reference for any discussion of American entry into World War II. Bruce M. Russett, *No Clear and Present Danger* (1972), is an interesting exercise in counterfactual history, suggesting that an Axis victory in Europe and Asia would not have threatened American national interests.

There are numerous general works on World War II. Herbert Feis, *Churchill, Roosevelt, and Stalin: The War They Waged and the Peace They Sought* (1957), richly details great power diplomacy from Feis's dual vantage of public official and historian. Gabriel Kolko, *The Politics of War* (1968), offers a very different analysis that is both more global and more radical in nature. Gaddis Smith, *American Diplomacy during the Second World War, 1941–1945* (1965), is a good synthesis that works well in the classroom. Robert A. Divine, *Second Chance: The Triumph of Internationalism in America during World War II* (1967), chronicles the continuing battle between internationalism and isolationism. Eric Larrabee, *Commander in Chief: Franklin Delano Roosevelt, His Lieutenants, and Their War* (1987), is a fascinating treatment of his subjects, while Gore Vidal, *Washington, D.C.* (1967), is a wonderful fictional account of the same powers-that-be. On Russian-American relations, see Mark Stoler, *The Politics of the Second Front* (1977); Keith Sainsbury, *The Turning Point* (1985), on the 1943 summits; Diane Shaver Clemens, *Yalta* (1970), the standard account of that controversial wartime conference; and Russell D. Buhite, *Decision at Yalta* (1986), for a more critical rendition of that same event. On relations with the declining British Empire, see Christopher Thorne, *Allies of a Kind* (1977), and John J. Sbrega, *Anglo-American Relations and Colonialism in East Asia, 1941–1945* (1983). The Asian war is also covered in provocative fashion by Akira Iriye, *Power and Culture: The Japanese-American War, 1941–1945* (1981), a seminal work by a distinguished scholar, and John W. Dower, *War without Mercy* (1986), a brilliant and controversial look at the role of racism among both the Americans and the Japanese. The military side of planning for the postwar period is well covered in Michael Sherry, *Preparing for the Next War* (1977), though political and economic planning has yet to receive its proper attention. Sherry's book should be supplemented by his more recent *The Rise of American Air Power* (1987). David Wyman, *The Abandonment of the Jews* (1984), is the standard treatment of a sad chapter in American diplomatic history.

Chapter 3

The origins of the Cold War have been hotly debated by historians for three decades. In addition to the general works on the Cold War, see Thomas G. Paterson, *Soviet-American Confrontation* (1973), for a critical view of American policy and an analysis of the economic dimension to the early Cold War. Daniel Yergin, *Shattered Peace: The Origins of the Cold War and the National Security State* (1977), blames the Cold War on splits within the American governing elite, while John L. Gaddis, *The United States and the Origins of Cold War* (1972), ultimately blames the Soviets for choosing confrontation even though no public pressures required them to do so. Melvyn P. Leffler, "The American Conception of National Security and the Beginnings of the Cold War," *American Historical Review* 89 (1984), stresses American geostrategic considerations that were concerned with far more than any potential Russian threat. Robert L. Messer, "World War II and the Coming of the Cold War," in John M. Carroll and George C. Herring, eds., *Modern American Diplomacy* (1986), is a fine synthesis by James F. Byrnes' biographer.

On the nuclear age and atomic diplomacy, Lloyd C. Gardner, "The Atomic Temptation," in Gardner, ed., *Redefining the Past* (1986), is an insightful overview and a good point of departure. Herbert Feis, *The Atomic Bomb and the End of World War II* (1966), is a well-researched defense of American nuclear policy by a distinguished historian and former State Department official. It should be supplemented with his *From Trust to Terror: The Onset of the Cold War, 1945–1950* (1970). Gar Alperovitz, *Atomic Diplomacy* (1985), once so controversial and now widely accepted, analyzes the dropping of the atomic bombs on Japan partly as an act of anti-Soviet intimidation. Relatedly, Barton J. Bernstein's recent "A Postwar Myth: Five Hundred Thousand U.S. Lives Saved," *Bulletin of Atomic Scientists* 42 (1986), raises questions about the official explanation that the atomic raids were aimed at saving a half-million American lives. Martin Sherwin, *A World Destroyed* (1975), describes the Manhattan Project that created the first atomic bomb, centering on Anglo-American affairs and relations between scientists and the political-military bureaucracy. Paul Boyer's wonderful *By the Bomb's Early Light* (1986), analyzes the impact of the bomb and the nuclear threat on American popular thought and culture. Gregg Herken, *The Winning Weapon* (1981), carries the story of atomic diplomacy onward to the 1950s, while John S. Gilkeson, Jr., *Gathering Rare Ores: The Diplomacy of Uranium Acquisition, 1943–1954* (1987), does the same with a more narrow but fascinating subject.

In 1946, relations with Great Britain were almost more important than those with the Soviet Union. William H. McNeill, *America, Britain and Russia . . . 1941–1946* (1955), now three decades old, still retains great value for its insights. Two more contemporary accounts take advantage of more recent documentation on both sides of the Atlantic to offer very substantial yet different interpretations of that special relationship: Terry H. Anderson, *The United States, Great Britain and the Cold War, 1944–1947* (1981), and Robert M. Hathaway, *Ambiguous Partnership: Britain and America, 1944–1947* (1981). G. M. Alexander, *The Prelude to the Truman Doctrine: British Policy in Greece, 1944–1947* (1984), provides an even more detailed focus on the crucial Greek revolution.

On Soviet-American relations, Herbert Feis, *Between War and Peace: The Postdam Conference* (1960), is the standard treatment for that crucial end-of-the-war summit meeting. Joseph G. Whelen, *Soviet Diplomacy and Negotiating Behavior* (1982), offers the most knowledgeable analysis of policy moves on the Russian side. Patricia Dawson Ward, *The Threat of Peace* (1979), is a fascinating narrative of the ill-fated foreign ministers' meetings that were so important in the early Cold War.

On Germany, the key area at stake in the early Russo-American schism, John Gimbel, *The American Occupation of Germany: Politics and the Military, 1945–1949* (1968), is still the standard history. More provocative and enlightening, however, is Bruce Kuklick, *American Policy and the Division of Germany*

(1972), focusing on the pivotal and divisive issue of economic reparations. Even more critical of United States policy, and its reindustrialization and remilitarization of Germany, is Carolyn Eisenberg, "U.S. Policy in Post-War Germany: The Conservative Reaction," *Science and Society* 46 (1982). Henry Blumenthal, the acknowledged authority on Franco-American relations, provides the background for French attitudes toward Germany in his *Illusion and Reality in Franco-American Diplomacy, 1914–1945* (1986).

On the early Cold War in Asia, Akira Iriye, *The Cold War in Asia* (1974), provides the best general overview. On the Chinese civil war and American policy, Kenneth Chern, *Dilemma in China, 1945* (1980), nicely dissects divided American opinion about options at the end of World War II, while Herbert Feis, *The China Tangle* (1956), carries the story forward with his still useful study of the 1946 mission of George Marshall to China. Gary Hess, *The U.S. Emergence as a Southeast Asian Power, 1940–1950* (1986), is the best regional study of the area that would later spawn the Vietnam War. More focused is Robert J. McMahon, *Colonialism and the Cold War* (1981), an excellent analysis of the crucial but often neglected nation of Indonesia.

On the central issue of the dollar gap and the imbalance in the global economy, Fred L. Block, *The Origins of International Economic Disorder* (1977), is a brilliant and readable introduction to a complex topic by one of our foremost intellectuals. For this early period of the Cold War, it should be supplemented with Richard Gardner, *Sterling Dollar Diplomacy* (1969), excellent on the British side. Robert A. Pollard, *Economic Security and the Origins of the Cold War* (1986), has some interesting notions about the role of economics in the early Cold War.

Chapter 4

The two best general accounts of the 1947 to 1950 period are very different in focus and interpretation. John L. Gaddis, *Strategies of Containment* (1982), emphasizes American policymakers and their changing definition and implementation of the containment policy toward Russia. Joyce and Gabriel Kolbo, *The Limits of Power* (1972), has a more global focus and is far more critical of American policy, especially its "reverse" courses in Japan and Germany.

On the British crisis and the Near East, D. C. Watt, *Succeeding John Bull: The United States and Great Britain* (1975), is an interesting overview of the transfer of power from declining Great Britain to newly hegemonic America. Examining a narrower time frame is William R. Louis's dense and informative study, *Imperialism at Bay: The United States and the Decolonization of the British Empire* (1978). More focused geographically is his excellent *The British Empire in the Middle East, 1945–1951* (1984). On the Truman Doctrine, which resulted from the British crisis, the best history from the American perspective is Lawrence S. Wittner, *American Intervention in Greece, 1943–1949* (1982). Also important is Richard Freeland, *The Truman Doctrine and the Origins of McCarthyism* (1971), for its probing analysis of the relationship between domestic politics and foreign policy. Two superb books provide the economic and regional context for the 1947 crisis. Nathan Godfried, *Bridging the Gap between Rich and Poor: American Economic Development Policy toward the Arab East, 1942–1949* (1987), is an excellent introduction to modernization model variations that underlie American approaches to the Middle East and to the Third World in general. David S. Painter, *Oil and the American Century: The Political Economy of U.S. Foreign Oil Policy, 1941–1954* (1986), parallels the Godfried book in some respects and again offers information and insights on not only the Middle East but Latin America as well.

On the pivotal European theater in 1948–49, the standard treatment of the Marshall Plan is now Michael J. Hogan's wonderful *The Marshall Plan* (1987), excellent for its analysis of corporatism and productionism at work. It should be supplemented with Alan S. Milward, *The Reconstruction of Western Europe, 1945–1951* (1984), which emphasizes European initiatives and questions the direct importance of the Marshall Plan. John W. Young, *Britain, France, and the Unity of Europe, 1945–1947* (1984), is a useful study of the antecedents of European economic and military integration efforts. On NATO, Lawrence Kaplan, *The United States and NATO* (1984), is best on the American side, while Timothy Ireland, *Creating the Entangling Alliance* (1981), looks at it from the European angle of vision. On the German crisis and the Berlin blockade, Avi Schlaim, *The United States and the Berlin Blockade, 1948–1949* (1985), is perhaps the most solid of numerous monographs. Daniel F. Harrington, "The Berlin Blockade Revisited," *International History Review* 6 (1984), is the best short synthesis and is a good introduction to the growing body of literature on this subject.

On Asia, Japanese reindustrialization, the Chinese revolution, and the war in Indochina have all received increasing scholarly attention. On Japan, Howard Schonberger, "U.S. Policy in Post-War Japan: The Retreat from Liberalism," *Science and Society* 46 (1982), is a pathbreaking interpretation. More ambitious in scope, and significant for its insights into both Japanese policy and the roots of the Vietnam War, is William S. Borden's superb *The Pacific Alliance* (1984). Michael Schaller, *The American Occupation of Japan* (1985), covers some of the same ground but adds a strategic dimension. On China, Nancy B. Tucker, *Patterns in the Dust* (1983), is an impressive piece of research on initial American reactions to the communist triumph in China. An appropriate supplement to it is June M. Grasso, *Harry Truman's Two-China Policy, 1948–1950* (1987), which contains fascinating new information on United States relations with Taiwan. Robert Blum, *Drawing the Line* (1982), stresses the application of the containment policy to China and its significance for early American involvement in Indochina. On that vital topic, Andrew J. Rotter's recent *The Path to Vietnam: Origins of the American Commitment to Southeast Asia* (1987), is indispensible, especially on the importance of Southeast Asia to American programs for economic recovery in Europe. For the region as a whole, Russell D. Buhite, *Soviet-American Relations in Asia, 1945–1954* (1981), offers a useful overview.

On domestic opinion and the emerging Cold War, see Ronald Radosh, *Prophets on the Right* (1975), especially his treatment of Robert A. Taft. Radosh, *American Labor and U.S. Foreign Policy* (1969), also has relevant information, especially on the role of conservative labor leaders and the implementation of

American policy overseas. Mary McAuliffe, *Crisis on the Left: Cold War Politics and American Liberals, 1947–1954* (1978), is the best history of the schism between ADA Cold War liberals and PCA dissenters. Lawrence Wittner, *Rebels against War: The American Peace Movement, 1941–1960* (1974), is required reading for understanding the persistent antiwar movement in the United States during the World War II and Cold War eras.

Chapter 5

Bruce Cumings is the acknowledged authority on the Korea War. See his *The Origins of the Korean War* (1981), which establishes the background through 1948; volume two is due for 1989 release. His own essay in *Child of Conflict* (1983), which he edited, is brilliant. Burton I. Kaufman, *The Korean War* (1986), provides the best short history of the Korean War, while William S. Stueck, Jr., *The Road to Confrontation* (1981), is useful for congressional opinion and influence. On America's involvement in the final French phase of the Vietnam War, consult Lloyd C. Gardner, *Approaching Vietnam: From World War II through Dienbienphu* (1988). Graham Greene's wonderful novel, *The Quiet American* (1955), deftly analyzes the destructiveness of American innocence abroad. The early chapters of George C. Herring, *America's Longest War* (1986), provide a useful context. William Borden's *The Pacific Alliance* (1984), is crucial on the role of Japanese reconstruction in early United States involvement, while Jon Halliday, *A Political History of Japanese Capitalism* (1975), provides the Japanese domestic context for that reconstruction.

On Latin America, Cole Blasier, *The Hovering Giant* (1976), offers an interesting, comparative overview, especially for Cuba, Bolivia, and Guatemala. Richard Immerman, *The CIA in Guatemala* (1982), and Stephen Kinzer and Stephen Schlesinger, *Bitter Fruit* (1982), are provocative and informative accounts of the American covert action in Guatemala in 1954. On the Middle East, Nathan Godfried, *Bridging the Gap between Rich and Poor* (1987), provides the essential economic framework. On the 1956 Suez crisis, two excellent studies are essential: Chester L. Cooper, *The Lion's Last Roar: Suez, 1956* (1978), and Donald Neff, *Warriors at Suez* (1981). William J. Burns, *Economic Aid and American Policy toward Egypt, 1955–1981* (1985), is an interesting microcosm of the transformation of Egyptian-American relations from confrontation to collaboration. On the related 1956 crisis in Hungary, Bennett Kovrig levels the *Myth of Liberation* (1973). Audrey Kurth Cronin, *Great Power Politics and the Struggle over Austria, 1945–1955* (1986), climaxing with the Austrian peace treaty, is indispensible background for the crisis in central Europe, while Adam Ulam, *Expansion and Coexistence: The History of Soviet Foreign Policy, 1917–1967* (1968), helps furnish the longer, more global context.

Among the many excellent books on McCarthyism and American foreign policy, see especially Robert Griffith, *The Politics of Fear: Joseph R. McCarthy and the Senate* (1978), and Athan Theoharis, *Seeds of Repression* (1971), one of his many fine works on the subject. Steven M. Gillon, *Politics and Vision: The ADA and American Liberalism, 1947–1985* (1987), picks up the crisis on the left where the McAuliffe volume (Crisis on the Left [1978]) puts it down.

Burton Kaufman's excellent study of Eisenhower's foreign aid policies, *Trade and Aid* (1982), is essential to understanding a crucial topic.

Also see the important biographical citations, especially on Eisenhower and Dulles.

Chapter 6

The late Eisenhower years saw both the triumph of economic internationalism and the initial signs of American economic erosion, into which Fred Block's superb overview, *The Origins of International Economic Disorder* (1977), provides enormous insight. Mira Wilkins, *The Maturing of Multinational Enterprise: American Business Abroad from 1914 to 1970* (1974), provides encyclopedic information on the expansion of American-owned multinational corporations into Europe and the Third World in the 1950s and 1960s. Richard J. Barnet and Ronald Müller, *Global Reach: The Power of Multinational Corporations* (1974), is a provocative application of dependency theory to the understanding of those same companies. John W. Evans, *The Kennedy Round in American Trade Policy* (1975), is the best account of a crucial but tardy effort to lower global tariff walls.

Michael R. Beschloss, *Mayday: Eisenhower, Khrushchev, and the U-2 Affair* (1986), is a wonderfully written, informative chronicle of Russian-American relations in the second Eisenhower administration, climaxing with the failed final summit meetings in Paris. Bernard J. Firestone, *The Quest for Nuclear Stability: John F. Kennedy and the Soviet Union* (1982), picks up the narrative thread in the Kennedy years, focusing on the nuclear test ban treaty. Frank Costigliola's fine article, "The Failed Design: Kennedy, de Gaulle, and the Struggle for Europe," *Diplomatic History* 8 (1984), says more than much longer volumes about one of the most persistently important subjects since 1945.

As Kennedy anticipated, the periphery provided much of the focus for American policy concerns during the 1960s. Richard Barnet, *Intervention and Revolution* (1968), offers a critical appraisal of those policies in general. On the central subject of escalation of American intervention, in Vietnam specifically, the literature is voluminous and still growing. George C. Herring, *America's Longest War* (1968), is the best overview, though Stanley Karnow, *Vietnam: A History* (1984), contains useful additional information. George McT. Kahin, *Intervention* (1986), is the best-researched and most scholarly account. Frances Fitzgerald, *Fire in the Lake: The Vietnamese and the Americans in Vietnam* (1972), is a popular, sometimes moving analysis that attempts, with mixed success, to view events from Vietnamese as well as American perspectives. Perhaps more successful is Gabriel Kolko, *Anatomy of a Revolution* (1985), based in part on extensive research in postwar Vietnam itself. The essays by Williams, McCormick, Gardner and LaFeber in William A. Williams, et al., eds., *American in Vietnam* (1985), constitute a good short survey of American policy, while its documents are quite revealing. Harry Summers, Jr., *On Strategy: A Critical Analysis of the Vietnam War* (1981), is the most controversial rendering of American military strategy and its implementation, while Ronald H. Spector, *United States Army in Vietnam* (1983), is unquestionably the most balanced and scholarly. Thomas R. H. Havens, *Fire across the Sea: The Vietnam War and Japan, 1965–1975* (1987), contains invaluable information on Japan's ambivalent relationship to the conflict raging in its former sphere of influence. Loren Baritz, *Backfire: A History of How American Culture Led Us into Vietnam and Made Us Fight the Way We Did* (1985), advances some interesting notions about American culture and the war, while Neil Sheehan's recent *A Bright Shining Lie: John Paul Vann and America in Vietnam* (1988), offers a fruitful approach so unique that it defies comparison. On more specific facets, see Stephen E. Pelz, "John F. Kennedy's 1961 Vietnam War Decision," *Journal of Strategic Studies* 4 (1981); Ellen J. Hammer, *A Death in November: America in Vietnam, 1963* (1987), on the overthrow of the Diem regime; Larry Berman, *Planning a Tragedy* (1982), on the escalation in early 1965; relatedly, James Clay Thompson, *Rolling Thunder: Understanding Policy and Program Failure* (1980); Gareth Porter, "After Geneva: Subverting Laotian Neutrality," in Nina S. Adam and Aldred W. McCoy, eds., *Laos: War and Revolution* (1970), on the parallel conflict in Laos; and Goran Rystad, *Prisoners of the Past?: The Munich Syndrome and Makers of American Foreign Policy in the Cold War* (1982), on the Johnson administration and the President's misuse of the lessons of history.

Nearly as important as the Vietnam War was American involvement throughout Latin America. The best general studies are Graham H. Stuart and James L. Tigner, *Latin America and the United States* (1975), impressive in its detail, and Samuel L. Bailey, *The United States and the Development of South America, 1945–1975* (1976), more focused in its time frame. Richard E. Welch, Jr., *Response to Revolution: The United States and the Cuban Revolution, 1959–1961* (1985), provides useful new information on early American reactions to the Castro revolution in Cuba, while Graham Allison's analysis of the 1962 Cuban missile crisis, *Essence of Decision* (1971), is important for its model of decisionmaking. On Kennedy's Alliance for Progress program, see Jerome Levinson and Juan de Onís, *The Alliance That Lost Its Way* (1970). Phyllis Parker, *Brazil and the Quiet Intervention, 1964* (1979), is the best account yet of American involvement in toppling the Goulart government. Also impressive and enlightening is Piero Gleijesis, *The Dominican Crisis* (1978), on an American military intervention in 1965 that initially prompted as much domestic American reaction as the escalation in Vietnam.

On Africa and the Middle East there are several important works that help decipher key developments such as the Congo crisis or the Six Days War. On Africa, the best general study is Peter Duignan and L. H. Gann, *The United States and Africa: A History* (1984). Thomas J. Noer, *Cold War and Black Liberation: The United States and White Rule in Africa, 1948–1968* (1985), is a very important contribution to a neglected topic. Richard D. Mahoney, *JFK: Ordeal in Africa* (1983), is perhaps the most narrowly focused. On the Middle East, Nadav Safran, *From War to War: The Arab-Israeli Confrontation, 1948–1967* (1969), is the standard history, one that nicely portrays the changing nature of United States-Israeli relations.

On the politics of the space race, Walter A. McDougall, *The Heavens and the Earth: A Political History of the Space Age* (1985), is breathtaking in its scope and impressive in its insights. On public opinion and foreign policy, Montague Kern, Patricia Levering, and Ralph A. Levering, *The Kennedy Crisis: The Press, the Presidency, and Foreign Policy* (1985), is quite useful.

Chapter 7

In general, the literature from 1968 onward tends to be thinner, less substantial. In part this reflects the relative paucity of manuscript and archival sources; in part it reflects the more journalistic, less scholarly training of many writers; and in part it reflects the difficulty of gaining a detached perspective on people and events that have been observed or experienced first hand. Nonetheless, our knowledge and understanding of recent history fares reasonably well despite these obstacles.

Raymond Garthoff, *Détente and Confrontation* (1985), commissioned by the Brookings Institution, is easily the most valuable overview of the 1970s and 1980s, impressive in its detailed documentation and its author's many suggestive insights. Other general accounts of the Nixon era, often critical in nature, include Franz Schurmann, *The Foreign Policies of Richard Nixon: The Grand Design* (1987); Jonathan Schell, *The Time of Illusion* (1976); Seymour Hersch's popular but controversial treatment of Henry Kissinger, *The Price of Power* (1983); and Garry Wills' brilliant and imaginative *Nixon Agonistes* (1970).

On détente and triangular diplomacy, in addition to Garthoff see Robert S. Litwak, *Détente and the Nixon Doctrine* (1984). The Soviet perspective receives useful attention in Jonathan Steele, *Soviet Power: The Kremlin's Foreign Policy—Brezhnev to Andropov* (1985), and in Adam Ulam's updating of earlier work, *Dangerous Relations: The Soviet Union in World Politics, 1970–1982* (1983). On the Sino-American leg of the triangle, Robert Sutter, *China Watch: Sino-American Reconciliation* (1978), does an impressive job of putting the topic in its long-term perspective. Maurice Meisner, *Mao's China and After: A History of the People's Republic* (1986), the best general history, provides crucial insights into the Chinese domestic context.

On the final stages of the Vietnam War, see William Shawcross, *Sideshow: Kissinger, Nixon, and the Destruction of Cambodia* (1979), especially on the tragic expansion of the war. On the peace negotiations at Paris, consult Gareth Porter, *A Peace Denied* (1975). For a biting retrospective on the lessons and legacies of the war, read Earl C. Ravenal, *Never Again* (1978). On domestic dissent, Todd Gitlin, *The Sixties* (1987), offers an empathetic portrayal, while Irwin Unger, *The Movement* (1974), is more critical. Two quantitative studies are helpful in connecting domestic political opinion and Vietnam policy: Melvin Small, *Johnson, Nixon, and the Doves* (1988), and Ole Holsti and James R. Roseneau, *American Leadership in World Affairs: Vietnam and the Breakdown of Consensus* (1984).

On the Middle East, scene of a fourth Arab-Israeli war and the OPEC oil shock, Robert Stookey, *America and the Arab States* (1975), is a solid general history. Seth Tillman, *The United States and the Middle East* (1982), is both sweeping and challenging. Cheryl Rubenberg, *Israel and the American National*

Interest (1986), offers a critical account of its subject, while Gary Sick, *All Fall Down: America's Tragic Encounter with Iran* (1985), provides historical background for the 1979 Iranian revolution.

On Africa, Henry Jackson, *From the Congo to Soweto: U.S. Foreign Policy toward Africa since 1960* (1982), is a good general history of this subject covering the 1960s and 1970s. John A. Marcum, *The Angolan Revolution* (1978), is very informative on the most significant African national movement in the 1970s and 1980s. Anthony Lake, *The "Tar Baby" Option: American Policy toward Southern Rhodesia* (1976), contains some stunning material on the Kissinger approach to African independence movements.

On Latin America, James Petras and Morris Morley, *The United States and Chile* (1975), is a sharp critique of American policy and the overthrow of the Allende regime. The distinguished Arthur P. Whitaker puts Chile in larger regional context in his *The United States and the Southern Cone: Argentina, Chile, and Uruguay* (1976). Stephen G. Rabe, *The Road to OPEC: United States Relations with Venezuela* (1982), is wonderfully enlightening both on U.S.-Venezuelan relations and on the larger issue of world petroleum.

Finally, David Calleo, *The Imperious Economy* (1982), is an important book that provides, from a different perspective, the kind of sweep and imagination about the international economy that Fred Block's work did for the earlier period. It should be supplemented by Robert Gilpin, *The Political Economy of International Relations* (1987), important in its own right.

Chapter 8

Raymond Garthoff, *Détente and Confrontation* (1985), is again the most important single source on the transition from détente to confrontation in the Carter period. Fred Halliday, *The Making of the Second Cold War* (1983), is a stimulating analysis from a radical perspective. More orthodox but quite useful is *Morality, Reason and Power: American Diplomacy in the Carter Years* (1986), by Gaddis Smith, a productive and respected scholar. Melvyn P. Leffler, "From the Truman Doctrine to the Carter Doctrine," *Diplomatic History* 7 (1985), does an excellent job of putting Carter's policies in historical perspective. Stanley Hoffmann, *Primacy or World Order* (1978), is an interesting analysis of Carter's "world order" politics, from the vantage point of both scholar and participant. More specific is Philip Hanson, *Trade and Technology in Soviet-Western Relations* (1981), an informative study of a crucial dimension in détente and its demise, while Strobe Talbott, *Endgame: The Inside Story of SALT II* (1979), is a fascinating account of the second unratified, strategic arms limitations treaty. Robert G. Sutter's richly researched *The China Quandary* (1985), helps put Carter's one-sided tilt toward China in context; Richard Barnet's sweeping study of the complex Euro-American connection, *The Alliance* (1983), does the same for the missile diplomacy in Europe.

Carter's human rights diplomacy ultimately figured in the Cold War revival. The best general study is Sandy Vogelgesang, *American Dream, American*

Nightmare (1980). Lars Schoultz, *Human Rights and U.S. Policy towards Latin America* (1981) is focused more on an area of particular concern for human rights advocates. Michael T. Klare and Cynthia Arnson, *Supplying Repression: U.S. Support for Authoritarian Regimes Abroad* (1981), argues, from a very different perspective, that American support for Third World military dictatorships remained the norm for Carter's policy.

Power politics within American society played an enormously important role in creating the conflicting tendencies between coexistence and competition in world affairs. Edward Tivnan, *The Lobby: Jewish Political Power and American Foreign Policy* (1987), is perhaps the best study of an important interest group. Stephen A. Garrett, *From Potsdam to Poland* (1986), is good on Eastern European ethnic groups in American society and their impact on public policy. Richard Melansen, *Writing History and Making Policy* (1983), sees the differently perceived lessons of the Vietnam War as having an important role in the ideological realignments of the post-Vietnam era. Alan Wolfe, *America's Impasse* (1981), is necessary for understanding the relationship of domestic politics, differential economic rewards, and foreign policy tendencies.

A major reason for the death of détente was that Russia and America differed over the implementation of coexistence in the Third World. Many of their differences centered on the "arc of crisis" in Southwest Asia and Northeast Africa. Among a growing body of works, the following provide good introductions to their specific topics in that area: on the Afghan revolution and the Soviet intervention, Anthony Arnold, *Afghanistan* (1981); on the Shah and the Iranian revolution, Barry Rubin, *Paved with Good Intentions* (1977), and R. K. Ramazani, *The United States and Iran: The Patterns of Influence* (1982); on the complex interplay of Israel, the Arab states, and the Palestinians, Barry Rubin, *The Arab States and the Palestine Conflict* (1981), and William B. Quandt, *Camp David* (1986); and on the Ethiopian crisis and Russo-Cuban involvement, David A. Korn, *Ethiopia, the United States, and the Soviet Union* (1986).

Latin America was the other major Third World focus for United States policy. The Panama Canal treaty was important both for American policy and for its effect on domestic politics and its foreign policy orientations. Walter LaFeber, *The Panama Canal* (1978), provides the best historical development and is particularly strong on the diplomatic side of events. J. Michael Hogan, *The Panama Canal in American Politics* (1986), is a valuable complement, especially strong on domestic political configurations. Morris Morley, *Imperial State and Revolution: The United States and Cuba, 1952–1985* (1987), is important to understanding U.S.-Cuban relations, and the transition from quasi-normalization in the early Carter administration to harsh confrontation in Africa and the Caribbean by its end. For the revolutions in El Salvador and Nicaragua, and initial American reactions to them, Walter LaFeber, *Inevitable Revolutions: The United States in Central America* (1983), provides the soundest historical grounding.

Chapter 9

A number of general studies have relevance to the Reagan years. Two are especially brilliant and useful. Nigel Harris, *The End of the Third World* (1986), is a superb account of the redivision of world economic labor that provides the essential external context for America's reassessment of its future options. Mike Davis, *Prisoners of the American Dream* (1986), is a provocative study of the internal sectoral and sectional changes that also figure so heavily in the decline of American hegemony. It should be supplemented by Kenneth M. Dolbeare, *Democracy at Risk: The Political Economy of Renewal* (1984), a significant work. Garry Wills, *Reagan's America* (1987), is less stimulating than his earlier Nixon book, but still quite insightful. Two useful books deal with the general phenomena of symbolic politics and policy: David Green, *Shaping Political Consciousness: The Language of Politics in America from McKinley to Reagan* (1988), a provocative overview, and Robert Dalleck, *Ronald Reagan: The Politics of Symbolism* (1984), a more narrowly focused study.

The central feature of Reagan foreign policy during the first five years was its militarization. On the interaction of military programs and domestic politics, see Desmond Ball, *Politics and Force Levels* (1981). Stephen J. Cimbala, *The Reagan Defense Program* (1986), has very helpful data on military spending between 1981 and 1985. Paul Stares, *Space and National Defense* (1987), is the accepted authority on the evolution of the Star Wars SDI program. Strobe Talbott, *The Master of the Game: Paul Nitze and the Nuclear Peace* (1988), is a classic insider narrative of a fascinating and still unfinished story. Diana Johnstone, *The Politics of Euromissiles* (1985), is the best current treatment of that crucial topic.

Most of the renewed Cold War focused and often floundered on Third World crises. In the Middle East, the Lebanon crises and the Palestinian uprising in Israel have provided center stage for the complex interrelationships between the United States, Israel, the Arab states, Palestinians, and American Jews. Steven L. Spiegel, *The Other Arab-Israel Conflict* (1985), emphasizes the domestic American context. Itamar Rabinovich, *The War for Lebanon* (1984), is a very informative introduction. Noam Chomsky, *The Fateful Triangle: The United States, Israel and the Palestinians* (1984), is a blistering and controversial critique by the noted linguist and political activist. On the reemergent crisis in South Africa, the best historical overview is Christopher Coker, *The United States and South Africa, 1968–1985* (1986). On the ouster of the Marcos regime in the Philippines and the subsequent social strife, see Raymond Bonner, *Waltzing with a Dictator* (1987), and Robert Shaplen, *The Unfinished Revolution* (1987).

Finally, there is a growing literature on the Reagan effort to roll back revolution in Central America. Walter LaFeber's *Inevitable Revolutions* is the most useful overview, but other volumes are important. Most have centered on Nicaragua, the Sandinista revolution, and the American-backed *contras*. E. Bradford Burns, *At War in Nicaragua* (1987), provides a useful introduction from a distinguished Latin Americanist. Mary B. Vanderlaan, *Revolution and Foreign Policy in Nicaragua* (1986), is excellent on the pre-1979 period, dating back to the mid-nineteenth century, while Karl Bermann, *Under the Big Stick* (1985), is especially strong on events in Nicaragua since 1979. Thomas W. Walker, *Nicaragua* (1986), is an insightful analysis by a first-rate political scientist with first-hand experience in Nicaragua. In addition, see Frank Brodhead and Edward S. Herman, *Demonstration Elections* (1984), not only for its treatment of El Salvador, but also for its general analysis of the way "demonstration" elections are structured to legitimize regimes sorely lacking in that quality.

Chapter 10

Scholarly material on the past half-decade is quite thin and needs to be supplemented with careful reading in contemporary newspapers and journals like the *New York Times*, the *Washington Post*, the *Wall Street Journal*, the *Economist*, and *Foreign Affairs*.

On the end of the Cold War, begin with Michael Hogan, ed., *The End of the Cold War* (1992), for the most balanced approach. John Lewis Gaddis, *The United States and the End of the Cold War* (1992), a collection of previously published articles, is a solid representation of neorealism. Michael Beschloss and Strobe Talbott, *At the Highest Levels: The Intimate Story of the End of the Cold War* (1993), focuses too narrowly on the Bush-Gorbachev relationship but is a gold mine of information.

On the conflict in the Persian Gulf, Michael Palmer, *Guardians of the Gulf* (1992), provides the best historical context. Stephen Graubard, *Mr. Bush's War: Adventures in the Politics of Illusion* (1992), is highly critical of President Bush's political motivations in opting for war. Haim Bresheeth and Nira Yuval-Davis, eds., *The Gulf War and the New World Order* (1993), is a good cross-section of leftist opinion on the Gulf War. Lawrence Freedman and Efraim Karsh, *The Gulf Conflict, 1990–1991: Diplomacy and War in the New World Order* (1992), is informative if somewhat uncritical. Alex Danchen and Dan Keohane, eds. *International Perspectives on the Gulf Conflict, 1990–1991* (1994), is rather unfocused but has some good pieces, like Avi Shlain's on Israel and the Gulf War.

On specific issues, the most useful works are those that provide an historical backdrop to the current period. Fred Halliday, *From Kabul to Managua* (1989), does so on Russian-American relations. Frank Costigliola, *France and the United States: The Cold Alliance since World War II* (1992), and Rene Schwok, *U.S.-EC Relations in the Post–Cold War Era* (1991), do so for U.S. relations with Western Europe. On the historical context of key crisis events, see Misha Glenny, *The Fall of Yugoslavia*, Walter LaFeber, *The Panama Canal: The Crisis in Historical Perspective* (1990), and Brenda Gayle Plummer, *Haiti and the United States* (1992).

Speculating on the post–Cold War era has become a booming cottage industry. Paul Kennedy, *Preparing for the Twenty-first Century* (1993), while less thoughtful than his *The Rise and Fall of Great Powers*, does touch all the important bases. Robert Tucker and David Hendrickson, *The Imperial Temptation: The New World Order and America's Purpose* (1992), is provocative. The authors in Charles Kegley and Kenneth Schwar, eds., *After the Cold War* (1992), represent a good mix of policymakers, academics, and peace activists. And finally, Geir Lundestad and Odd Arne Westad, eds., *Beyond the Cold War: Future Dimensions in International Relations* (1993)—a product of the Nobel Institute—stresses religious, class, and North-South conflict in the years ahead.

Index

Geneva Accords, 110, 113, 114, 115, 117, 120, 147, 148, 151
Geneva Summit, 108–11, 119
Georgia, secession of, 243
German Democratic Republic (East Germany), 110, 135, 174, 240, 244
Germany, 21, 22, 25, 27, 55, 169, 193; and American hegemony, 252; as beneficiary of the Cold War, 242; and Brussels Pact, 108; and a common market, 79; and Croatia, 254; and currency reform, 80; economic power of, 157, 164; and European Defense Community, 132; and hegemony, 6; and Marshall Plan, 132; and nationalism, 54, 251; and NATO, 87, 107, 108, 109, 132, 244; Nazi regime in, 30, 33; neutralization of, 93, 132; and nuclear nonproliferation treaty, 173; and Poland, 174; rearmament of, 68, 87, 96, 106–8; recession in, 239–40; reindustrialization of, 39, 57, 68, 80; reparations of, 22, 25, 39, 68; reunification of, 237, 240, 244; revanchism of, 61, 68; and Soviet Union, 30, 40, 68, 80, 242, 244; threat of a permanent division of, 133; and Tripartite Pact, 31; and United States, 65, 244, 249, 250; and world markets, 238; and Yalta system, 38, 39
Glasnost, 234, 235, 243
Global warming, 241
Goldwater, Barry, 156, 198
Gorbachev, Mikhail, 232, 242, 243; and American intervention in the Gulf, 248; and American support, 244–45; and *glasnost* and *perestroika*, 235; and summits, 230, 231; and "third way" economic policy, 245
Goulart, João, 146
Great Britain, 21, 34, 35, 56, 61, 72, 75, 169; and Aswan Dam project, 122–23; as banking and credit center, 22; Brussels Treaty, 87; and Common Market, 79, 128, 131; and crisis of 1947 in Greece and Turkey, 75; and dollar gap, 90, 93; European Defense Community, 107; and

Four-Power Pacific Treaty, 26; and Geneva Summit, 108–11; and Gulf War, 250; as hegemonic center (1815–70), 6, 18; and Labor party government, 56, 74; loan from United States (1946), 55, 56; and Manhattan Project, 45; and militarization, 95; as part of "Outer Seven," 140; and offer of Polaris missiles, 131; and Skybolt missile program, 131; strategy of, in World War II, 34–35; and super-fighter aircraft, 235; and United States, 249, 250; and world markets, 54; and Yalta Conference, 38
Great Depression, 28, 30, 50, 150, 162, 237, 243, 257; causes of, 29
"Greater China," and Japan, 244
Greater East Asian Co-Prosperity Sphere, 5, 31, 112, 116
Great Leap Forward, 137, 166
Great Society, 9–10, 158, 196
Greece, 83, 85, 165, 181; civil war in, 66, 68, 75; and Cyprus, 181; and Great Britain, 61, 72; and NATO pact, 87; and Soviet Union, 66, 108
Greek and Turkey crisis, 75
Green Berets, 138, 150, 152
Greene, Graham, 138
Grenada, 221, 226
Gromyko, Andrei, 173, 184
Gross world product (GWP), 238
Groves, Leslie R., 43
G-7 group of industrial nations, 246, 255
Guatemala, 122, 142, 226; and Arbenz regime, 118; and human rights, 201; and United States, 121, 220
Gulf of Tonkin crisis, 152, 153, 160
Gulf War. *See* Persian Gulf War
Guyana, 137, 146

Haig, Alexander M., 13, 217
Haiti, anarchy and repression in, 251
Halberstam, David, 150
Hansen, Alvin, 52
Harrington, Michael, *The Other America*, 157
H-bomb, 44, 93, 94, 96, 101, 109, 131
Hegemony, 4–7; decline of, 256; definition of, 5; domestic context of, 7–12

Tito, Josip, 64, 65, 68, 111, 118, 122, 123, 170
Trade acts (1962, 1974), 127, 180
Trade deficits, 51, 127, 128, 227
Triangular diplomacy, 171, 195, 205
Trilateral Commission, 189, 199
Trujillo, Rafael, 147
Truman, Harry S., 15, 58, 69, 84, 93, 111, 134; and Americans for Democratic Action, 71; and atomic bomb, 43, 44–45; and James F. Byrnes, 67; and Congress, 76, 77, 86; and dollar gap, 93; and Dulles, 100; and Economic Cooperation Administration, 82; and the Fair Deal, 157; and German rearmament, 106; "get tough" policy of, 41; and Indochina, 117–18; and MacArthur, 104; and Marshall Plan, 85; and NSC-68, 97; and reconstruction loan to Soviet Union, 41; speech to Congress on Greece, 75, 77; and Soviet atomic bomb, 93; and Soviet proposal of armistice in Korea, 104; and Stalin, 44; and Vietnam, French control of, 99; and Henry Wallace, 69; and Yalta Conference, 65; and U.S. aid to France, 113
Truman Doctrine, 8, 66, 72, 75, 80, 83, 87, 96, 123; anticommunism of, 76, 77, 85; and dollar gap crisis, 75, 76, 93; and Eisenhower Doctrine, 139; globalism of, 21, 76, 77; innovations of, 88
Truman-MacArthur controversy, 104
Tshombe, Moise, 141
Turkey, 77, 83, 165; and Baghdad Pact, 120; and Great Britain, 61, 72, 75; and Greece, 181; and Kurdistan, 251; and NATO pact, 87; and Soviet Union, 61, 65–66, 75, 77, 108; and U.S. missiles in, 145

Ukraine, secession of, 243
Ultranationalists, German, 241
Unemployment: in Europe, 240; in Soviet Union, 243
Unions: American, 8, 82–84, 96; marginalization of, 240
United Nations (UN), 102, 137, 253, 255; and cease-fire in Iran-Iraq War,

253; and Congo, 140–41; Economic Commission for Europe (UNECE), 78; and end of American hegemony, 246; General Assembly, 49, 79, 124; Secretariat, 255; Security Council, 40, 49, 65, 253; and world order, 238
United States, 20, 21, 74, 111, 170, 193, 239, 254; and Allende, 201; and an Amerasian bloc, 256; antiwar movement in, 152; and ANZUS pact, 100; army of, 87, 129, 133, 187; and Aswan Dam project, 122–23; and atomic bomb, 43, 44–45, 65, 66, 91, 93, 131, 205, 230; and Baghdad Pact, 120; and Brezhnev Doctrine, 169, and Brussels Treaty, 87; and "Christmas bombings," 178; budget and trade deficits, 246; Commerce Department of, 28; and Common Market, 113, 126, 127; and Nicaraguan contras, 122, 220; and Conference on Security and Cooperation in Europe, 175; and Cuban missile crisis, 144–45; and détente with Soviet Union, 11, 167, 168; and Diem, 148; and dollar gap crisis, 94; domestic dissent in, 155; and Duarte, 220; economic supremacy of, 9, 19, 47, 161, 169; educational and infrastructural weakness, 246; foreign military bases of, 87, 120, 205, 210, 226; and Geneva Accords, 148; and Geneva Summit, 108–11; and Germany, 25, 41, 68, 80, 93, 107, 108, 126, 244, 249, 250; as global policeman, 23, 49, 134, 138, 140, 144, 148, 155, 159, 186, 189; gold reserves of, 127, 162; and retention of Gorbachev, 244–45; and Great Britain, 19, 33, 47, 55, 56, 249, 250; gross national product of, 157, 219, 227; and Gulf War, 250; and Hitler, 37; and 1956 crisis in Hungary, 11; and military coup against Hussein, 251; and industry, 47, 191–92; and INF treaty, 224; and integrationism, 111; and International Monetary Fund, 53; and internationalism, 23, 68, 69, 156; and overseas

for Reconstruction and Development
World monetary system, 169
World-system, 1–4, 5, 29, 49, 88, 91, 252, 256; and China, 93, 101; and neutralism, 120; and Soviet Union, 93; and United States, 19, 47, 92, 155
World War II, 17, 33, 34–35, 243, 249

Yalta Conference, 38–41, 45, 53, 58, 62, 65

Yeltsin, Boris, 243, 245
Yemen, 139, 204
Yom Kippur War. *See* October War
Young, Andrew, 202
Yugoslavia, 66, 68, 76, 119, 170, 181, 254; civil war, 237, 245, 250, 251, 253, 255; and war with Croatia, 253; Serbian, 254; and Soviet Union, 65, 108, 111; and United States, 200

Zaire, 165, 188, 201, 202

Library of Congress Cataloging-in-Publication Data

McCormick, Thomas J.
    America's half-century : United States foreign policy in the Cold War and after /
Thomas J. McCormick. — 2nd ed.
        p.   cm. — (The American moment)
    Includes bibliographical references and index.
    ISBN 0-8018-5010-X (hc : alk. paper). — ISBN 0-8018-5011-8 (pbk : alk. paper)
    1. United States—Foreign relations—1945–1989.   2. United States—Foreign
relations—1989–   3. World politics—1945–   I. Title. II. Series.
E744.M416   1995
327.73'009'045—dc20   94-34698